An Army of Lions

POLITICS AND CULTURE IN MODERN AMERICA

SERIES EDITORS
Margot Canaday, Glenda Gilmore,
Michael Kazin, and Thomas J. Sugrue

Volumes in the series narrate and analyze political and social change in the broadest dimensions from 1865 to the present, including ideas about the ways people have sought and wielded power in the public sphere and the language and institutions of politics at all levels—local, national, and transnational. The series is motivated by a desire to reverse the fragmentation of modern U.S. history and to encourage synthetic perspectives on social movements and the state, on gender, race, and labor, and on intellectual history and popular culture.

An Army of Lions

The Civil Rights Struggle Before the NAACP

Shawn Leigh Alexander

PENN

UNIVERSITY OF PENNSYLVANIA PRESS

PHILADELPHIA

Published by
University of Pennsylvania Press
Philadelphia, Pennsylvania 19104–4112
www.upenn.edu/pennpress

Printed in the United States of America on acid-free paper
10 9 8 7 6 5 4 3 2 1

Library of Congress Cataloging-in-Publication Data

Alexander, Shawn Leigh.
An army of lions : the civil rights struggle before the NAACP / Shawn Leigh Alexander.
p. cm. — (Politics and culture in modern America)
Includes bibliographical references and index.
ISBN 978-0-8122-4375-8 (hardcover : alk. paper)
1. African Americans—Civil rights—History—19th century. 2. African Americans—Civil rights—History—20th century. 3. Civil rights movements—Civil rights—History—19th century. 4. Civil rights movements—Civil rights—History—20th century. 5. African Americans—Politics and government—19th century. 6. African Americans—Politics and government—20th century. 7. African Americans—Social conditions—To 1964. 8. United States—Race relations—History—19th century. 9. United States—Race relations—History—20th century. I. Title. II. Series: Politics and culture in modern America.
E185.61.A437 2011
323.1196'073—dc23 2011023615

For Kelly

As the agitation which culminated in the abolition of African slavery in this country covered a period of fifty years, so may we expect that before the rights conferred upon us by the war amendments are fully conceded, a full century will have passed away. We have undertaken no child's play. We have undertaken a serious work which will tax and exhaust the best intelligence and energy of the race for the next century.

—T. Thomas Fortune

NYA, January 25, 1890

Contents

Preface

> Agitate and act until something is done. While we are resting on our oars, seemingly content with expressing our indignation by resolutions at the outrages which daily occur, others are presuming upon this inaction of our rights—nay upon life itself.
>
> —Iola (Ida B. Wells)

"The Negro must organize," wrote Brooklyn-based African American lawyer T. McCants Stewart in 1889. "He must be peaceable, but if . . . forced to fight," argued Stewart, invoking two famous Civil War battles involving African American Union troops, "he must do so with the same pluck, energy and spirit which he displayed at Fort Fisher and Battery Wagner; and if he must die, let him make his death so costly to the whites in blood and fire as to force the conservative and moral white elements of the South to stand up for peace, and to insist upon equal and exact justice to all men alike." These "fighting words" were written in response to Stewart's confidant, journalist and political activist T. Thomas Fortune and Fortune's call to assemble a national convention of the local branches of the Afro-American League and form the country's first national civil rights organization.[1]

Fortune's desire for a national civil rights organization resonated with African Americans in the late 1880s. After the 1876 election of Rutherford B. Hayes—one of the most contentious and hotly disputed elections in American history—southern states, backed by violence, intimidation, and the invocation of white supremacist racial politics, rewrote their constitutions and passed legislation stripping African American citizens of their civil, social, and political rights. At the same time, black citizens' rights in the North were also being increasingly curbed. African American leaders and activists responded in many ways ranging widely from self-help and racial solidarity to economic nationalism, emigration, and political agitation.

This book chronicles the response of black organizations, particularly civil rights organizations, to the rise of racial segregation and violence in the age of Jim Crow—the period from the 1880s through the first decade of the twentieth century. As such, it provides the first full-length study of the major local and national civil rights organizations of the era: the Afro-American League, the National Afro-American Council, the Constitution League, the Committee of Twelve, and the Niagara Movement. Though unappreciated or understudied, these organizations laid the institutional, ideological, and political groundwork for the establishment of the National Association for the Advancement of Colored People (NAACP) in 1909.[2]

An Army of Lions is also about the people who fought and continued to fight when their position in American society became increasingly tenuous and victory was not foreseeable. This pioneering group was comprised of individuals who understood, as scholar activist William S. Scarborough argued in 1889, that "Southern outrages and Northern proscription make inactivity on our part almost a crime." Rather than succumbing to these rising injustices, black activists during the late nineteenth century organized "as a means of self-protection."[3] All the individuals and organizations in this study upheld the validity of the Reconstruction-era civil rights amendments as these amendments were being stripped from federal and state constitutions, and as racial discrimination, disfranchisement, and mob violence curtailed and limited modes of political redress and protest. These individuals used propaganda, moral suasion, boycotts, lobbying, and electoral office as well as the call for self-defense to end disfranchisement and contest racial violence. But while they wielded a wide range of weapons, the courts were key in their pursuit of justice. In the process, the Afro-American League, as well as the organizations that formed in its wake, created the legal strategy that became the foundation of the NAACP's struggle for civil rights in the twentieth century.

An Army of Lions also reveals the shifting views, changing allegiances, and competition for support and resources among leading African American intellectuals and activists as Jim Crow dawned and developed. In this era, I argue the vitality of the protest tradition in African American social and political thought did not disappear or diminish. Rather, the philosophies of legal redress, racial solidarity, self-help, economic development, educational reform, and emigration were all vibrant and intermingled. This is particularly demonstrated in the study of the Afro-American League and the Afro-American Council, both of which were active for nearly two decades during the "nadir," and which at various times counted nearly every leading African

American within their ranks as they debated the racial climate of the nation and tried to formulate a program for racial advancement within their comprehensive platform.

When asked about civil rights organizations, most Americans immediately think of the NAACP. Scholars might begin with the Niagara Movement, led by W. E. B. Du Bois, William Monroe Trotter, and Frederick McGhee, to identify important precursors, but few mention prior organizations, and if they do, they largely tend to dismiss these groups as relatively insignificant paper organizations that rarely put their politics into action. One reason for this is that Du Bois has mistakenly become central to our understanding of this period of African American history. His leadership role in the Niagara Movement, for example, has obscured how others have perceived and studied the era. As a result, scholars have often agreed with Du Bois's and historian Herbert Aptheker's assertion that only the Niagara Movement influenced the founding of the NAACP.[4]

An Army of Lions challenges this assumption by revisiting the organizations that preceded both the Niagara Movement and the NAACP. In shifting attention away from Du Bois and his leadership of the Niagara Movement, this study shows that the Afro-American League, the first national civil rights organization, and its successor, the National Afro-American Council, were the harbingers of the NAACP. The civil rights activities of the groups chronicled—including challenges to disfranchisement legislation in the southern states, attempts to pass anti-lynching legislation, local branches' filings of numerous anti-discrimination cases in New York, Minnesota, Washington, Wisconsin, Florida, California, and other areas—clearly show that these organizations were much more active and well organized on both the national and local levels than previously acknowledged. Moreover, the Afro-American Council did not collapse after the Niagara Movement was formed, as previous scholars have argued. Rather, as Du Bois himself acknowledged in 1905, the creation of the Niagara Movement breathed new life into the "older Negro organizations," including the Council.[5]

A secondary aim of this study is to highlight the roles of a wider range of intellectuals and activists—some forgotten, some not—such as T. Thomas Fortune, Bishop Alexander Walters, Ida B. Wells-Barnett, Mary Church Terrell, Jesse Lawson, Lewis G. Jordan, Kelly Miller, George H. White, Frederick McGhee, Archibald Grimké, and Booker T. Washington in this nascent civil rights effort. *An Army of Lions* explores the way in which the participation of these activists in the organizations mentioned above contributed to the foundation of the NAACP. In particular, it reconsiders Washington's civil rights activity while transforming our understanding of African American civil rights organizing during a period that has become synonymous with accommodation. Washington was much more involved in the activity of these organizations than previously thought.[6] "Washington," as August Meier argued nearly half a century ago, "was surreptitiously engaged in undermining the American race system by a direct attack upon disfranchisement and segregation." The picture that emerges from a careful study of Washington's work and activities within these organizations "is distinctly at variance with the ingratiating mask he presented to the world."[7]

While *An Army of Lions* helps further our understanding of an important chapter in the story of African Americans' struggle for social, civil, and political equality, it is not a depiction of a long, continuous civil rights movement. [8] These individuals and organizations and their activities did not constitute a movement in the sense that scholars understand the post-World War II American civil rights movement. Although there was certainly continuity in struggle, the activities of the organizations discussed here did not continue uninterrupted into the twentieth century with both national and local support. Nonetheless, the individuals and organizations discussed in this book do help us reconsider our understanding of African American civil rights activity during Jim Crow by demonstrating that there was active agitation during "the age of accommodation."

An Army of Lions highlights how this early civil rights activism provided a bridge of ideas and activists that helped create a template for many of the activities the NAACP has developed over the past century. In fact, it argues that the League and the organizations it spawned provided the ideological and strategic blueprint of the NAACP. The methods of agitation, legal redress, and moral suasion utilized by these early activists and organizations became the model for many of the better-known civil rights organizations of the twentieth century. The creation of the NAACP, therefore, represented a significant realignment or adjustment rather than a major paradigm shift.

There were multiple reasons for this realignment. First, the organizations formed prior to the NAACP, particularly the Afro-American League and the Afro-American Council, were never able to gain the support of the masses. As Booker T. Washington warned T. Thomas Fortune in 1887 while offering his support of the development of the League, "beware of forming on the mountaintop, do not forget the valleys."[9] This issue plagued the League and the Council, as well as the other organizations formed before the NAACP.

Even Fortune, upon speaking at the creation of the Council in 1898, expressed concern regarding the lack of support and activity on behalf of the masses. Similarly, when resigning from the group in 1904, Fortune cited this continuing problem as one of his reasons for doing so. Three years later, during his final months at the *Age* in late 1907, he published an editorial lamenting that "the Niagara Movement and the National Afro-American Council are both in the air by a thread of hope that the mass of the people will wake up and do something."[10]

The inability of these early organizations to attract mass support was due, in part, to the tenuous financial situation that each encountered. The NAACP did not solve this enduring problem, but was able to survive better than its predecessors due in large measure to external financial support. The major fiscal problem faced by pre-NAACP organizations was the high price of membership or annual dues at a time when the masses of African Americans were struggling just to survive the economic impact of white supremacy. Each of the earlier organizations charged a five-dollar annual membership fee, a sum that during this time was high for professionals as well as the masses. Learning from this mistake and staked with some limited white financial support, the NAACP initially set membership dues at one dollar for associates and two dollars for contributors—fees that were more manageable and would became even more so over time.

The pre-NAACP organizations' inability to effectively disseminate information to members and the general public about their activities also greatly limited the support they garnered. The organizations needed a well-distributed mouthpiece or organ to publicize their activities and to spell out their policies and organizational goals. Like the Abolitionist movement before it, the Afro-American Council attempted this when organizing in 1898, but was limited by both a lack of funding and the regional fissures within the organization. Based on a proposal of William A. Pledger of the *Atlanta Age*, the organization sought to create a Washington, D.C.– based newspaper to publish general news and to be used as the Council's propaganda machine. While this endeavor never got off the ground, W. E. B. Du Bois picked up the idea with the Niagara Movement, publishing both *The Moon* and *The Horizon*. He then carried and expanded upon this idea after the formation of the NAACP by creating *The Crisis*. As historian Patricia Sullivan explains, "Du Bois believed that future of the NAACP, indeed its very survival, depended upon securing a firm base among black Americans and organizing them around a common vision of political and social struggle."[11] *The Crisis* was central to this endeavor. "We are trying something which has not often been done," Du Bois indicated, and "that is to spread propaganda over a wide space where there is no territorial unity. We are trying to bring together people who have never seen each other, but simply have racial discrimination as a point of contact."[12] Unlike the other organizations, Du Bois, the NAACP, and *The Crisis* were successful in spreading their message and unifying the second generation removed from slavery to help build support for the creation of local branches of the NAACP.

Booker T. Washington and his looming presence on the scene—most importantly within the Afro-American Council—also played a major role in the realignment that led to the creation of the NAACP. Washington's public position of accommodation as well as his perceived attempts to control the Afro-American Council by steering it toward a "conservative" position helped galvanize open opposition to the Council. As this study demonstrates, Washington likely agreed with many of the positions and strategies of the civil rights organizations, but was locked into maintaining a public stance of accommodation due to his dependence on conservative northern philanthropists and moderate southern whites. In fact, perhaps the main reason the Afro-American Council did not become *the* civil rights organization was due to the many members who knew of Washington's full "radical" involvement in the Council not being allowed by Washington to discuss this activity publicly. Washington's activities in the organization's court cases and strategies were much deeper, "radical," and forward-looking than previously acknowledged. However, for contemporaries who were unaware of Washington's covert activities within the organization, or even for many who were aware but resented his public silence, his presence and power became too much to stomach. The Wizard's publicly "conservative" policies in the wake of deteriorating racial conditions thus had come to trump individual understanding of the man, his sympathies, and his presence within a *civil rights* organization. As a result, Washington's demand for discretion regarding his public and private roles as well as his feuds with other civil rights leaders prevented the Council's leaders from bringing individuals such as Trotter and other Niagaraites into the fold, in St. Paul and Louisville in particular. Moreover, after 1906 and Brownsville, many of Washington's allies within the organizations refused to allow him to dictate policy and approach and began seeking to form new organizations or alliances not subject to his oversight.

An additional issue that plagued the precursors of the NAACP, as well as the organization itself (but not to the same detriment), was personality struggles and the clashing of egos. According to the *Colored American* after the Afro-American Council's 1903 Louisville convention, the problem could be characterized as "cerebral elephantiasis." The clamoring for a voice and the desperate desire of many to be *the* leader greatly hindered the development and day-to-day workings of race organizations in the late nineteenth and early twentieth centuries. "We have a condition," Fortune explained in the *Colored American Magazine* shortly after his 1904 resignation from the Council, "in which every man feels that he is as good and knows as much as his neighbor, and refuses to follow if not allowed to lead. Demoralization, therefore, paralyzes the thought and action of the race. That is the situation to-day."[13] The Afro-American League and Council were particularly weighed down by this phenomenon. While each organization provided a debating platform for the influential leadership ideals and strategies proposed by T. Thomas Fortune, Ida B. Wells-Barnett, Mary Church Terrell, Henry McNeal Turner, Booker T. Washington, W. E. B. Du Bois, Alexander Walters, William Monroe Trotter, and others, debate often failed to produce a "functional consensus" among the "deeply divided intraracial ideals related to the fulfillment of black citizenship in American democracy."[14] Because of this inability to reach a practical accord, the debating frequently highlighted hairline cracks that often grew to cavernous proportions until both sides were so blinded by their own positions that they were within only shouting rather than talking distance of each other. This repeatedly led to splintering and the development of similar, yet rival organizations that competed for the same funds and attention from members of the race.

Yet despite the myriad issues that plagued pre-NAACP civil rights organizations, these groups still were able to fashion a rich and multifaceted legacy of struggle and networks of activists that later converged with the formation of the NAACP. *An Army of Lions* is thus a history of the individuals involved with these early organizations who formed a group of activists that, as T. Thomas Fortune claimed in 1890, knew their rights and had "the courage to defend them."[15]

On completion of this work, it became obvious that no serious engagement with the history of civil rights activists could be complete without such individuals as T. Thomas Fortune, J. C. Price, T. McCants Stewart, Ida B. Wells-Barnett, Henry McNeal Turner, Bishop Alexander Walters, Mary Church Terrell, John Mitchell, Jr., George H. White, William Monroe Trotter, Frederick McGhee, Jesse Lawson, Lewis G. Jordan, J. Douglass Wetmore, W. E. B. Du Bois *and* Booker T. Washington. I believe that such a statement will become clearer as you read about the activities and events contained in *An Army of Lions*. All of these individuals were active in the Afro-American League, the National Afro-American Council, and the organizations that developed in their wake prior to the creation of the NAACP. Their efforts had a decisive impact on the development of future civil rights activism, especially the Afro-American League and Council's "go into the courts and fight it out" approach.[16] These individuals and their colleagues were "convinced of the necessity of *organization*," and believed that only a well-organized group of African Americans could "successfully combat the direst and deadliest of all foes to human progress, and equal citizenship, viz. *American prejudice*."[17]

Chapter 1

Aceldama and the Black Response

> The Freedman is dying 'mid carnage and gore
> God of our fathers!—hast thou given us o'er
> In this bloody embrace, to these tigers a prey?
> Let vengeance be thine!—thou wilt repay.
> Away with the thought!—for this is no dream;
> They war against civil rights!—that is their theme.
> But soon will they cringe, as we know full well
> The crisis has come and the tolling bells tell
> We will not yield, not in fear of the grave,
> The rights that belong to the free and the brave.
> —Henry McNeal Turner, 1881

Racial tensions in Danville, Virginia, a town of eight thousand with a slight black majority, were on the rise during the state election of 1883. Early in the campaign, several newspapers ran an editorial cartoon depicting white school children being paddled by an African American schoolmaster.[1] The cartoon played on the fears of the white community, which had lost some political control to the African American community in the previous election. In 1882, blacks had gained both a majority in the city council and a healthy share of the law enforcement positions, and had begun to dominate the public market under an African American superintendent. Despite continued white control of key political positions—mayor, police chief, city sergeant, commissioner of revenue, etc.—the dominant rhetoric surrounding the election was that Danville's "black government" must be defeated.[2]

Amid this rising racial tension, a group of prominent white businessmen issued the "Danville Circular." The notice sought to "lay before [the public] a few facts from which [they could] form some idea of the injustice and humiliation to which our white people have been subjected and are daily undergoing by the domination and misrule of the radical or Negro party in absolute power."[3] Seeking to rally support for the white Conservative-Democratic party in the coming election, business leaders claimed in the circular that the black population paid only a fraction of the tax dollars paid by white citizens, yet disproportionately benefited from the expenditure of tax revenues. The business leaders also grumbled that white men were being arrested by African American policemen for the most frivolous acts and were typically brought "to the Mayor's office followed by swarms of jeering and hooting and mocking Negroes, and tried, fined and lectured and imprisoned by a Negro justice and then followed to the jail by the same insulting rabble."[4] Finally, the circular complained that African Americans perpetually lied to whites, and that they "infest the streets and sidewalks in squads, hover about public houses, and sleep on the doorsteps of the storehouses and the benches of the market place. They also impede the travel of ladies and gentlemen, very frequently forcing them from the sidewalk into the street."[5]

It was within this context that racial violence and terrorism commenced in Danville on November 3, 1883. Just three days before the election, a black man apparently jostled a white male on the sidewalk as they attempted to pass one another. According to reports, words were exchanged, and the white male drew his revolver and opened fire. More gunfire and scuffling occurred; when the dust and powder had settled, three African Americans lay dead with six others wounded. Four whites were wounded and one killed.[6] White vigilantes, in what became known as the Danville Riot, took control of the town and warned blacks not to be on the streets on Election Day. Proclaiming victory in advance, the vigilantes declared that they would win "votes or no votes, with double barrel shotguns, breach loading shotguns and Smith and Wesson double-action."[7]

Events such as the Danville Riot were repeated throughout the South in the post-Reconstruction period. A generation removed from slavery, African America remained locked in a brawl with the larger American society over its very existence. While a number of white Americans prospered during the Gilded Age and the Progressive Era by benefiting from limited political, social, and economic reforms, conditions for African Americans reached their lowest point in the post-Emancipation era. In such a climate, a small cadre of blacks began grasping the need for organization in the fight to stop the reversal of African American civil and political rights. In turn, this group began calling for the formation of a national civil rights organization. Those involved in the movement to create this organization represented a new generation of blacks born in the last days of slavery or the first years of emancipation. They understood the rights guaranteed by the Reconstruction amendments and were willing to defend them. Together, they actively worked to expand the national government's policies to cater to their needs while remaining politically independent. They understood the necessity of organizing from within the African American community, and used global politics, public memory, and the press to achieve their goals.

* * *

Through violence, intimidation, and the invocation of racial politics, Danville's white minority was successful in reducing the number of black voters and reclaiming its position of power in the city's political and economic sectors. The events of Danville in the autumn of 1883 offer a poignant illustration of the ways in which southern states had been systematically overturning the limited power that African Americans had gained during Reconstruction. Since 1876 and the election of Rutherford B. Hayes, the South had resumed its plans for racial and social engineering to the extent allowed by the U.S. Constitution, existing laws, and northern public opinion.[8] Violence was a key element in the redemption of white control. As historian Edward Ayers noted, unprosecuted white lawlessness and the "violence of lynching was a way for white people to reconcile weak governments with a demand for an impossibly high level of racial mastery, a way of terrorizing blacks into acquiescence."[9]

The violence and intimidation against blacks employed throughout the history of the United States had not stopped during Reconstruction. In 1884, African American journalist T. Thomas Fortune declared, "it is not necessary . . . to recapitulate the incidents of Reconstruction history which naturally led up to the finality of 1876. It is sufficient to know that anarchy prevailed in every Southern State; that a black man's life was not worth the having; that armed bodies of men openly defied the Constitution of the United States and nullified each and every one of its guarantees of citizenship to the colored man." Fortune also asserted that it is important to remember that the Republican Party permitted armed insurrection during Reconstruction, and in that period "thousands of black men . . . were shot down like sheep and that not *one* of the impudent assassins was ever hung by the neck until he was dead."[10]

The mob violence and lynching from 1868–1876 that Fortune discussed in his 1884 article became more pervasive in the South and took on an even more savage character in the post-Reconstruction era. During the 1880s, the practice of lynching became transformed from acts of extrajudicial "justice" that harbored no particular racial overtones into a systematic, ritualistic ceremony where thousands of blacks of all ages and genders would be slowly executed by mutilation, torture, and burning in a public forum. By 1882, lynching had become a national problem, and both the *Chicago Tribune* and the Tuskegee Institute began keeping records of the acts of violence. Northern politicians and the public, however, were reluctant to involve themselves in any form of southern affairs as public sentiment increasingly favored the burying of the "bloody shirt." With the nation's energy directed toward reunification, the status and protection of African America became only a negligible factor in that process.[11]

This reign of terror against black individuals and the community throughout the South was accompanied by the slow, methodical creation of a system of de jure and de facto segregation now known as Jim Crow.[12] Although the Civil Rights Act of 1875 guaranteed African Americans full and equal enjoyment of public accommodations, theaters, and other public amusement, the "law was disregarded with impunity."[13] As early as 1877, the young black journalist John E. Bruce remarked that though the black American had been freed and enfranchised, "he is only nominally free. His rights are abridged; he is an American only in name. The doors of public schools are closed against his children, [and] common carriers, hotel and places of amusement, refuse to recognize him as a free man; no matter what his rank or station may be, he cannot enjoy the privileges which the Constitution . . . guarantees to the humblest citizen."[14]

Even while individuals such as Bruce chastised the nation for the slow and methodical encroachment on black rights, such encroachments continued to expand despite judicial questioning of the constitutionality of segregation. Beginning with Tennessee in 1881, states had steadily been passing statutes segregating African Americans on railroad cars, in depots, and on wharves. By 1880, five major cases concerning African American civil rights had reached the Supreme Court—two of them dealing with discrimination in inns and hotels, two with theaters, and one with railroad cars.[15]

African Americans responded to these social conditions in numerous ways, including the promotion of self-help, racial solidarity, economic nationalism, emigration, and political agitation. Around 1883, new individuals appeared on the scene who challenged the strategies of the older black leadership and aimed at gaining and defending civil and political equality. For example, in that year T. Thomas Fortune became the head editor of the *New York Globe*. Fortune, born a slave in Florida, watched his father, Emmanuel Fortune, and his Republican colleagues struggle against nefarious forces during Reconstruction. Soon after the election of Hayes and the end of Reconstruction, the younger Fortune left the South, settled in New York, and founded the *New York Globe* (subsequently named the *Freeman* and the *Age*), which quickly became the most widely read black paper of the era. Using the memory of his youth in Reconstruction Florida and his newspaper as his pulpit, the sometimes-cantankerous Fortune became one of the most outspoken critics of southern racism, a promoter of racial solidarity and race pride, and an uncompromising advocate for the civil and political rights of African Americans. He castigated disfranchisement, election fraud, both of the political parties, mob violence, the convict lease system, inequities in school funding, and the rise of segregation.[16]

* * *

During this same period, vocal editors such as Harry C. Smith and W. Calvin Chase began publishing the *Cleveland Gazette* and the *Washington Bee* respectively. Others such as T. McCants Stewart, Richard T. Greener, John E. Bruce, John Mitchell, Jr., William S. Scarborough, Booker T. Washington, Fannie Barrier Williams, Ferdinand L. Barnett, and Ida B. Wells began assuming leadership roles.[17] As Richard T. Greener, Harvard University's first black graduate, observed, "young Africa, stronger in the pocket, expresses its contempt for the lofty airs of the old, decayed colored aristocracy." This new group, though not cohesive, generally turned its energies inward, promoting self-determination and race enhancement.[18]

Extremely important in this group of "young Africa" was the large crowd of journalists, such as Fortune, Wells, Bruce, Mitchell, and Chase among others, who were gaining more respect during the period. As African American elected officials progressively lost the fragile footing they held in the political arena during the post-Reconstruction era, the black press increasingly became the voice of the race, expressing racial pride and encouragement as well as attacking all forms of racism and exploitation. From the late 1880s into the first decade of the twentieth century, the black press became more and more important as a voice in the community, and the editors of the increasing number of black newspapers and journals commanded more respect and gained a greater following because of the perspicacity and range of their analysis.[19] Through their actions, the editors of the period often became active participants and leading organizers in the political activity of the race.

However, one month prior to the violence of Danville, this group of individuals—and black America as a whole—was dealt a judicial blow that confirmed the "revolution gone backward" previously signaled by unprosecuted violence in places such as Danville.[20] In mid-October of 1883, the Supreme Court reached a decision on the five cases (commonly referred to as the "Civil Rights Cases") that had been pending since 1880. In a four-to-one decision, the Court ruled that neither the Thirteenth nor Fourteenth Amendment authorized the public accommodations sections of the Civil Rights Act.[21] This decision removed one of the few remaining restraints on southern discriminatory practices; in conjunction with the spread of lynching and mob rule, it made many within the black community believe, as John E. Bruce declared six years earlier, that blacks were "Americans only in name."[22]

Not surprisingly, the African American response to the decision was forceful and indignant. "The colored people of the United States," Fortune declared, "feel to-day as if they had been baptized in ice water." Fortune wondered further whether the U.S. government was worthy of the respect and loyalty of the black community.[23] African Methodist Episcopal Church (AME) bishop Henry McNeal Turner, the fiery emigration supporter and former state legislator from Georgia, provided the answer when he professed that the decision "absolves the negro's allegiance to the general government, makes the American flag to him a rag of contempt instead of a symbol of liberty."[24] John E. Bruce, the irascible nationalist leaning freelance journalist, joined the chorus, observing that there was "a class of half-educated people belonging to the superior race in this country, who are devoting all their energies, and what little intellect God has given them . . . to demonstrate that the Negro isn't as good as a white man." Months later, he noted that "in this so-called land of the free and home of the brave it is a common thing for us to speak of it as Our Country," yet "socially and politically it is not our country but simply our abiding place . . . we are permitted to exercise the right of citizenship only when the exercise of such a right conforms to the ideas of the dominant race."[25] Bruce proposed remedies to enable African Americans to survive the difficult times, asserting that education would "unlock the door," and that the accumulation of wealth would "push it open enough for any Negro to pass through with ease."[26] He believed that if African Americans organized around these issues in a united front, they would accomplish a great deal.

Bruce's fellow newspaperman Fortune agreed. Organization was needed—and in a form in which the community had no prior experience. Following the Supreme Court decision, the young editor began agitating for a long-range solution to the race question, proclaiming "We are aliens in our native land. . . . The colored people have been told emphatically that they have the ballot, and if they can not use it can't be helped. We are placed at the mercy of every lawless ruffian; we are declared to be the victims of infamous injustice without redress."[27]

The situation, in Fortune's estimation, called for immediate action—something he did not see coming from either of the two major political parties. "I desire not to be unjust: I desire to render unto to Caesar the things that are Caesar's," he argued. The time had arrived, he intoned, "when colored men should stop and think. That's all—*stop and think*." He insisted that he knew his rights and had "the courage to protest when [his] rights [were] outraged," proclaiming "I do care" which party "sacrifices my rights, abuses my confidence, outrages my feelings—*I protest!*" Fortune wanted the race to have the same position, and called for the community to organize with "unity of counsel and of purpose," because "when we have these," he argued, "we can force from demagogues and fanatics all the just rights which the Constitution guarantees to us."[28]

Evoking rallying cries of "no more Danvilles" and "Race First Then Party," Fortune called on the community to create a national black civil rights organization that could effectively and systematically protest lynch law, mob violence, segregation, the penal system, and the inequitable distribution of school funds. It would stand as an "uncompromising defense of the race with which we are identified." "Let us agitate! *agitate!* AGITATE! until the protest shall wake the nation from its indifference," Fortune declared.[29] "You must fight your own battles," he urged. "You must come together. Brave men, men of brains—these must come to the front, and laying aside all selfish and personal aims labor for the upbuilding of the race and the full concession to us of each every right guaranteed to us by the Constitution of the United States. And the masses must sustain such men." He concluded: "*Our rights, our liberties, must be forced from the States, the counties, the municipalities. . . . Will you do it! Dare you do it!*"[30]

* * *

Fortune's idea of self-help and racial solidarity through protest and agitation in response to the white community's indifference and hostility was not necessarily new. The convention movement, beginning in Philadelphia in 1830, met irregularly on the national and state levels for nearly sixty years to formulate plans for solving the problems that faced the race. Over time, the conventions advocated the abolition of slavery through moral suasion, political action, and armed revolt. Before the Civil War, some delegates had also promoted the notion of emigration. In the post-emancipation years, the conventions, dominated largely by politicians, were concerned mostly with civil rights and the enforcement of the Fifteenth Amendment, with some later emphasis on self-help, land ownership, and migration out of the South.[31]

Yet despite the nearly annual gatherings of the conventions, Fortune believed that the movement had not accomplished much, and its approach of holding meetings and making proclamations before returning home to do little or nothing had run its course. Fortune's plan was a new model—a permanent organization that would not ask, but rather demand that justice be done. A national civil rights association that would meet annually in convention, but would be based in local and state branches throughout the country, to fight not only racism in general, but to contest discrimination and mob violence in the local, state, and federal courts as well as the halls of Congress and the office of the U.S. president. This new model, once constructed, would become the form in which African American protest would formulate again and again throughout the nineteenth and twentieth centuries, most directly in the Afro-American League, the Afro-American Council, the Committee of Twelve, the Niagara Movement, and the National Association for the Advancement of Colored People.

Initially, despite the continued deterioration of black rights, there was little response to Fortune's call for the creation of a national organization. Three years after his original appeal, however, Fortune had become a more determined and better-prepared advocate. In the spring of 1887, he again proposed the formation of a national league that would fuse together the small efforts of various individuals and groups. There come "periods in the history of every people," he declared, "when the necessity of their affairs makes it imperative that they take such steps as shall show to the world that they are worthy to be free, and therefore, entitled to the sympathy of all mankind and to . . . justice and fair play."[32]

From the pages of the *Freeman,* Fortune pleaded for "every man and woman to take hold and do his duty."[33] Black Americans "needed to take hold of this problem" for themselves and make so much noise that all the world shall know the wrongs [they] suffer and [their] determination to right those wrongs."[34] His friend and supporter, Brooklyn-based lawyer T. McCants Stewart, a freeborn South Carolinian who had taught at Liberia College before returning to New York to practice law, agreed and encouraged the idea of creating a race organization to coordinate the efforts of the population as they directly attacked the discrimination in the nation. Stewart sought a coordinated effort of "colored men with leather stomachs to continue going into places where" they were refused "until 'the boss' and his guests" were "accustomed to entertain and lunch with 'the brother in black.' "[35]

Fortune certainly approved of this direct-action campaign, but both he and Stewart knew that the struggle would have to be waged on many fronts while its supporters utilized a variety of political impulses and tactics. Fortune drew for example on the Irish struggle as a source of inspiration for the black community. The Irish in America and Ireland, as Fortune understood their situation, had kept their fight in the press and gained the sympathy of the world through their actions. In the 1880s, thousands of Irish Americans rallied in support of an organization known as the American Land League, formed to bolster both struggles in Ireland and the Irish National Land League. Fortune believed that the actions of these Irish laborers in Ireland and America could serve as a model for organization of black America. He prodded African American readers to follow the Irish example in which the Irish "make themselves heard by their lung power, by the length of their purse strings, and by the intelligence with which they cast their ballots, and by the confidence they place in the men who have the ability and the courage to champion their cause either with argument or dynamite."[36] As he saw no similar movement taking place in the African American struggle, he proposed the creation of a Protective League to see if members of the race could not put their "shoulders to the wheel and . . . compel the concession of those constitutional rights" that were denied them.[37]

Fortune further proposed that his "Afro-American National League" be patterned after the Irish National League, an outgrowth of the Irish National Land League that began in 1879 under the leadership of Michael Davitt. The

Irish National Land League was organized to challenge the maltreatment of Irish tenant farmers by their landlords and British rulers, but Davitt, influenced by Henry George, also began promoting land nationalization.[38] Many members disagreed with this emphasis and shifted their loyalty to another leader, Charles Parnell, who ultimately formed the Irish National League. The ideology and direction of the Irish National League was seen as a compromise between the two leaders' views on the land question, with the new organization placing home rule rather than land reform as its top priority.[39]

Inspired by the Irish firebrands Davitt and Parnell and their struggle, in an 1886 editorial Fortune called for African Americans able to throw their weight and money behind the Irish cause. "The colored people," he explained to his readers, "know what oppression is, for they have been, they are now, oppressed; it is manifestly right and proper, therefore, that they should sympathize with oppressed people under whatever government such may be found. . . . We have an honest sympathy for the Irish people in the parliamentary fight, and it would be a wise step if those of us who can afford to do so would contribute something to the Fund now being raised to assist Mr. Parnell in his parliamentary battles."[40]

Fortune's linking of the African American struggle to the battle taking place in Ireland occurred while Parnell, Davitt, Henry George, and Irish-American journalist Patrick Ford were at their peak of popularity. In the mid-to-late 1880s, George and Ford made great strides in persuading the Irish-American community that the Irish Land League struggle was not just something in the homeland, but one that affected the world. In their speeches and writings they drew clear parallels between the situation in Ireland—land monopolization, social unrest, degraded farmers and laborers, and hollow democratic institutions—and conditions in the United States. Fortune was particularly drawn to the universality of Irish Americans' struggle against accumulated undemocratic power. He concurred with Ford when the latter intoned from his paper, *Irish World*, that the struggle in Ireland is the "same as the struggle in America—a contest against legalized forms of oppressions."[41]

Fortune proposed the creation of the Afro-American League nearly a year and a half after calling upon the black community to lend its support to Parnell and the Irish National Land League. Like the Irish and Irish Americans, he wanted Afro-Americans to make themselves heard by argument or dynamite. He rhetorically asked, "How would we proceed in this important matter? . . . Let the entire race in this country organize into a Protective

League; let it be organized on the same plan [as] that [of] the Irish National League."[42] Fortune's proposal received immediate recognition from the Irish American incendiary John Boyle O'Reilly. O'Reilly, the editor of the Boston-based *Pilot* and a supporter of the Irish National League, declared that the forming of "the Afro-American League to protect the interests of our colored fellow citizens is a step in the right direction. . . . The colored American element can become the strongest political race in the country. Every self-respecting black man and woman should join the League."[43]

One week after making the second call for a national organization, Fortune published a list of grievances upon which his proposed Afro-American League would focus its attention. They included challenges to lynching and mob rule as well as the suppression of black suffrage. Third on the list was a challenge to the unequal distribution of funds allotted to black versus white schools. A fourth grievance concerned the South's deplorable penitentiary system, including chain gangs and convict lease programs. Another point of contention was the increasingly discriminatory practices of the Southern railroads. Finally, Fortune believed that the League had to challenge the growing practice of denying blacks access to public accommodations.[44]

Fortune did not believe that the creation of such an uncompromising organization would be easy, and understood that Southern members would likely experience extreme and violent reactions from whites. Because the association's activities were of such importance, however, Fortune held that nothing should prevent its members from arousing public opinion and advocating for social change. He went so far as to acknowledge that the use of force by Afro-Americans to protect themselves and their right to voice their grievances might be necessary in some circumstances. "We propose to accomplish our purpose by the peaceful methods of agitation, through the ballot and the courts," the fiery editor declared, "but if others use the weapons of violence to combat our peaceful arguments it is not for us to run away from violence."[45]

Mrs. A. E. J., supporter of the League idea, concurred with Fortune's sentiments, as the final three stanzas of her poem, "A Woman's Plea for the League," demonstrates:

Brave Attucks, aye, and L'Ouverture,
Nat Turner, and the rest,
A record left that will endure
Old Time's severest test.
Then let their memories spur you on,

To fight for Liberty;
You have it not, save empty name;
You have it not,—and who're to blame?
Your reason answers,—"We!"

Yes, we may bleed, and we may die.
What cares our brother race?
We're "naught but Negroes"—Man, Oh fie!
Go, hide your craven face,
If you can find it in your heart,
Against a cause so just
To raise your voice, to take the part
Of those who'll thrust the poisoned dart
Of scorn deep in your breast!
We've more men, brave enough to die,
If need be, for the cause.
We've women too, who'll join the cry
For Justice, backed by laws.
But what's the good of naught but words;
Join hands, each bold brave knight;
Come let us all, with deeds and words,
And heart to heart, bound with race cords,
"The League" will the fight.[46]

Echoing the commitment demonstrated in the above poem, much of the black community and press responded favorably to Fortune's call for the creation of a united organization. The young principal of Tuskegee Institute, Booker T. Washington, expressed his enthusiasm by writing, "Push the battle to the gate. Let there be no hold-up until a League shall be found in every village."[47] Ardent editor of the *Memphis Free Speech* Ida B. Wells called the League idea "the grandest ever originated by colored men." She declared that the race had "reached a stage in the world's history where [they could] no longer be passive onlookers, but must join the fray for [their] recognition, or be stigmatized forever as a race of cowards." She continued by summarizing the hideous outrages of the nation: "Innocent men (supposed to be so until proven guilty) and women are victims of mob and lynch law; cultured and refined ladies and gentlemen are being insulted and proscribed on the railways every way and every day we turn there is this insulting prosecution to be met." For Wells, the way to challenge such a situation was to establish and maintain the Afro-American League and fight a passionate and coordinated struggle against racial injustice.[48]

John Mitchell, Jr., the outspoken editor of the *Richmond Planet*, was also among the many who responded favorably to the proposition of organizing a league.[49] Mitchell, born a slave in Virginia amid the Civil War, became a local politician, businessman, and newspaper editor. Through his pithy yet passionate editorials, Mitchell continually protested all forms of racial discrimination, contested lynching, and promoted black education and uplift. Following Fortune's call, Mitchell urged his readers, and black America in general, to "follow words with action. . . . Let the cry for organization go forth until the country is girdled with organizations of colored men who will be able to demand recognition and force the respect due the law by all men."[50] Mitchell was so encouraged by the prospects of the League that he quickly created the first local branch in Richmond, Virginia, on June 22, 1887.[51]

As favorably as much of the community reacted to the League idea, a number of individuals did not see the prospects of such an organization in the same glorious light. In an article entitled "Must the League Wait?" Fortune summarized many of the arguments against its creation. He believed that there had been so little organization prior to this time because "Everybody suspected everybody else of harboring treacherous designs." Second, he noticed that many individuals expressed reservations because they believed such an organization "would provoke the wrath of Southern whites and therefore precipitate bloodshed and other violence." Many were convinced that African Americans were too "poor and dependent and courageless to sustain" such an onslaught.[52] Finally, Fortune quoted the sentiments of Marshall W. Taylor, editor of the *Southwestern Christian Advocate*, to highlight the anti-League sentiment that irked the politically independent editor the most. Taylor suggested "that it would be well to defer the organizations until about the time of the inauguration of our next President."[53]

For Fortune, these criticisms were "nonsense," especially the final comment. He believed there was "no reason in the world why the great interests of the race should be allowed to wait on the motions" of the future president or the Republican Party.[54] It was not lost on him, however, that there was enough sentiment against the creation of the League that the building of the organization might have to be put on the back burner for a while. Nonetheless, he believed that such a civil rights group would develop. It "may come as a slow growth," he proclaimed, but "we believe it will come; in fact we believe it must come."[55]

Through his newspaper, Fortune continued to try to instill members of the race with the "self-reliance and mutual confidence" needed to solidify the Afro-American League. In the same issue where he surmised that the League might have to be put on hold, he published an outline of organization and a constitution for the proposed group.[56] In this projected constitution, he proclaimed that the organization would educate the public on the problems African Americans and the nation face and would appeal to the country's court system to protect the legal and constitutional rights of the nation's black citizens. Fortune now, however, steered clear from his earlier support for self-defense, a tactical concession that might have satisfied conservative elements in the black community without blunting previously circulated promises of retaliation. Finally, he claimed that the Afro-American League should be nonpartisan because the political parties had only swindled the black voters since the passage of the Fifteenth Amendment. By adopting a nonpartisan stance, Fortune felt that the League might use the black vote to influence politicians into supporting issues of importance to the black community.[57]

* * *

Encouraged by the creation of state leagues in Connecticut, Pennsylvania, Virginia, and Alabama, and despite his earlier reservations regarding the possibility of immediately creating a national organization, Fortune proposed that a national meeting of the League be held in Richmond, Virginia, for early December 1887.[58] With the subsequent formation of yet another state League in Kansas and his publication of organizational plans, Fortune was optimistic that branches would soon develop throughout the country.[59]

However, his optimism proved to be premature. Despite his continued promotion of the League idea, the development of the organization on a national level came to a halt and the proposed national meeting never took place. Limited local and state Leagues, as Marshall Taylor had suggested, may very well have had something to do with the election of Benjamin Harrison and the return of the Republican Party to the White House. Despite repeated calls for African Americans to take an independent stance in politics, the majority continued to cast their ballots and fate with the Republican side. Generally speaking, African Americans were elated with the election of Harrison and the Republican Party's control of Congress.[60]

Harrison, however, did not enter office with as strong a stance on African American rights as the black community had hoped. Even before his inauguration, many African Americans had begun to express doubts concerning his effectiveness, and his subordination of the race issue to that of the tariff left many blacks pessimistic. To many within the community, Harrison, like Hayes before him, was promising "ex-confederates control of the South."[61]

Furthermore, early in the Harrison Administration, many African Americans began to question whether the Republican Party could or would affect real change in the country—something it had failed to do since the election of Hayes.[62] Despite Republican control of the executive and legislative branches of the federal government, African Americans continued to witness the deterioration of the minimal political footing they had maintained during Reconstruction. They persistently suffered from mob and lynch violence. As John Quincy Adams of the *St. Paul Western Appeal* asserted nine months after Harrison's inauguration, the defeat of the Democratic ticket had so maddened southern whites that they increasingly unleashed their true feelings toward the African American population. Unfettered racial violence, Adams opined, "reveals the fact that the white men of the South hate the Negro citizens with a hatred that is implacable, malignant, and undying. So deep and strong is this hatred," proclaimed the editor, "that grave senators are lead by it to the perpretration [sic] of deeds that would put Jessie James to the blush."[63]

Appeals to the federal government for intervention or some other form of relief continually fell upon deaf ears. The always-provocative Henry McNeal Turner contended that Harrison was "giving as much attention to the wails and dying groans of the Negro South and West as he is to the bark of a dog."[64]

It was in this climate that Fortune's Afro-American League idea began to gain currency. With no external help in sight, the African American community once again turned inward to discover the solace and strength to struggle against this "Hell-born anaconda" seeking to destroy the black population, especially in the South.[65] Throughout its two-year hiatus, the League idea had never really died: development had continued on the local and state level even if it failed to materialize on the national stage.[66] With continued outrages occurring against blacks throughout the country, Fortune took the opportunity in January 1889 to reinsert into the public debate his desire for the creation of a national civil rights organization.

At the end of 1888, a lynching party was organized in Mississippi following a scuffle between a black male and a white male. The African American had refused to step aside as the white male passed on the walkway. After the tussle, the black men of the community, rather than waiting around idly for the anticipated response, laid in ambush and fired upon the "lynching party of white rascals, killing a few of them." Fortune condemned the Northern white press for blaming the incident on the black community, stating "colored men do not attack white men except for very provoking cause." Moreover, he called for the black population of the South to stand with their guns. If whites "resort to the gun and the torch . . . let the colored men do the same, and if blood must flow like water and bonfires be made of valuable property, so be it all around, for what is fair for the white man to do to teach the Negro his place is fair for the Negro to do to teach the white man his place." The heated editor then revived the idea of his national organization, believing that no headway would be made against the injustices served upon the race until such a body was developed. "The Irish people never could bring John Bull to his proud knees until they combined in a compact organization," Fortune noted. Black America "shall make very little headway against the cussedness of Uncle Jonathan until [they] adopt that leaf of Irish history for Home Rule and absolute justice."[67]

A few months later, William E. Matthews, successful lawyer and real-estate broker in the Washington, D.C. area, wrote Fortune expressing his desire to resuscitate the League idea.[68] According to historian Robert Factor, Matthews through his connections with the African Methodist Episcopal Church and his affiliation with literary and historical societies in Washington, New York, and Maryland played an important supporting role in relighting the spark for the Afro-American League idea.[69] Matthews' efforts were aided by the *Detroit Plaindealer*'s publishing his letter in the pages of their weekly, then printing the correspondence in a circular sent to various black leaders and sympathetic whites asking for their ideas concerning such an endeavor.[70] In October 1889, Fortune republished his "Outline of Organization" and proposed constitution of the national association, and Leagues quickly began to be organized throughout the country.[71] By the fall of 1889, more than forty local and state organizations had been created.[72]

Once again, Ida B. Wells was among the first to speak out in support of the creation of a national civil rights organization. "[I]n light of recent events," she remarked, "the thinking men of the race are beginning to realize more forcibly than ever that our only hope is union. Congress seems powerless to help us, the State Executive machinery is unwilling to do so," and the only hope is for the race to turn inward for strength and address the nation as one unified body.[73] Robert Pelham, editor of the *Detroit Plaindealer*, seconded

Wells's thoughts, noting "a spontaneous outburst of approval to the sentiment that the time for patience and meekness is past, and that now is the time for action. Action that will not alienate, but bring to the cause of the race, friends. . . . Public opinion is stiring [sic] up the hearts of the liberty loving people. . . . Act! Agitate! Organize!"[74]

In the same issue of the *Age* in which Wells's comments appeared, Fortune published an editorial entitled "The Supreme Effort," explaining that it behooved African American citizens to organize for self-protection and to appeal to the best sentiment of the American people for justice. He believed that "the heart of the Nation is true to the sublime principle of justice" and that, properly appealed to, it would "arouse and shake itself as a lion when injustice has been denuded of the specious glamour in which it delights to parade." He proposed that victory would be won by wearing the public out with persistence, and that the League, like the abolitionist movement before it, would besiege "legislatures and Governors and courts of law with petitions and protests" until the African American community was blessed with the "baptism of justice" accorded them by the Constitution of the United States. African Americans, he declared, had "talked long enough."[75] It was now time to act. He again called for a national meeting of the Afro-American Leagues and other clubs or societies desiring to cooperate in the movement for a national organization, and scheduled a meeting in Nashville, Tennessee, on January 15, 1890.[76]

Many throughout the nation concurred with Fortune's sentiment, and to demonstrate the growing interest, the following week's *Age* was filled with a number of letters and selections from other papers throughout the country expressing support for the creation of a national civil rights organization. An excerpt from a sermon by the pastor of Detroit, Michigan's Bethel Church, James M. Henderson, demonstrates the enthusiasm for the proposed assembling of the Leagues. The idea "to centralize and unify the mighty forces of the race and lead the willing to victory," Henderson acknowledged, "is an ambition as grand as any that ever inspired noblest deed. . . . with a loud hurrah the enthusiastic clans are gathering from cold and bleak Minnesota to the Rio Grande, from New England to the Golden Gate eager eyes are reading the Fortune Constitution and earnest voices are crying out for the formation of leagues." "Let the people," Henderson told his congregation, "gather in the log schoolhouse, the hall, the church, or the forest if need be and with a steady hand let a million black men subscribe to the Magna Charta of our day."[77]

Despite the enthusiasm for the national convention, there remained a handful of issues that divided League supporters: the proposed name for the organization, the location of the meeting, and the makeup of League leadership. The name of the group, for example, was questioned by a contingent from the Washington, D.C. and Philadelphia areas. On November 16, 1889, W. Calvin Chase, the somewhat erratic, recalcitrant editor of the intensely Republican *Washington Bee*, who lived by the message of his paper's masthead "honey for friends, stings for enemies," ran an editorial claiming that there "are a great number of leading colored men in this country in favor of organization, [but] they are opposed to the name 'Afro-American League.'"[78] Chase argued that the proposed national body should be called the Equal Rights League of the United States, judging that such a name change would not "discriminate against the whites . . . [and that they would create] an organization whereby all good Americans can be members."[79]

Central to this argument was the distaste of Chase and others for the term *Afro-American* as opposed to Negro, colored, or black. Fortune was one of the strongest supporters of the term Afro-American, but Chase did not believe that the term was proper and, at this time, preferred the term colored. Harry Smith of the *Cleveland Gazette* responded forcefully to Chase's suggestion for a name change, stating that the name of the League would not be changed with his constituency's consent. "[Y]ou will not have to scratch around in the ashes to know what the Afro-American League stands for," he added. "The equal rights of American citizens is its alpha and omega."[80]

Regarding the second element of Chase's argument, "the discrimination of whites," Fortune simply asked who had drawn the colored line first. Fortune, in his initial call, had claimed that the organization was necessary because it had been "thoroughly demonstrated that the white people of this country have determined to leave the colored man alone to fight his battles."[81] Having turned its back on the black community, the white population had consistently drawn the color line.[82] Fortune, therefore, did not see any particular problem with creating an all-black organization. That did not mean, however, that whites should be excluded from the struggle. Rather, a particular goal of the League was to appeal to the best sentiment of the white population, and in coordinated efforts with them, to effect change in America.[83] Fortune, for example, had invited author and supporter of African American civil rights George Washington Cable to attend the national convention, and did not believe that the name of the organization would inhibit like-minded individuals of either race from coordinating their efforts to end the injustices that African Americans suffered daily. [84]

The question of leadership was another issue that accompanied the growth of the League idea, inspiring debate in the months before the first national conference. In October 1889, black newspapers carried a series of exchanges between William E. Matthews and lawyer and former minister to Haiti John Mercer Langston. Matthews discussed the need for the Afro-American League and urged Langston to support and lead such an organization. Matthews claimed that "a brave sagacious man is required to head this movement and organize the race into one potential whole," and believed that Langston was "qualified by temperament, training, high courage, and wide acquaintanceship with the needs of the race" for such a position.[85] In a lengthy response, Langston reported that he hopefully would "assume authority" without "offence to any one," and thanked Matthews for the opportunity to be appointed to such a manly position.[86]

In the issue of the *Age* that carried Langston's response, Fortune published an editorial calling for the Leagues to meet and to select their national leadership. It appears that one of the main problems that Fortune and others had with the unilateral selection of Langston as president of the League was that the process was undemocratic. More important, neither Matthews nor Langston at that point were members of any local or state League.[87] "If it shall please the branch Leagues after permanent organization, to elect Mr. Langston president," Fortune explained, "it will please us well; but it would be unjust to have branches already organized to have one man or a dozen who do not represent any organized branch of the League designate the chief officer."[88]

Fortune's call for the supporters of League to settle the leadership question at a national convention did not quiet the discussion. In fact, the editor's name was also tossed into the ring as a proposed candidate for the position. Many opposed Langston's bid for the presidency of the League not only due to his lack of membership in the organization, but because of his loyalty to the Republican Party. Also, while a defender of the race, Langston was not known as a "race man." Unlike Fortune, who called for "race first, then party," to many Leaguers Langston appeared willing to subordinate the issue of the race for the betterment of the Party.

League supporter Josephine Turpin Washington, a Howard University graduate and freelance journalist, did not see Matthews's preference for John Mercer Langston as League president as constituting the choice of the people. She agreed with Fortune that the decision should be made by the supporters of the League at a national conference. That aside, she threw her support behind

Fortune, whom she believed was the "natural and appropriate leader of the movement which is the product of his own fertile brain." She declared, "regardless of the fact that the honor is peculiarly due him, he is the possessor of such qualities especially needful in such leadership! He is young, progressive, bold, independent, keen of insight, varied in experience and of wide acquaintanceship." Besides, Washington asserted, he is "essentially a race man, subordinating personal interests, party allegiance, everything, to what he conceives to be the good of the race."[89]

At that time Fortune felt that the organization could do better than electing him the first president of the organization. He informed Philadelphia-based AME bishop William Heard, who also had supported him for the presidency, that he did not seek the office and would not express the desire for such a position. Fortune reiterated his wish that the individuals who had supported the movement and built the Leagues on the local and state levels select the leadership of the national organization.[90] Although there continued to be some debate in the national newspapers over the issue, the subject of presidency was put on hold until the convening of the national convention.

In the month leading up to the meeting, a final spark of controversy emerged concerning the proposed holding of the national convention in Nashville, Tennessee. As noted earlier, Tennessee had led the nation in the creation of post-Civil War de jure segregation. In 1870, the state passed a statute against intermarriage, which quickly became the model for every southern state. Again, in 1881, the Volunteer State led the way as it adopted the first Jim Crow law, which segregated African Americans on railroad cars, in depots, and on wharves. After the Supreme Court ruling in 1883 on the Civil Rights Cases, Tennessee, like other southern states, passed additional Jim Crow laws resulting in the segregating of public and private establishments, including hotels, restaurants, theaters, parks, libraries, and barbershops.[91]

A number of individuals objected to the national convention being held in Tennessee because they believed the delegates would not be treated fairly. The *Detroit Plaindealer*'s Robert Pelham explained that he was "somewhat fearful of Nashville" for several reasons. The delegates could not "expect the sentiment of the city to be with" them. Furthermore, the Nashville press was decidedly against Afro-Americans, refusing to speak of them except in demeaning terms such as "darky" or "coon." Nor could the group expect the Associated Press to give the convention solid, positive coverage.[92] Ferdinand L. Barnett, prominent Chicago attorney and editor, who himself was born to free parents in Nashville in 1859 before his family moved to Canada and later

Chicago, also expressed dissatisfaction "with the naming of Nashville . . . as the place for holding the conference," and believed the meeting should "be held in some Northern city, or at least north of Mason and Dixon's line where the members would feel free to express their opinion."[93]

In fact, almost everyone who wrote to Fortune and the *Age* expressed dissatisfaction with the choice of Nashville as the location of the convention. Interestingly, however, no one suggested that the holding of the convention in Nashville or another southern city might provide opportunities for initiating legal test cases against discrimination. In late November the majority opinion won out: the location of the national convention was changed to Chicago, where it was believed that "the difficulties" would "be entirely removed."[94] The change of venue and Fortune's call for the convention was signed by eighteen individuals from thirteen different locations, including Fortune, Alexander Walters, J. Gordon Street, William A. Pledger, Robert Pelham, Jr., Edward E. Cooper, Harry C. Smith, John Mitchell, Jr., Magnus L. Robinson, J. C. Price, John C. Dancy, William C. Chase, Thomas T. Symmons, Ferdinand L. Barnett, William B. Richie, Van N. Williams, B. Prillerman, and William H. Heard.[95]

Fortune believed that League supporters represented a kind of "New Negro," an "Afro-American agitator."[96] The latter phrase was coined by Henry W. Grady, the editor of the *Atlanta Constitution* and an advocate of the "New South," who believed that the American Race Problem was caused by the "Afro-American agitator, stirring" up strife, while the majority of the black population were "happy in their cabin homes, tilling their own land by day, and at night taking from their children the helpful message their State sends them from the schoolhouse door." The *Age* editor rhetorically asked why a group of two hundred African Americans had only recently congregated in Grady's own city of Atlanta to protest the horrible condition of the race in the Peach State. They came, Fortune explained, to denounce the suppression of the vote, the reign of mob and lynch violence, and the universal denial of African Americans' civil rights. Fortune believed such a thing as an Afro-American agitator existed, but denied that this activist was stirring up strife among a peaceful and content population. To the contrary, the Afro-American agitator had appropriately recognized the true conditions of the race in America and was "taking steps forth to the contention for absolute justice under the Constitution."[97]

Fortune contended that this rising Afro-American agitator was sounding "the death knell of the shuffling, cringing creature in black who for two centuries and a half had given the right of way to white men." He proclaimed that "in no uncertain voice that a new man in black, a freeman every inch, standing erect and undaunted, an American from head to foot, had taken the place of the miserable creature." This New Negro, he argued, "*looks like a man!* . . . bears no resemblance to a slave, or coward, or an ignoramus." "His mission," Fortune contended, "is to force the concession to him of absolute justice under State and Federal Constitutions." The Afro-American agitator, he concluded, had come "to stay, and the Afro-American League [was] the fortress of his strength."[98]

* * *

The momentum continued to build, and Fortune moved closer to fulfilling his six-year-old dream of creating a national civil rights organization. In 1884, Fortune had asked if anyone in the black community dared to stand with him to protest "when [their] rights are outraged." Throughout the 1880s, as the black community's political, social, and economic conditions continued to weaken, he and his supporters incessantly promoted the League idea. For inspiration, they drew on the Irish struggle in the United States and in Ireland, a fight in which they recognized the universal struggle against oppression. They also pulled in their own history, recalling in their campaigns the memory of the struggle against slavery, the abolitionist tradition, and the brave rebellious spirit of individuals such as Crispus Attucks and Toussaint L'Ouverture. After several years of campaigning, Fortune now stood with a group of activists prepared to perfect the nation's first civil rights organization: a group of Afro-American agitators willing to put forth the type of eternal vigilance and manly protest necessary to achieve racial equality. At the end of the decade, Fortune had a right to believe that the race was moving away from being "freeman in name—slaves in fact." The Afro-American agitator was on the rise.[99]

Chapter 2

"Stand Their Ground on This Civil Rights Business"

> The Irish National League has lessened the burden upon poor Ireland, and the prospective Negro National League will lessen our political proscription and social discrimination and teach the white Negro–haters . . . that the Negro is a man . . . and that we will receive the justice due us . . . by concentration and by our manly efforts.
>
> —Howard L. Smith

> Colored men of America, you are to answer whether or not you are ready to pitch an endless battle for the rights of manhood and womanhood.
>
> —W. H. Bonaparte

A few weeks after T. Thomas Fortune's strong rejoinder to *Atlanta Constitution* editor Henry Grady, the Afro-American agitator's quest to create a national civil rights organization finally came to fruition. The importance of the founding meeting, as Fortune noted, could neither have been easily estimated nor come at a more opportune time. The country was continuing upon its rapid course of obliterating the civil rights legislation of the Reconstruction period. While the situation had not yet reached the "nadir," the nation was well on its way toward fully "betraying the Negro." Southern states were steadily passing discriminatory legislation and were on the verge of systematically removing black voters—beginning with new provisions to the

Mississippi constitution. Moreover, northern and western blacks continued to face de facto discrimination as many whites ignored state civil rights laws or individually simply practiced various forms of discrimination. This rise of a national white supremacy was backed by a markedly increased amount of lynching and mob violence. The Afro-American League was positioning itself to be the group to stand united against this rising tide of violence and discrimination.[1]

The League's activities during this period were extremely important, but its significance is too often downplayed in studies of African American history. While the organization is frequently mentioned in the context of the African American community's response to Jim Crow, it is regularly depicted as being a failure because it lasted only a few years on the national level and did not mount any national challenges to an increasingly restrictive system of segregation. Despite its seemingly short tenure, however, the League and its activities were far more significant than historians have acknowledged. Its efforts on the local and national level demonstrate continued struggle by African Americans fighting against the odds and in the face of widespread hostility to prevent their rights from being constrained. Moreover, the actions of League supporters throughout the country set the model by which African American protest would formulate again and again throughout the nineteenth and twentieth centuries.

The history of the Afro-American League, then, reveals the success and failures of a segment of the black community attempting to create an organized response to its deteriorating social condition. The group did not challenge the growing de jure segregation of the South head-on; instead it concentrated its efforts on the de facto discrimination in the North. Among other incidents, the League tested discrimination in restaurants in Minnesota and in New York. It also successfully opposed attempts to segregate schools in Ohio and discriminatory insurance rates in New York. In its lone southern case, the League initiated a suit against the separate coach laws in Tennessee. While actively struggling against rising discrimination, the League also fought to gain widespread support among the leadership class of the community and the masses while laboring to obtain a financial foothold in the midst of the creation of rival organizations and opposition to the League idea.

Detractors were prevalent during the formation of the organization. Fortune believed that those who prophesized the movement's quick demise were the same "croaking ravens who have pulled the race back since the war."[2] In his estimation, myopic, selfish activities of the League's critics had to fail because the organization would and must succeed for the good of the race. Fortune proclaimed: "No race ever had before in the history of mankind greater cause for organization, for self-reliance, for self-help than Afro-Americans." The white public, Fortune asserted, had formed "a league to rob [Afro-Americans] of social, civil and material liberty, and are working hand in hand, in utter defiance of the Federal Constitution, to accomplish their outrageous purpose." It was now time for the black community to form its own organization to protect their rights that were "suspended in the balance."[3]

An editorial published by Levi J. Coppin in his *AME Church Review* passionately supported Fortune and tried to invigorate the delegates preparing to attend the Chicago event. The League movement, Coppin claimed, "is one of the most remarkable and significant manifestations of awakened manhood shown by the race since or before the war. The unanimity with which the people have responded to the call for national organization effectually disposes of the belief, long current and firmly rooted, that the Afro-American was constitutionally incapable of grasping the potentialities of co-operation and of turning them to advantage." Moreover, the League's formation "marks a tremendous advance in all the elements of strong, resourceful and aggressive manhood," and Coppin believed that the participants would "place the imperiled rights and interests of the race before all other considerations of whatever sort, and will contend for them, whatever circumstance of trial or danger may befall them in the work."[4]

In the midst of this fanfare, 141 delegates from twenty-one states descended upon Chicago.[5] The delegates were representatives of what might be called the African American middle class.[6] They included ministers, journalists, lawyers, educators, and a few low-level politicians, all of whom represented members of a new burgeoning class that, unlike the older black elite, were not dependent on white customers for their positions in society. Rather, they were a "newer rising group of men [and women] that formed the backbone of the entrepreneurial and professional group that depended" on the black market, and would in the coming years become the economic and social elite of the community.[7] They represented a leadership class that believed that self-help and racial solidarity, along with a direct attack on America's growing racial apartheid, was the proper course of action.

This group, however, was not fully represented at the initial meeting. While African American women comprised a significant portion of this emerging class, and Fortune believed that black female participation was central to the League's success, no female delegates were present at the convention.[8] Black women had not been restricted from participating in League activity, as demonstrated by the outspoken support and activities of Ida B. Wells and Josephine Turpin Washington during the group's formation. Moreover, the Afro-American League's belief in the necessity and encouragement of black female participation placed some of its leadership at the forefront of recognizing the efficacy of black women assuming a greater role in the public sphere. Debate raged throughout the community in the late nineteenth and early twentieth centuries as women such as Wells, Washington, Anna Julia Cooper, Mary Church Terrell, Lucy Laney, Fannie B. Williams, Fannie Helen Burroughs, and Charlotte Hawkins Brown (many of whose activities would include involvement in the League and later the Afro-American Council) began assuming greater roles in public affairs. Nonetheless, there was no universal agreement on the roles women could or should assume in the public sphere, and despite female representatives to the local and state organizations, the state leagues did not nominate any female delegates to participate in the first national gathering of the group.[9]

* * *

On a cold Chicago morning, with justice and racial pride on their minds, the delegates to the Afro-American League's first convention arrived and launched the historic and greatly anticipated meeting. After formalizing the organizational structure of the new group in the first session, the delegates convened for the afternoon to see the stage adorned with three portraits: Frederick Douglass in the center flanked by those of J. E. W. Thomas of the Illinois legislature and T. Thomas Fortune. From this stage, Fortune delivered an address six years in the making. Setting the tone for the event, he declared that the delegation was meeting in Chicago "as representatives of 8,000,000 freemen, who know our rights and have the courage to defend them. We have met here to-day to emphasize the fact that the past condition of dependence and helplessness upon men who have used us for selfish and unholy purposes, who have murdered and robbed and outraged us must be reversed."[10]

Fortune viewed those in attendance as the direct and rightful heirs of the abolitionist movement. It was only fitting, he averred, that they had convened "upon such historic ground" as Illinois, for "it was here that Elijah Lovejoy, the first martyr of freedom's sacred cause, died that we might be free." It was here too, he underscored, "that Abraham Lincoln lived, and in this soil that he sleeps."[11] Fortune invoked the names of those two martyrs of freedom and "of the black heroes who died at Battery Wagner, Fort Pillow and the awful crater at Petersburg" to conjure up the spirit of their cause, "universal emancipation," and to enthuse the delegation "with the devotion to high principle which William Garrison emphasized when he exclaimed, 'I am in earnest; I will not equivocate. I will not retreat a single inch—and I will be heard.'"[12]

Standing on these same principles, Fortune congratulated the new abolitionists for arousing themselves from "the lethargy of the past." He then set a militant tone for the convention by declaring that blacks ought not to stand idly by as they are stripped of their rights.[13] Afro-Americans, he asserted in a tone usually associated with the "New Negro" of the twentieth century, must "fight fire with fire," as "It is time to face the enemy and fight inch by inch for every right [that the white man] denies us."[14] Employing some of the same language that he had used in June 1887 to advocate for black self-defense, he declared:

> all those men who have profited by our disorganization and fattened on our labor by class and corporate legislation, will oppose this Afro-American League movement. [And] they may resort to the coward[ly] argument of violence; but are we to remain forever inactive, the victims . . . ? No, sir. We propose to accomplish our purposes by the peaceful methods of agitation, through the ballot and the courts, but if others use the weapons of violence to combat our peaceful arguments, it is not for us to run away from violence. . . . Attucks, the black patriot—he was no coward! Toussaint L'Ouverture—he was no coward! Nat Turner—he was no coward! . . . . If we have work to do, let us do it. And if there comes violence, let those who oppose our just cause "throw the first stone."[15]

The Afro-American League, in Fortune's framing, would fight under the banner of truth, justice, the federal constitution, and honest manhood. Planting themselves firmly on these truths and under such a political framework, they would "fight down opposition, drive caste intolerance to the wall, crush out mob and lynch law, throttle individual insolence and arrogance, vindicate the right of [black] women to the decent respect of lawless rowdies, and achieve at last the victory which crowns the labors of the patient, resourceful, and the uncompromising warrior." The Afro-American agitator believed that the organization would, once and for all, lead African Americans out of "the house of bondage into the freedom of absolute justice under the

Constitution."[16] The delegation rose with a thunder of applause at the close of Fortune's address and quickly moved to have the speech published as the guiding sentiment of the new organization. Over the next two days, delegates heard from a number of leading spokesmen of the race, all of who echoed Fortune's call as to the need for a permanent organization.

One of the most eventful and humorous speeches of the convention came when H. C. C. Astwood, recently of New York, formerly of Louisiana, and a former consul in Trinidad under President Arthur and consul to Saint Domingo in Cleveland's first administration, presented a set of resolutions to be sent to Congress.[17] Astwood satirically claimed that an alternative to the southern problem existed. He asserted that, since the existence of the large African American population in most of the nation's southern states made the "situation painful and uncomfortable for the small minority of white fellow citizens therein," the new organization should petition Congress for one million dollars "to furnish the unhappy white citizens . . . who may desire to settle in other and more favored States, free from Afro-American majorities, with free transportation and lunch by the way to any of the States north of the Mason and Dixon line."[18] Astwood added that Congress should designate Senator John Tyler Morgan of Alabama, Senator Wade Hampton of South Carolina, and Senator Randall L. Gibson of Tennessee "to be the 'Moses' to lead the unhappy people out of the States of their misfortune."[19] The resolution was unanimously adopted with one alteration: a delegate from Georgia proposed that Senator George G. Vest of Missouri be added to the list of individuals responsible for leading their distraught constituencies to the Promised Land.[20]

The other speakers during the three-day conference, less humorous in their tone but no less serious of the gravity of the situation, agreed with the issues laid forth by Fortune in his opening address. Each spoke of the necessity to create positive methods for solving the so-called Negro Problem, calling for the building of favorable public opinion toward the black population, the promotion of vocational and higher education, and the need to protest against the increasing discrimination and use of violence against the African American community that was occurring throughout the nation.[21]

All delegates agreed on the need for a permanent organization. The committee on the constitution created, and the delegation adopted, a document mirroring Fortune's 1887 organizational proposal. This provided for the formation of a politically nonpartisan body whose objectives were to protest, investigate, and create an impartial report on lynching and other outrages perpetuated against blacks, as well as test the constitutionality of the growing Jim Crow system. Finally, despite the all-black and all-male composition of the convention, the League's constitution proclaimed the organization to be open to all persons over the age of eighteen without regard to race or gender.[22]

The convention closed with the election of its permanent officers. Joseph Charles Price—president and founder of Livingston College, an AME Zion institution in North Carolina, who had gained a national reputation among blacks and whites as an educator and a speaker—was nominated as president, defeating Fortune and Reverend Joshua A. Brockett of the St. Paul AME Church of Cambridge, Massachusetts, who was also a member of the local Cambridge Colored League.[23] Fortune, however, was overwhelmingly elected secretary. The convention then adjourned and the delegates set out to return to their local and state branches. Determined to push forward the ideas set forth in the constitution of the newly formed national civil rights organization, the delegates vowed to reconvene at a national convention to be held in Knoxville, Tennessee, in July 1891. Additionally, a committee headed by H. C. C. Astwood traveled to Washington to present President Harrison with the Address to the Nation and a letter detailing the conditions faced by the African American population in the South.[24]

In the early days of 1890, therefore, as the nation continued to move down the path of a national white supremacy order, the country's first national civil rights organization was launched. Fortune and the other delegates believed they had created an organization that would be able to do what the earlier convention movement did not: provide an apparatus for sustained activity. The League was designed to be a continuous institutionalized convention in the form of a national association to effectively and systematically challenge the rise of segregation, protest lynch law and mob violence, and limit the spread of disfranchisement. The actions of these delegates in Chicago and League supporters throughout the country set the model by which African American protest would formulate again and again throughout the nineteenth and twentieth centuries.

The historic civil rights convention received largely negative, if uneven, coverage in the white press. Chicago newspapers spoke of Fortune as "the New York coon" whom they accused of working for the Democratic Party.[25] *The Nation* viewed the League's purpose as a separatist one that sought "class legislation." Consistent with its position on the Supreme Court's 1883 decision, *The Nation* believed that African Americans were citizens and had their rights protected by the Constitution. It called for blacks to cease their plea to "be the special favorite of the laws."[26] *The Appeal*, edited by convention delegate John Quincy Adams in St. Paul, Minnesota, responded directly to *The Nation*. Adams protested that the present condition of black America was unlike that of all other segments of the country. "The Irish-Americans . . . and other naturalized Americans," maintained Adams, "are accorded all the rights which are denied to the native born Americans of African descent." Therefore, until blacks' rights are "protected in the ordinary modes by which other men's rights were protected" there would be a need and desire for an organization such as the Afro-American League.[27]

State and local leagues throughout the nation could not have agreed more. What began in 1884 by a young editor in New York as a call for black unity against the rising tide of discrimination and racial violence had evolved into a moment of revolutionary change and political redefinition for black America. Only a generation removed from slavery, blacks had organized a national civil rights group to defend themselves and speak truth to power. This organization sought to challenge the developing concepts of a new American civil and political society (including notions of segregation, disfranchisement, and creation of a racial state) in the post-Reconstruction era. Echoing the words of Fortune in his convention address, the members of the League "knew their rights and had the courage to defend them."[28]

With this new collective attitude and sense of purpose, the delegates returned to their states primed to initiate activity regarding the issues discussed in Chicago. Groups were formed in New York, Massachusetts, Virginia, North Carolina, Tennessee, Missouri, California, Wisconsin, Minnesota, Indiana, Illinois, Michigan, Nebraska, Connecticut, Pennsylvania, Georgia, South Carolina, Iowa, and Colorado, among other areas. Activity in the states ranged from the simple formation of local groups to the initiation of civil rights cases against those perpetrating the various types of discrimination that African Americans experienced at the local and state levels.

Some of the earliest post-convention League activity occurred in Wisconsin. In November 1889, immediately following Fortune's call for the creation of a national organization, African Americans in the Badger State had organized the Wisconsin Civil Rights League and promptly framed the Civil Rights Bill, which they sent off to the state assembly.[29] The Civil Rights League also supported the discrimination case of Owen Howell, a resident of Milwaukee who had been refused admission into the parquet of the Bijou Opera House.[30] Amid this flurry of activity, the group agreed to merge with the Afro-American League and quickly prepared to send delegates to the Chicago convention.

Black Wisconsiners responded positively to the national conference. Upon returning to the area, representatives quickly formed a state League and sought to expand the number of local groups in the region.[31] After an immediate outburst of activity, however, the group's momentum seemed to lag. On May 9, 1890, William T. Green, a Canadian immigrant, lawyer, and vice president of the Wisconsin organization, issued a rallying cry to state and national supporters. Published in the *Detroit Plaindealer*, Green's letter chided the members of the organization for their apparent "indifference." He reminded them of the Afro-American League's purpose, and invited those who had become lax in their support for the League idea to "read the blood curdling accounts of the way in which our men, women, and children are being chained and driven like cattle in the prison pens of the South, read of the Barnwell massacre; read the statistics of the murdered Afro-Americans, whose blood like that of Abel crieth out from the ground, not to God alone, but to the sympathies of their fellow men."[32]

Green then asked black Wisconsiners to notice how "Afro-Americans are frozen out of every legitimate employment save the most menial." He further noted that the state had a governor who appeared willing to sign the Civil Rights Bill, but the black population had failed to organize and support its passage by the legislature. "Afro-Americans are being driven to the gallery of a theatre like dogs in a wood shed, told at the threshold of the hostelries no Nigger need apply," Green maintained.[33] He implored them to "unite, organize and in [their] unity devise some means to do away with these absurdities."[34]

The Wisconsin community responded to Green's admonitions. Over the next few months, the group continued to struggle to get the Civil Rights Bill passed through the Assembly and to support Owen Howell's suit against Jacob Litt, proprietor of the Bijou Opera House.[35] During the final week of June, the League celebrated a victory when a jury awarded Howell nearly two hundred dollars in damages.[36] The members of the Wisconsin League's executive committee vowed to stay by Howell's side if Litt appealed the decision. As William T. Green explained, "that is what we have organized for, to defend and protect each other's interests and political rights."[37] The group also urged African Americans in Wisconsin and throughout the country to "stand up for their rights like other citizens and not hesitate to prosecute any and all persons who in defiance of humanity and law refuse them the treatment of civilized beings."[38]

It was thus at the state and local levels that the Afro-American League made its first stand. League members from the Badger State demonstrated that the community was no longer willing to beg and plead for its rights, but intended to demand and press for them. For the Afro-American League, the victory in Wisconsin showed that the organization was not just a political mouthpiece that only met in conventions on the national stage. Rather, the members of the organization had proven willing to actively protest for their rights on the local level.

Ohio was another place where the Afro-American League attempted to take root and grapple with the "knotty problems that beset the Afro-American" population.[39] Following the Chicago convention, Harry Smith, a journalist and Republican-appointed politician who would later serve in the Ohio state legislature from 1894 to 1898 and 1900 to 1902, immediately began in his influential *Cleveland Gazette* to promote the formation of local branches, declaring that one or more Leagues should be formed in "every city, town or village in the State of Ohio having ten or more Afro-Americans." Smith declared it was time to "act!".[40]

In particular, Smith called upon League chapters to organize to challenge recently proposed legislation calling for the segregation of the state's schools. [41] Ohio House Bill No. 458 proposed that separate schools be established for black children. If a local school board lacked a majority in favor of the segregated school system, the board could unite districts to allow a desired number of pupils so as to create a separate school.[42] Smith called on the state's black population, and especially the local Leagues, to stand up against this discriminatory legislation.[43] He cried, "let *every* community do its duty in this matter. Hold meetings and denounce such legislation. Send representative men to your members of the Assembly and leave no stone unturned that will contribute in the least to the ignominious defeat of the unjust and retrogressive measure. It is a stab at our vital interests which should arouse to action leading men, our churches, societies and especially our Afro-American leagues."[44]

With a rallying cry calling for the defeat of the separate school legislation, African Americans began organizing throughout Ohio under the banner of the League. In late March 1890, a local League was organized in Ashtabula County and promptly drafted a petition that was sent to Representative John P. Green, a prominent Cleveland attorney, Republican politician, and League member, to be read before the House. Declaring that black citizens stood against any "law that discriminates in favor of, or against, any class of . . . citizens," the petitioners vowed to withdraw support for any party or men who would not "oppose such unjust and cruel discrimination."[45] Another petition was drafted and sent from a newly formed League in Lebanon, Ohio. In concurrence with sentiments expressed by the citizens of Ashtabula County, the document declared that "any and all, who by word or act lend or give encouragement to such legislation . . . shall be deemed traitors" to the race.[46]

With support for its organization at a peak, the Ohio delegates of the national convention called for a statewide conference of local Leagues to be held on May 20, 1890, in Columbus.[47] Roughly one month before the state convention, one of those delegates, Henry Lee of Oberlin, published a rallying letter in the *Gazette*. In Lee's estimation, the meeting of the Leagues was of great importance since the "status of the Afro-American in this country is approaching an important crisis" of which House legislation for segregated schools in Ohio was just one small indication of the trouble. He called for the convention to adapt the motto, "*Advance*, Forward, Onward, and Upward" as the time had come for African Americans to "plant the standard of [their] manhood upon the highest peaks of American citizenship and maintain them there or die in the attempt. Every attempt at the regulation based upon the simple color of the skin must be met with the undeniable rights of American citizenship." Therefore, "in the name of the race" he called upon his fellow citizens to "Arouse! Arouse! Fall in line! Leave the plow, the storehouse, the shop, the bench, the office, and strike one manly and telling blow for our race, citizenship, our civil rights and full justice."[48]

The highlights of the state convention included the censuring of ex-Mississippi Senator and current Recorder of Deeds Blanche Kelso Bruce for having replaced African American clerks in his office with white workers. Leaguers also sent an address to the House Legislature elucidating the purpose of the organization at the state and national levels. The delegates claimed they had assembled to secure their rights and call attention to any discrimination on the basis of color at the local, state, or national level, and that they would petition the state assembly to uphold and defend the rights and privileges guaranteed to all citizens of the nation. Consistent with the sentiments of the local Leagues leading up to the convention, the address to the legislature deprecated "any efforts . . . to modify the present system of mixed schools in Ohio."[49]

But after the state convention, the Ohio League seemed to languish. Initially Henry Smith expressed disappointment with the convention turnout and selection of state officers.[50] Then the group and its activities virtually disappeared from the pages of his newspaper until he published an open letter to League members from national president J. C. Price in October 1890 that decried the deplorable state of the organization in Ohio.[51]

Other local Leagues were also struggling. For example, as Ohio's organizing efforts were suffering, Washington, D.C.'s local League also suffered somewhat of a setback, though of a different nature—one that illustrated the competition for limited recourses in black activist circles. A few weeks after the Chicago convention, many of the older Republican politicians and patronage seekers—including P. B. S. Pinchback, John Mercer Langston, John M. Townsend, and Edward P. McCabe—held a separate conference and formed the independent American Citizen's Equal Rights Association (ACERA). With the exception of the nonpartisan clause of the League's constitution, the group's declarations echoed the sentiments of the League.[52]

The immediate feeling of many African American leaders was that to survive, the two organizations needed to merge. Many believed that multiple organizations with virtually the same purpose competing for funds from the black community would knock heads and weaken each other financially. Members of the ACERA understood this and named J. C. Price, president of the Afro-American League, the chairman of the conference. Furthermore, on the final day of proceedings, the members of ACERA resolved to take steps to unite the two groups. A full merger of the two organizations, however, never occurred because the issues that prompted the original creation of the group were never resolved, and the ACERA continued to exist as an autonomous organization.[53]

Despite the creation of the ACERA and the draining off of some of the League's Washington, D.C. membership, the local League did manage to win support in the region. On April 4, 1890, the local League held a meeting at the Second Baptist Church where John E. Bruce delivered a passionate speech entitled "Blot on the Escutcheon."[54] Bruce captivated his audience by skillfully outlining the "Negro Problem (so called)," and black America's distinct position of being honored with a hollow title of "American citizen."[55] He declared that blacks possessed "all the rights of citizens in the abstract," but were denied basic accommodations in the public sector, segregated in the public school system, and discriminated against by "Christian white men" in the housing sector."[56] After setting the stage, Bruce turned to challenge his audience and stir them to action. The "blot on the escutcheon," he proclaimed, "consists of the failure of the General Government to enforce the laws upon the statute books."[57] Bruce fully understood that a united effort by black America would force the national government to cease being "passive and indifferent" to the injustices perpetuated against nearly eight million of its citizens.[58]

"The solution to the problem" Bruce emphasized, was in the hands of Afro-America:

> Talk won't solve it; promises and threats won't solve it; the assimilation of the races will not solve it. The Negro must preserve his race identity, must unite his energies, talent and money, and make common cause. He must, in order to get justice from white men, show them that he is entitled to it not as a privilege, but as a common right vouchsafed to all by Almighty God. Unity and harmony of sentiment and feeling, of act and deed, are the levers that must of necessity overturn American caste-prejudice. In organization, co-operation and agitation the Negro will come nearer to the solution of the white man's problem than by meekly submitting to injustice and wrong at the hands of those who are responsible for our condition; who murder our defenseless brethren, for daring to be men.[59]

"Organization, co-operation and agitation" had been the words the Afro-American League used to inspire participation in their united effort to end segregation and the deadly mob violence sweeping the nation. In the early months of the national organization, the group had leveled attacks on civil rights violations and inspired cooperation in their efforts. These efforts, however, focused mainly on violations of civil rights legislation that already existed in the North rather than the growing de jure segregation of the South. While the organization understood the necessity of challenging the southern system and followed the activity of southern members, it attempted to create test cases in the North to set a series of precedents that would enable it to move south and challenge the developing Jim Crow system. At the same time, the national organization sought to raise monies to create a defense fund for the larger southern struggle.

Questions regarding the merit of this strategy surfaced soon after the Washington, D.C. meeting when the local Leagues of Michigan converged on Detroit to form a state organization. During the months leading up to the state convention, supporters of the Michigan League attempted to awaken the state's African American population. In March, Michigan's black community received a setback when a Michigan circuit court ruled against African American William Ferguson's suit versus a restaurant owner, George H. Gies, who had denied the plaintiff equal accommodations because of the color of his skin. Six years before the famous Louisiana case, *Plessy v. Ferguson*, and at a time when the separate but equal doctrine was gaining strength in the lower courts throughout the nation, the Wayne county circuit court ruled that a "public restaurant keeper has a right to so control his business that he may keep separate tables for ladies and for gentlemen, for white persons and for colored."[60]

Daniel Augustus Straker, Ferguson's attorney and a recent migrant to Detroit from South Carolina where he was an important legal and political figure, urged the black population of Michigan to be "up and doing for danger is ahead," and he held that the William Ferguson case and others like it were causes demanding the support of the National Afro-American League. Robert Pelham of the Detroit *Plaindealer* agreed with Straker's call for action, but believed that the fight and financial burden of the legal battle should fall upon the shoulders of the local and state organizations. This way, the national group could concentrate its energies and funds "where they will be most needed—in the South."[61] Unconcerned as to whether the national or the state organization should lead that activity, Michigan African Americans heeded the call of Straker and Pelham, forming Leagues in a number of counties throughout the state.[62]

Movement toward a state convention, however, was not as smooth. Those forming the League in Michigan dealt with a thorny issue that had plagued the formation of the national organization and continued to fester as state groups convened. In many states, individuals were unwilling to support the Afro-American League because of the nonpartisan clause of the group's constitution. The League had not done its job to sufficiently explain the basis for this clause, nor had they identified exactly who would be affected by the regulation. Robert Pelham attempted to remedy these oversights by stating in the *Plaindealer* that the League was a "non-partisan organization, although it leaves to local leagues the privilege of taking such action in politics as they may see fit." Thus, all supporters of the League idea were invited to become members of the local, state, and national organizations "irrespective of race, politics, color or sex."[63] After this clarification, local Leaguers fell in line and marched "on to Detroit," where 157 delegates assembled to create the Michigan Afro-American League.[64]

The clear highlight of the convention came during the address given by D. Augustus Straker, chairman of the proceedings. Emphasizing the reasons for the gathering, Straker called upon delegates to declare their constitutional rights anew and "demand their enforcement, and never cease demanding on all occasions until they are conceded to us and we enjoy them fully and equally with all of our fellow citizens." He also called for the convention to denounce "the recent outrages perpetuated upon [southern blacks] by cut throats and lynchers" and such events as "the Barnwell Massacre," asking for the creation of a federal court to sit in Washington, away from the influence of the states, to try those responsible for the butchery occurring throughout the country. Appealing for unity within the African American community, Straker felt it was "useless to hold State conventions or National Leagues unless [blacks are] united in purpose and plan so that an insult to one of our brethren in the South is an insult to us. A right denied in South Carolina, must find resentment here, a lynching committed there must be denounced here in Michigan." Straker, to thunderous applause, concluded, "let our complaints be heard on the hill top and in the valley and from shore to shore in State and county conventions and leagues until we get justice and equal rights, the doors of industry be opened to us, the public places of refreshment and amusement know no distinction between their patrons."[65]

Emboldened, delegates returned to their respective counties and set forth in putting energies toward the cause of the League idea. Soon after the convention, Reverend David A. Graham, president of the Michigan League, minister in Kalamazoo, and father of Shirley Graham Du Bois, outlined his vision of the state organization's role in the activities of the national group.[66] He echoed Straker's sentiments that an attack on any member of the race must be viewed as an attack on the whole community, and believed that Michigan Leaguers needed to create a legal defense fund to bring practitioners of racial violence or discrimination to justice. Graham realized it was doubtful that the group would succeed in getting a capital punishment decision in a lynching case, but believed that it would get some justice, and that it would only take a few cases to teach the "South that 'Negro' organization is not to be scoffed at" and "that lynchings would be followed with earnest prosecutions." He argued that this approach would force southerners to become weary of their general discrimination against the Afro-American population, and forecasted that the organization would be able to raise twenty-five thousand dollars for their cause within the next year.[67]

However, black communities in Michigan failed to echo Graham's enthusiasm. Over the next few months, the group struggled to persuade blacks in the state that membership in the Afro-American League did not require renouncing their political affiliation. A further setback occurred when Reverend

Graham departed the state, leaving the organization without a president.[68] Therefore, despite the Michigan organization's continued growth, and its success in gaining a favorable decision in the appeal of the *Ferguson v. Gies* case (when in October 1890, the state supreme court overturned the Wayne county court ruling), the group failed to capitalize on the victory and never established a unified effort across the state.[69]

This, however, was not the case in New York. In the spring of 1890, during roughly the same time as the Washington, D.C. meeting and the flurry of action in Michigan, League activity began developing in the New York region. Before the convention, the movement managed to create a number of locals throughout the state, but its main activity centered in and around New York City, with branch leadership in the hands of T. McCants Stewart, Reverend Alexander Walters, and T. Thomas Fortune. After the convention, the New York Afro-American League attempted to introduce a civil rights bill into the state legislature. Stewart, a freeborn Charlestonian who had received his law degree at the University of South Carolina during Reconstruction before relocating to New York and becoming a confidant of Fortune, placed finishing touches on a bill calling for graduated penalties: for the first violation, a one hundred dollar fine; for later violations, license revocation and imprisonment.[70]

While the civil rights bill was pending, members of New York state branches lent their support to another piece of antidiscrimination legislation seeking to prevent race-based prejudice in insurance prices.[71] With these two pieces of proposed legislation on the minds of New York League supporters, the state organization held its founding convention on May 22 and 23, 1890, in Rochester, the longtime home city of Frederick Douglass. The elected officers of the state organization included Fortune, president; T. McCants Stewart, counsel; Reverend Alexander Walters, head of the executive committee; and Mrs. A. M. Tracy, member of the executive committee. On the second day of the proceedings, Tracy urged women to join the organization. Calling upon the men of the League to support the work of black women, she satirically reminded her audience that "the men must have the women with them in the work of the league, for it is written that it is not good for man to be alone."[72]

The importance of the civil rights legislation, which had dominated the organization's activity prior to the convention, was noted in the resolutions passed by the state League and signed by Fortune, Walters, Tracy, and others. One resolution vowed that the group would pressure the legislature to pass a law to insure equal treatment for all citizens without regard to race.[73] Yet despite the League's pressure and commitment, the civil rights bill was dead by the summer months. With its failure, businesses across the state remained free to strengthen de facto segregation.[74]

Fortune, possibly in response to the escalation of discrimination in the state, entered the Trainer Hotel on June 4, 1890, and requested to be served a beer. When the bartender leaned across the counter and informed him that the establishment did not serve blacks, Fortune reportedly replied, "See here, young fellow, you will fill my order, and if you do not, I will remain here and ornament your establishment until you close in the morning." After some discussion with the bartender, the proprietor, and a police officer, Fortune was arrested for disturbing the peace, being intoxicated, and engaging in disorderly conduct.[75]

The following morning, Fortune appeared in court with his friend T. McCants Stewart as his counsel. After some hue and cry, Stewart managed to get the charges dropped, but the two firebrands were not satisfied with the small victory. Immediately they set to work and called on the legislative committee of the state Afro-American League to aid them in filing suit against the Trainer Hotel. As Fortune exclaimed on the first page of that week's *Age*: "I submit that I would expect nothing less than such treatment in a hotel anywhere in the South, and in any court of justice in the South, but I . . . am astonished to find such treatment accorded an Afro-American in New York City. Close up the line," he declared, "and let us fight for our civil as well as our political rights. Hold up the hands of the Afro-American League. Put money in its treasury. Let us stand together and fight."[76]

Within a week, the most significant activity of the Afro-American League had begun. Fortune and Stewart decided that they were not going to "sit down and swallow the insult," for that would have been totally inconsistent with their support for the creation of the Afro-American League. Rather, they believed Fortune's civil rights incident should serve as a test case to challenge the increased discrimination in the state of New York and set a precedent to challenge the growing civil rights violations throughout the nation.[77] As John Mitchell explained in his *Richmond Planet*, "win or lose the case must necessarily awaken a wide-spread interest in the country, and thereby create a sentiment against this discrimination as well as set an example which citizens in other prejudiced States might do well to follow."[78] The two New Yorkers agreed and therefore filed a suit with the New York Supreme Court for damages of ten thousand dollars against the proprietor and manager of the Trainer Hotel.[79]

Across the nation, black citizens rallied in support of the New York editor's cause. John C. Dancy, League supporter and editor of the North Carolina-based *Star of Zion*, believed that Fortune should "wear [his] imprisonment as a badge of honor" and that the black community must rally behind and assist the effort. John Mitchell concurred, warning the African American community from the pages of the *Planet* that they must "sooner or later . . . learn to stand by their leaders, especially those who have the manhood to contend for the rights of the race." Further support resulted from a call to the state Leagues issued by the president and the attorney of the National League, J. C. Price and Edward Morris, that urged members to throw their weight and finances behind Fortune's cause.[80] Reverend William J. Simmons of the *American Baptist* offered more temperate support, declaring: "While we would prefer that Mr. Fortune abstain from the use of such a beverage, yet it is a shame that a man of his ability and position should be refused entertainment on account of color."[81] What the editor of the *American Baptist* and many others who wrote to the *Age* in support of Fortune understood was that the case was about more than a beer. As George Knox of the *Indianapolis Freeman* proclaimed, "there is no better time than now to test the question of the Negro's civil rights in the courts."[82]

Fortune's case against the Trainer Hotel can be seen as the origin of the legal strategy employed by a national civil rights organization to arouse national sentiment around a local case that could create precedent to challenge de facto and de jure discrimination throughout the country—one later popularized by the NAACP. The Afro-American League's attempt to use this sort of strategy is the genesis of the tactics other civil rights organizations that formed in its wake would continue to employ. In many respects, it could be argued that the origin of *Brown v. Board of Education* has its roots in Fortune's case and this struggle (or from a bar to *Brown*, if you will).

While Fortune and his lawyers moved against Trainer, the League pressed forward on both local and national levels. In October 1890, the executive committee of the movement met while president J. C. Price once again sent out an open letter to the Leagues outlining the structure of the organization and discussing its importance. He congratulated those who had formed state Leagues for their foresight and self-reliance and urged others to follow in their footsteps in creating an "ORGANIZED PROTEST against the color line."[83] He held that if blacks failed "to possess the manhood and patriotism to stand up in the defense of [their] Constitutional rights, and protest long, loud and unitedly against their continual infringement," they "were unworthy of their heritage as American citizens and deserve to have fastened on [them] the wrongs of which many . . . complain."[84] Finally, he believed that the creation of the Leagues was an example of the type of self-help that the African American community needed. Blacks, in his opinion, had "looked too constantly at the influences *without* . . . and not enough at the forces *within*," and that the movement represented the type of organized "*power*" needed to gain recognition in America.[85]

However, despite some local success—the initiation of Fortune's challenge to the discrimination policy in New York and the optimism exuded in J. C. Price's letter—the Afro-American League languished as it neared its one-year national anniversary. The frustration regarding the situation at the local level was ironically revealed in the same issue of the *Cleveland Gazette* that contained president Price's letter. The state of the Ohio organization was "deplorable," according to the paper's editor, who urged his constituents to take note of the sentiments presented in the president's address and to fire up the leagues.[86]

Reverend James M. Henderson, the popular pastor of Bethel Church in Detroit, echoed similar sentiments via an article published in the *Detroit Plaindealer*. Henderson believed that apathy, not agitation, was the watchword of the League movement, but alleged that the responsibility lay on the shoulders of president Price. Fortune responded by asserting that the responsibility for any apathy within the movement actually lay in the hands of the local and state leaders, not with the presidency of the organization. The editor noted, "one cannot carry the League on his shoulders. Nothing can be done without money, and enough money had not been paid in by local leagues to pay for the stamps, stationery and printing of the Secretary's office alone." Fortune appealed to his readers and the supporters of the League to not grow impatient, as the organization could not take on the manifestation of a "giant in a day or a year."[87]

Fortune believed that the larger community would support the group if local leaders educated the masses on the importance of the movement. Those placed in organizational authority would then have the mass-based support needed to sustain challenges to ensure African Americans their political and social rights. As Fortune observed, old sentiments of dependence and victim status died hard, but were dying nonetheless. With education he believed that the community would stop looking outside of itself for the "relief that [could] only be obtained from within," and that the old slave mentality would be supplanted "by a manlier and more rational sentiment—a sentiment of self-reliance and self-help and mutual dependence."[88]

The absence of mass support was central to problems faced by the organization, but a lack of publicity of the group's activities greatly contributed to this and may have been the group's greatest flaw. The committee on legislation was responsible for collecting, collating, and publishing information about the conditions of African Americans and of challenges to them. However, the activities of the various local and state branches received hardly any coverage at all outside their respective regions, thereby disconnecting local readers from the broader struggle. Take, for example, the Ohio campaign against segregated schools and Fortune's suit against Trainer. Neither event was given a considerable amount of coverage outside of the respective states. In fact, the Ohio League's campaign was not mentioned in any of the newspapers controlled by supporters of the organization except for Harry Smith's *Cleveland Gazette*. The *Detroit Plaindealer*, under the guidance of Leaguers Robert Pelham and William Anderson, provided the best coverage of League activity nationally, but it too failed to seize upon the successes of the group to drum up greater support. Moreover, although the *Indianapolis Freeman*, under control of George Knox, spilled considerable ink in support of Fortune's Trainer case, it was never able to translate coverage into increased League membership either in Indiana or nationally. With greater publicity accorded to the legal cases or the broader struggles of the Afro-American League, the local leaders might have been better able to attract support from the masses who, in turn, would have been more actively apprised of the activities of the organization at the local and national levels.

One region of the country that attempted to arouse widespread support for the organization was St. Paul, Minnesota. Fortune's 1887 call for the creation of a protective league fell upon receptive ears in the Saintly City. By the 1880s, St. Paul's growing black population began to feel and resent the subtle effects of de facto segregation.[89] A month prior to Fortune's call for the creation of a national civil rights organization, William Hazel, a stained-glass artist who at the time was visiting the city, was denied accommodations at the Astoria and Clarendon hotels.[90] Arrested after protesting the incident, Hazel filed suit against the proprietors of the Clarendon hotel seeking two thousand dollars in damages.[91] In October, a jury ruled in favor of Hazel, but awarded him a hollow recompense of only twenty-five dollars.[92] The black community of St. Paul viewed the decision as an outrage as they knew such a verdict would not act as a deterrent against future acts of discrimination. They therefore decided to take matters into their own hands by creating a protective organization—the Minnesota Protective and Industrial League—to oversee any future infringements on the rights of St. Paul's black citizens.[93] It is not known whether the Minnesota Protective and Industrial League was connected to Fortune's League idea, but when an Afro-American League formed in the city in 1889, the previous organization disappeared and many of its members joined the new group.[94]

From its initial inception, the St. Paul branch of the Afro-American League attempted to draw the whole community into the organization. After the national convention of the League in Chicago, which was attended by two members of the local branch's executive committee (*St. Paul Appeal* editor John Quincy Adams, and attorney Frederick McGhee, a recent migrant to the city from Chicago), the St. Paul group decided to hold a public demonstration to stimulate interest in the League.[95] The leaders of the local League decided upon Emancipation Day as the opportune date to hold a "monster . . . demonstration" celebrating the progress of the race since Lincoln's Proclamation, to acknowledge the hurdles left to leap over to gain full equality, and to highlight the League's program.[96]

At the moderately attended event, both McGhee and Archbishop John Ireland, leader of the local Catholic church and supporter of black rights, gave judicious addresses on the issue of social and political equality. McGhee acknowledged that blacks had made tremendous strides in the past twenty-eight years, yet a fully equal society remained a distant objective. Bishop Ireland was a bit more forceful: he condemned local incidents of discrimination and declared "color is the merest accident . . . let all people in America be equal socially and politically."[97]

Despite the flash of radicalism in Ireland's address, nothing really came of the Emancipation Day demonstration because the local Afro-American League failed to propose any new strategies for fighting discrimination. Whether the group gained a significant increase in membership is unknown. This overall weakness and symbolic nature of the event was not lost on William Hazel, who had by this point resettled in the area. He called the affair a grand example of humbuggery, noting that the Afro-American League proposed a meeting to "do something [and the] result . . . [was] nothing."[98]

The firebrand Hazel believed that the League both in St. Paul and on the national level was bankrupt, both financially and ideologically. He noted that the national organization had been unsuccessful in mounting a significant challenge to any legislation not in the best interests of the race. On the local level, Hazel pointed out that over the past year, the group had failed to throw its weight behind any act of discrimination, including his newest suit against the Delicatessen Restaurant. As a member of the opposition, Hazel called for a change in the leadership of the St. Paul League and for a more proactive approach to achieving "perfect freedom."[99]

Hazel's frustration with the League did not last for long: by the spring he had joined its ranks. By that time, he had also reached an amicable out-of-court settlement with the Delicatessen, to which the *Appeal*, the St. Paul voice of the Afro-American League, gave sufficient press coverage.[100] After joining, Hazel threw his weight behind the group and, along with other supporters of the League such as McGhee and Adams, called for the creation of a state branch.[101]

Around the time of Hazel's settlement with the Delicatessen Restaurant, the Wisconsin League was riding a wild roller coaster with its efforts to push the state legislature to pass the Civil Rights Bill it had drawn up nearly two years prior. Led by the activities of the Milwaukee branch, the Wisconsin group remained active throughout the year. In late January 1891, it held a large banquet to gather supporters of the organization and inform them of the issues that black people faced in Wisconsin and throughout the nation.[102] Then in February, the League sent representatives to Madison to address the judiciary committee concerning the necessity of the Civil Rights Bill.

After a persuasive argument for the bill by William T. Green, the lead representative of the group, the Leaguers left the capital city with the belief that they had the upper hand and that it was only a matter of time before the group celebrated the passage of the Civil Rights Bill. The champagne was taken off ice, however, when Democrats on the judiciary committee removed references to a number of public places, including "theaters, restaurants, barber shops, and saloons," leaving inns as the only facilities affected by the Bill.[103] The executive committee of the state organization responded by sending a "petition to the legislature to allow [the Bill] to be withdrawn as the passage" of such legislation "would do more injury than good."[104] The League's plea was ignored, but the group continued to attempt to influence the legislature as the Bill made its way to the state senate. Four months after these strange events, the Wisconsin League celebrated the defeat of the Civil Rights Bill, vowing to return to the Assembly with a stronger piece of legislation and greater Republican support.[105]

While the Wisconsin League was experiencing trials and tribulations, the New York League gained its greatest victory to date. As already mentioned, the New York group, spearheaded by the Albany branch, had been promoting legislation to end insurance discrimination. In March 1891, the New York Assembly unanimously passed the Chase-Ward Bill, and the following month the governor signed it into law; the bill prohibited insurance companies from "making any distinction and discrimination between white and colored persons . . . as to the premium or rates charged for policies."[106] Fortune used this successful campaign as an attempt to silence critics of the League. He believed that the victory spoke "thunder tones" as to the purpose of the organization. The movement, the editor declared, was designed to "secure enaction [sic] of this and many other just measures for the relief of our people."[107] The "thunder tones," however, did not echo very far: no pro-League newspapers outside of New York even commented on the victory.

The legislative committee of the organization had again failed to promote the successes of the various branches of the League. While the branches and state groups gathered to coordinate their activities for the coming national convention, none of the campaigns of the previous year were used to stimulate interest in the organization. The newspapers controlled by League supporters neither discussed Fortune's case nor addressed the activity in Michigan, Ohio, Wisconsin, Connecticut or Nebraska.[108] Without such promotion, it is understandable why many African Americans questioned the actual purpose of the Afro-American League.

Tensions and skepticism remained, particularly as the organization moved toward its national convention. The selection of Tennessee as the location of the second national convention once again sparked controversy. In March 1891, the state had passed separate coach legislation that officially created the Jim Crow railcar.[109] A number of the state Leagues expressed hesitation about participating in the convention if their delegates would have to suffer such a humiliating experience as being seated in segregated railcars.

The Minnesota League was one of the groups that expressed concern about the location of the national meeting. It held a mass meeting on June 24 to discuss proper action toward the convention and Tennessee's separate coach legislation.[110] The group, led by the St. Paul branch, issued a protest and petitioned the executive committee of the National League to change the place of the convention to a location where "laws are not a shame and a disgrace to all sense of justice and right." Furthermore, Frederick McGhee offered a suggestion, which was adopted by the state organization. McGhee, reviving the call of former Michigan League president and current McGhee colleague in Minnesota, Reverend David A. Graham, believed that a fund should be started for the "purpose of testing the validity of [Tennessee's] statute" and that the League should "lend their utmost efforts to procure subscribers" to the defense fund.[111] Such an open challenge to the developing southern Jim

Crow system was the first of its kind by the organization, but members failed to address the seemingly contradictory nature of their two positions.

Despite the convictions of the Minnesota branch, the location of the convention was not changed and delegates descended upon Knoxville for the second annual national meeting of the Afro-American League. The conference was met with less fanfare than the first convention, and the number of delegates dropped considerably—from 141 to thirty-two, with only twelve states represented, down from twenty-one the previous year. Part of the reason given for the lackluster turnout was, as the St. Paul delegation and others claimed, that members did not want to be Jim Crowed.[112] Another reason for the poor attendance concerned funding. As the New York League announced before the event, many of its state's delegates were forced to remain home because their local branches failed to amass enough funds to defray the delegates' expenses.[113]

At the convention, the League wrestled with issues that would come to define its success—and ultimate failure. Many within the organization believed that its slow growth resulted from the nonpartisan orientation of the organization. In their estimation, this was the reason major political leaders such as John Mercer Langston, Frederick Douglass, Blanche K. Bruce, and P. B. S. Pinchback failed to identify themselves with the League.[114] The delegation therefore voted to eliminate the nonpartisan clause. Although it did not become an official supporter of either party, the organization's national leaders were no longer encouraged to remove themselves from political positions.[115] Other topics discussed at the conference dealt with the continued, unchecked lynch and mob violence in the South, the existence of a system of taxation without representation in the southern states, and the growing convict lease program in the region. Ida B. Wells spoke to the delegation urging Afro-American women to join the organization and to press on with their fathers and brothers in the struggle against the injustices the race suffered.[116] The delegates also joined the Afro-American Press Association in recommending that President Harrison appoint an Afro-American to at least one of the nine appellate judgeships.[117] Finally, the group condemned the growing separate car system. John R. Lynch, ex-Mississippi congressman, sent a letter to the delegation declaring this to be the paramount concern of the organization, and that the group's position on the "matter should be outspoken and unmistakable. It should be emphatically declared that the political party which countenances and tolerates such odious legislation, and which will not favor the abrogation and repeal of such laws, wherever, they exist, will receive no support from colored persons in any part of the country."[118]

Concurring with Lynch's sentiments, the delegates declared the practice to be a "gratuitous indignity—an insult to [their] manhood, and [they] believe[d] it to be a violation of constitutional and common law."[119] They called on the entire race, and especially the members of the League, to "use all lawful means to break down the iniquity." With their newly elected president, T. Thomas Fortune, the organization closed its second annual convention by singing "John Brown's Body" and by promising to raise their voices and use their influence, power, and vote "to do away with this outrageous, disgraceful, offensive and inhuman class legislation."[120]

* * *

In her account of the Knoxville meeting, Ida B. Wells pertinently criticized the organization. She believed that J. C. Price had done nothing to promote the League during his presidency, and she looked forward to seeing how the organization developed under Fortune. She was disappointed, however, that the group had failed to map out the explicit work of the membership for the ensuing year. In Wells's estimation, "a handful of men, with no report of work accomplished, no one in the field to spread it, no plan of work laid out—no intelligent direction—meet and by their child's play illustrate in their own doings the truth of the saying that Negroes have no capacity for organization." At the same time, "a whole race is lynched, proscribed, intimidated, deprived of its political and civil rights, herded into boxes (by courtesy called separate cars) which bring the blush of humiliation to every self-respecting man's cheek—and we sit tamely by without using the only means—that of thorough organization and earnest work to prevent it." "No wonder," she contended, "the world at large splits us with impunity."[121]

The greatest failure of the organization in the first year of its existence was its inability to publicize its activities on the national level, but Wells's criticisms also rang true. The League did view the confronting of separate car laws as one of its highest priorities, but failed to outline a clear strategy for attacking the legislation. With no clear-cut plan and only a list of resolutions, how did the organization differ from the groups that Fortune perceived as passive, rhetorical conventions that did very little to aid in securing African Americans their political and civil rights? The League had to change: it had to attack the legislation that stood in the way of black rights and publicize that struggle to gain the support of the masses. In its first year, the organization was comprised mostly of northern middle-class members dominated by entrepreneurs and ministers. The League had to find some way to enlist the support of the larger black community—in particular, the southern agrarian population, which suffered the most from race-specific legislation and lynch law.

William Anderson of the *Detroit Plaindealer*, and now secretary of the League, concurred with Wells's sentiment, proclaiming that "indignation over the separate car law is rampant, and any movement on the part of the League looking toward testing its constitutionality in the United States Supreme Court, would be rapturously hailed and aided."[122] Wells took the next step in pushing the League's political agenda. On her return to Chattanooga from the Knoxville meeting, she had been forced to ride in a Jim Crow car and sit in a segregated waiting room. In late July, she wrote Fortune, urging that the League take action against the unjust system.[123] There would be no disagreement, as the League had recently taken on a similar case involving Reverend William H. Heard, a League member and AME minister from Philadelphia who had experienced similar treatment in Tennessee. Heard had been forced to ride in a segregated car despite his purchase of a first-class ticket. The League, under the guidance of attorney Captain Judson W. Lyons of Augusta, Georgia, had filed a suit in the name of Heard against the Pullman Company and the Nashville, Chattanooga and St. Louis Railway.[124]

Yet rather than lending support to the Heard case, the Knoxville, Tennessee branch mobilized to take steps of its own against its state's separate coach law. The group resolved to petition the governor to call a special session of the legislature to review the provisions of the law, with the intent being to repeal the legislation. The branch also called upon other state branches to lend cooperation and assistance as they formed an organized protest against present race discrimination.[125]

Shortly after the National League initiated the Heard case and the Knoxville branch lodged its protests in Tennessee, the New York City branch held a rally at Reverend Alexander Walters's Zion Church against the Jim Crow car system. According to reports, five hundred people attended, including former congressman John Mercer Langston.[126] In his address, Langston argued that the race needed lawyers more than preachers, and asserted that if African Americans truly wanted their rights, they would put enough money into the treasury of the Afro-American League to challenge the increasing Jim Crow legislation. Most important, they should immediately provide sufficient funds for the League to return to Tennessee and challenge the constitutionality of that state's separate coach legislation.[127] Another supporter of the cause was John Lynch. Although he was unable to attend the rally, he sent a statement addressing the separate coach legislation and commending the League's efforts to challenge the unjust system. At the end of the meeting, a resolution was passed that denounced the present course of various state legislatures throughout the country and vowed to continue to agitate on the matter.[128]

In this spirit, League chapters formed throughout the nation. In Atlanta, Georgia, for instance, a new group formed under the guidance of R. L. Lovinggood that declared it would fight "to break down color bars" and obtain for Afro-Americans "an equal chance with others in the avocations of life."[129] On the other coast, 150 African Americans convened at California Hall in San Francisco to form the first Afro-American League in the state. The delegates of the convention elected San Franciscan Theophilus B. Morton as president of the new branch and vowed to influence local and state politics "to benefit our people in maintaining their political rights." The local organization also encouraged investment in "race"-based businesses, manufacturing, and other enterprises employing African Americans.[130]

As momentum was building throughout the country, members of the Minnesota branch, led by the St. Paul contingent, convened to outline and implement their own plan to challenge the constitutionality of the separate car laws.[131] Rallying around the defense of their delegate to the Knoxville conference, Samuel Hardy, these citizens of Minnesota met at Pilgrim Baptist Church in St. Paul to discuss the matter and read letters from T. Thomas Fortune and Ida B. Wells encouraging them to challenge the unjust legislation; they initially raised around $150 for the suit and elected a committee to advance the case.[132]

The following week in New York, the Afro-American League drew first blood. Fortune and Heard met with the Pullman Palace Car Company on August 28, 1891 to negotiate a partial settlement in the Heard case. After some discussion, the parties agreed upon a settlement of $250 in damages and the discharge of conductor Kellogg, the railway man who had discriminated against Reverend Heard on his return to Philadelphia.[133] The settlement was seen as a success despite not bringing about any changes in legislation. As a result, the suit against the Nashville, Chattanooga and St. Louis Railway proceeded.

Before the League could move forward, however, the group needed greater assistance. Fortune exclaimed, "we need money, and plenty of it, and the local leagues must furnish it. If they do not, how can they expect the officers of the League to undertake and prosecute even the important matters now at hand? The local leagues must do their duty."[134] A couple of weeks later Fortune again pleaded with the community to support the League financially. "Talk is cheap and law is expensive," he declared. "We the race, do a great deal of unnecessary and profitless talk. The League is out to succeed, but a half a dozen men cannot make it succeed. It requires the brains and the energies of the entire race."[135] The Milwaukee League concurred, publishing the fact that it had sent the national office the "necessary sum" and hoped that "many other leagues follow Milwaukee's lead . . . as nothing can be accomplished without funds."[136]

While Fortune and the Milwaukee branch pleaded with the black community for funds, the *Langston City Herald* of the Oklahoma Territory offered fifty dollars toward the testing of the constitutionality of the separate coach legislation, but only if fifty of the "leading Afro-American journals would do the same."[137] Why this money was not offered to aid the Afro-American League in its existing case is unknown. Some of the motivation may have had to do with the fact that, as far as the public understood, Reverend Heard had not contributed to his own suit. "How much of the amount that was gained for [Heard]," Pelham of the *Plaindealer* wondered, "was turned over to the treasury of the League to carry on the other" suit?[138] The editor believed that all damages awarded should be returned to the group to help "carry on its warfare."[139] William Anderson, secretary of the national organization and close associate of Pelham, was well aware that Heard had not contributed any of the damages to help fund the suit against the Nashville, Chattanooga and Saint Louis Railway. However, it is unclear whether he even received any of the damages awarded to him in the settlement.

What occurred in Minnesota, however, was even more confusing. While the League pressed ahead on the Heard case, drumming up support and pleading for money, members of the St. Paul branch organized a new group at their August 25th meeting and began soliciting funds for their own suit rather than supporting the Heard case and the national organization.[140] The St. Paul group claimed that the Minnesota Civil Rights Committee was "formed for the purpose of devising means for testing the constitutionality of the separate coach acts."[141] What was the purpose of the Afro-American League? What was the purpose of the Heard case, for which the national office was soliciting funds? The intentions of the St. Paul branch were certainly unknown to either Fortune or Wells who, as noted earlier, wrote separately to the St. Paul group encouraging it to instigate a challenge to the Jim Crow system or to throw their weight behind the League's efforts.[142] Neither of the activists, however, anticipated that the St. Paul contingent would form a separate organization to do so.

This situation had been revealed when Fortune wrote a congratulatory comment in the *Age* for the actions taken by what he believed was the St. Paul branch of the Afro-American League.[143] In his brief remark, Fortune took issue with the statement by Frederick McGhee that the national office of the League had failed to take action against the legislation that was sweeping the South. He stated that he had informed the St. Paul lawyer of the Heard case against the Nashville, Chattanooga and St. Louis Railway and of the satisfactory settlement in the case against the Pullman Company when McGhee contacted him about the case of Samuel Hardy. He also warned about the difficulties of proceeding in the case without any money in the organization's treasury.[144] Nowhere did Fortune mention that the League had decided against instituting the Heard suit. While Fortune responded that it was "tomfoolery" to proceed without money, the organization did not fold up its tent as McGhee and the Minnesota Civil Rights Committee implied. Rather, the League continued in the remaining months of the year to call for money to support this and other efforts.[145] John Quincy Adams of the *Appeal* responded to Fortune's comments by stating that the actions were not by the Afro-American League of Minnesota but by the Civil Rights Committee of Minnesota, and that the committee was meeting considerable success and was getting hold of money, "the lever which moves the world and which MUST be used in the matter now on hand."[146]

Once again the problem seems to have been a lack of communication. Though Fortune continued to call for money in the *Age*, few papers supporting the League reprinted the calls or followed the progress of the Heard case. The *Appeal*, however, constantly gave coverage to the letters received by the Civil Rights Committee secretary, William Hazel, and kept a running total of the subscriptions sent to aid the Hardy case.[147] One of the letters was by Josephine St. Pierre Ruffin, a League supporter from Boston, who wrote to Hazel and the Committee expressing her enthusiasm for their case and praising them for crystallizing something that the National League had failed to get off the ground.[148] Wells and D. Augustus Straker, both supporters of the League, also praised the Minnesota Committee.[149]

The Minnesota Civil Rights Committee did such a good job promoting the suit that it overshadowed the League and, in many respects, took whatever momentum the organization may have gained with its favorable decision in the Heard-Pullman case. When forming a new organization in St. Paul, the Committee expressed its desire to see the "National Afro-American League . . . take some action in the premises" since the group had "all the machinery of organization necessary." Why then did its members start up their own organization?[150] Why not pursue a suit as the St. Paul branch or the Minnesota branch of the League, as Fortune believed they were doing when he endorsed their actions initially in a letter that was read at the opening meeting of the Minnesota Civil Rights Committee and later published in the *Age*?

While perhaps a bit of stretch, the creation of the Minnesota Civil Rights Committee could very well have sounded the death knell of the Afro-American League. But why would members of the organization form a new group and virtually pull the resources and momentum away from the national movement? The answer remains unknown. The Afro-American League struggled to survive the year while Fortune continued to call upon local branches to lend their financial support to the activities of the group and looked forward to the organization's attempt to challenge the constitutionality of the Jim Crow System in a southern court.

While the League was struggling to scrape together enough money to challenge the Heard case, the organization received news that Fortune had won his suit against the Trainer Hotel.[151] After nearly a year and a half, the Fortune-Trainer suit had finally come before the New York Supreme Court. An all-white jury notwithstanding, Fortune and his defense team, led by T. McCants Stewart, secured a victory. Although the decision set little or no precedent to challenge the unjust legislation being passed throughout the nation, the trial was filled with symbolic ramifications.

The magnitude of the case was revealed in counselor Stewart's opening remarks when he made a forthright proclamation in defense of African Americans' civil and political rights. He reminded the jury of the progress that the nation had made during the last five decades and jogged their memory that they lived in a state that joined a number of other states in 1868 to amend the national Constitution to include the Fourteenth Amendment. Likewise, he reminded the jurors that their own state constitution contained similar clauses. Yet Stewart further argued that the Trainer suit had little to do with social rights. He recapped the state's 1873 Civil Rights Act, impressing upon the jury that social rights were not related to civil rights, which were those at issue in the case.[152] He stated "every man is Czar in the social empire; but every man in our democracy has to yield obedience to the law in his relation to the public and the State." Moreover, "the intelligent Afro-American does not bother his head any more about social equality that you do about the man in the moon. What he rightly insists upon . . . is that he shall enjoy without let or hindrance every public, every civil and every political right guaranteed him by the Constitution and the law of the land," adding that this was what the suit was about and this was what the "Afro-American have been contending for more than a generation."[153]

After all arguments were heard, the jury took fewer than twenty minutes to rule in Fortune's favor, agreeing to a total settlement of $1,016.23.[154] The court bustled with excitement as the fact sunk in that Fortune had won a victory despite a Tammany Hall judge and an all-white jury. The trial garnered widespread attention in the nation's black community. Many, including Booker T. Washington who was in town raising money for Tuskegee, hurried to the front of the courtroom to congratulate the editor and his counsel.[155]

Congratulatory letters also began flooding into Stewart's and Fortune's offices. Many of them acknowledged the greater significance of the victory for the race and the Afro-American League. Reverend Alexander Walters was one of the first to send his best wishes, stating that he considered the victory "an important advantage not only for yourself but likewise for the race. With a few more victories like the Heard affair and your case against Trainer, your great interest in the race will be acknowledged by all the race."[156] Professor William V. Tunnell of Howard University believed that Fortune's victory had vindicated the League idea. Judge J. Pennoyer Jones of Arkansas thought it was now time to take the momentum and turn toward the "'Jim Crow Car' outrage." Finally, John Mercer Langston believed that Fortune had taught the race "and the country that at last the law, the judge, the jury, the lawyer and the courthouse" are what African Americans needed in vindicating their claims.[157]

Yet even with the Trainer Hotel victory, the race did not seem to be in a position to put its weight—and more importantly, its financial support—behind a legal defense strategy. Despite the favorable reaction by many to Fortune's success, the League continued to languish at the national level. Some of the local branches continued to meet, and a few persisted in instituting challenges against the increasing Jim Crow legislation. In Milwaukee, a strong League presence continued; as the year ended the organization had money left in its local coffers and vowed to continue the struggle for the rights of blacks as American citizens and "never weaken until victory" was won.[158] Finally, just prior to their December meeting, the Milwaukee group, as it had done after the Chicago convention, attempted to rally League supporters both in the state of Wisconsin and throughout the country. The Milwaukee executive committee declared "it would be a shame . . . and a stigma upon the race if the league is permitted to collapse because of a want of interest." It then asked, "what can we ever expect to accomplish if we never make a start, or are you satisfied to ride in Jim Crow cars when you go South and are you delighted by being told that you cannot sit where you please in a theater, or are you content being debarred the privilege of dining in first-class restaurant or hotel because your skin is black?" "Does not the thought of what our race suffers in the South arouse one spark of indignation and a desire to alleviate their condition as well as our own?" argued the Milwaukee committee. "Then why not come together," it concluded, and "show the world we are a race who can and do resent the humiliations, the injustices, practiced upon us?"[159]

Robert Pelham echoed the sentiments of the Milwaukee League. Since the Knoxville convention, his paper had been publishing a series of articles written under the nom de plume "puncture," aimed at addressing specific criticisms of the Afro-American League and setting the record straight regarding the creation of the organization.[160] Then, during the final months of the year, Pelham tried to "gather the clans" to promote the growth of the group and its activities. In October 1891, he reprinted a letter sent to League secretary William Anderson from an African American living in the "back wood counties of Arkansas." The individual claimed that blacks had to be careful in his region as it was "of frequent occurrence here for colored men and women to be taken from their homes and whipped for almost nothing, or because he or she exercised the privileges of manhood and womanhood." Despite the risks, this individual was ready to participate in League activity—"even at the risk of life." "This is the ring of true metal," Anderson declared, "when the Afro-Americans all over the country arrive at this point, the prejudices and intolerance of the North and South will cease to assume the aggravating form of the present." He then called upon "all church organizations, all social and literary societies, all secret and benefit organizations, whose purpose is for the welfare of the people, and all manner and condition of men are wanted to help the Afro-American League in its effort to create the public sentiment that will secure justice."[161]

Despite Anderson's impassioned call, there is no evidence that the League rallied to the beat of his drum. Sporadic local activity, such as that in Milwaukee, could be seen, but no sign of a national mobilization. Moreover, the scramble for supporters of civil rights at the national level became more congested by the end of 1891. Not only were the Afro-American League and the

American Citizen's Equal Rights Association competing for followers, but former carpetbagger and League supporter Albion W. Tourgée had formed the National Civil Rights Association.[162] Evidently Tourgée had determined that the Afro-American League was no longer effective and that the black population was unable to organize for its own defense. When the League formed, Tourgée, the author of *A Fool's Errand*, wrote a long letter to the convention congratulating participants on their efforts and presenting his thoughts on organization.[163] He had also written supporters of the League idea prior to the national convention to welcome their actions as "the first step the race has attempted of its own motion toward self-assertive freedom—the only freedom that can ever be relied upon to give results.[164]

The new organization gained praise from some African Americans, but once again, as with the American Citizen's Equal Rights Association and the Minnesota Civil Rights Committee, the National Citizen's Rights Association's goals or tactics differed little from those of the Afro-American League. With this little difference among the groups, a number of individuals wondered why yet another organization had formed. Yet despite these reservations, Tourgée and his followers continued on their course and began instituting their own challenges against the growing outrages throughout the country.[165]

As the year came to a close, both the Afro-American League and the Minnesota Civil Rights Committee of Minnesota continued soliciting funds for their respective legal battles. Toward the final months of the year, Fortune became more embittered and his attitude cautionary regarding the success that the League might gain over the next year in the face of financial problems. The situation was not new, for Fortune had been begging for funding for the entire life of the organization. As late as October 1891 he lamented that "the Afro-American League [was] not a self-sustaining organization by a good many dollars. On the contrary it is, financially, one of the poorest organizations of the kind in the world."[166]

Secretary William Anderson, however, was not ready to throw in the towel as far as the League idea was concerned. In response to criticism from the *Pennsylvania Statesman*, he noted that since the "inception of the Afro-American League there have been formed thirteen state organizations . . . and local leagues have been formed in nearly every state of the Union." The reason the Leagues had not accomplished more, Anderson believed, was because the "executive committees have not had energy enough to push matters, and make their local leagues a factor in their communities . . . yet there are many local organizations that are doing much good." Moreover, in the two years of its existence the League had accomplished some good, although "its influence in some communities has been more beneficial than in others, according to the activity displayed there in." The Afro-American League started and "won suits at law, it has been the medium by which business enterprises have been started, it has moulded sentiment and for these reasons organizations" like the League were needed and should be supported by the community as a whole.[167]

Activity did continue on the local level. In February 1892, John Mitchell, Jr., urged the creation of Leagues throughout Virginia, Kentucky, and other southern states for the purpose of forming "a united and solid front" against the separate car legislation. He urged the League supporters to "organize to make [their] peaceful protests against injustice more effective. Organize to promote [their] material welfare! Organize to elevate the moral and industrial needs of the people!"[168]

In Milwaukee, the local organization propelled the League into new territory by moving directly into mainstream politics. Following the Knoxville convention, the group saw no contradiction in being a member of the League and participating in politics. The group, in turn, moved to support League member John J. Miles as a candidate for nomination for alderman of the Fourth Ward and campaigned for Miles outside of the League circle, urging African Americans living in the ward to rally behind him in his efforts to become Milwaukee's first black alderman.[169] Additional activity was expressed by the League's assembling state conventions, which continued in a number of locations including Michigan and Nebraska.[170]

* * *

Throughout 1892 the country continued to backpedal away from Reconstruction legislation. Jim Crow laws, represented especially by the enactment of separate coach acts sweeping the South, multiplied. Responding to this action, the League raised funds for the Heard case, attempted to organize against separate coach legislation, and formed groups in regions such as Madisonville, Kentucky, as late as July 1892.[171] Yet despite the group's efforts, Jim Crow continued to spread throughout the South, and de facto segregation increasingly gained momentum in the North.

On many levels, however, the expanding de facto and de jure segregation was not the most pressing concern of African Americans. Lynching and mob violence was the issue that alarmed the black community most as death tolls increasingly mounted. By 1892, the frequency of such heinous crimes had rapidly increased. Between 1889 and 1893 nearly seven hundred people were killed, a number not seen before or again in the years of the New South.[172] One of the main reasons for the League's formation was the defense of the African American population from such terrorization, and during 1892 several local branches began actively organizing against these crimes against humanity.

How to attack this terrorism and bloodshed, however, posed something of a problem for League members. Some believed that the group should revitalize the aspect of the original League constitution that promoted emigration to a safer and more comfortable region of the country, especially the North or West. Yet others seemed to think that public outcry and the creation of public sentiment against such barbarism was the route to end the terror.[173] In the midst of this discussion, a number of African Americans put forth an eloquent appeal for the black community to conduct a day of prayer and reflection. Since state authorities were indifferent and the national authorities found themselves unable or unwilling to protect "their native citizens murdered upon American soil," the petitioners believed that the only place the community could turn to at the moment was the "Lord God . . . to him, who has the power to enlighten and soften men's hearts . . . and who brought Israel out of bondage."[174]

However, the Afro-American League did not issue this appeal, and many of its supporters believed that there would be no need for such a passive act as a day of fasting and reflection if more people had taken up the League's ideas and funded its causes. Nevertheless, some Leagues around the country joined their communities in honoring the call and helping to organize the events on the day of fasting, May 31, 1892. For example, Albert W. Hill, president of the Michigan Afro-American League, published a passionate call to utilize the day of fasting as a springboard for future organizing. "The time has now come for action," he declared.

> To the League, the Negro of the South looks for aid and protection. He stands today with strained, listening ear waiting for some brave words from you which will convince him that you have not forgotten him or the resolutions you made when the League was formed.
>
> Lynched without a trial upon the slightest suspicion of guilt; forced to abandon property, the fruits of years of toil and self denial, if he has

> the manhood to defend himself; hunted down by bands of armed assassins, in the full of day, in the abused name of law and order and under the lying pretense of honest citizenship; intimidated, terrorized and proscribed; impoverished by laws, the makers of which with damnable frankness, unblushingly admit, were made only for him; unarmed and defenseless, he appeals to you to devise some means of profound peace the slaughter of men and women because they are black. If you are men you will not allow this cry for aid to go unheeded. If you care for your brother in the South and do not want him again to sink to the level of the slave, show by your presence . . . that you are determined no longer to calmly submit to unjustice and outrage.[175]

Gatherings were held in a number of states, including Indiana, Illinois, Minnesota, and Michigan. At these convocations, the Afro-American League was well represented. In Michigan, the League dominated the proceedings, with Reverend James M. Henderson, Albert Hill, and D. Augustus Straker addressing the audience gathered at Bethel Church. Straker's speech was concise and motivating. He told the audience, "We indict the white race of American citizens for injustice towards us not only for the period of more than two hundred and fifty years, during which time we physically endured an inhuman bondage, which deprived us of life, of liberty, or human happiness, of the wages of the sweat of our brow; the children, the offspring of our blood, the mother, the agent of our being, the wife, the consummation of our affections the brother, the sister the relative, but we complain that although we are no longer slaves, but freemen . . . we are oppressed and denied our rights . . . we are discriminated against." He asserted that "the courts of justice turn a deaf ear to our cries for protection, the dog is set upon us to drink our blood for human satisfaction; the public places of accommodation, and in the method of travel we are scorned and condemned as lepers. Oh, God! Wilt thou hear us!"

Straker claimed that the League had gathered to draft a petition to Congress and to unify with other groups such as Tourgée's American Citizen's Rights Association to emancipate blacks from "wrong and oppression." He further declared that "the colored citizen has reached the conclusion that to maintain his rights, to defend himself against oppression, to protect his home and the lives of his kindred from lynch law in all and any of its shapes or forms is worth dying for." Finally, Straker recommended that neither he nor any other African American who had as much heritage in America as any other citizen of the country should sing "Sweet Land of Liberty" until "liberty is in more than words possessed and enjoyed by every citizen black or white."[176]

These sentiments were shared by members of the Minnesota Afro-American League and the Minnesota Civil Rights Committee who gathered at Tuner Hall in St. Paul to observe the day of fasting and prayer. The group passed resolutions similar to those expressed by Straker, and the proceedings were capped off by Rosa Hazard Hazel, wife of William Hazel, singing a song she composed to the tune of "America."

O Country, tis for thee
Pledged to fair Liberty –
For thee we cry;
Land where our fathers came,
Land of our mothers' shame,
Land of our toil and pain,
Must thou too die?
Die to the sense of wrong,
While on they lips, the song
Of liberty!
False to thy sacred trust!
False to thy hallowed dust!
False to thy true and just
Who dies for thee?
Shame on thy starry crown![177]

Following the events of May 31, 1892, a number of local Leagues continued their efforts to organize their membership against lynch and mob violence and the growing Jim Crow system. But the fact that the national organization failed to convene for its third annual conference in Philadelphia provided more reliable evidence that the Afro-American League was falling apart. A few new Leagues were formed in Tennessee, Kentucky, and Pennsylvania, but as Robert Pelham stated in the *Plaindealer* in September, "it will take time for the people to generally take up with the movement for as a mass they fail to realize their condition. For the present, those interested in the league or kindred organizations must be content with slow growth, and sow assiduously the seed of the movement that will in time ripen and bear rich fruit."[178]

Over the next year, some supporters of the League worked tirelessly to promote the ideas and actions that had been proposed by the organization at its inaugural meeting in Chicago. Some new branches even developed in areas such as Los Angeles, but the League on the national level had fallen so much from the scene that George Knox of the *Indianapolis Freeman* asked if the League were dead. In his editorial, Knox called out, "if not, let the word go 'round, and if it but sleeps, let it be aroused, for there is work . . . it becomes the Negro to stir himself for himself."[179] Knox explained that there had been "a successful effort in some . . . states, to keep life and activity in the anatomy of local League organizations." That fact notwithstanding, "the national body, as an intact organization, has long since gone glimmering." He proposed that a call go forth, and that the group begin to organize on the state level to prepare for a national gathering, for "a veritable hell is staring the Negro in the face . . . [and] he must swim or perish."[180]

President Fortune did not respond to the editorial, but Bishop Henry McNeal Turner subsequently called for African Americans to convene in Cincinnati, Ohio, to discuss the best course of action for the race, including "African repatriation or Negro nationalization elsewhere."[181] One month later, Fortune announced the death of the League. He listed indifference on the part of the so-called race leadership, lack of support by the masses, and financial problems as reasons for its demise.[182]

Fortune's labeling of the organization as defunct may have been premature, however, as the desire for some type of organized defense against the "veritable hell" experienced by black Americans was apparent by the numbers who descended on Cincinnati for Turner's convention.[183] Moreover, the cooling embers of the League idea were kept aflame by the activities of various local Leagues throughout the nation. Encouraged, in the summer of 1894 Fortune called upon local Leagues to rally and form state conventions so that the national organization could again assemble on the national stage.[184] In response to continued acts of lynching and mob violence throughout the nation, he wished to support the anti-lynching campaign begun in 1892 by Ida B. Wells, which was beginning to reach an international audience.

Wells, who similar to Fortune was born a slave in 1862 in Holly Springs, Mississippi, had watched her parents struggle against wicked forces in the immediate years after emancipation. Like so many black families, however, the Wellses did not fold up their tents; instead they fought back whenever possible and carved out a life for themselves. Young Wells watched the actions of her parents and the community and strove to educate herself and follow in their footsteps. Then at the age of sixteen, following the death of her parents and infant brother in a yellow fever epidemic, she dropped out of Shaw University, later Rust College, to teach school and care for her remaining siblings. Later she relocated to Memphis, Tennessee, where she taught and eventually became a journalist—writing initially for the *Living Way*, a Baptist weekly, and later the militant *Free Speech*, which she co-owned. Her activist career began in earnest in 1883 when she refused to leave a first-class ladies car on the Chesapeake, Ohio, and Southwestern Railway. This action was taken after the Supreme Court's 1883 overturning of the Civil Rights Act of 1875, which also inspired so many of her contemporaries to take action. Wells took her case to court; though she won at the lower levels in 1884, the Tennessee Supreme Court overturned the decision in 1887. After the defeat, Wells did not stop agitating for social, civil, and political rights. Like Fortune, she took to the editorial pen and used the pages of her newspaper to campaign vigorously against the white supremacy that was rapidly growing throughout the nation.

Following the lynching of her close friend, Thomas Moss, and his two associates, Calvin McDowell and Lee Stewart, Wells began investigating the brutal acts of lynching that had been on the rise in the South.[185] In her findings, Wells shattered the myth of rape touted as the central reason for the lynching of black males. In May 1892 she published an editorial in her newspaper listing a number of lynchings that had taken place since the previous issue. Wells's editorial warned, "nobody in this section of the country believes the old threadbare lie that Negro men rape white women. If Southern white men are not careful, they will over-reach themselves and public sentiment will have a reaction; a conclusion will then be reached which will be very damaging to the moral reputation of their women."[186] After the publication of the editorial, a mob of white citizens in Memphis destroyed the offices of the *Free Speech* and threatened the life of Wells and anyone involved with the paper's publication. After hearing of the events back in Memphis, Wells, who had been visiting New York, decided not to return to the South and joined Fortune's staff at the *New York Age*.

Publishing her findings in the *Age* brought Wells a wider audience. In October 1892 she published a pamphlet, *Southern Horrors: Lynch Law in All Its Phases*, which one scholar has called the "point of origin in American critical thought on lynching and racism."[187] Wells then stepped up her publications and addresses on the issue of lynching, and in April 1893, she traveled to England for the purpose of internationalizing the issue. Wells, like the abolitionists before her, understood the importance of making the atrocities of America known worldwide. Already, her *Southern Horrors* pamphlet had been republished in England as *U.S. Atrocities*. Upon her return, she attended the Columbia Exposition in Chicago where she, Frederick Douglass, and Ferdinand Barnett published and distributed *The Reason Why the Colored American Is Not in the Columbian Exposition*, a pamphlet which further brought the plight of African Americans to the world stage.

It is at this moment, when Wells's anti-lynching campaign was gaining strength and a worldwide audience, that Fortune called for the National Afro-American League to reorganize. As Wells prepared to embark on another trip to England, Fortune declared that the race had reached a period in its "contention for justice under the Federal Constitution . . . when a decent regard for the opinions of mankind demands that we should enter a concerted and emphatic protest against the mob spirit abroad the Republic, and . . . break down the testimony given by Miss Ida B. Wells to the British public as to the extent of race prejudice and mob violence in the United States."[188] A meeting of the League on the national level, he insisted, was necessary to ensure that the

> British public may not be deceived by the avalanche of misrepresentations which is now being poured into Great Britain by white men of the South, who feel that they are being injured in their financial standing before the world by the plain, blunt, truthful statement of the facts which has been made to the British public by a woman of the race whose reputation is being assailed with all malignancy and mendacity which desperate men employ in a hopeless and dishonorable cause.[189]

For such a purpose, Fortune believed it necessary to "gather the clans," but he allowed only two weeks for this action to be completed. A few Leagues gathered, including a meeting with a rousing endorsement for Wells and the League in Boston, but due to the short notice, the majority of the local Leagues were unable to activate themselves. The Afro-American League once again folded at the national level. Such a situation prompted the once-supportive George Knox to proclaim that the Afro-American League was "dead, sir! dead as a door nail, we know not the power great enough to re-illumine its ashes and once more galvanize it into life." Therefore, despite an occasional glimmer of activity at the local level and continued public references to Fortune as president of the Afro-American League, after July 1894 the group no longer held a place on the national stage.[190]

* * *

With the increased need for a national organization in 1894, why did the Afro-American League fail to regroup on the national level? Aside from its financial troubles, T. Thomas Fortune raised one of the major problems with the Afro-American League when he first called for its formation. In October 1887 he noted that the Afro-American community had never had a "great popular leader in the sense that we speak of Parnell or Gladstone . . . a leader whom the people trusted and would sustain as loyally in the day of defeat as in the day of victory." Fortune believed this was true because black America was comprised of "a race of leaders!" Every man regarded himself as a "natural captain and therefore scorns to be led or advised." To be successful, the race would have to move away from being an army of "self-exalted generals" and learn the "great principle of co-operation,"[191]

The Afro-American League was envisioned as an association that would facilitate coordination of the community's strengths and abilities for the purpose of securing full citizenship rights. The stated goals of the organization were to bring together the race under one unified front. However, from the start the League was unable to unify the race. The group both failed to attract mass support and to unify those supporters who aspired to be leaders of the race. No one truly disagreed with the end goal of the organization—forcing the U.S. government to uphold the rights of African Americans guaranteed by the Constitution and bringing about an end to mob and lynch law—but many disagreed on the path that the organization should take. As Ida B. Wells remarked in her response to the *Detroit Plaindealer*'s 1889 circular, "dissensions among . . . leaders will prevent the [League's] organization."[192]

Wells was certainly correct regarding the Afro-American League. From the beginning, the organization competed with the American Citizens' Equal Rights Association, founded a month after the League's creation. Then, as the League was struggling to gain a foothold in the community, the Civil Rights Committee of Minnesota and the National Civil Rights Association joined the fray, two other organizations competing for financial support that had similar platforms. Fortune considered it foolish for the organizations to continue struggling against one another rather than unifying their resources and efforts. As Robert Pelham noted, "The Afro-American is not rich, by any means, and in supporting more than one National body of this kind there is a useless waste of expense entailed upon the people in keeping up the organizations. The money thus wasted could be better used in solving the questions that should be of interest to every Afro-American."[193]

Another factor that undermined the growth of the Afro-American League was the absence of backing from powerful figures in the black community. Many scholars have noted the lack of support from politicians such as John Mercer Langston, Blanche K. Bruce, and Frederick Douglass. However, as damaging as this may have been, it did not really lead to the destruction of the organization. As noted earlier, Langston supported the League's actions on several accounts. He may have never become a full member of the organization, but like John R. Lynch, he visibly offered encouragement to the group in the beginning and supported both the Fortune and Heard cases.

The real problem was that the League failed to attract the masses. The organization was top-heavy, and although aspects of its platform were designed to aid the majority, especially in the South, none of those ideals ever translated into practice. Responding to the *Detroit Plaindealer*'s circular, Booker T. Washington remarked, "An organization of the kind I am sure can be made to serve a good end if it can in some way be made to *reach* and *interest* the masses of the colored people. Most conferences, conventions, etc., heretofore have reached only the 'mountain peaks,' leaving 'the great Alpine range of humanity and activity below.' "[194] The League failed to heed Washington's advice.

More important, the organization failed to enlist the support of individuals and institutions in contact with the masses. Though the AME Church was well represented in the ranks of the organization, especially in the South, the Baptist Church had no direct association with the group or its activities. The League also failed to gain the full support of the secret societies and beneficial associations on the rise in the late nineteenth century. Moreover, the group failed to fully draw upon African American women. When the group assembled on the national stage, Fortune remarked that unless "the women of the race take hold of the Afro-American League it will never be the power it should be."[195] The observation turned out to be true, but Fortune's blame was likely misplaced.

Without larger support from the religious community, the secret societies, and black women, the League was unable to carry out its program.[196] And to complicate matters, the organization's downfall was also marked by the incapacity to coordinate publicity surrounding its efforts. Though the League had the support of key editors at influential black newspapers, the activities of the League were rarely discussed in black publications outside the immediate region where its activities were concentrated at any given time. Such lapses contributed to the group's inability to gain widespread appeal.

Finally, the growing group of young intellectual and professionals who nominally supported the development of the Afro-American League effectively deserted Fortune and the few active supporters of the League. Many of the ostensible supporters espoused rhetoric with no follow-up. Those seemingly prepared for action had leadership aspirations of their own and organized even more groups, further dividing the minds, actions, attention, and resources of the African American community.[197] Apparently the race was not quite ready to coordinate its efforts in "an endless battle for the rights of manhood and womanhood." Thus, successes of the various local branches notwithstanding, the National Afro-American League "practically died in the act of being born."[198] Yet despite its collapse, many of the League's strategies would not die. In the years ahead, the League idea would be further developed as others attempted to bring into existence a viable national civil rights organization.

Chapter 3

Interregnum and Resurrection

> The time demands the revising of the Afro-American League. . . . the fire is not out . . . it is the duty of every well thinking Negro to advocate the awakening of this laudable body and advance the true principals of strength and unison.
>
> —Charles Hall

While the Afro-American League collapsed on the national stage the reasons for its existence—the spread of disfranchisement, segregation, and racial violence—did not disappear. In fact, during the 1890s, the social and political forces that created the need for the Afro-American League actually became more enveloping. During the decade, lynchings rose to an average of more than one hundred per year, and segregation gained national legal sanction with the Supreme Court's *Plessy v. Ferguson* decision. With this unceasing growth of a national white supremacy African Americans continued to attempt to organize to secure and protect their citizenship rights, but at the same time other strategies developed to complement the overall push to gain security and recognition in a nation that continually denied both to the black community. During this period, a number of individuals and organizations attempted to fill the void left by the Afro-American League while others created programs that would work in concurrence with the League's civil rights activism. These individuals and organizations included the likes of Booker T. Washington, Ida B. Wells, the National Association of Colored Women's Clubs, and the National Federation of Colored Men. However, despite the actions and efforts of these individuals and organizations, as the decade proceeded and blacks' rights were continually violated (often with the use of violence as a tool of physical and psychological control), the resounding call was for the community to again create a national organization based on the platform of the Afro-American League to secure and protect the citizenship rights of African Americans. The calls became so numerous that by the final years of the decade, the League idea was resurrected in the form of a new organization, the Afro-American Council, and many of the voices that had risen in the interregnum joined forces with the cadre of individuals who had kept the idea alive to try to perfect this new national civil rights organization.

* * *

In the early 1890s, in the wake of the Afro-American League's collapse and before the rise of the Afro-American Council, black Americans continued to face deteriorating conditions. The rise of racial violence especially became the pressing issue within the black community. While both federal and state governments persistently ignored the nearly daily reports of the barbarous activity, Ida B. Wells, as well as a number of other black newspaper editors, continued to expose the disgraceful practice. Wells, the former League activist, in particular served as a thorn festering in the side of white America's conscience, and almost single-handedly internationalized the anti-lynching crusade.[1] Many, especially African Americans, praised her tireless activity and ardent support for the defenseless. Abraham Kendrick, for instance, celebrated Wells's courageous activism in a poem published in the *Indianapolis Freeman*:

> By and by up springs a woman,
> Rushes boldly to the front;
> Shouting, "I will board the vessel,
> And for justice I will hunt."[2]

Not everyone, however, was pleased with the international attention that Wells's campaign garnered. In 1895, a year after T. Thomas Fortune tried to revitalize the League nationally in support of Wells's anti-lynching activity, James Jacks, president of the Missouri Press Association, attacked the lonely warrior. Jacks had received a letter from Florence Belgarnie, secretary of the British Anti-Lynching Committee, soliciting the help of American journalists in the battle against lynching. Jacks replied to Belgarnie by attacking African Americans in general and black women in particular: "The Negroes in this country are wholly devoid of morality," he proclaimed. "They know nothing of it," Jacks continued, "except as they learn by being caught for flagrant violations of law." Black women like Wells, he asserted, were "prostitutes and all . . . natural liars and thieves. . . . . Out of 200 in this vicinity it is doubtful there are a dozen virtuous women of that number who are not daily thieving from the white people."[3]

Once knowledge of Jacks's letter reached American shores, black women resolved to take action on their own terms and speak against such libel. Their stance was hardly new: African American women had been active in the public sphere since the abolitionist movement and had been increasing their activity in recent years. Moreover, for a number of years black women had formed clubs promoting self-help and the racial uplift of black communities. Several of these early clubs sponsored night schools that offered courses in literature, history, and art as well as industrial skills such as sewing, housekeeping, cooking, and gardening. Many clubs also provided nurseries and other day-to-day assistance for working mothers.[4] Women involved in the clubs believed that black women would lead the masses to a position of self-reliance. As Anna Julia Cooper, educator, author, activist, and cofounder of the Colored Women's League said in her 1892 *A Voice from The South*, "Only the Black Woman can say 'When and where I enter, . . . then and there the whole Negro race enters with me.'"[5] Club women, in turn, took this principle to heart by putting it into action.

After the outrage produced by Jacks's letter, many in this disjointed club movement began to realize that a national organization was needed to coordinate their efforts and fight against the defamation of the African American community in general, and black women in particular. In 1895, two such organizations were formed: the National League of Colored Women and the National Federation of Afro-American Women. In the summer of the following year, the two merged into a new organization, the National Association of Colored Women (NACW). The association, adopting the motto "Lifting as We Climb," was dedicated to raising the level of the home, moral, and civil lives of the black community. Like its affiliates, the NACW called for the creation of nurseries and industrial classes to aid mothers and black women in general. The organization also promoted temperance, relief for the poor, and women's suffrage.[6] Their overarching objective was to aid the race in becoming self-reliant and independent.

Though no longer a national presence, the Afro-American League continued on the local level, and many of its chapters supported Wells and the club movement. Nowhere was this support demonstrated more strongly than in Omaha, Nebraska, where a resolution condemning Jacks's comments and expressing "no fear" for supporting the "anti-lynching cause" was passed during the organization's July meeting. The Omaha branch further endorsed the action of the National Convention of Club Women and sent with their local representatives a copy of their resolution of support, which claimed full "co-operation" in what the new organization proposed to do "for the elevation of mankind."[7]

The message of racial uplift and self-reliance espoused by the women's movement was similar to that of another former League supporter, Booker T. Washington.[8] Washington, born a slave and educated at Hampton Institute in Virginia, was becoming a leading voice in the black community during the 1890s.[9] In 1881, he became the principal of Tuskegee Normal and Industrial Institute in Alabama, an all-black school teaching self-determination, which quickly equaled other black institutions of the day. Tuskegee emphasized industrial education and economic independence in an area dominated by sharecropping. The school soon became larger than the town as Washington bought surrounding farmland and sold it at low rates to create a community of land and homeowners. The Institute and its surrounding community became the model black town, an example of Washington's vision of self-reliant communities that could turn segregation into autonomous development and economic opportunity through separation and strength in numbers.

Washington's subsequent transformation into *the* black leader, however, took him and his influence beyond the grounds of Tuskegee. On September 18, 1895, he gave a speech at the Cotton States and International Exposition in Atlanta, which is now famously known as the Atlanta Compromise. In it, Washington opined that if left alone, blacks could prosper and contribute greatly to the nation as a whole. In an attempt to disarm southern whites, Washington declared that agitation for social equality was not where African Americans needed to put their energies, and that in "purely social" matters the races could "be as separate as the fingers, yet one as the hand in all things essential to mutual progress."[10] In return for relinquishing the demand for immediate civil and political rights, Washington called on whites to remove any barriers to black economic advancement as the two races worked together, but separately to uplift the South and the nation. After the Atlanta Exposition address and the death of Frederick Douglass earlier that year, Washington was made the principal negotiator between the races. Andrew Carnegie, William Baldwin, and other white philanthropists gave money to uplift the race, and Washington allocated the funds to areas that he saw fit, such as the promotion of black businesses and support of other black schools. He also became a key political advisor for many Republican politicians, including Theodore Roosevelt, who looked to Washington as his foremost confidant on race issues after his election to the presidency.

Washington's public philosophy—a renunciation of rights, silence on abuses, and disparagement of higher education—that gained him his place as *the* leader, however, could not be sustained as white racism failed to lessen, lynching continued to rise, and Jim Crow became solidified in the decade after Washington's Atlanta address. Such action was not directly Washington's fault, but despite his secret support for challenges to segregation and occasional public vocal challenges to discrimination, for many he came to symbolize steady deterioration of black rights.

* * *

During the mid-1890s, often referred to as the beginning of an interregnum in the struggle for black political rights, the Afro-American League continued fighting at the local level. Furthermore, in the wake of the failure of the League on the national stage, many supporters began lending their support and energies to other nascent protective or civil rights organizations. This period has been viewed as a time in which a neo-abolitionist spark was unable to kick-start any sort of organized black, white, or interracial response to the deteriorating conditions of the black community. But at the same time, many continued to search for the proper fuel. While Washington's public message of "accommodation" dominated the rhetoric of race relations, a certain cadre of individuals continued to try to create a less accommodating national civil rights organization. These individuals in turn advanced the struggle started by the League by maintaining local activities of League branches and by starting a new group built upon the foundation provided by T. Thomas Fortune's League.

In late 1895, a few months after Washington's address, a new civil rights association formed. The National Federation of Colored Men of the United States was organized by a number of former Afro-American League supporters, including George L. Knox, editor of the *Indianapolis Freeman*; Chicago attorney Edward H. Morris; and Detroit attorney D. Augustus Straker; it mirrored the League in a number of ways, focusing on the principles of political and legal agitation for black rights.[11] The Federation grew out of a conference of Colored Men held in Detroit in December 1895. The group elected Straker its president, organized the nation into districts, and sought to attack the worsening conditions through coordinated activity. In the published resolutions, the Federation proposed focusing on mob and lynch violence and the continued disfranchisement of African American men; at the same time it also promised to push for equal employment for black workers in the industrial sector of the nation.[12]

In its first year of existence, the Federation focused largely on lynching, especially lobbying efforts to get the federal government to be more concerned and take greater action. While not tied to any particular political party, the Federation acknowledged that the most heinous violations against the black population took place in the South, an area dominated by the Democratic Party. Therefore, like many of the previously organized efforts of African Americans, it focused its lobbying efforts on the Republican Party. With the coming of the 1896 presidential election, the Federation pressured the Republican Party by seeking to get an anti-lynching plank inserted into its platform.

The need to elicit support from political parties for a federal anti-lynching law was not new, but the hypocrisy of Congress's refusal to issue such legislation became ever more apparent during the 1896 campaign. In the early months of the year, Congress passed a law forbidding prizefighting anywhere in the United States. Even before the federal legislation, governors throughout the nation, especially in the South, were calling special sessions to enact laws and mobilize "the militia to resist the daring encounter of two bloody boxers." Harry Smith of the *Cleveland Gazette* in highlighting the selective morality of such leaders declared, "we behold the power of great states thundering their deadly decrees against an offensive sport, while scenes of the most outrageous brutality and inhumanity, unsurpassed in wickedness and atrocity, are perpetuated under their eyes, and nothing is done to bring the villains to justice." "Not content with the unlawful taking of a prisoner's life," he asserted, "they subject him to bloody torture, hacking off parts of the body, gashing it here and there, mutilating and tearing asunder the shivering victim while they hold up to public gaze the bleeding trophy." Smith questioned whether state representatives had shown any concern for these hideous crimes, but sarcastically retorted that surely since the outrageous prizefighting had now been made an unlawful practice, legislatures throughout the country would move to make lynching and mob violence a similar unlawful act.[13] Smith made clear that mob rule and good government could not coexist. The sooner the federal government became aware of this practicality and moved to hold the states accountable for lawlessness, the faster the nation would join the ranks of civilized governments.[14]

In addition to lynching, the rise of de facto and de jure segregation nationally in the spring of 1896 was another issue of concern for the black community. According to Richard T. Greener, South Carolina attorney and Federation member, "lynching the body is not half as deplorable, nor one tithe as demoralizing as the persistent attempt north and south to degrade an entire race."[15] Greener was reacting to the continued growth of de facto and de jure segregation sweeping the country since the overturning of the Civil Rights Bill in 1883.

The rise of white supremacy was a national issue, not just a southern phenomenon, as was demonstrated during its brief tenure by the Afro-American League's attacks on de facto segregation and discrimination in the North. In the final decade of the century, discrimination and racial tensions increased in the North as black voters were minimized, labor unions drew the color line, and public schools moved toward segregation. By the mid-1890s an uncompromising white supremacy was sweeping the country, bolstered by among other things, the Supreme Court 1883 ruling and an increasingly ambivalent Republican Party, especially on the federal level.[16]

In May 1896, the Supreme Court again stated its opinion on the matter in *Plessy v. Ferguson*, which approved the doctrine of separate but equal accommodations. Justice Henry B. Brown, delivering the majority decision, ruled, "the object of the [Fourteenth] amendment was undoubtedly to enforce the absolute equality of the two races before the law." Subsequently, "in the nature of things it could not have been intended to abolish distinctions based upon color, or to enforce social, as distinguished from political equality, or a commingling of the two races upon terms unsatisfactory to either." Brown added that laws that permitted, or even required, separation, did not "necessarily imply inferiority of either race to the other."[17]

The ruling, however, was not unanimous. Justice John Marshall Harlan delivered a scorching dissent prophesying that the judgment would prove as "pernicious as the decision made by" the Court "in the *Dred Scott* case."[18] In the black press, one of the strongest condemnations of the ruling came from Bishop Henry McNeal Turner, who stated in his *Voice of Missions* that Judge Taney's *Dred Scott* decision was a "bagatelle" compared to this piece of "judicial jugglery."[19] Turner also sent an open letter to other African American newspapers urging the black communities to voice their anger with the decision. Few put their words on paper, but Richard T. Greener did, and he agreed with Turner's assessment. Fearing that the Court's opinion in the *Plessy* case would prove to be more sweeping than Taney's dictum, Greener urged the race to stand up and act; he was afraid a worse fight was still to come, but that a "new Baptism of courage and defiance and self-assertion may be the position of the 'new Negro.' "[20]

Augustus Straker and other members of the Federation agreed with their associate's sentiments and took their case to the Republican convention. At the national convention in St. Louis, Missouri, in June 1896, Straker and the other representatives of the Federation urged the GOP's executive committee to include a plank in the party's platform condemning lynching and pledging to eliminate it once and for all when in control of the government.[21] Straker, Greener, and the other Federation representatives also took the opportunity to make their position on racial discrimination in public facilities and the recent *Plessy* decision known. "We view with alarm the recent decision of the Supreme Court," Straker noted, "in which the unjust and nefarious method of discriminating among passengers traveling in steamcars, within several Southern states, because of race and color, and not even of condition, since no distinction is made between the clean and the unclean, the rich and the poor, has been upheld by law, and we are determined no longer to be discriminated against, as American citizens." He asserted, "We are American citizens, whether white, brown, mulatto, black, or any other shade of color, and the Constitution nowhere upholds the passing of any law . . . [and the decision of the Court in *Plessy*] is a violation of Article XIV of the Constitution."[22] Quoting the deceased advocate of black rights Charles Sumner, Straker reminded those in attendance that " 'Equivalents are not equality,' " while declaring that the Federation would fight against all laws that draw distinctions between citizens. He told the Republican Party that the Federation shuddered to think about the future, "for [blacks] are not cravens, nor cowards, and will not always submit to such injustice, believing that a minority with God, is a majority in the battle for right."[23]

Straker and the other representatives of the Federation left their meeting with the Executive Committee satisfied that the Republican Party understood their stance on racial discrimination and would subsequently take action against lynching and its perpetrators once ex-governor McKinley took office.[24] In the end, however, their optimism proved unfounded. The Republican Party failed to issue a strong position against racial discrimination and took no firmer a stance against lynching than it had in 1892. While the Party condemned the act, it failed to make any concessions or to pass special legislation to end the practice. Moreover, the request of the Federation for a congressional discussion about the implementation of anti-lynching legislation did not come to fruition for another four years.[25]

* * *

Despite the Federation's belief that it could gain the support of the people and the ear of the new administration, the group never achieved the national prominence it desired. Just a few short months after the Republican convention, individuals began calling for the revival of the Afro-American League to fill this perceived void. In August 1896, William Calvin Chase, the editor of the *Washington Bee*, began advocating for an organization that brought together the local Leagues still operating and the new groups popping up—an organization that he believed would take the form of a revitalized Afro-American League.[26] For Chase, it was time for the African American population to "decide whether they are men or pigmies," and he believed that the League idea provided the best opportunity for the race "to stand up like men."[27]

A number of African Americans supported Chase's proposal. The editors of the *Virginia Leader* seconded the *Bee*'s nomination of Fortune as the rightful leader of the national League while claiming that they had already secured twenty names to start a local League in Alexandria. The *Leader* called on others in the African American press to "unite and organize a league in their towns." Such action, they believed, would make the organization successful in every state.[28]

By mid-November, Chase had organized a local League in the District of Columbia and proposed having the community organize groups throughout the District as an example of a united front in the race's quest for recognition of their citizenship. The *Bee* editor also received more endorsements from individuals outside the region. James L. Goodall, for instance, wrote Chase; Goodall was chairman of the Pennsylvania Afro-American League, an organization he had formed a few years prior, which now boasted a membership of five thousand.

Such news encouraged Chase, who continued to pound the press with calls for organization. The following week he again called for the creation of an African American united front across the nation; "disorganized forces of Afro-Americans", he believed, enabled "those who have power to ignore their just claims. Our children, wives, and husbands are butchered without cause or provocation, the unjust discrimination in our public inns on the railroads should call for immediate and strong organizations throughout the country."[29]

Fortune agreed. In a letter to Chase, he applauded efforts to revitalize the League idea. Fortune believed that the organization was a "positive necessity," but cautioned that people might still not be ready to support the institution. "A movement like the league," he explained, intended "to do for us what the Home Rule movement under Charles Stewart Parnell did for Irishmen—force respect and justice from their fellowmen and from the government—can only succeed by the united efforts of the people." In Fortune's view, this was the only question holding back the League. He urged Chase and his supporters to ponder the question while testing the support of the masses. He agreed, however, to call for a national convention as president of the League if that question were answered in the affirmative.[30]

Benjamin F. Stewart of Lancaster, Pennsylvania, seconded the need for mass support and greater unity. Stewart, the former chairman of the Pennsylvania League, urged Chase and others to slow their preparation for a national convention. He believed that the past problems of African American organizations lay in the actions of national conventions, which he saw as having been convened on the national stage before proper organizational work had been done. As a result, when the delegates left the conventions, they had no real structure or firm base to turn to. Stewart called upon the League movement to build wisely, getting "city, county and state organizations, and then [the League] will have the foundation upon which a national organization can stand and accomplish good" for every African American.[31]

Stewart's assessment of the problems that had hampered black organizations in the past echoed Fortune's ideas. When Fortune originally called for the creation of the Afro-American League, he insisted that the organization break the model set by the conventions of blacks before and after the Civil War by doing more than just holding protest rallies and passing resolutions. The League, or any other group that wanted to organize for the rights of black Americans, needed to have the masses and leaders working together for the people rather than for glory and status. "Are we Brave Men or Cowards?" Fortune asked in an 1894 *Monthly Review* article: "the great need of the times is well directed agitation which will vex the soul of the nation until it shall be aroused to a sense of its duty." But who would provoke this agitation, he asked. The national failure of the League taught the race a lot, but the question was whether the community was willing to take note of the lessons.

What was needed, both then and now, was a "League, national in character, with a hundred thousand members who would support it loyally. . . ." Such an organization, he asserted, "could in time bring about the correction of every wrong, of every injustice, of every outrage perpetuated upon the race." To do this, however, the race "must have men good to lead, and men good to follow, all of whom will back up their protestations with money necessary to keep the legal machinery of the nation hot, working in our behalf."[32] The opportunity, he maintained, was there for the taking, but he questioned whether blacks were willing or able to seize the moment.

Fortune's comments demonstrate the frustration and skepticism that existed within the African American community at the time. Many in the community understood that some sort of organization was needed to stop the continued growth of segregation and mob violence that was rising at an unparalleled level. The League was designed to be a continuous institutionalized convention in the form of a national association to effectively and systematically challenge the rise of segregation, protest lynch law and mob violence, and limit the spread of disfranchisement. Though it was not completely successful as a national organization, the idea and structure of the group was the model that many continued to look at to organize the race. The questions, which were the same for Fortune in 1884 and 1894, were whether the community would assist an organization such as the League and whether the leaders of the race would cooperate in the development of such a group.

Such skepticism remained in 1896. Was the race ready? Was it finally ready to do what they "refused [six] years ago?"[33] In the months following Chase and Stewart's discussion about the revival of the League, the *Bee* received information about local Leagues forming throughout the country, including California, Delaware, Rhode Island, Virginia, and the District of Columbia.[34] Chase then called on Fortune to issue a request that all states organize and assemble in a national convention in the city of Philadelphia for the third annual convention of the original Afro-American League.[35] Chase believed that the "colored man [was] no longer the fool," and that a convention in the early part of 1897 would demonstrate the race's wish for proper recognition from the federal government and desire for self-protection.[36]

Fortune, however, never called the national meeting. Although nothing in the surviving historical record helps explain this inaction, it is likely that he did not believe the masses were sufficiently behind the organization.[37] Throughout 1897, Leagues continued to organize, and a number of the local and state groups met in state conventions from the spring into the fall. But

Fortune did not perceive a national organization as being truly viable "because the masses" did not "care a rap about the organization."[38]

Despite Fortune's lack of support, local Leagues met at the state level—Pennsylvania and Rhode Island, for example, gathered in May and August respectively. The California League was especially active and had much to celebrate when it gathered. During the early months of the year the group, led by League president and Bay area resident Theophilus Morton, began pressuring San Francisco assemblyman Henry C. Dibble to introduce the state's first civil rights bill. Since its inception, the organization had been chronicling the racial discrimination experienced by black Californians, especially by describing these experiences in the pages of League member John J. Neimore's *Eagle*. By the early months of 1897, the group decided its top priority was ending the indignities the black population suffered throughout the state. In March, its efforts were rewarded when the California legislature passed the Dibble bill, which prohibited discrimination in all "accommodations, advantages, facilities and privileges of inns, restaurants, hotels, eating houses, barber shops, bath houses, theaters, skating rinks, and all other places of public accommodation or amusement."[39]

Other Leagues elsewhere were not as successful, but kept the idea of the necessity of a national civil rights organization in the minds of those reading their annual reports in selected newspapers. W. Calvin Chase, moreover, had not given up on the League. He tried one last time to urge Fortune to call a national meeting in Philadelphia after Pennsylvania's successful state convention in Lancaster, but the latter again failed to see the utility of such an exercise without sufficient mass support.[40]

Chase grew frustrated and was no longer willing to wait for Fortune to act. In May 1897, he supported the actions of George W. Murray, John W. Cromwell, and Dr. J. N. Johnson in the formation of the Negro National Protective Association in Washington, D.C. The new organization, of which little is known, mirrored the Afro-American League. The nonpartisan group stood for black rights, but also supported the notion of uplift through education, black businesses, and social reform.[41]

Despite the refusal of Fortune to revive the League on the national level, and the formation by Chase and his colleagues of a new organization, the idea of the League refused to die. Actually, with conditions continuing to deteriorate for the African American community, the need increased for a unified effort to fight the growing proscription and violence. Everywhere African American men or women turned they were met with hostility. Black men were being disfranchised throughout the South while the Supreme Court was preparing to hear the arguments in *Williams v. Mississippi*, a case regarding a state's right to impose a poll tax and literacy requirements for voting. When legal means proved ineffective, black officeholders, voters, and their allies were subjected to extralegal forms of terrorism and abuse. This dangerous situation was demonstrated in the spring of 1898 when Frazier B. Baker and Isaiah H. Loftin—the postmasters of Lake City, South Carolina, and Hogansville, Georgia, respectively—were murdered for attempting to exercise their political rights.[42]

In response, in that spring Bishop Alexander Walters urged Fortune to call a meeting of like-minded individuals who understood the necessity of reviving the national civil rights and protective organization. Walters, born a slave in Kentucky, quickly rose in the ranks of the AME Zion church, holding pastor positions in Louisville, San Francisco, Chattanooga, and Knoxville before becoming the pastor in 1888 of the Mother AME Zion Church in New York City. Four years later, at age thirty-four, Walters became the youngest bishop of the AME Zion Church. It is during these early years in New York that Walters became an active participant in the thriving Brooklyn black community and an ally and friend of Fortune. Walters was a leader in the New York Afro-American League working alongside Fortune and Stewart in the victories of the state and local branches, and in the absence of a national organization continued to work on the local level.

On March 10, 1898, the dynamic race advocate sent the following open letter to the *New York Age*:

> Fellow Citizens: The late outrages perpetrated against Postmasters Loften [Loftin] of Hogansville, Georgia, and Baker of Lake City, South Carolina, for no other reason than their race and color and having no reason to believe from past experience that the perpetrators will be brought to justice; and further, because there is a determined effort on the part of the white labor unions of the country to exclude the Negro from the industrial avenues in which he can make an honest living, it became absolutely necessary that we organize for self-protection.[43]

Like W. Calvin Chase several years earlier, Walters strongly encouraged Fortune as the president of the League to call a meeting at an early date for the purpose of evaluating the present state of the race and suggesting remedies.[44]

Having already failed twice, Fortune remained reluctant to issue the call to resurrect the League. He informed Bishop Walters that if over one hundred signatures could be collected, he would again assemble the group.[45] Others were also hesitant to make another attempt at forming a national civil rights organization. Edward E. Cooper of the *Colored American* spoke for many throughout the country when he asked, "The necessity for a strong protective organization was never greater than it is today, but are conditions more favorable to such a combine now that they were in 1890?" Cooper questioned whether the race had "accumulated any larger stock of wisdom by repeated failures and a defrauded citizenship" and whether the leaders of the race were "better prepared to bury ancient hatchets, and to work in unison." If such a situation existed, Cooper believed that the League was worth reviving. But if the League was to be "established, men, money, and mind must be set to work, and these forces must work in harmony." Because, he warned, the race had no "time to play at the old childish games," it was imperative that its members have an organization that actually stood for something.[46]

The "old childish games" were the same that Fortune and others had discussed since the original call of the formation of the Afro-American League. Aside from mass support, many supporters of a national civil rights organization wondered if individuals would finally set aside their differences to work for the betterment of the race. As Fortune had stated many times, such an effort as the League needed "good men to lead and good men to follow." Many in the community feared that the organization contained many men with ideas and desires to lead, but few who were willing to follow.

Despite this cautious attitude, it did not take long for enthusiasm about the League to build. Writing in the *Illinois Record* on April 30, 1898, managing editor and Afro-American League supporter Charles Hall called for the reorganization of the League. Hall had sent letters out to various individuals throughout the nation asking if there was an interest and support for this "valuable organization."[47] According to Hall, there was an overwhelming endorsement for the group, and he asserted that if Fortune made the call, people would come. Moreover, by May, Edward Cooper was coming around and again saw the use of reorganizing the group; however, he cautioned that since the United States was currently involved in its conflict over Cuba, League supporters should proceed slowly and delay a national meeting until the war quieted down or ended altogether.[48] Cooper and his colleagues believed that the public had its eyes and ears tuned into the war and would not take favorably any agitation on the home shores. "True, separate coach laws are still here; the work of disenfranchising the race goes industriously on; and the other forms of color proscription show no signs of amelioration," they explained. "But these ills cannot be remedied by spasmodic action, nor by inopportune agitation." They further argued that "when we hold an expensive convention, and attempt to mass the Negro intellect of the nation at a given point, we want the undivided attention of the populace, and a mental condition that will insure dispassionate judgment. It will not help our cause to fly off at a tangent and lay ourselves open to the charge of disloyalty . . . when the American heart . . . is centered upon . . . a foreign foe."[49]

While many League cohorts may have agreed with the ideas articulated by Cooper, they maintained their support for the organization and continued their organizational efforts on the local level. In St. Paul and Minneapolis, Minnesota, local activists went forward in creating an organization designed to uphold the community's civil rights.[50] During the summer months, the citizens of the Twin Cities, led by many members of the original Afro-American League including William and Rosa Hazel, John Quincy Adams, and Frederick McGhee, organized the Afro-American Law Enforcement League. This group set out to pick up where the League and the Minnesota Equal Rights Association had left off in the early 1890s.[51]

As July rolled in and Minnesota's Enforcement League picked up steam, Copper posited that war fever was abating, and that within the next few months the League should gather on the national stage. In his opinion, Washington, D.C., was the logical place for such a meeting, but recognized that the ultimate decision was Fortune's.[52] Still many supporters agreed that the time for a national convention had come, and that to bolster attendance the meeting should be held somewhere centrally located.

Amid this increase in support for a national meeting, supporters again began convening at the state level. In addition to the Minnesota group, in late July 1898 the California League, now consisting of one thousand members, called a statewide convention to devise a plan for greater unification among the race, thus enabling them to bond together in a struggle against racial discrimination within the state.[53] Likewise, the Leagues of Illinois also convened during the month "to unite the various sections" of the state organization.[54]

The following month, Fortune emerged to reassert his position on the revival of the National Afro-American League. Since March, Bishop Walters had collected signatures in support of his call, and by August, he had nearly

125 signatures.[55] Walters constantly sent Fortune the signatures as a symbol of the race's support for the League idea. Yet Fortune was still as reluctant to rekindle the Afro-American League at the national level as he had been when W. Calvin Chase made a similar appeal in 1896.

In an open letter to Walters, Fortune explained that he had given the bishop's request "long and faithful consideration," but concluded that the popular sentiment behind the request was not great enough to justify a national convention. According to Fortune, there was "just as much need of the Afro-American League to-day as there was in 1890," but as in 1893 and 1896, he did not believe that the "masses of the race are any more ready and willing to organize" to sustain the group on the local, state, and national levels.[56] He agreed, however, to call a general race conference in Rochester, New York, on September 15, 1898, to discuss the existing conditions of the race and the actions the community should take in response to the worsening state of affairs. Rochester was chosen as the meeting site to coincide with the unveiling of the Frederick Douglass monument, which Bishop Walters had suggested as being a logical location and time.[57]

Fortune surprised much of the country with both aspects of his decision, but many supporters of the League idea still recognized a need for the conference and lent their support to his guarded response. Edward Cooper expressed the sentiments of many by stating, "We have had our fill of popgun movements, and flashes in the pan. . . . Though the call was liberally signed, there was a noticeable absence of the names of a number of leaders whose influence and money are absolutely essential to the success of a national engine of protection."[58] He concluded by agreeing with Fortune's compromise because it would "test the temper of the race in a positive manner, and may crystallize into action."[59]

The consensus was clear: no matter how cautious individuals were, an organization devoted to the rights of African Americans was necessary. Since the collapse of the League on the national level, the conditions of the black community had continued to deteriorate. With the failure of both third-party politics in the Populist movement and the fusion movement between black Republicans and the Populists, the decline of the Knights of Labor, and the collapse of the Farmer's Alliance, the community increasingly looked to itself to stand up for its rights. Yet what type of organization should be created? Political solutions had failed thus far, but the codification and enforcement of political and civil rights were essential starting points in the attack on white supremacy. Those seeking to revive a national civil rights organization understood that they had to find a new approach, and they met in Rochester, New York, in the fall of 1898 to attempt to hash these issues out.

* * *

When many prominent African Americans met in Rochester to pay tribute to Frederick Douglass at the unveiling of a monument in his honor, the specter of southern disfranchisement weighed heavy on their minds.[60] The day after the commemoration, a racially mixed delegation met in the city's common council chambers to discuss the state of the race as well as the reactivation of a national civil rights organization.[61] After the opening invocation and introductions by Mayor George E. Warner and John W. Thompson, a local businessman who had spearheaded the commemoration and along with Walters had encouraged Fortune to hold the meeting in Rochester, the League president took to the podium to discuss the necessity for the meeting, but also to articulate why he was reluctant to call for the revival of the organization. Seemingly pleased with the strong female presence, Fortune began by stating that he would have nothing to do with the organization "unless the women are given a voice in its affairs." He went on to explain that he did not think that the population was ready for a national organization, "just as the Irish people were not prepared for organization when it was attempted." In his estimation, the race had not risen to the position it needed to sustain such a group, "for they had but thirty years in which to recover from 250 years of bondage." Yet, even though Fortune did not think that anyone could galvanize the masses, he saw the possibility and necessity of doing so. He was not certain, however, that the black community alone could inspire such a movement. The past actions of the community had almost persuaded him that African Americans could not "accomplish [their] object any more than [they] could the abolition of slavery unless white men and black men, the white women and the black women, join the movement."[62] Fortune's statement was as much a comment on the condition of black America as an attack on former abolitionists for abandoning blacks since Reconstruction. Moreover, it was more of a rallying cry for the revival of a neo-abolitionist movement, much like the speech he had given in Chicago in 1890.

Fortune then turned his attention to the continued deterioration of black rights and the increased acceptance of the southern racial position and Social Darwinist ideas.[63] The *Age* editor warned that this course of events would inspire revolution, which would emerge out of the expansion of the nation's racial hostilities into the newly acquired territories of Cuba, Puerto Rico, and the Philippines. This revolution would also develop because of the related expansion of mob law in the South.[64]

Finally, Fortune addressed the problem of miscegenation laws. These laws, he argued, were unjust and impractical as those in love would circumvent them. Besides, the African American population had been victims of, rather than the cause of, this situation that the country so feared. He urged everyone to look down South and see "the yellow color of the people," noting "the black man did not make the yellow color. Whose fault is it"?[65]

The editor argued that situations such as these—the continued destruction of black rights and the unfair miscegenation laws, as well as the deterioration of African American schools and the augmentation of Social Darwinist ideas in America and abroad— were "sufficient provocation to have an association for the uplift of the race." Bishop Walters concurred, and the delegates moved to outlining their plans for organization.[66]

After much deliberation, the group decided that it was better to form a new organization rather than try to revive the League. However, the new organization, the Afro-American Council, mirrored the former organization in everything but name. The Council was an organization that placed agitation for black rights as a central objective, but emphasized economic and moral development as well as race pride and solidarity. The delegation originally elected Fortune as president, John C. Dancy as vice-president, Ida B. Wells-Barnett as secretary, and John W. Thompson as treasurer.[67] But after the selections, Fortune surprised many by announcing that he could not be president of the organization because he had little faith that the race could support the movement. Wells-Barnett immediately moved to have Fortune removed as president, and the delegation selected Walters to succeed him. The *Age* editor, however, then agreed to chair the Executive Committee.[68]

As the organization concluded its proceedings, former U.S. minister to Liberia John H. Smythe addressed the chair and declared that he could not support an organization that "opposed separate schools and favored mixed marriages."[69] The delegation then voted on Smythe's status within the organization, concluding that he could not be a member of the newly formed Afro-American Council while holding such views. The convention concluded with Smythe formally severing ties with the group.

Following the Rochester meeting, many offered their support to the new organization. However, Fortune's refusal to take the presidency and Smythe's comments on separate marriages and schools sparked heated debate. Both George Knox of the *Indianapolis Freeman* and Edward Cooper of the *Colored American* demanded that the *Age* editor explain his actions.[70] Knox even published a humorous poem calling out the New York editor in the pages of his *Freeman*:

> Timothy T!
> Rude you B!
> One can not C!
> The reason Y!
> Not even I!
> Your inconsisten(C)y!
> T! T! Thomas Fortune![71]

Fortune obliged the public, responding in an open letter to the *Colored American* that he had been consistent in his position. When he called the conference, Fortune explained, he lacked confidence in the race's ability to sustain a national civil rights organization, and he had repeated that position in his address to the delegation at the Rochester meeting and once again when the group chose him as the president. Once Ida B. Wells-Barnett suggested that the president of the group should have faith in the race and in the work of the organization, the editor agreed, and naturally withdrew from the presidency. Fortune also cited poor health and financial woes as contributing factors that led to his decision. Ultimately he did not want the weight of the organization to fall upon one person, namely himself, as he felt had been the case with the Afro-American League.[72] Fortune's explanation seems to have satisfied the public, and the press dropped the issue after his open letter.

The Smythe incident, however, did not die as quickly. Directly following the conference, Fortune ran an article entitled "Separate Legislation Humbug." In this piece he declared it an "insult for any Afro-American to appear in a race assembly of honest men and women and unblushingly declare that he believes in the two evils which are the very bases of all our civil disability and moral degradation."[73] The separate school legislation, he noted, "embodies the inception and concatenation of all the separate civil legislation under which the race staggers." According to Fortune, "The man who endorses the separate school infamy must perforce endorse all the other parts of the separate machinery of legislation which weighs down the race."[74]

On the separate marriage laws, Fortune saw no need to regulate a purely personal matter. As far as "preserving the Negro race type [was] concerned," Fortune urged Smythe to go "through the country, or confine his investigations to the city of Richmond and count the fatherless yellow children with black mothers he meets." In the end, Fortune saw the Smythes of the country as "dead weight on the progress of the race," and believed that their attitudes did nothing to aid the race in its quest to gain full citizenship rights.[75]

The general sentiment regarding Smythe's comments was that they had no place at the conference. As Edward Cooper of the *Colored American* asked, "what is to be gained by agitating such questions, especially at this time, when the life, property and civil status of the race hang so threateningly in the balance? We fail to see any benefit in bringing up intermarriage or mixed schools as a drawn issue."[76] Many editors, who focused on the intermarriage issue over school legislation, felt that the problem would resolve itself. Alexander Manning of the *Indianapolis World* advised that one could advocate for the races to "select partners only among themselves," but should not try to force individuals by "vexatious legislation." He believed that it would turn out like Prohibition: "temperance is desirable but it can't be enforced by law."[77] Intermarriage, as Cooper explained, was a personal preference. "The law should have nothing to do with it, for or against and the right of outsiders to object is just about as binding as one's opinion of persons who insist upon eating onions, garlic, or limburger cheese . . . and no amount of agitation" will change "individual tastes."[78]

A number of editors and individuals, however, came out in defense of Smythe.[79] John E. Bruce, for example, a supporter of the Council and a close friend of Fortune, did not see how the members of the organization could ever expect to popularize its "pet schemes of solving the race problem." "The best class of white women," averred the petulant nationalist, "do not seek matrimonial alliances with black men or yellow men who have Negro blood in their veins."[80] Furthermore, he saw no reason the "excellent and well meaning gentleman of the Council should seek to destroy the race type by encouraging our men to marry poor and sometimes ignorant Irish, English, German, and Scotch women, and our women to marry white libertines, native and foreign."[81]

Bruce's position was a response to Fortune and many others' belief at the time that amalgamation would ultimately solve the race problem.[82] In spite of the speechmaking at the meeting in Rochester, however, biological amalgamation was not unanimously endorsed by Council members. Nowhere did the delegation state that amalgamation was either a "scheme" or official position of the group. The organization simply would not oppose intermarriage, as Fortune and others explained, for reasons of both moral and political principle. If the group approved legislation limiting personal relations, it would set a precedent that would likely be expanded into other areas.

On the issue of mixed schools, Bruce saw no need for them because the students would suffer and black teachers "would have a very poor showing at the hands of school boards." He favored "separate schools when taught by competent Negro men or women." In his *Colored American* editorial, Bruce explained that he did not believe a "Negro child has nearly as much respect for and interest in his race who is taught in a mixed school, to defy the white race at the expense of his own race, as he would have if taught in a Negro school." He argued that if a child were educated in a white school or environment, "he grows up to manhood as ignorant of the Negro and his history . . . as the white boy. After he has arrived at manhood he discovers that he has reached the end of the social equality of the school room, and like that Pactoius Prime he is 'only a nigger.'"[83]

Many members of the Council were sympathetic to Bruce's sentiments on the lack of equality in the integrated education system. And many likely agreed with his nationalistic stance regarding the quality of education the students received in the mixed schools. Similar to his position on intermarriage, however, Bruce had oversimplified the organization's position. The authorities, as Fortune indicated in his September 29, 1898 article, would view the acceptance of any separate legislation as endorsement of all "other parts of the separate machinery of legislation which weighs down the race."[84] He and others in Rochester pragmatically understood their acceptance of Jim Crow marriages and education would be used by lawmakers and the white public as justification for the spread of legal segregation.

While the Smythe controversy abated, the Council got down to business. The delegates of the Rochester meeting went to their respective communities to form local and state organizations. As Cooper explained, there were high hopes for the group under Bishop Walter's able leadership. Finally, he encouraged all "Race-loving Negroes every where" to "get in line for the Afro-American Council."[85]

Just a few months after the Rochester meeting, the black community was offered a chance to show its support for the organization when Walters called on the Council to assemble in Washington on December 29, 1898, inviting those who enrolled in the organization at its formation in Rochester and all signers of the original call as well as those sympathetic to the object of the group. Most importantly, Walters encouraged interested parties who came to the city to contribute five dollars annually toward carrying out the purposes of the Council.[86] This plea by Walters for a mandatory fee to participate in the proceedings of the group constituted a shift in the approach of a national civil rights organization as the Council was determined not to fail because of a lack of funds as had the Afro-American League.

The reason for calling a special meeting in such close proximity to the Rochester conference, Walters explained, was to allow the group to shore up the organization. It would give individuals who had wished to be at the Rochester meeting, but could not because of location or previous obligations, the opportunity to show their support for the new national civil rights organization.[87] Furthermore, the "continuation of brutal lynchings, unjust discriminations on railroads and in hotels, restaurants and labor unions, the disenfranchisement of Afro-Americans in several southern states, and a host of other obstacles which are thrown in the way of [black America's] moral, financial, educational progress, [made] it absolutely necessary" for African Americans to organize "and perpetuate an organization for self-protection."[88]

The necessity of organizing for self-protection had rapidly increased in the short time since the creation of the Council. Racial violence and the continued growth of Jim Crow had mushroomed during the final months of 1898. In Wilmington, North Carolina, for instance, racial tensions exploded in November. African Americans in the city and throughout the state had continued to hold public offices and actually gained political influence during the 1894 election with the victory of the Fusionists, a coalition of Republicans and Populists who "restored local democracy to heavily black towns and counties."[89] Determined to regain control in the 1898 elections, the Democrats created a campaign based on the fear of "negro domination," which included images of African American males as sex-craved predators seeking the precious white women of the region.

During this "safety at home" campaign, Alexander Manly published an editorial in his *Daily Record* on August 1898 condemning white men for the sexual exploitation of black women and suggesting that white women only claimed rape when their affairs across the color line became public knowledge.[90] Such statements added fodder to the intense campaign. This tension increased when John C. Dancy returned from the Rochester meeting of the Afro-American Council the following month having joined an organization in opposition to legislation preventing interracial marriages. At the time, Dancy, the collector of customs at Wilmington, held one of the highest paid political positions of the state. Democrats, however, noted Dancy's support of the Council as an example of how black men would use politics and power to gain entrance into white men's homes and the bedrooms of their women.[91]

In this volatile climate the Democrats gained victory in the November elections. The Democratic success resulted largely from the fact that the Fusionists were afraid to campaign and blacks feared going to the polls due to threatened reprisals. The speech of the newly elected mayor of Wilmington Alfred Moore Waddell on the eve of the election simply and effectively explained the situation. He told his audience, "You are Anglo Saxons. You are armed and prepared, and you will do your duty. . . . Go to the polls tomorrow, and if you find the negro out voting, tell him to leave the polls, and if he refuses, kill him. We shall win tomorrow, if we have to do it with guns."[92]

A mere political victory, however, did not satisfy the Democrats. Less than a week after the election, white Democrats, in the form of the "White Declaration of Independence," ordered the resignations of all African Americans and Fusionists still in office, urged employers to fire black employees, and demanded that Alex Manly and others leave the city immediately.[93] When elements of the community failed to react in a timely matter—one day—mobs descended on the black community and burned to the ground the home of Manly's newspaper, the Love and Charity Hall. The mob also strip-searched black women for weapons, killed at least a dozen black men, and forced some 1,500 black residents to flee for their lives—including Manly and Dancy.[94]

A number of black residents of the city of Wilmington and greater North Carolina wrote to President McKinley asking for aid and protection, but he did not respond.[95] The president's silence concerning these acts of violence, as well as his failure to comment either on the Supreme Court's decision in April in *Williams v. Mississippi*, which upheld the use of a poll tax and literacy requirements, or on the Louisiana legislature's enactment of the "Grandfather Clause," did not gain him any allies in the African American community.[96] Further disfavor with McKinley came when he went on a tour of the South and remained silent on the continued deterioration of black rights and the growth of racial violence in the region. It was under these circumstances that the Afro-American Council planned its meeting in Washington, D.C.

With the blatantly open violence of Wilmington and the continued growth of white supremacy in the north and south, those gathering in Washington understood that they needed to finalize and expand the organization they had set up in Rochester into one that would stand up for black rights and be unafraid to attack anyone who seemingly stood in the way of those rights. To accomplish this, they needed to expand their delegation by bridging the ideological gaps that existed in the community and try to create a flourishing organization that spoke to all in their attempt to secure the common goal of full social, civil, and political equality. In short, the Council needed to find common ground among the ideologies of political protest, racial solidarity, and self-help.

* * *

One week before the meeting, T. Thomas Fortune gave an address to a mass gathering sponsored by the Negro National Protective Association at the AME Zion Church in Washington, D.C. Fortune agreed to attend the Council meeting despite his feelings about the potential success of such an organization. As Fortune had explained to his friend Booker T. Washington a few weeks earlier, he was going to attend the convention to prevent them "*from doing anything foolish*."[97] This statement, however, loses some of its initial bite in the light of the editor's rhetoric at the Zion church meeting, where the speech he gave did not come close to the accommodationist positions associated with Washington and his Tuskegee Institute.

Fortune opened his address by thanking Reverend Dr. William J. Howard, the pastor of the Zion church, who had commenced the conference with an invocation praying for President McKinley. The *Age* editor explained that the president certainly needed God's blessing, for if "ever a man had wandered farther away from the faith than the President of United States he would like to know it."[98] Fortune noted that he did not care for McKinley and believed that the president was turning his back on the African American population that had helped put him in office. Fortune further declared that he came to Washington "to fight the President. He has gone back on us. I want the man whom I fought for to fight for me, and if he don't I feel like stabbing him."[99] The editor was greatly disturbed that McKinley was leisurely touring the South, "glorifying rebellion, mobocracy, and the murder of women and children" while decorating Confederate graves.[100] Fortune also was bothered by the lack of meetings between African American representatives and the president during his southern tour in spite of the fact that African Americans composed the majority of the population in many of the cities the president visited.[101]

Fortune, responding to the events in Wilmington, claimed that if only a few African Americans agreed with his positions, there would have been an equal number of deaths occurring across the color line. While blacks may not have had "Winchester rifles they had pitch pine, and, while the whites were killing," blacks should have been "burning."[102] The editor also scoffed at the notion recently pushed in Wilmington that the male African American population was replete with rapists. "If ever there was a race of rapists," he said, "it is the white men of the south." Then with a large degree of sarcasm, he added, "there is nothing purer and grander in all the world than the white womanhood in the south" and that "if the colored women do not measure up to the same standard it is because of the lascivious white men who have had their way there for more than 200 years."[103] Fortune also lambasted the Supreme Court for the decision it had recently rendered in *Williams v. Mississippi.* Having gone to the District to prevent the Council "*from doing anything foolish,*" Fortune achieved virtually the opposite: the rhetoric that would come out of the Council meeting seemed tame in comparison to his public address.[104]

It was in such a situation that Bishop Walters made his final call for all religious organizations, secret and non-secret societies, educational institutions, and groups who sought as their objective the amelioration of the conditions of black America to send delegates to Washington.[105] He believed that the outlook for the African American population was grim: "Truly, the outlook is gloomy. But we have seen gloomier times than the present (a short while before the war, when the fugitive slave was passed) and we were brought triumphantly through by the God of armies." What bothered the bishop most, however, was the attitude of some in the African American community that blacks should not unite for their self-protection. "They advise us to stay silent," he said, "and let the white men have their way—burn, hang, rob, insult, and discriminate against us in every way, and we are to kiss the hand that smites us." In response to such sentiment, Walters exclaimed, "nay, nay, my brethren, the time has come when the Negroes must unite." Picking up on the content of Fortune's speech earlier in the week, Walters concluded "the President of the United States, whose duty it is to see that the citizens are protected, has abandoned us to our fate." To face such a situation, he reasoned, the community must not stay silent. If it did it would "surrender all that has been given us as citizens and we shall prove ourselves unworthy of the name of freemen." Walters proposed that Afro-Americans should gather in Washington to show the world that, since the president and a number of southern governors had abandoned black America, "we (10,000,000 Afro-Americans) have decided by the assistance of God to help ourselves."[106]

Walters called for these individuals to come to Washington to support a platform that resembled the one set forth by T. Thomas Fortune's 1887 call for the creation of the Afro-American League. It went further than the original League program, however, by including the proposal that the organization would push for fair African American representation in state and local governments. Walters also proposed that the Council devise methods to "raise funds to prosecute all perpetrators of lynchings and other outrages and to test the constitutionality of laws enacted by some of the southern states" that have as their objective the disenfranchisement of and discrimination against African America. The developing organization, Walters explained, would seek the reformation of the penal system, push for healthy emigration from a terror-ridden section" of the country, and encourage industrial and higher education as well as the creation of business enterprises. Furthermore, the new group demanded that "moneys be appropriated by the federal government (which should have been done at the time of our emancipation) to supplement the school funds of the southern states" and recommended certain days of protest throughout the year, focusing on fasting and prayer to bring light upon black America's fight for equal rights.[107]

With Wilmington and the calls of Fortune and Walters weighing heavily on his mind, *Colored American* editor and secretary of the local Council Edward Cooper shored up the final preparations to receive the delegates. On December 29, 1898, at 11 A.M., envoys representing the "church, the school house, the store, the press, the professions, [and] the farm" and coming from Virginia, New York, New Jersey, California, Georgia, North Carolina, Ohio, Illinois, Iowa, Louisiana, Mississippi, Michigan, and other locations assembled at the Metropolitan Baptist Church.[108] With approximately one hundred bona fide delegates enrolled, Walters called the Council to order.

In his first presidential address, Walters moved to set the tone and temper of the developing organization. "It is our misfortune to live amidst a people whose laws, traditions, and prejudices have been against us for centuries," he began. "Indeed, it has ever been the policy of a certain class of Americans to keep the Negro down."[109] He then outlined the achievements of the race—including the struggle to defend the country in every conflict since the Revolutionary War, the battle for emancipation over great opposition, and the fight for enfranchisement—and reaffirmed the right of African

Americans to agitate against the backpedaling of the nation from these achievements. He also condemned President McKinley for failing to speak out against the continued deterioration of black rights and perpetuation of racial violence, noting, "There has always been confusion, strife, and often bloodshed, just before the successful consummation of great movements; but the leaders did not back down. . . . Christianity met with opposition. . . . All sorts of obstacles were employed to hinder the progress of the anti-slavery movement, but did the leaders abandon the field? No."[110]

Walters could not understand black community leaders and friends who advised blacks to be quiet and let whites have their way with them.[111] He explained that the community could not afford to remain silent when the U.S. president, elected with black votes, refused to comment on atrocities committed against blacks, or when the governor of Illinois sanctioned the slaughter of black laborers who threatened to cross the picket line. Afro-Americans must not stay quiet when mobs ravished black communities throughout the South and the southern states stripped the population of its vote. Nor should silence exist while black women were insulted and thousands of women, men, and children were "burned at the stake, hung to the limbs of trees, and shot like dogs or at the least robbed of their meager earnings."[112] To remain silent under such circumstances "would be unworthy of the name freemen."[113] "There can be no real peace in America until, this problem is solved," the bishop said. He also advised the community to complement their agitation for full manhood rights with self-reliance. Education, according to Walters, was a key to finding a solution: "Education is the sun whose powerful rays of character, industry, self-reliance, and patience, will ultimately melt that the tremendous iceberg of American prejudice, which has chilled us for more than two centuries."[114] He did not think the community could be exposed to too much sun, which should come in the form of "all educational agencies, whether classical, scientific, industrial, or otherwise."[115]

In his address, Walters also emphasized the importance of industry. He believed that the community had to focus on farming and industry, the "foundation of the superstructure." "The Negro farmer" he argued, would "create a position for the Negro merchant, and the Negro farmer and merchant will create a position for the Negro manufacturer. . . . [S]upport for the Negro minister, doctor, lawyer, and all professional men" would necessarily follow.[116] In addition, Walters called on the white population to "remove the ban of prejudice [and] open the doors of factories, mills, and machine shops and give [black workers] a fair chance." At the same time, he did not believe that blacks should merely wait for white prejudice to subside. Instead, he urged the community to take advantage of all available opportunities along the way. Despite the fact that African Americans had been robbed of thousands of dollars, they had "accumulated over $400,000,000 worth of property real and personal." African Americans, he counseled, should "continue to buy land and to build and improve homes, thus becoming more independent."[117] He also encouraged African Americans to continue to agitate for their full manhood rights, to put forth responsible leadership for elected office, and to make their voices heard when atrocities occurred.[118]

The delegation responded to Walters's address with tremendous applause. The president's speech set the tone of the convention and outlined the organizational framework of the Afro-American Council, which merged two growing schools of black thought regarding the approach to solving the race problem. It blended the approach espoused by Booker T. Washington and others of economic, educational, and internal development being the solution to the race problem with that of others such as Ida B. Wells-Barnett who believed that agitation, political activity, publicity, and protest were necessary to gain full citizenship rights, equality, and justice. The Council, as symbolized by Walters's address, sought to negotiate with these two camps by giving each ideological stance equal weight and value in the organization's platform in recognition that neither could be successful on its own nor should be abandoned for the other.

Later that evening when the Council reconvened, Wells-Barnett, delivering one of the strongest addresses of the conference, spoke to an audience of nearly fifteen hundred people on the subject of "Mob Violence and Anarchy, North and South." She linked recent riots in Wilmington, North Carolina, and the slaughter of black laborers in Virden, Illinois, with the murders of the postmasters in Georgia and South Carolina, and demanded that the administration—which she believed was more concerned with the national decoration of Confederate graves than the rights of blacks—respond affirmatively. The greatest struggle and most troubling matter in the recent events, Wells-Barnett argued, had been the "indifference manifested by the people of the North to these wrongs."[119]

Reminiscent of her comments made at the Afro-American League's second annual convention, Wells-Barnett insisted that "if this gathering means anything it means that we have at last come to a point in our race history where we must do something for ourselves, and do it now." The African American community needed to "educate the white people out of their 250 years of slave history." "The white people of the North," she argued, "are not so much indifferent as ignorant." The Council secretary then demanded that the group move to conduct a hearing before the people of the North, especially the congressmen from the region, to educate them on the situation and to force the politicians to uphold the Fourteenth Amendment and "cut down the basis of representation in the South to accord with the actual number of voters."[120]

Wells-Barnett also commented on the state of black politics, expressing the opinion that Washington "made a great mistake in imagining that the black people could gain their rights merely by making themselves factors in industrial life." Like Walters before her, Wells-Barnett understood that the struggle for equality had to pursue a multipronged approach, which included industrial development, accumulation of wealth, moral uplift, and consistent agitation for suffrage rights and full protection under the U.S. Constitution. The delegation gave Wells-Barnett a standing ovation and a Chautauqua salute at the end of her address.[121] Henry P. Cheatham, recorder of deeds for the District of Columbia, was given the unenviable task of following Wells-Barnett; he closed the evening session with a far more moderate and measured speech.

The delegation met again the following day, with the afternoon sessions dominated by a discussion centering on a public organizational endorsement or condemnation of the McKinley administration. This discussion was most certainly fueled by the remarks of Fortune, Walters, and Wells-Barnett condemning the president for ignoring the plight of black Americans. After a long and lively debate, the so-called administrationists won out. This group claimed that there was no real need to endorse or oppose the administration because the sentiments of the organization concerning the failures of McKinley and his silence would appear in the group's address to the nation regardless of whether they formally denounced the administration.[122]

After this long deliberation, John P. Green, a Republican state legislator from Ohio, stated that President McKinley had been advised by a few African Americans not to mention the violence in North Carolina and South Carolina in his annual message to Congress. This remark immediately provoked an angry response from the delegation, spearheaded by Fortune, who called for the names of these "Black Judases."[123] Green responded that he did not have to give any names, and the audience's anger increased. Finally, the delegation agreed to adjourn into committees, with Green providing the names of the traitors in the Committee on Address, to which he belonged.

When the Council reconvened for its evening and final session, attendance had swelled to nearly three thousand.[124] After a number of other addresses, Fortune rose to read the Council's address to the country. Before beginning, however, he announced that Green was unable to provide the names of those who had advised McKinley to stay silent. The audience immediately erupted into hysterical laughter.[125] Fortune then read the formal statement of the Council, declaring its strong support for the principle of equality for all citizens of the United States regardless of "color, nativity, politics, or religion."[126] Echoing the opinion of its president the day prior, the Council members believed that they needed to promote a two-pronged attack: "There are certain things which those of us who live in the South can accomplish, and certain other things which those of us who live in the North can accomplish. We may take different methods to reach the same ends, but the results will be for the common advantage."[127] Those in the North should agitate, through "protest, petition, and . . . political conduct," while southern blacks should focus more on "education and internal development." Although the Council called for a split in emphasis throughout the country, its members stressed that they would not "sacrifice one principle of manhood or citizen right." There was not one right guaranteed by the federal government that they did not claim, and not one denied by the state constitutions that they did not propose to fight.[128]

The address identified nine areas for the nation and the Afro-American Council to immediately address. One of these issues included the growing campaigns of southern governments to disfranchise the black population. The organization called on the federal government to reduce the congressional representation of those states as mandated by Section 2 of Article 14 of the Constitution. Second, the Council called upon the nation to take action against those perpetuating violence against blacks, including calling upon McKinley to adjust his record of silence on this vital matter in order to redeem the honor of America. Third, the organization denounced the existence of separate railway car legislation, opining that the government should do something about such laws if for no other reason than that the railway companies defrauded consumers monetarily by the practice because the value of a ticket purchased in the North did not have the same worth once the train rolled across the Mason-Dixon line.[129]

The address also called for the reform of the southern penal systems, the equitable distribution of educational funds in the South, and the promotion of industrial and higher education. It also proposed the geographical dispersal of the race away from violent and economically stagnant regions. Finally, the group encouraged the development of various business enterprises, which along with education represented the "strongest levers in the uplifting of the race."[130]

In essence, though the organization chose a different name, the Council was the revival of the Afro-American League. The objectives declared in the Council's constitution were almost identical to those of the League, and the new organization picked up where the League's activities had ended. As had the League, the Council set up local bureaus to address the various needs of the black population, including those dealing with immigration, education, business, legal action, newspaper, vital statistics, anti-lynching, legislation, ministerial, and literary issues.[131]

The administration of the Council, however, differed from its previous incarnation. In an attempt to accumulate funds and avert the previous fiscal failures of the League, the new group imposed a five-dollar fee for each voting delegate to the national conference, with an option of life membership upon the payment of fifty dollars.[132] Also, the post of financial secretary became the only salaried position, and the Executive Committee was now composed of three members of each state or territorial branch, with one of these three members required to be a woman.[133] The organization then chose its officers. Bishop Walters was again voted as president, Ida B. Wells-Barnett as financial secretary, John W. Thompson as treasurer, and T. Thomas Fortune as chairman of the Executive Committee.[134]

With the selection of the permanent officers and the drafting of the constitution of the Afro-American Council, African Americans had recreated a national civil rights organization that possessed an ambitious, multilayered plan to address the variety of conditions affecting the race throughout the country. The Council was a recreation of Fortune's original plan for the Afro-American League—a permanent organization that would demand justice and be an apparatus for sustained activity throughout the nation. The actions of these delegates in the District of Columbia and supporters throughout the country continued the model of African American protest set forth by Fortune and the League: one that would be reused and modified again and again throughout the twentieth century.

After solidifying the organization, the members adjourned the special session of the Council, determined to right the wrongs done to them by various forces, including the complicit federal government. The delegates set out to develop the organization in their various locales, and sent a contingent to the White House to demand a hearing with the president, hoping to force him to understand their position and to place demands on his administration. Many began falling in line with the Afro-American Council, and hopes were high that the race would mobilize support for a national civil rights organization determined to secure social, economic, and political equality for African Americans. With these high hopes, it was now the Council's responsibility to figure out how to advocate for black rights during a period in which political and social conditions continued to deteriorate and when many were looking inward to devise a more self-reliant response to the situation. It would be a difficult challenge, but those associated with the budding organization understood the seriousness of the situation and had already begun seeking the balance necessary to secure their rights.

Chapter 4

Not Just "A Bubble in Soap Water"

> With intelligent organization, the Negro race can become a great power in the business and political world, and if he would be wise in his day and generation he would begin NOW to lay the foundation of an organization through which he will be enabled to find the key to the solution of all the problems with which the essayists and theorists of the race are struggling in the effort to find a patent plan for the redemption and salvation of his race.
>
> —John Edward Bruce

> Let all, old and young, male and female, join hands and hearts in the prosecution of this work until there are no race problems to solve, no lynchers to condemn, no rapists to be hanged, no barriers to be removed, yes press on until there is no North, no South, no East, no West, but one indissoluble union, all striving to make more glorious our country.
>
> —Representative George H. White

According to the editor of the *Richmond Planet*, John Mitchell, Jr., the conclusion of the Afro-American Council's first national convention marked the "beginning of a new era."[1] Most involved with the convention and those who read of the proceedings in the nation's black newspapers concurred. Wielding strong symbolic value, the meeting demonstrated that the race was coming together in a firm and organized manner, taking matters into its own hands, and agitating for change. Built on the same principals as its predecessor the Afro-American League, those associated with the Council wanted to create a permanent national civil rights association that would meet annually in convention, but that would be based in local and state branches throughout the country, whose purpose would be to fight not only racism in general, but to contest discrimination and mob violence by using the local, state, and federal courts as well as the halls of Congress and the office of the U.S. president.

The new national civil rights organization, however, braced for a long, difficult struggle. The growing forms of segregation and discrimination in the North and South that had been steadily building in the 1890s were firmly entrenched by the turn of the century. Moreover, the lynching and mob violence used to back white supremacy had become more pervasive. With this difficult terrain to navigate, the Council had to be a flexible organization that could modify its tactics and strategies to meet the challenges of the changing environment. All involved understood that it would be a difficult task, but at least initially Council supporters seemed up to the undertaking. Most supporters of the Council were eager to use the momentum of the organization's successful convention to push their agenda. It was imperative that the group demonstrate that it was not another race organization that met once a year and failed to put any political positions into action. Quickly local branches sprung to action, holding meetings and outlining how the organization could grow and be an effective voice for the African American community.

The first order of business was to make demands on the federal government. Immediately following the Council convention in Washington, a delegation requested a meeting with President McKinley. After some hesitation, the president agreed to meet the delegation in a private roundtable discussion. John Mitchell, Jr., chosen as the spokesman, read portions of the organization's national address to the president, deliberately stressing the provisions related to lynchings and the recent outrages in the southern states.[2]

Though not mentioned by name, McKinley could not have misunderstood the message. Fortune, Walters, and Wells-Barnett's frustration with his silence regarding the upsurge of racial violence in the Carolinas and Illinois during his southern tour had been well publicized, and McKinley was undoubtedly aware of these individuals' opposition. But according to the *Planet*'s coverage of the meeting, the delegation aired their frustrations during a twenty-minute conversation and left the meeting satisfied.[3]

Such satisfaction was relative. The delegates desired only a commitment from the president to demonstrate concern for the lives and well-being of African American citizens. As Edward Cooper explained in his *Colored American*, the Council's appeals to the president were not for armed intervention: "Moral suasion is what we want, and we would be glad to see it applied for the Negro's benefit as earnestly as Mr. McKinley is applying it to wipe out the Mason's and Dixon's line."[4] Cooper, however, was skeptical that the president would actually speak on the issue. But as Cooper later indicated, he was largely pleased with the meeting and believed that the committee made a "marked impression upon the President," optimistically telling readers to "watch things" in the immediate future.[5]

Cooper's excitement, guarded as it may have been, marked the general mood of those around the country watching the activities of the Council. Anticipation was in the air, and many believed that the black community would throw its weight behind the Council and make it a great success. As Alexander Manning of the *Indianapolis World* stated, the Council "deserves the praise of every well-thinking Negro who has the interest of his race at heart throughout the country, for its manly stand and success in not allowing the convention to be gobbled up, body and soul, and captured by a lot of office seekers, office holders and political job lots." The Council, in the eyes of many, had proven itself to be an organization for the race and not just a party—an organization that was not afraid to present its stance to the powers that be.[6]

Not everyone, however, was as impressed by the activities of the Council. Those in charge of the *Chicago Record*, for example, believed that the convention had changed little. According to the *Record*'s description, the conference was a sideshow, full of disturbances and disgraceful disorder. The paper's editors believed that the delegates had actually done a disservice to the race by convening in Washington, arguing that "Instead of four hundred Negroes spending fifteen or twenty dollars each for the purpose of passing a few windy resolutions that have no more effect on the condition of affairs than a jay bird flying between the earth and the sun, has on the solar system they could have contributed ten dollars each to the promotion of some worthy race enterprise."[7] John Lay Thompson of the *Iowa State Bystander* concurred, suggesting that the race would be far better off saving its money, organizing businesses, and venturing toward solving the race problem through the accumulation of wealth. The editors of both papers, however, failed to report that the Council supported the development of businesses and the accumulation of wealth along with its demand for political rights. Moreover, neither editor offered an alternative organizational plan.

* * *

Praise and criticism aside, the issue that seemed to dominate conversations about the Council's activities after the convention was the election of Ida B. Wells-Barnett to the post of organizational secretary. A supporter of the Afro-American League and an earlier advocate for reviving the civil rights organization, Wells-Barnett was elected by her peers as the group's secretary. Confusion ensued, however, when Richard W. Thompson of Washington, D.C. claimed that the Council had elected him recording secretary.[8]

Adding to this confusion was the declaration of Edward Copper that the one mistake of the new civil rights organization was the election of Wells-Barnett to an executive position. Cooper claimed he meant no disrespect to Wells-Barnett or her capabilities, but believed that a man should hold the position of secretary.[9] Calling her election "an extremely unfortunate mistake," he proposed that she take charge instead of a national women's auxiliary.

Cooper's suggestion was counter to the position of the Afro-American Council. As was the case during the formation of the Afro-American League, many members of the Council believed that in order for the organization to be successful, African American women needed to assume a primary role. Wells-Barnett's nomination to such a prominent position in the organization was thus a demonstration of this continuing commitment as well as an example of the respect many of her peers had for her and her activism. Cooper's comments demonstrate there was no universal agreement on the roles of women in the Council or on their place in public affairs in general. A number of Council supporters, however, were willing to speak out against Cooper and the other objectors, and to push for a more-gendered equal participation in the developing civil rights organization.

For instance, responding to Cooper's charges, George Knox asserted that Cooper's position was preposterous and asked that all accept Wells-Barnett as the Council's secretary through her term. In a further attempt to quell dissent, Knox's colleague, *Freeman* associate editor Monroe A. Majors, a physician and author of the 1893 publication *Noted Negro Women: Their Triumphs and Activities*, remarked that the secretary "without a doubt is accredited as one of our leading celebrities . . . known today throughout the two continents [and by] retaining her position much dignity and usefulness beyond the seas will be the outcome."[10] Knox and Major's opinion won out: Wells-Barnett continued to hold her post as Council secretary. Moreover, staying consistent with the Afro-American League's position, all branches had to have at least one female representative in the leadership of the organization.

After this controversy, Council members moved onto more pressing issues, one of which was to set up a committee to work in concert with Dr. Samuel S. H. Washington of Birmingham, Alabama, who was organizing a lobby group to challenge that state's recent attempt to disfranchise its black citizens in its upcoming "unconstitutional Constitutional Convention."[11] Another was to attract allies. To that end, executive committee member and librarian at the Library of Congress Daniel Murray published an organizational outline of the group in a local white newspaper, the *Washington Evening Star*. Murray explained that the Council was modeled after the great abolitionist organizations and was seeking to "appeal to the Christian hearts and consciences of the American people."[12] Echoing the discussion of the national convention, he affirmed that one of the primary objectives of the Council was to seek the "enactment of a law reducing the representation in the Congress and the electoral college" of states that have "bogus constitutions" and deprive African Americans of the franchise.[13] He also advised supporters to boycott the railroad, arguing that due to economic necessity, this course of action would force the end of unjust segregation.

Finally, Murray suggested that the Council focus on serving as a political watchdog. Though the organization was nonpartisan, he proposed that the group keep an eye on federal appointments and "oppose the preferment of men who have taken an open stand of hostility toward" African Americans.[14] As he explained, "no man would openly abuse the Irish, or the Germans, or be the author of invidious or unfriendly legislation toward them" because of their political voice. Murray proposed that the council take heed of the practices of the immigrant communities and begin using them to their own advantage.

The idea struck a chord, and a few weeks after the *Evening Star* published Murray's article, John Edward Bruce (aka Bruce Grit), freelance journalist and steady League and Council supporter, published a favorable review and series of comments in the *Colored American*. Bruce praised the Council's work, agreeing with Murray that the most effective means of solving the race problem was through organization, and that the most logical organization for the job was the Council. Addressing specific points raised by Murray, Bruce affirmed that the Council should begin its struggle by attempting to restrict the congressional representation of those southern states that disfranchise African Americans. As Bruce explained, "The time for the Negro to enter a vigorous and manly and effective protest against this system of political fraud is NOW!" And the way to make the "system odious is through [organization] and agitation long continued and persistent. The man who fraudently [sic] occupies a seat in Congress is a thief and ought to be branded as a thief by those whom he robs of the opportunity to be heard in their own defense by representatives of their own choice." He also backed Murray's call to work as one against oppression, supporting Murray's position that the public be careful of how they read statements attacking the Council as many were working to undermine its effectiveness. Finally, the feisty journalist called on the African American to remember the axiom "an army divided is an army defeated."[15]

No local branch of the organization heeded the words of Murray and Bruce better than Murray's own Council No. 1 in Washington, D.C. The week after Murray published his article in the *Evening Star*, the congressional librarian presided over a special session of Council No. 1. One of the strongest branches at the national convention, it sought to capitalize on that showing by spearheading action. Jesse Lawson spoke to the District members and called upon them to organize a movement second only to that of the national body. He and his colleagues believed that the existence of a strong Council branch in the nation's capital was vitally important in the larger organization's attempts to affect federal policy.

Born in Maryland in 1856 and educated at Howard University and Howard Law School, Lawson was currently a vice president of the Council, but he would go on to serve on many committees during the organization's history and would become a vitally important force behind its efforts. As with other members of the D.C. branch, Lawson was employed by the federal government, in his case at the Bureau of Pensions. He was also John Mercer Langston's attorney in Langston's 1889 contest regarding seating the House of Representatives. In addition, Lawson edited the *Colored American* from 1893 to 1897, founded the National Sociological Society in 1903, and with his wife Rosetta, founded the Inter-Denominational Bible College, later Frelinghuysen University.[16]

In his address to his fellow Council branch members, Lawson outlined the importance of the African American labor force in the nation's economy.

As he explained, 95 percent of the black population belonged to the industrial and agricultural labor force. Without their cooperation, the nation would not solve its current labor troubles. Lawson stressed that blacks were without representation on the Industrial Commission, which Congress had created in June 1898, and therefore recommended that the Council pressure Congress to create a special commission to "inquire into the industrial condition of the colored people of the United States, and to suggest legislation that will tend to help them in their laudable aim to obtain a comfortable living. . . ."[17] The delegation unanimously endorsed Lawson's suggestions, and after the meeting created a steering committee to map out a plan for local action. It also agreed to hold monthly meetings within the city and designed plans to aid in the development of other branches throughout the region.[18]

Criticism of such activities was swift. In Richmond, the *Virginia Times* took note of the Washington, D.C. meeting in its January 31 issue. Under the caption "A Cry from Macedonia," its white editors attacked the Council, particularly the D.C. branch, for excessive dependence on the federal government. They claimed that African Americans erroneously believed they were wards of the federal government. The editors declared that blacks were "by nature a Nationalist" as they cared "little for State government, but had supreme respect for the Federal Government."[19] The paper continued to misconstrue the words and actions of the Council by proclaiming that the mantra of the organization was to call "upon the government to enact some special class legislation in favor of the Negro because of the color of his skin" and to "help the Negro to make a living and to accumulate wealth."[20]

John Mitchell, Jr., editor of the *Richmond Planet*, took exception to the *Times*' characterization of the African American population in general and the Afro-American Council in particular. On the first issue, the outspoken editor simply asked how the *Times* could expect the black population to be anything other than "Nationalist." The reason for the black community's nationalist tendencies, he explained, was "written on every street-corner, in every eating-saloon, and at every election booth." The federal government, he reminded critics, had produced the Emancipation Proclamation, the Fifteenth Amendment, and the Civil Rights Bill, while states continued to enact "all kinds of humiliating laws to his [the black community's] detriment and aggravation."[21]

As to the issue of the African American community looking to the federal government for a handout, Mitchell simply replied that the *Times* was "in error." Blacks had turned to the government because of the conditions they faced and because existing laws were being openly flouted or eviscerated. Moreover, for "250 years" the government had permitted members of the race "to be robbed of his manhood, despoiled of his virtue, and stripped of his possessions." On these grounds, the editor reasoned, the government is "morally responsible for the advancement of a people thus despoiled."[22] To further his argument, Mitchell asked the editors of the *Times* to look at the pages of their own paper, where a proposal requesting that the U.S. government give the leaders of the Cuban military three million dollars to disburse among their soldiers if they disbanded and moved into civilian life had been praised by the *Times* on the second page of the same issue in which the newspaper criticized the Afro-American Council.[23] The editor of the *Planet* asked, "for what is this money to be paid?" He then answered his rhetorical question: "to enable the Cuban soldiers to have funds with which to begin life as citizens upon the plantations of Cuba . . . 'Forty acres and a mule' for the Cubans." Black Americans had never received the forty acres promised to them at the conclusion of the Civil War, but instead became "a white man's mule and he is paid as a dray-man to drive it."[24]

The Council, Mitchell explained, was only asking the government to do what was morally right—to pass such "legislation as would tend to help [blacks] in their laudable aims to earn a comfortable living."[25] He called on the government to uphold the Reconstruction Amendments to the Constitution and to give black Americans their just reparation for the years of toil under the lash—their three million dollars, and their forty acres and a mule. These were not special laws in the eyes of Mitchell and other supporters of the Council, but rather morally just legislation.

Besides the unjustified attack by the *Richmond Times*, another issue with ramifications for the national organization emerged out of the local Washington, D.C. meeting. Following the national convention, Bishop Walters had instructed Daniel Murray to form a Legal and Legislative Bureau to advise the Council on methods of procedure in testing laws restricting the rights of African Americans. During the same local session at which Lawson spoke, Murray assembled the Bureau, appointed North Carolina representative George H. White as general counsel, and a number of Council members around the country as assistant counselors.[26]

Similar to the consensus that emerged following the national convention, Murray and his colleagues saw an immediate need to reduce the congressional representation of those states that through legislation had deprived African American voters of the franchise. Murray and the bureau understood that little action would result if they failed to produce solid evidence to support their claims. For that reason, the group focused on the upcoming census to gain an accurate count of the African American population as well as the number of qualified black voters in particular states that had passed laws disfranchising black citizens. With these figures in hand, the Council would then call on Congress to pass legislation forcing states to elect representatives based on the accurate number of citizens who were enfranchised.[27]

With the creation of the Council's Legal Bureau, Murray wrote Illinois representative Albert J. Hopkins, chairman of the Census Committee, explaining that the Council wished for the Committee to add an amendment to its pending census legislation that would call on the census takers to table the number of qualified voters in each state. The Council appealed to Hopkins on a partisan basis. "The southern section of the country," Murray reminded him, "has a large excess of power in the determination of the policy of the government by reason of the large voiceless population in that section." With a few votes "gathered here and there in the country at large, they have been able to shape the policy, make laws and control the destiny of this Nation."[28]

On February 1, 1899, Murray met with Hopkins, who according to the director of the Council's legal and legislative bureau "entered enthusiastically into the aims and objects of the Council to reduce proportionately the representation" of states that had limited the suffrage guaranteed by the Fourteenth and Fifteenth Amendments. Hopkins, however, did not envision that the Committee would endorse the Council's amendment, nor did he "deem it prudent to put anything in the bill of a partisan nature."[29] This setback did not deter Murray, who scheduled a larger meeting with Hopkins that would include other members of the Council and the legal bureau. According to Murray, the meeting was cordial and lengthy, but the two sides could not agree on the necessity or viability of inserting the Council's amendment into the new census legislation.[30]

Despite its initial failure, the Bureau did not give up on its fight to reduce the representation of those southern states that had passed disfranchising legislation. Moreover, much of the Bureau's frustration with Hopkins dissipated because Edgar Crumpacker, a representative from Indiana and member of the Census Committee, introduced his own bill embodying the essential features of the Bureau's amendment. Following the bill's introduction, Murray immediately recommended that the Council endorse it.[31]

Murray and the Bureau also turned their attention to Lake City, South Carolina, where postmaster Frazier Baker had been murdered. Since his death, Baker's position had lain vacant, and during the early months of 1899 citizens of the region had called for the office to reopen. South Carolina representative James Norton proposed that the postmaster general install a white clergyman, a Mr. Curtis, to replace the slain Baker. Once the news spread about these efforts, Murray, George White, P. B. S. Pinchback, and Reuben S. Smith sent a letter of protest to the postmaster general. They explained that Norton's suggestion was "distasteful to almost every colored man in the United States, and would be regarded as a virtual abandonment" of the Republican Party principles.[32] The cosigners asserted that any action taken that replaced Baker with a white postmaster would invite additional instances of murderous opposition to African American officeholders in the South. Rather, they proposed the creation of an interracial committee of Lake City citizens to select a competent black citizen to replace Baker and to assure the protection of the new postmaster, or that the office be kept closed.[33]

While members of the Legal and Legislative Bureau were combating the activities in South Carolina, they also moved to lay the groundwork for one of its most celebrated cases, a constitutional challenge to the Louisiana election law. In the Louisiana constitution of 1898, the state legislature established new residency, educational, and property requirements for voting. In addition to these provisions, the constitution established the grandfather clause, which exempted from the requirement persons whose ancestors had not voted on or before January 1, 1867. Since African Americans had been denied the right to vote prior to that date, the exemption was intended to limit disfranchisement to blacks within the state. The new Louisiana constitution violated the Fourteenth and Fifteenth Amendments, and the Legal and Legislative Bureau strategized to challenge the constitutionality of this election law before similar measures spread across other southern states.[34]

The Bureau's fears were justified. North Carolina sought to implement a grandfather-type law in the November elections, while other states were also considering altering their constitutions.[35] Such actions frightened supporters of the Council, who understood that these laws were unjust, but could be fought. As Edward Cooper declared from the pages of his *Colored American*, "Set this down and stick to it: The election laws of Louisiana and North

Carolina are unconstitutional."[36] The Council's Legal Bureau took the "wicked" actions of the southland seriously and believed that a challenge to such legislation should be one of the first suits to come from the office of the new Bureau.

As the strategic planning began, detractors arose. W. Calvin Chase, editor of the *Washington Bee* and outspoken supporter of reviving the Afro-American League, began to voice his disapproval of the new race organization. Chase believed that the organization had become race specific, asserting that the Council "has too much color to it to be a success." Furthermore, Chase was troubled by the fact that many of the members of the Council were of the Methodist faith, and complained that many of its leaders were Methodist bishops who had no following and therefore would fail in their endeavors. Chief among these leaders was Bishop Walters, president of the Council, whom Chase described as "an eratic [sic], vacillating leader who is . . . impetuous and rattle brain[ed]."[37] The reasons for Chase's frustration with the Council are unknown. One may certainly assume that he was not of the Methodist faith, but other than that, his tirade was based on no real logic. One possible explanation for his reservations about the organization may lie with his own recent attempt to launch a civil rights group, the National Equal Protection Association. This endeavor gained virtually no support, and the group had effectively disappeared by the time the Council was formed.[38]

In any case, members of the Council paid no attention to Chase's angry outbursts. The only publication to offer even a cursory comment was the *Colored American*. The week after Chase's remarks, Edward Cooper published a passing editorial in it acknowledging that Reverend William Bishop Johnson, editor of the *National Baptist Magazine*, had come forward with a "ringing endorsement of the Afro-American Council" in the pages of his journal.[39] Moreover, both Reverend Johnson and Reverend Elias Camp Morris, president of the National Baptist Association, played prominent rolls in the Council's convention. Cooper then asserted that such an endorsement "repudiates the charge of a few nincompoops that the great movement is an exclusive Methodist concern."[40]

* * *

Events in the weeks that followed debate of the Council's legislative strategy caused Chase and members of the Council to forget such petty aspersions. A few days after Cooper published his response, hell broke loose in Georgia as the dark cloud of white terrorism and brutality descended over the nation. On Sunday, April 23, 1899, the small white Christian communities of Palmetto and Newman, Georgia, participated in one of the most heinous crimes of the century: the murder of Sam Hose.[41]

Hose was a laborer who had begun working on the farm of Alfred Cranford sometime in 1898. On April 11, 1899, Hose asked Cranford for some time off and an advance in salary to allow Hose to return to his hometown to visit his ill mother. Cranford refused and the two got into a verbal argument. The following day, Cranford approached Hose, who was chopping some wood, and recommenced the argument. At some juncture in the quarrel, Cranford's anger reached the point that he drew his pistol and threatened Hose. In self-defense, Hose hit Cranford with the axe that he was using, killing him instantly. As he appreciated the gravity of the situation, Hose immediately fled the scene.[42]

Once word of Cranford's death spread, the white community quickly formed a posse to hunt down Hose. Newspapers of the region stirred the frenzy by publishing biased accounts of the incident that transformed Sam Hose the laborer into Sam Hose the black beast-rapist. Many of the reports had Hose entering Cranford's home, killing Alfred, grabbing an infant child from the arms of Mrs. Cranford, and throwing the baby against the wall before forcing its mother "to submit to the most shameful outrage which one of her sex can suffer."[43] Moreover, many papers began tying Hose to a number of crimes, including other murders, throughout the state. Similar to many other cases throughout the South, the press's exaggeration of the events in the Sam Hose affair added to the white community's fear of the "black beast" and served as a warped justification for their desire to capture and enact brutal retribution.[44]

On April 22, 1899, nearly ten days after Cranford's death, two brothers captured Hose some seventy-five miles away from Palmetto on the farm where his mother lived. In an effort to collect the reward money, the following day his captors transported their prisoner back to the Atlanta region. En route, individuals on the train identified Hose. After some discussion at one of the stops, Hose's captors were persuaded to alter their plans so as to take their captive to the town of Newman, near the Cranford farm. There a mob chained Hose to a pine tree. Once a crowd of Sunday worshippers teemed around the directors of the lynching in a carnival-type atmosphere, they began their slow methodical torture of the victim. It lasted nearly thirty minutes, during which they mutilated Hose, cutting off his ears, fingers, and genitals before covering his blood-soaked body with kerosene and burning him to death.[45]

After Hose's corpse had cooled, the crowd, including four thousand who sped in from Atlanta on special trains, dug among the ashes for souvenirs. When thrill-seekers had carted off all recognizable signs of the victim, the feverish horde set their sights on the pine to which the mob had bound its villain. Once the tree was chopped into small transportable pieces, the chain that had bound Hose to that tree was distributed link by link to those still seeking a memento to remember their Sunday excursion.[46]

News of the horrendous scene in Georgia spread quickly, with a number of the nation's leading papers carrying descriptions of the event. In its discussion of the lynching, the black press let its anger be heard as editors lashed out against the barbaric incident. W. C. Martin screamed from the pages of his Kansas City-based *American Citizen*, "The only thing to have placed this Georgia mob on a plane with the lowest order of savages was to have eaten their victim's flesh as they cut it off with their knives."[47] John Lay Thompson of the *Iowa State Bystander* appealed to America's sense of leadership in the world, noting "the government and American Christians can talk about the inhuman treatment of Cuba by Spain, the horrors of the Russian serfs and peasants, the cannibals, head-hunters of Simons, and the shocking butchery of Americans; but what think you about the United States suffering her own citizens to be hung, butchered and the bodies burned, the crisping parts of the charred body cut into pieces and sold as souvenirs?"[48] In a variety of ways, many of the African American editors throughout the country echoed the words expressed in the pages of the *Bystander* and the *American Citizen*. The one thing they all agreed upon was that action had to be taken to end the heinous act of lynching.

A few days after the Hose lynching, Bishop Walters addressed a large audience at the New Jersey Methodist Conference in his hometown of Jersey City, New Jersey. The Council president took a hard stand against the brutal acts, commenting on the dubiousness of Southern men's claim that they were only resorting to lynching to protect their women from the lasciviousness of black men. As Walters explained, "This cry [that] we must protect our Southern white women, is leading us on to another bloody struggle; it is the Southern white man's subterfuge to satiate his implacable hatred for the negro."[49] Walters added that "the Cubans and the Filipinos on whom we have spent so much money and shed so much blood to free from Spanish oppression, were never treated as barbarously in time of peace by that government as some Negroes have been in the states of Arkansas, Texas, North Carolina, South Carolina, and Georgia." In such a climate, the bishop bluntly stated "it is rather amusing to intelligent Afro-Americans to read in the great dailies and weeklies of our country about [efforts of] Americans to give to the Cubans and Filipinos an equitable and beneficent government, when they are powerless to secure life and liberty to their citizens at home."[50]

In concluding his address, Walters returned to his prophesy of another bloody conflict on the nation's horizon. "The greatest problem of America today," he asserted, "is not the currency question nor the colonial processions, but how to avoid the racial war at home. You cannot forever, keep the Negro out of his rights. Slavery made a coward of him for 250 years, he was taught to fear the white man."[51] However, Walters exclaimed, "he is rapidly emerging from such slavish fear, and ere long will contend for his rights as bravely as any other man." "In the name of the almighty God," he cried out, "what are we to do but fight and die?"[52]

Not all agreed with Walters's sentiments. John E. Bruce believed that an act of violence would end with the extermination of the African American population. "I am no more of [a] coward than is Bishop Walters," proclaimed Bruce, "but I am not ready to subscribe to this sentiment, great as seems the justification." According to the fiery journalist, the African American community was not ready for such action. Unlike Walters, Bruce did not think that many whites would "aid him in a crusade against the lawless white mobs of the south." "There isn't a more clannish or united race on earth than the American whites," Bruce argued. He assumed that a war of the races would end in the annihilation of the black community and "a closer communion of the white men North and South . . . [since] the sympathy of the white men of the North would very naturally go out to their kinsmen by blood and marriage in the South." To justify this prognostication, Bruce called on his readers to look at the means that the white men in both the North and South had utilized to trounce the Native American population and the actions they were currently employing in Cuba and the Philippines.[53]

Walters, if away from an attentive, easily excitable audience, may have agreed with Bruce. He and many of his fellow clergymen active in the Council came up with a more peaceful attempt to get the country to focus its attention on the abhorrent crimes being committed in the southern section of the nation at a rate of over one hundred times a year. Citing the many atrocities that African Americans were suffering, including being deprived of their citizenship rights guaranteed by the Fourteenth Amendment and being executed without the privilege of being tried by a jury of their peers, Walters called on the black population to observe Friday, June 2, 1899, as a day of prayer and fasting. He also asked the ministers and churches of all denominations to set aside the following Sabbath, June 4, for prayer and remarks on the subject of lynching.[54] Bishop Walters and the Council believed that if a sufficient number of African Americans and their parishes participated on June 2 and the following Sabbath, the event would demonstrate to the nation the solidarity of the black population in seeking an end to the brutal act of lynching and would, it was hoped, prick the conscience of America.

During the month between Walters's call and the actual day of prayer and fasting, a number of local Councils met to continue pushing forward with the organization's agenda. Gertrude Mossell, journalist, author of *The Work of Afro-American Women*, and active member of the Philadelphia Council, expressed enthusiasm concerning the future of the branch, noting that it had successfully accumulated money for its treasury and increased the interest in the organization in the Quaker City.[55] The Philadelphia organization received a boost with Walters's call for the day of prayer and fasting. The week following his appeal, Walters traveled to the city to speak to a joint meeting of the local Afro-American Council and the Methodist Preacher's Union, a white organization. According to Mossell, in that address Walters brilliantly recounted the barbarities practiced upon the black citizens of the South and appealed to the Christian sensibility of the audience to find a peaceful end to the bloody butchery. Moreover, because the Council president so elegantly represented the race's cause, Mossell suspected that the local organization would gain some strong white alliances in its struggles.[56]

The District of Columbia branch also held a public meeting that May. The principal speaker for the event was Congressman George H. White, who kept with the general theme that was preoccupying the black community at the moment—lynching. He opened his address by stating at "no time in the history of our freedom has the effort been made to mould public sentiment against us and our progress so strongly as now." But he assured the audience that the African American community would "not down at the bidding of any man or set of men and it would be well that all the bloody host of lynchers and assassins all over this country should learn this now."[57] White presented a series of statistics that refuted the charge that African Americans were lynched for rape and the protection of the white home. The congressman charged that the majority of blacks murdered in the South were killed for no other reason except "desire of blood."[58] "But with all this mobocracy," White continued, "God still lives and his heralds of the cross cry aloud" throughout this nation. Echoing Walters's position, White believed that God would stir an interracial coalition to wipe the inhuman atrocities out of existence. He reasoned that the "lance must be placed at this festering sore which tends to sap out the life blood before the putrifying [sic] cancer destroys our body politic."[59] White then turned his attention to other activities of the Council. He encouraged his audience to flood into the community to teach the race to diversify its development of the trades and professions. He desired a healthy balance between the two goals, trusting that once the community achieved this diversification, it would be better able to organize for the benefit of itself, as he believed the white race had been doing for a number of years. Finally, Congressman White praised African American women for their leadership in the development of the race and for the central role they exercised in developing and sustaining black organizations.[60]

Despite the interest demonstrated in areas such as Philadelphia and Washington, D.C., not everyone was enthusiastic about the Council and its method of bringing the nation's attention to the horrors of lynching. W. Calvin Chase was again one of the first to voice his dissatisfaction with the planned event. Chase did not see what effect prayer would have on the "cut-throats, lynchers, and murderers,"[61] and believed that African Americans had prayed too much and now needed to strike when struck. What Chase failed to offer, however, was a strategic plan to implement a self-defense strategy. Nor did he say what African Americans should do when whites reacted.

Even though Chase failed to produce a logical and strategic alternative, individuals throughout the nation agreed with his position. Julius F. Taylor, editor of the *Salt Lake Broad Ax*, affirmed that those who believed in prayer should be held in the highest regard. But he also insisted that "the negro must not expect to have his wrongs righted by praying, fasting and singing, but he must rely on his own strong arm to accomplish that objective. For it has been said by those of olden times that whoever would be free must himself strike the first blow."[62] Mrs. C. C. Steward, editor of the *Ship*, was in complete agreement. From the pages of her paper, the Virginian made it clear that "the white man knows how to shoot and keeps his Winchesters. He teaches his wife and baby boy to shoot." This lesson, she believed, was what "the negro needs to learn," calling on the Council to "couple that" advice with its prayers.[63] Steward was convinced that "a good-double barrel rifle and plenty of ammunition will go a great deal further in protecting our families from being mobbed and lynched than all the prayers which can be sent up to heaven."[64]

These editors, however, had missed the central issue of the Council's plan. Neither Walters nor any member of the Council truly believed that prayer was going to end lynching. By acting in solidarity and producing a national day of reflection, they sought to appeal to the moral conscience of Americans who did not participate in the dreadful act, but were complicit in its continuance. *Richmond Planet* editor John Mitchell, Jr., summed up the argument: that Chase thinks, "we have prayed too much and fought too little. As we understood it the prayer meeting was to move Jehovah and that class of people who take no part in such barbarities."[65] Then in a jab aimed at Chase, Mitchell concluded by pointing out "Brother Chase says nothing about the fasting [and] of course drinking is not prohibited."[66]

Regardless of detractors, many supporters throughout the country understood the necessity of the day of prayer and fasting and aligned themselves with Mitchell, Walters, and the remaining Council supporters. In the weeks prior to the event, local Councils throughout the nation began preparing for the occasion. For example, groups in Topeka, Richmond, Washington, D.C., Philadelphia, and Indianapolis all promoted the Council's day of prayer and reflection and made preparations to hold local services.[67]

Organizing for the day of prayer, however, was not the only issue concerning Council members. One week before the day of reflection, P. B. S. Pinchback, chairman of the Council's Literary Bureau, called a meeting of his department. The Literary Bureau was set up by the national organization with its objective being to publish and disseminate material that would agitate for African Americans' civil rights and educate the general public about the race's struggle. Members of the Bureau included, among others, Pinchback, T. Thomas Fortune, Lucy E. Moten, John Mitchell, Jr., Ida B. Wells-Barnett, Cyrus Field Adams, John E. Bruce, and Lewis H. Douglass, son of Frederick Douglass.[68] During the final week of May, the committee drafted and sent a letter to southern governors on behalf of the Council and the entire black population. The Literary Bureau appealed to the governors to use the power of their office to guarantee that justice was meted out to all alike within their jurisdiction. They also beseeched public officials to see to it that sentencing and punishment for crimes only be carried out by officially constituted agents of the law.[69] While the members of the committee certainly did not expect to get the full unprejudiced attention of the southern politicians, the dissemination of the letter on the eve of the national day of prayer constituted prudent action. By appealing to both the federal and state governments, the Council was able to demonstrate that it had exhausted all other formal alternatives. Thus the organization was able to defuse criticism that might have come from various circles throughout the country once it staged such a public display of protest.

As the newspapers carried the information about the petitions during the first weekend of June, Council members throughout the country gathered together to reflect on the atrocities that the race faced nearly every day and to pray for some amount of relief from the evils. Acknowledging the event, the *Colored American* published a poem by Council supporter John E. Bruce. Entitled, "The Hour of Prayer," the poem captured the mood of the black community and brought to light the issues that moved the Council and its supporters to protest:

"Gather to your solemn meeting,
Ye who weep for human woe;
God is never tired of greeting
Those who seek his face below—
Sought for humbly,
Rich his mercies ever flow,"

Pray for those who're helpless, friendless
Spurned and hated for the deeds
Of the vicious, and the aimless,
Who are progress oft impede
Lord in mercy
These thy aid most sorely need.

Pray for those who've felt the power
Of a race whose proud boast is,
That this Christian land of ours
Unto all doth justice,
Let it look on thee and live.

Pray for hearts pierced through with sorrow
Burdened down with woe and grief
Pray for sold whom the tomorrow

Offers but a slight relief,
Heaven hear us,
And defend us, Help, O, help our blind belief

"Pray with tears for proud oppressors
Trampling on the North they hate,
Pray for reprobate professors
Hastening to a darker fate,
Oh let mercy
Check them, ere it be too late."[70]

In addition to observing the day of prayer and fasting on Friday, June 2, 1899, the Council called on ministers throughout the country to preach special sermons on the following Sabbath. Among the many ministers who complied with the Council's request were Bishop Henry McNeal Turner of Georgia, Bishop Benjamin Tanner of Philadelphia, Bishops Cicero Richardson Harris and James Walker Hood of North Carolina, Reverend Francis Grimké of the District of Columbia, and Reverend David A. Graham of Indianapolis.[71]

Graham's sermon represented the general sentiment of those who supported the Council's call to use the pulpit for moral suasion. In his homily, Graham outlined how "evil showed itself at every turn" under the Mason and Dixon Line, describing how blacks were denied access to restaurants and forced to use separate waiting rooms, ticket windows, and street and railroad cars while being denied admission to churches, cemeteries, and parks. Although these inconveniences were deplorable, he declared that they were not the worst evil. "The greatest affliction," he asserted, was the "lack of trial by jury when accused of a crime," and the way lynching was replacing the courtroom in the sentencing of an accused African American. Reverend Graham used the remainder of his sermon to argue that African Americans needed to challenge the injustice and cruelty of whites, expose the fallacies used to justify mob trials, and bring pressure for the rule of law to be upheld throughout the South.[72] In the end, what Reverend Graham and the other ministers who observed the Council's call were asking their congregations to do was to lend their support to the civil rights organization in its effort to expose the hypocrisy and brutality of the South and to gain favorable legislation to end the deplorable act of lynching.

* * *

After the organization's successful weekend of reflection, most supporters of the Council were eager to use the momentum to push their agenda, organize, and put action behind rhetoric. It was imperative that the group demonstrate that it was not another race organization that met once a year and failed to put any political positions into action. Quickly the local branches sprung to action, holding meetings, preparing for the Council's annual convention, and outlining how the organization could grow and be an effective voice for the African American community.

This movement was first demonstrated the week after the day of prayer, when the Albany, New York branch held its monthly meeting. At the event, John E. Bruce outlined the means by which he believed the group could become a success. Bruce asserted that the black community needed to turn inward to solve the race problem. "The Negro in America today," he explained, "hangs upon the cross of suffering and is being taunted by his critics in press and pulpit on his inability to save himself."[73] He urged his audience to unite and organize under the Council. "There is only room in this country for one *great* Negro organization," he said, and "until the Negro, en masse, has learned the value and the use of organization as a means to an end, he will ever be a divided and important factor in all the relations which join him to the other elements of the citizenship."[74] Therefore, the African American community's salvation lay within itself, and the Council was the organization best suited to bring about deliverance. Bruce also urged his audience to stop filling the pockets of white businessmen and to form cooperatives for self-sufficiency and respectability.[75]

Bruce, echoing George White's address in Washington, D.C. the previous month, asserted that the Council was the only group to lead the race in these endeavors. Alongside its struggle for civil and political rights, it was the lone organization to encourage enterprising men in business and the professions. Under the leadership of Bishop Walters, the Council was the organization that believed "the magic word Money! And its twin sister Power! Are to be the great levers of this modern Goliaths—prejudice and proscription."[76] In short, the path to salvation was simple, and could be expressed in two words: "hanging together." The question, however, was whether the black American had the "good sense or the courage to try this plan." If so, Bruce asserted, "let him put his manhood to the test by sustaining not only with his mouth, but with his moral and substantial support the work and mission of the Afro-American Council."[77]

Bruce's address was enthusiastically received by the Albany branch and was soon published in the *Colored American* and as a pamphlet promoting the activities of the Afro-American Council. Shortly after its publication, local branches of the Council began meeting for their July sessions. Preparations also began for the group's second annual convention to be held in Chicago during August 1899. In early July, the Chicago Council held a meeting with Walters and local members of the steering committee at the office of Ferdinand Barnett to solidify the preparations for the national meeting.[78]

The Philadelphia branch was also active in the month leading up to the national convention. After the July meeting, Gertrude Mossell published a proposal calling on the national organization to create two new fact-finding commissions—one devoted to health issues, the other to crime. Regarding the need to compile vital statistics, she was concerned about the recent rise of tuberculosis throughout the nation and the negative public perception of those who had contracted the disease. She called for the Council to create a commission to investigate the disease in the black community and then "prepare literature warning and teaching our people how to avoid the conditions leading to the contraction of such diseases."[79] In regards to the commission on criminal activity, Mossell asked the Council to appoint several researchers—W. E. B. Du Bois and Hightower T. Kealing were suggested—to study the criminal element of the black community scientifically and sociologically. With such a study published yearly and presented at the Council's annual convention, Mossell hoped to better understand the root causes of crime while fashioning means to deter it. She also wished to have the intellectual and statistical firepower, in a similar vein to Du Bois's Atlanta University Studies and the American Negro Academy's Occasional Papers, to respond to the negative pictures of black Americans set forth in white newspapers and journals throughout the nation. If the Council followed her advice, Mossell felt that within a decade such scientific studies would bring about a vast change in the way African Americans were being portrayed and thereby improve relations between the two races.

In the months leading up to the annual convention, the District of Columbia Council worked on issues similar to those suggested by Mossell and the Philadelphia group. In conjunction with the attempt by the Council's Legal Bureau to get the Census Bureau to accurately count the number of eligible voters in each state, the local organization created a committee consisting of Daniel Murray, Minor Normal School principal Lucy E. Moten, and Howard University professor Kelly Miller to lobby the Census Bureau to appoint an African American as a special agent "to collect all the statistics available bearing upon the moral, intellectual, and material status" of the black population.[80] The Council believed that census law allowed for such information to be gathered. However, to ensure that the director of the Census Bureau had the power to appoint an agent to collect the information, the Council discussed with the director the importance of having an amendment secured to section eight of the law. In the end, as in the Council's previous encounter with the Census Bureau, the director indicated that he saw the merit of such an exercise, but did not feel that it was necessary at this time. The Council's committee members agreed to meet with the census director again soon and continued lobbying for their cause.

Along with the activity in Philadelphia, Chicago, and Washington, D.C., state Councils representing Illinois, Iowa, Indiana, New York, Virginia, Kansas, Ohio, Minnesota, Missouri, Texas, and California chose their state delegates for the second annual conference. This conference, to be held in Chicago in conjunction with the National Association of Colored Women's annual meeting, was the most diverse the race had ever assembled.[81] Prominent individuals from all walks of life were scheduled to speak, including Du Bois, Henry McNeal Turner, Josephine St. P. Ruffin, George White, Fannie Barrier Williams, Robert Pelham, Reverend Reverdy Ransom, J. Silone Yates, Ida B. Wells-Barnett, John Mitchell, Jr., and Fortune.[82]

A number of the editors and communities threw their support behind the upcoming conference, but W. Calvin Chase of the *Washington Bee* once again opposed the gathering. It appears "that there will be another Negro 'war whoop,' under the auspices of an alleged Afro-American Council," the editor observed. He complained that the black community never heard voices being raised when Democrats held the office, and did not understand why "these minstrel shows" had to occur under a Republican administration.[83]

Such criticism lends a greater understanding of Chase's frustration with the Council. His aggravation with the group was due as much to a clash of personalities as it was an expression of party politics and his political leanings. He accused many in the organization of being "office seekers," but his defensive stance against any criticism of the Republican Party demonstrated that he was catering to the Republican administration.[84] This position actually placed him in line with his earlier condemnation of the Afro-American League in 1890, which revolved around the organization's nonpartisan position.[85]

Chase's crosstown rival, Edward Cooper, lodged the only response to the contemptuous remarks. He explained in his *Colored American* that the Council "is not a political organization. It is designed to work on non-partisan lines, to develop a larger life for the Negro through any agency from which assistance can be obtained—republican, democratic, populist, or denominational." The meeting of the Council, added Cooper, "is not held especially to pass upon the merits or demerits of the administration, except in the most incidental way, and simply as one of the many forces worthy of notice."[86]

This response did not quell Chase's criticism of the Council. The following week, he returned with a harsher display of wordplay, portraying the Council meeting in the following manner:

> The great national Negro minstrel show, otherwise known as the Afro-American Council . . . will convene in Chicago, Ill., in a few days. . . . The interlocutor, Bishop W. B. Walters [sic], will not have his principal end man, Editor Fortune, present, who generally amuses his hearers by his many acrobatic utterances on politics. Some of the tambourine bishops will be present, no doubt, because their churches object to them attending other kind [sic] of minstrel performances. . . . The assistant interlocutor, Mrs. Ida Wells Barnette [sic], will make a stump speech on lynching, while our genial friend, Editor John Mitchell, will introduce his new version of Uncle Tom's Cabin and convince the few that will attend that "lynching must go."[87]

In contrast, Cooper depicted the upcoming meeting and the Council as the most important event for the race in 1899. "The Afro-American Council," asserted Cooper, "is now the recognized national protective organization of the race. It is so considered by the President, leading members of Congress, some of our ablest jurists and many of the leading officials of the states throughout the Union; also by our religious denominations, press, and benevolent societies." In addition, Cooper was certain that the convention was of great importance and needed the support of all "thoughtful men and women of the race" because the session would "doubtless inaugurate a policy which will be pursued by the race for years to come."[88]

* * *

Amid this journalistic jousting in the District of Columbia, the men and women of the Afro-American Council and the National Association of Colored Women (NACW) converged upon Chicago to demonstrate the strength of organization and to outline a strategy for the moral, educational, political, and economic uplift of the race. Meeting first, the NACW held a successful convention in Quinn Chapel AME from August 14 through August 17, 1899, with about 175 delegates. Central to the discussion at the conference was the necessity of working with children. An afternoon session, for example, was devoted to need for clubwomen to get involved with the creation and support of kindergartens.[89] In addition to this discussion, a number of other papers were delivered, including those presented by individuals who were members of the both the NACW and the Afro-American Council—counting among others, Mary Church Terrell, Fannie Barrier Williams, Josephine Silone Yates, and Elizabeth C. Carter—on various subjects, such as southern discriminatory separate-coach laws, which the clubwomen condemned.[90]

On the day that the NACW closed its convention, the Council, with many NACW members present, gathered at Reverend Reverdy Ransom's Bethel AME Church on Thirteenth and Dearborn Streets. Fifty-three delegates from thirty-seven states attended the Chicago convention, with hundreds of spectators filling the church pews and aisles to hear the proceedings. The delegates mainly represented the professions, especially those of an educational, medical, journalistic, and ministerial bent. Conspicuously absent from the proceedings were Council supporters Judson W. Lyons, Henry P. Cheatham, John P. Green, George H. White, P. B. S. Pinchback, and Booker T. Washington, who had been in the city to attend the NACW convention. T. Thomas Fortune also failed to come to Chicago, but was known to be ill at the time.[91]

Much of the proceedings were dedicated to academic papers and addresses devoted to the moral, educational, political, and economic uplift of the race. Among the individuals addressing the convention were eight delegates from the NACW convention, including Mary Church Terrell, Elizabeth C. Carter, and Josephine Silone Yates. Additional papers were given by W. E. B. Du Bois ("Business Enterprises of the Race and How to Foster Them"), Ferdinand Barnett ("Disfranchisement"), and Edward E. Brown ("Lynching").[92] Besides these addresses, individuals spoke on the exclusion of African Americans from labor unions and industry and on the federal government and protection and migration and emigration.[93]

Henry McNeal Turner, its foremost supporter at that time, broached the subject of emigration at the convention. Turner asserted his belief that African Americans had no real future in the United States and that the race would only find solace in a nation of its own.[94] Such a position was a slap in the face to the Council, an organization advocating for the social and political rights of the black community in the United States—not in a country in Africa, South America, or the Caribbean. Reflecting this position, nearly everyone who followed Bishop Turner criticized his position. Furthermore, for the first time in the Council's history, the organization deemed it appropriate to adopt a resolution firmly asserting its desire to stay in the United States. The convention resolved that:

> since we and our fathers and our father's fathers were born on American soil, have fought and bled for American liberty, and have toiled for American wealth, it is just proper that we should enjoy rights and share the duties of American citizens, and we declare it to be our unalterable resolution to strive by all proper and manly means to vindicate our privileges and fulfill our duties rights here in the land of our birth.[95]

In addition to the resolution on emigration, the delegates, through the initiative of Reverend Ransom, drew up a diktat on the practices of organized labor. The group's decree echoed the position of Jesse Lawson in his address to the Washington, D.C. branch back in February as it called upon the government to appoint an African American to the recently organized Industrial Commission. The members of the Council, however, did not expect the organization to wait for the government to act. Instead, they called for the creation of a committee to work with labor leaders and the Industrial Commission in an attempt to bring about a "spirit of fraternity and co-operation" with or without representation on the Commission.[96] In addition, the Council agreed to aid and encourage black laborers desiring to become skilled workers.[97]

The Council also passed a resolution regarding state and federal enforcement of the Fifteenth Amendment. J. D. Mohoney of Pittsburgh, who introduced the resolution, called for the state and national governments to be held responsible for paving a "path to the ballot box [for African Americans] as straight, smooth, and safe as that of any other American citizen."[98] In addition, the Council endorsed a resolution calling on the federal government to prevent the heinous crimes of lynching, arguing that the government must "see that the lives and property of its citizens are not taken from them without due process of law, and to this end we shall solemnly demand such national and constitutional legislation as shall at least secure as great protection from mob violence." The passage of such legislation, the Council asserted, was in the power and interest of Congress and would "prevent justice in America from becoming a byword and a mockery."[99]

On the issue of the government's responsibility in the matter of domestic terrorism, there was some debate regarding how strongly to hold President McKinley and his administration accountable for their failure to act against the pervasiveness of lynching. The convention basically divided into three factions similar to those that had surfaced at the Washington, D.C. meeting back in December. One group wanted to publicly condemn McKinley for remaining silent, another was prepared to wait and see what the president would do, and the third believed that any condemnation of the Republican president was contrary to the nonpartisan position of the organization.[100]

Given such divisions, the Council did not condemn McKinley, but did issue a broader criticism of public officials who had "not used their station to voice the best conscience of the nation in regard to mob violence and the fair treatment of justly deserving men."[101] The delegation also attached to this resolution a bill drafted by Boston attorney Edward E. Brown, which declared "lynching to be a crime against the general government and empowers the president to interfere in any state or territory to prevent such crimes."[102]

Another issue inciting much debate among the delegates of the Council concerned the political and education direction and policies that the race should pursue. Booker T. Washington's role in such policies consumed a great deal of the discussion after Reverdy Ransom called for the delegation to denounce Washington. The local minister believed that the Council should speak out against the sage of Tuskegee because of his perceived antipolitical stance and his failure to attend the Council meeting after speaking at the NACW convention.[103]

The delegates, however, did not know that T. Thomas Fortune had written to Washington advising him to avoid the convention. It was an election year, and President McKinley, like all of his predecessors, had done little to combat the mob violence that terrorized the black South. He also had been reluctant to accept black volunteers to fight in the Spanish-America War.[104] Washington, however, remained on favorable terms with the president, thereby raising the ire of numerous Council members. Given the possibility that the convention might condemn the McKinley administration, Fortune did not believe that the Tuskegee principal should place himself in such a precarious position.[105]

In the end, the delegates were unable to get a resolution passed condemning the Wizard of Tuskegee. Many in fact came to the principal's defense and recognized the importance of his actions for the moral and educational uplift of the race. For example, W. E. B. Du Bois, director of the Council's Business Bureau, went on record deploring the attacks on Washington, declaring that the Tuskegee president was "one of the greatest men of our race."[106] Council president Bishop Walters summed up the position of many within the organization—one that aligned him with Fortune's initial reasoning for encouraging Washington to avoid the meeting—by remarking that "Mr. Washington's relation to people of both races in the North and the South, made it impracticable for him to connect himself with the discussions of an organization which might be radical in its utterances to the destruction of his usefulness in connection with many classes."[107]

While many agreed that the Council should take no action to condemn or censure Washington, a number of resolutions conflicted with the Tuskegee principal's public positions, as was underscored by the assertions of Walters, Fortune, and others that Washington's presence at the convention might have hurt his national position as intermediary between the races. Furthermore, the Council's address to the nation was a strong statement to which Washington would have been unable or unwilling to affix his name.

In that address, penned by District of Columbia Council member Jesse Lawson, the Council summarized its positions and outlined them in strong language to the country. During a period of international expansion, the address highlighted the nationalism and patriotism of the African American community, the advances of the race, and the civilized nature of black America. "When the white men were away fighting to dethrone the stars and stripes and to erect in its stead the emblem of the Southern Confederacy," Lawson observed, "we had their women at our mercy and could have slain them, but our superior nature asserted itself and not a hair of their heads was harmed." "On which side of the balance," Lawson rhetorically asked, "should superiority be placed?"[108] In addition, the address condemned the acts of violence and called for whites to end this barbarous activity: "The race problem in America is not with the Afro-American. The white people made the problem and they must solve it." The Council leaned heavily on the government to lead in this struggle by passing legislation and properly enforcing existing laws. Finally, the address called on the government to create a commission to investigate the condition of African Americans in industry. Echoing calls from the legal and legislative bureau, it also called for a fair and accurate count of black Americans in the forthcoming census.[109]

With the adoption of the address and the reelection of Bishop Walters as president, the Council closed its second annual conference. As expected, the organization garnered a decent amount of coverage in the press, with a majority of black newspapers expressing praise, anticipation, and eagerness for its efforts. Not all were convinced, however. Chief among its detractors was editor W. Calvin Chase of the *Washington Bee*. Picking up right where he left off before the conference, Chase again ridiculed the Council and its promoters. Believing that the organization would have a short future, he characterized the Council as "a bubble in soap water," warning his readers that the organization was doing more harm than good.[110]

Labeling the organization "the Afro-Farce Council," Alexander Manning of the *Indianapolis World* was also critical, while not wholly in accord with Chase. Unlike Chase, Manning did not have any problems with the makeup of the organization or the conference resolutions; what he took exception to was "the holding up of the delegates for $5 a piece."[111] Although Manning understood that the fee helped to underwrite expenses incurred by the Council, he felt that its generous size left the organization for sale to the highest bidder.

Other than these two attacks, the Council received favorable press following the convention. But many newspapers, black as well as white, did express opinions on the Booker T. Washington issue. Though the delegation had squashed Ransom's move to denounce the Wizard, some white newspapers printed stories that falsely claimed that the Council had repudiated the Tuskegee principal.[112] When Washington was asked about this while he was in Saratoga, New York, he expressed surprise at the news. In words echoing the sentiment of Bishop Walters at the convention, he explained that when he left Chicago, he was in "understanding with all the leading spirits of the council, from President Walters down, as to the good that" the organization could accomplish. He added that many in the black community wished him to become involved in political activity, but that he would continue to work on the "moral, educational, and industrial development" of the race. All the same, Washington did not believe that the supporters of the Council were wrong for promoting greater political activity.[113]

Following Washington's statement, Reverend Reverdy Ransom asserted that the Tuskegee man had met with the leaders of the Council and stated his position on how the organization should proceed. This, according to Ransom, was the reason that he challenged the leader. If Washington had a message to convey to the group, the reverend believed that he should have attended the session.[114] Ransom did not agree with Washington's position of deemphasizing political action in the struggle for African Americans' social and political equality, and believed that the Council needed to declare its independence from Washington and his position.[115]

Ransom's position ignored the fact that the Council, as stated at the founding convention of the organization, believed in a two-pronged approach to the struggle—political agitation and moral and educational uplift. The Council did not deem it necessary to condemn one of the approaches as long as it was still viable and the other was not stifled. At this juncture in 1899, neither tactic was muffled as the Council endorsed both. This position was evident in the resolutions, the final drafts of which were drafted primarily by Du Bois, as well as the national address written by Jesse Lawson. Furthermore, public statements by the Council demonstrated that Washington had not controlled the organization.[116] Many supporters certainly understood this and agreed with John E. Bruce, who explained it was "gratifying to learn that the more thoughtful and intelligent Negro leaders in the Chicago convention" such as Henry McNeal Turner, Bishop George Clinton, and Du Bois agreed with this sentiment and "promptly repudiated the unwise attack." Washington, Bruce further contended, would doubtless, "survive all of his captious and flippant critics and especially that class of them who have done nothing to save talk and theorize."[117]

Most supporters of the organization were eager to put the issue behind them and get down to business in order to prove that the Afro-American Council would have a longer lifespan than "a bubble in soap water." Gertrude Mossell published a roaring endorsement of the Council in the *Colored American,* predicting great success for the organization. "[I]n the past," she stated, "it has been the policy of the race to organize, elect officers, do nothing throughout the year, quarrel continuously, and come together the second year united and in harmony upon but one issue to elect new officers, from the president down." The Council, in her eyes, had reversed this trend by working energetically throughout the year and reelecting a number of its officers. Furthermore, officers were chosen by Council members rather than by individuals propped up by whites for blacks to follow.[118]

The month after the convention, Walters called a meeting of the executive committee in the District of Columbia. First on the agenda was the election of Richard W. Thompson of Indiana to the position of secretary, following the resignation of Elizabeth Carter of Massachusetts.[119] The committee designated Washington, D.C., as the organization's headquarters and appointed a committee to present President McKinley "with portions of the Council's address . . . which urged the formation of a special industrial commission to inquire into the Negro's status in the labor world." The committee was also responsible for publishing the Council's address to the nation in pamphlet form and giving it wide circulation. Speaking to a reporter about the organization, Walters laid to rest the Washington controversy by explaining that the Council had not denounced the Tuskegee principal, and that it supported the work he was doing for the race. Declaring his political independence (possibly distancing himself and the Council from Washington's policies), Walters asserted that the Council was a political organization, but not a partisan group. He called for all interested in securing the rights of African Americans to "unite on the general proposition of race advancement, without surrendering the right to free and independent action as individuals."[120]

* * *

Following its first full convention, and less than a year after the formation of the group, the Afro-American Council had successfully planted itself on the national scene. The attention the organization was attracting, however, centered around its condemnation of President McKinley and its perceived criticism of Booker T. Washington. The national civil rights organization now had to firmly establish itself in the nation's consciousness as a group doing more than condemning the actions of the president and other race leaders. It was also necessary for the Council to demonstrate that it was not yet another race organization that met once a year and passed resolutions, but failed to translate political positions into action.

Such action was increasingly needed at the turn of the century. The white supremacy that had been steadily building throughout the nation in the 1890s had become entrenched in the nation's consciousness with the continued growth of de facto and de jure segregation and discrimination and the increased pervasiveness of lynching and mob violence. All of this was bolstered by, among other things, an increasingly ambivalent Republican party, especially on the federal level; a hostile state and federal court system; and the near ubiquitousness of "scientific" studies of race and ethnicity—largely done at white southern universites, but increasingly being published in national journals— suggesting that racism was justified.

In the months following the convention, with this increasingly hostile environment weighing on their minds, members of the Council began working on various strategies to dismantle Jim Crow and end racial violence. First and foremost among those plans was the organization's response to the lynch mobs that permeated the country. To that end, George H. White, Daniel Murray, and Edward Brown began strengthening the anti-lynching bill that Brown had presented to the organization in the Windy City.[121] In addition, one of the most outspoken advocates for the abolition of lynching, Ida B. Wells-Barnett, the recently elected director of the Council's new Anti-Lynching Bureau, called for ten thousand African Americans to join the Council.[122] By contributing twenty-five cents to the Anti-Lynching Bureau, each new member would aid in "agitating, investigating, and publishing facts and figures on the lynching evil."[123] In doing so, the Bureau hoped to arouse public sentiment, build mass support, and influence government bodies both nationally and locally as a means to pass legislation and demand enforcement of the law.

Shortly before the Council convention, Wells-Barnett and some of her Chicago associates had investigated the Sam Hose lynching. In order to bring about greater distribution of this information, Wells-Barnett published their findings in her most recent—the third in six years—anti-lynching pamphlet. As with her other works, *Lynch Law in Georgia* challenged popular notions regarding the justifications for lynching. This particular pamphlet offered a bleaker assessment of conditions in the South than Wells-Barnett's previous works. "The real purpose of these savage demonstrations," she asserted, "is to teach the Negro that in the South he has no rights that the law will enforce . . . that no matter what the white man does" African Americans cannot resist without drastic consequences.[124]

Despite this bleak outlook, Wells-Barnett firmly believed that continued agitation and the publication of facts about lynching were necessary. And with the aid of membership, Wells-Barnett argued that the Council's Anti-Lynching Bureau could revolutionize public sentiment regarding the dreadful activity and bring about justice.[125] The St. Paul branch of the Council concurred with Wells-Barnett's sentiment and began gathering signatures from supporters of anti-lynching legislation in Minnesota.[126] Also, through the efforts of Council supporters, members of the organization led by Jesse Lawson secured a hearing with President McKinley in early October 1899. At that meeting, delegates presented the president with the organization's national address and again stressed the need for the administration to pass legislation that would bring law and order to the country.[127]

These matters were at the center of a speech delivered by Bishop Walters before the Boston Afro-American Council at the North Russell Street AME Church the same month. Walters stressed the need for anti-lynching legislation and outlined the Council's plans to garner national support for such a measure. He also addressed the need for the nation to become aware of the deceitful legislation being passed throughout the South designed to disfranchise the black population. On this issue, the Council president discussed his organization's preparations and willingness to test the constitutionality of similar election laws in Mississippi, Louisiana, and South Carolina.[128]

In his Boston address, Walters quoted heavily from John L. Love's essay, "The Disfranchisement of the Negro," published as Occasional Paper no. 6 of the American Negro Academy. The Academy, formed in 1897, was essentially an educational society seeking to promote science, art, literature, and higher education; publish scholarly works; and defend the black population from vicious attacks.[129] Love's paper examined the measures that southern governments were using to disfranchise the black population, dissecting the recently revised constitutions of Mississippi, Louisiana, and South Carolina.[130] Walters was impressed by the paper and understood its value in the propaganda war against the injustices occurring throughout the country. Before speaking in Boston, he had written John Cromwell, the president of the Academy, requesting a thousand copies of Love's essay, which Walters planned to distribute to educate the public concerning the southern states' new legal restrictions on the voting and civil rights of African Americans.[131]

In the shadow of this positive flurry of activity, however, Walters caused a minor disturbance in the organization's affairs. As the presidential campaign of 1900 was beginning to heat up, in an interview with the *Washington Post* he called on the African American community to consider supporting the Democratic Party. This shift in allegiance was necessary, he believed, because Republicans continued to demonstrate a nonchalant attitude toward black voters and remained largely indifferent to lynching, disfranchisement, and the protection of African Americans' political and civil rights.[132]

Walters, however, was not calling for an all-out abandonment of the Republican Party—he certainly did not think that the Democratic Party, especially one dominated by southerners, would give African Americans a better shake. Rather, he was requesting that blacks pay close attention to the election, divide their vote, and increase their leverage as a bloc. If the Republican Party felt the effects of lost elections, it might pay greater attention to black voters. Walters thus believed that African Americans must consider all alternatives and alliances to make themselves and the issues they supported politically viable.[133]

Following the publication of Walters's interview, a number of black editors immediately challenged his suggestion. Chief among the detractors was perennial critic W. Calvin Chase. "Editor Fortune's idea was to have a strong race organization," Chase asserted, but "the preacher has killed the Council." He continued, "Whenever there are too many Methodist preachers mixed up in any institution, you can just come to the conclusion that pot-house politics must enter."[134] Chase called on the Republican officeholders within the "Democratic Organization" to abandon Walters and his sinking enterprise.[135] Recorder Henry P. Cheatham and Register Judson W. Lyons heeded the advice of the *Bee* and "vamoosed pack and baggage."[136]

Others associated with the Council immediately rushed to explain their position on Walters's strategy. Edward Cooper of the *Colored American*, for example, noted that the Council was comprised of individuals: administration and anti-administration Republicans, Democrats, people who believed that blacks should divide their vote, prohibitionists, officeholders, office seekers, and female suffragists. All were united for one cause, "race unity and race advancement along the lines of more liberal education, broader industrial opportunities, and grander citizenship."[137] Therefore, although Walters's suggestion was from an individual who happened to be the president of the Afro-American Council, he did not, in Cooper's mind, speak for the entire body of the organization; thus according to Cooper, the Council remained a "non-partisan and non-political organization."[138]

John E. Bruce agreed. In an article published in the *Colored American* under the title, "The Council Not Involved; The Individual Expression of Bishop Walters Does Not Compromise His Organization," Bruce stated that he did not see Walters's position as being especially "dangerous to the life of the Afro-American Council."[139] Bruce did not understand why all the "brethren and especially all the brethren in office, should constitute themselves the wet nurses of the Council, when the Council really isn't in need of wet nurses." Nor did he understand why members of the Council needed to speak out against the bishop when no official from the other group that Walters belonged to, the AME Zion church, had criticized him in print. Bruce believed that the "precipitate haste of these eminent and overzealous gentlemen to protect the good name of the Council is entirely uncalled for." And he believed the "Bishop's interview [was] all right and the Council [was] safe, thank God!" For, while the "constitution specifically provides that the Council shall be non-partisan as a deliberative body," Bruce asserted, "it does not inhibit its officers or members from expressing their views, political or religious." Therefore, in his call for blacks to divide their vote, Walters had taken "advantage of that unwritten clause to say a few things on his individual responsibility which have met with the approval of every Negro, who isn't afraid of his job, or his shadow."[140]

Walters and other members of the Council previously active in the Afro-American League must have experienced a bit of déjà vu regarding the dispute over the partisan nature of the organization.[141] Understandably frustrated with the diversion created by his *Washington Post* interview, Walters took matters into his own hands: he attempted to end the controversy by publishing an elegant defense of his position in the *Colored American*. "I notice that my interview," he wrote, "has greatly perturbed the equilibrium of some noted Afro-Americans, most especially Hon. Judson W. Lyons, the Afro-American spokesman for and defender of the administration."[142] Echoing Bruce, Walters noted that his individual position and the political nature of the Council had been mischaracterized and exaggerated. Nowhere in his statements, he said, had he "advised the Afro-Americans [sic] to bolt (go en masse) into the democratic party." Rather, he had simply advised blacks to "divide their vote where it would be to their advantage to do so."[143]

In regards to the Afro-American Council's nonpartisan nature, Walters argued that many were trying to pull the wool over the public's eyes regarding the true meaning of the Council's constitutional clause. To Walters, as with Cooper and Bruce, the clause meant that no one was "barred from membership in the Council because of his political faith, nor [was] the Council to indorse one political party to the exclusion of the other."[144] It did not mean, however, that the organization ignored political questions. If such an understanding were true, Walters argued, the organization would be unable to carry out its main objectives and would be rendered ineffective.[145] Walters believed that individuals such as Judson Lyons and Booker T. Washington, who continued to advise the race to wait for the "ruling classes, white men who are well disposed, men of influence and wealth, to make advances towards us," were speaking "nonsense."[146] African Americans, Walters asserted, "are the fellows who are down and need help," and they must "take the first initiative."[147] As the president of the Afro-American Council, a nonpartisan but political organization, Walters called for the black community to take matters into its own hands by making political alliances and decisions that would better its position and leverage.

Walters's defense seemed to silence many of his critics and set the community to thinking. Walters's letter, as Edward Cooper noted, has "been voted a 'bell-ringer'" and the "points he brings out are giving colored men food for reflection that will do him a great deal of good, and teach him a few valuable lessons in political duty."[148] The community should reevaluate the two parties every election, Cooper asserted, "to determine whether or not they stand for the things, which, in your judgment, seem best for the race and country at that particular time."[149]

After the controversy surrounding Walters's proposal began to dissipate, the organization started preparing for the Executive Committee's annual meeting in Washington, D.C. As the meeting approached, branches throughout the country kept up their activity, demonstrating through a range of actions that the Council was *the* organization that had a strategy for the moral, educational, political, and economic uplift of the race. The District of Columbia branch, for instance, continued to expand in numbers and established plans to distribute coal to the community during the coming winter.[150] In addition, the branch became directly involved in a discrimination case against the New Grand Opera House.[151] The proprietor of the facility, Plimpton B. Chase, was being sued by area public school teacher Nelson E. Weatherless for violating the civil rights act of the District by segregating the orchestra seating in Chase's theater.[152] The Council, led by Daniel Murray and Richard W. Thompson, unanimously adopted a series of resolutions to aid in the legal case against the opera house, pledging to support any other persons aggrieved by discrimination throughout the District.[153]

While the District branch became involved in the case against the "Jim Crow Grand," activity was also heating up on the opposite side of the country as the group's Seattle, Washington branch was organizing a protest against police discrimination. After a series of incidents involving female pickpockets, many of whom were black, local police chief William L. Meredith issued standing orders to arrest any "suspicious" black women in the Yesler-Jackson neighborhood. The black community began to protest after a number of innocent women were harassed and arrested. The Seattle Council held a number of meetings at the Sleeping Car Porter's Club and the AME Church, where they passed strong resolutions and created a committee to meet with Chief Meredith. During December, the group met with local law enforcement officials and aired their grievances. After the meeting, Meredith rescinded his order.[154]

* * *

In the shadow of this activity in the District of Columbia and Washington state, the Council's Executive Committee met during the closing days of 1899.[155] The Committee had a busy agenda, including an "investigation into the constitutionality of certain southern election laws, pushing of the [George] White bill to give the federal authorities jurisdiction in cases of lynching and public disorder . . . and the presentation of important facts and data before the Industrial Commission with hope of inspiring legislation."[156] With all this on their plate, members of the Council's Executive Committee met to map out a plan of attack for the organization for the coming year.

The Committee proceeded through its semi-annual meeting with no derailments, agreeing to support George White, who had worked with Daniel Murray and Edward Brown during the past several months on the anti-lynching bill Brown presented in Chicago, so as to pass the bill through Congress. Many on the Executive Committee agreed to collect petition signatures in support of this effort. Frederick McGhee of St. Paul, Minnesota, led this campaign by presenting a petition signed by one thousand citizens of Minnesota: a list that included the governor, leading judicial and state officials, and many business and professional men and women.[157] The Committee believed this to be a good beginning, but set a goal of accumulating fifteen thousand signatures.[158] The Committee also agreed to support the Crumpacker Bill designed to reduce southern representation and affirmed its pledge to challenge the Louisiana election law by urging members to return to their states to raise funds for legal expenses. In addition, the Committee agreed to support former Texas politician and current schoolteacher Robert L. Smith of Oakland, Texas, who was agitating against the lien system that forced farmers in his state and throughout the South into perpetual debt.[159] While aligning themselves with Smith, the Council also vowed to bring the matter before the Industrial Commission within the coming months.[160] At the conclusion of the Executive Committee meeting, the group held a joint reception with the American Negro Academy, which had met in the city during the same week.[161]

With a clear-cut outline of its activities for the coming year, the Afro-American Council was now an organization united in support of the rights of the race and deadly earnest in its endeavors. Through its efforts, the Council believed that if it had the right amount of organization, the nation would hear the issues of the race and nurture the goal of gaining social and civil equality for African Americans. As members of the Executive Committee left the nation's capital, they had every reason to believe that they were involved in an organization with more substance and a greater lifespan than a "bubble in soap water."

Jesse Lawson

George H. White

Frederick McGhee

Rev. Walter H. Brooks

Daniel Murray

J. C. Price

Booker T. Washington

Wilford H. Smith

T. Thomas Fortune

John Mitchell, Jr.

H. C. Smith

William Calvin Chase

Edward Elder Cooper

John E. Bruce

Ida B. Wells

Alexander Walters

Mary Church Terrell

W. E. B. Du Bois

William Monroe Trotter

J. D. Wetmore

Niagara Movement delegates, Harper's Ferry, West Virginia. Posed in front of Anthony Hall, Storer College. Courtesy Special Collections and Archives. W. E. B. Du Bois Library, University of Massachusetts Amherst.

Afro-American Council at the St. Paul convention. *St. Paul Appeal*, June 19, 1902. Courtesy Minnesota Historical Society.

Chapter 5

To Awaken the Conscience of America

Hail to this Council for inspiration,
For undaunted manhood, for equal rights,
A product—the black man's own creation
Led by such as Walters, as Arnett, White

Midst outrage, opposition and labor,
As a race let us struggle for the right,
Thus educate the hearts of our neighbor
Our oppressor, yea our brother in white.
—J. Francis Lee

It is because of our equality by nature that we appeal to
the conscience of the nation to recognize our manhood and treat
us as they treat other men, be they ever so white.
—Alexander Walters

As the twentieth century dawned, African Americans found themselves in a precarious situation. Throughout the country, black civil and political rights were being violated systematically while white vigilantes murdered roughly a hundred individuals annually. This growing system of Jim Crow and unmitigated racial violence was reinforced by, among other things, the increasing number of "scientific" studies of race and ethnicity—often categorizing the world according to its different ethnic groups and ranking them in terms of superiority—that suggested racism was justified.[1] African American activists responded to this white supremacy in numerous ways, but only one organization, the Afro-American Council, stood in firm opposition to this racial Armageddon. Building on the model set forth by the Afro-American League, the Council was an organization based in local and state branches throughout the country whose mandate was to fight not only racism in general, but to contest discrimination and mob violence working through the local, state, and federal courts and legislatures.

Though historians have paid scant attention to them throughout the years, the Council's activities during this period were extremely important. A vast majority of the individuals who scholars have deemed *leaders* of the race at the turn of the nineteenth and twentieth centuries were active in the organization at one point or another. Additionally, the activities of the group during the period on both the national and local levels highlight the daily grind of organizing. It was a slow and arduous process to build a test case to challenge the spread of disfranchisement while at the same time continuing constant lobbying of the federal government to gain favorable legislation to counter the disfranchising and discriminatory actions of the southern states. This action was maintained alongside multilayered attempts to end the disgraceful act of lynching by pursuing legislation, propaganda, and legal action on the national and local levels. All this took place while the Council tried to raise money and calibrate messages that would properly inform both the white and black communities, thus raising their consciousness on the necessity of righting these wrongs.

Coming off the successful December 1900 Executive Committee meeting, members of the Council took their leading role in this struggle very seriously. While interested in addressing issues deemed central to overturning the current situation, finding a means to finance political activity took precedence in the early days of 1900. Though the organization had successfully gained support throughout the country from a small cadre of budding black businessmen, entrepreneurs, ministers, and other professionals, it had not overcome the financial strains that plagued its predecessor, the Afro-American League. Like the League, the Council failed to gain mass support, and its members, though significant in number, seemed unwilling—or unable—to financially support the ambitious activities of the organization.

The leaders of the Council understood their dilemma and did not want the organization to falter on the national level as the League had done. The Council needed to firmly plant itself in the nation's consciousness to show the public that the group would do more than other organizations in the past. This mission was extremely difficult and without precedent. Years before the existence of a national civil rights organization with a paid staff of advocates, the Afro-American Council called on African Americans to place their hard-earned and often meager resources into an organization that could not promise immediate results. A strategy of challenging disfranchisement, the brutality of lynching, and the restriction of African American civil and social rights through legal means was not a glamorous struggle. Rather, the Council's work promised to be a laborious, time-consuming war of attrition that needed a steady flow of money and an effective means of communicating about the Council's activities to supporters. It would be an ambitious endeavor, but one that many in the organization's leadership felt was essential to the Council's survival and success.

With monetary constraints weighing heavily on their minds, the organization's Financial Committee sought to plant the seeds to properly grow the Council and its program. The committee, led by John H. Hannon, met at the home of Jesse Lawson to collect funds and put the plans of the national body into operation, particularly the group's legal challenges to Louisiana election law and Georgia's convict lease system.[2] "[T]he time," the Financial Committee declared in a circular appeal, "is now ripe for action on the part of the Afro-American Council, to justify its right to the continued support of the people, by taking steps to meet their laudable desire to test . . . the constitutional provisions in force in the state of Louisiana . . . operative solely upon American citizens of African decent." Such action, the committee argued, was the right of free men, and proclaimed that the world would judge the race's "fitness for citizenship . . . by unity of purpose to resist" every encroachment upon their rights. The committee ended this appeal by asking that every "man and woman in sympathy with the effort to bring before the courts" the protests of the Council "make a liberal contribution of money for that purpose" while also encouraging "others to do likewise."[3]

Following the meeting, the committee sent circulars titled "An Address to the People of the United States" to all race-loving men and women who might support the cause. Booker T. Washington was one of the first individuals to receive the appeal, and immediately sent one hundred dollars as well as confirmation to Jesse Lawson that he intended to support the effort in other ways as well. [4] Lawson graciously replied to the Wizard by thanking him for his support and explaining that his donation would remain anonymous, but added that the Council needed at "least $2000 in hand and the promise of three thousand dollars on demand from reliable sources" before action could begin.[5] Washington responded by putting out pleas of his own to sympathetic whites.[6]

Around the same time, independent journalist John E. Bruce also raised his voice in support of the organization, calling the Financial Committee's appeal a splendid plea to "the manhood and womanhood of the Negro race." To achieve victory in the fight for black rights, he encouraged all to send money to the Council's Financial Committee and outlined a plan, using Sunday collections, where he estimated the race could without even feeling it raise fifty to a hundred thousand dollars "in less than three months." With this war chest behind it, Bruce asserted that the Council could "make it very interesting for Southern nullifiers who believe that the Lord made the earth for his saints, and that they are the saints."[7]

Bruce, echoing the plan outlined by the group's Executive Committee, also appealed to clergymen and organizational leaders of the black community to send petitions signed by their supporters or congregations in support of George White's anti-lynching bill, which he was preparing to introduce to Congress.[8] Finally, Bruce called on the black electorate to use their vote in the coming election and hold those not supportive of black rights accountable. "Ask them to vote for Mr. White's anti-lynching bill and keep tab on 'em." If they failed, he averred, "lose them in the shuffle, when they pop up for re-election."[9]

Many supporters of the Council concurred with Bruce's exhortations and called for the community to heed his words and lend its support to the organization. The Woman's Loyal Union of New York City, an African American woman's club associated with the National Association of Colored Women, sprang into action immediately by circulating the Council's pamphlet to the "women's clubs," both white and black, "of Greater New York." They also began securing signatures in support of White's anti-lynching bill with the goal of returning the petition to Washington by autumn.[10]

The St. Paul and Minneapolis Afro-American Council affiliate, the Law Enforcement League, leaped into action as well, but with a distinctive approach. After local representative of the Executive Committee Frederick McGhee returned to the region, the group met to determine the best way to raise money for the Council's legal challenge of Louisiana's suffrage laws. After some discussion, it decided to produce a play starring McGhee entitled *A Social Glass*, and announced that it intended to donate all proceeds to the Council's treasury.[11]

* * *

While John E. Bruce offered his fundraising plan and the Minnesota Council used the arts to secure funding, the national organization pressed forward as well. On the national level, the group continued its laborious, dull process of lobbying the federal government and using the press to expose the white supremacy that was sweeping the nation as the Council hoped to gain public support and favorable legislation to end the discriminatory actions of the southern states. To this end, the District of Columbia Council, the lead branch in national affairs, appointed a committee led by George H. White to bring before the Industrial Commission "facts bearing upon the social and economic status of the Negro race."[12] This committee was created to document and expose the horrors of the convict-lease system, the discrimination practiced by labor unions, and the credit system that locked black agricultural workers into perpetual debt and created a kind of neo-slavery.[13]

White and the Council also pushed forward with the anti-lynching bill that he, Daniel Murray, and Edward E. Brown had drafted over the past year.[14] On January 20, 1900, White introduced his legislation to Congress: White Bill (H.R. 6963), which deemed any participation in a "lynching bee" a federal crime and demanded the repeal of all statues that conflicted with the proposed legislation.[15] White's congressional colleagues, however, virtually silenced the bill by preventing him from reading the text into the *Congressional Record* for "technical reasons," and then quickly burying the legislation in the House Judiciary Committee.[16]

Congress may have ignored and effectively filibustered Rep. White's bill, but this did not stop the Council from continuing to press the anti-lynching issue in other forums. Ida B. Wells-Barnett and the Anti-Lynching Bureau were at the center of the Council's multipronged attack. The Council, for example, attempted to institute the fundraising and educational plans Wells-Barnett had outlined after its national convention. Also, as White's bill went before Congress during the first few months of the year, Wells-Barnett embarked on a tour of the East Coast where she lectured on the "horrors of lynching" and raised money for the cause.[17]

Wells-Barnett also took her fight to the major journals of America. In publishing an article in the January issue of *Arena* magazine entitled "Lynch Law in America,"[18] Wells implied that the entire nation was responsible for these horrible crimes and noted that the perpetuation of such acts was destroying the moral fiber of the country.[19] She continued to highlight and challenge the erroneous idea often echoed by the press that the majority of those lynched were killed because of their inability to keep their hands off white women. As the director of the Anti-Lynching Bureau, Wells-Barnett had personally investigated a number of the cases and had found little evidence to support that claim, but cautioned that this did not mean that such an allegation might not be without foundation in specific instances. The "Negro," she explained, "has been too long associated with the white man not to have copied his vices as well as his effort to blacken his good name by asserting that assaults upon women are peculiar to his race. The negro has suffered far more from the commission of his crime against the women of his race by white men than the white race has ever suffered through *his* crimes."[20] After discrediting and satirically responding to the accusations of rape often used to justify lynching, Wells-Barnett announced that the Council's Anti-Lynching Bureau would continue to investigate and publish the facts to the world. She noted that lynching was having an effect on the image of America worldwide and in some realms the damage had already taken root. The world knew America by its moniker, "the land of the free and the home of the brave," but Wells-Barnett believed that many were beginning to question this image as the facts behind lynching were revealed. The world would not believe that brave men gathered "by thousands to torture and murder a single individual, so gagged and bound he cannot make even feeble resistance or defense."[21]

The Afro-American Council and its Anti-Lynching Bureau tried to reach the consciousness of America through the actions of Wells-Barnett and Rep. White. With hard-hitting articles such as "Lynch Law in America," White's pending bill, and lectures on the subject by bureau members—including Wells-Barnett, White, and the uncompromising editor of the *Richard Planet*, John Mitchell, Jr. —the Council, in effect, became the authority on lynching. This, in turn, allowed the Council to assert control over the counter-discourse regarding the issue. By effectively arguing that lynching was not an irregular act of violence but a ubiquitous part of the American culture, many within the organization believed that the Anti-Lynching Bureau could become the voice of the Council and its activities. With Wells-Barnett lecturing and publishing articles in mainstream white publications and White pressing his bill before Congress, the Council hoped to gain favorable attention and funds to support its activities.

In addition to these activities involving the issue of lynching, the Council maintained an active lobby in Washington, D.C. that likewise faced an uphill battle. For instance, the committee that had formed in Washington called on the Industrial Commission on February 10, 1900. Council representatives pressed the issues drawn up the previous month—the convict lease system, discrimination by labor unions, agricultural neo-slavery—but the Commission did nothing more than take their comments under advisement.[22]

Thwarted in these endeavors, the Council continued to solicit funds to support challenges to Louisiana's election laws. In late February, the group issued an official plea and, echoing Bruce's previous comments, again issued a call for all race-loving men and women to financially contribute to the cause. Furthermore, Walters and the Financial Committee placed the call in various black newspapers throughout the country as a means to collect funds for the organization and to acknowledge those who contributed in print.[23]

A month later, representatives of the race met in the District of Columbia to discuss the necessity of testing the suffrage legislation of various southern states. Those in attendance included White, T. Thomas Fortune, Edward Cooper, Daniel Murray, Jesse Lawson, William Calvin Chase, and, anonymously, Booker T. Washington.[24] Though the Council did not preside over the meeting, its members and influence dominated the proceedings. By the end of the summit, those present endorsed the activities of the Council, particularly its efforts to challenge the legality of the Louisiana constitution.[25]

With this larger acknowledgment of the Council's efforts and the gradual accumulation of funds, the organization continued the lengthy process of developing a case against legislation enacted by bigots. Meanwhile, local Councils continued to meet regularly and promote the activity of the organization. Local branches held monthly meetings in New York and Washington as well as in Indiana, where new branches had developed during the early part of 1900. The topics of discussion at these meetings included fund-raising activities for the Anti-Lynching and Legislative Bureaus of the organization and educational and political matters— including crime statistics, business enterprise, constitutional guarantees for African Americans, and the facts and figures surrounding the lynching epidemic.[26]

Congressional work continued as well. George White, for example, continued to press forward with attempts to get some type of anti-lynching legislation pushed through Congress. At the end of February, a little over a month after he first attempted to bring his bill before Congress, White began to address his colleagues during a debate over a tariff on Puerto Rican goods. After speaking briefly on the topic at hand, he quickly seized his opportunity and moved from the issue of the tax to mob violence and the necessity of anti-lynching legislation. In highlighting the imperative nature of the situation, White proclaimed that over the past thirty-five years, "50,000" African Americans had been "ignominiously murdered by mobs, [and] not 1 per cent of whom have been made to answer for their crimes in the courts of justice."[27]

Underscoring the manner in which Congress had discussed the unprosecuted murders of African Americans, White read into the *Congressional Record* the words of his white colleagues, including Mississippi's John S. Williams, Georgia's James M. Griggs, and Alabama's senator John T. Morgan concerning the issues of mob violence, the fitness of African Americans for citizenship, and the general characterization of black males as "monstrous black beasts."[28] White also read into the *Record* newspaper articles that countered the comments of his colleagues' characterization of the situation. After the scene was set, Representative White finally read into the *Record* the antilynching bill he and his Council colleagues had drafted, explaining to the House that there were but two questions for Congress to settle. The first was whether his congressional colleagues would "step aside from the consideration of economic questions, the all-absorbing idea of acquisition of new territory, and consider for a moment the rights of a portion of our citizens at home and the preservation of their lives?" Second, he asked whether Congress had the authority to enact a law to end the evils of mob and lynch violence—a rhetorical question that he addressed next.[29]

Central to White's argument were the beliefs of the well-respected Massachusetts lawyer and legal scholar Albert E. Pillsbury, who had previously offered a convincing argument for the constitutionality of a federal antilynching law. According to Pillsbury, the "legal proposition that the United States . . . has no power to protect [its citizens] in their lives within sight of its own capital" was "so monstrous that it is not to be conceded until affirmed by a final authority."[30] Dealing with the crime of lynching certainly could lie within the equity powers of the courts and government if, as many believed, the selling of liquor could be prevented and punished by a bill.[31] After reading from Pillsbury's letter, White concluded his speech to a polite "prolonged applause." But after he sat down, the House proceeded with the discussion of Puerto Rico as if he had never risen to address the session.[32]

Such a response did not deter supporters of the Council, who praised White's efforts to read the issue of mob violence into the public record. Furthermore, they called for the race to support White and the efforts of the Council to right the wrongs perpetuated throughout the nation against African Americans.[33]

Shortly after White's address to the House, Bishop Walters requested members of the race and of the Council to lend their support to another activity. In response to Annie Brown-Adams, the only surviving daughter of John Brown, Walters called upon African Americans to celebrate the Sage of

Ossawattomie's hundredth birthday on May 9, 1900.[34] Walters proclaimed that Brown deserved their praise because his "love of liberty was a consuming passion which caused him to abhor human slavery and to voluntarily yield up his life for the overthrow of that iniquitous institution." Furthermore, he had "demonstrated his loyalty to the race when he stopped to kiss a Negro child, on his way to the place of his execution." Walters, in turn, called upon every African American church, school, literary society, and "especially every Afro-American Council to hold exercises in honor of this grand old hero." Finally, he urged all lovers of liberty who created these celebrations to take up a collection in the name of Brown for the Council's activities against the Louisiana suffrage law and to aid Congressman White in his struggles to pass an anti-lynching bill.[35]

However, as the Council was experiencing a sense of momentum with White's bill, the growth of new branches, the development of the Louisiana case, and the excitement of celebrating John Brown Day, Walters sent shock waves through its ranks by announcing that he would not likely seek reelection as president of the organization at the Indianapolis Convention in August.[36] The bishop's commitments as a high-ranking official of the AME Zion Church, president of the Council, and lead representative to the upcoming Pan-African Conference had become too much to juggle.[37] However, the universal regret that greeted Walters's tentative decision was cushioned somewhat by Representative George H. White's verbal consent to seek the Council's presidency.[38]

On the heels of Bishop Walters's announcement, and just prior to the John Brown celebration, the District of Columbia branch held a very successful monthly meeting. Members of the local Council agreed to appeal to the political parties at the national conventions to insert a plank into their platforms calling for suffrage in the District of Columbia. The group also endorsed the newly formed Interstate Conference Commission, especially members W. G. Fearing and R. S. Smith, who had proposed a plan to push for the passage of the Chandler Bill. The bill advocated punishing anyone who denied citizens suffrage by reason of their color. The branch also formed a delegation, which included Jesse Lawson and P. B. S. Pinchback, among others, to monitor the Senate Committee on Privileges and Elections headed by Senator William E. Chandler of New Hampshire, and to stress the importance of such legislation.[39]

In the days that followed, members of the Washington, D.C. Council and branches throughout the nation assembled for the centennial celebration of John Brown's birthday. Bishop Walters presided over the festivities at the Metropolitan AME church in the nation's capital, opening the event with a reading of a number of biographical sketches of the martyr followed by the congregation's somber rendition of "John Brown's body lies moulding in the clay."[40] Archibald Grimké and Professor Kelly Miller followed Walters, with the latter reading a paper entitled the "Negro as a Religious, Social and Political Factor." The solemn-yet-warm celebration closed as Jesse Lawson briefly outlined the Council's current activities. As he passed the collection plate, he called upon those in attendance to honor Brown's work by supporting the Council's efforts in the Louisiana case.[41]

A few days after the meeting at the Metropolitan, the Albany, New York Council gathered at the Hamilton Street AME church. The gathering was a dual celebration of old John Brown and the passage of the Ellsberg School Bill, thoroughly endorsed by the state Council; the bill outlawed school discrimination throughout New York.[42] William H. Johnson, who called the meeting to order, explained the purpose of the gathering by endorsing Brown and his actions: "John Brown was not a fanatic as many would have us think. He was for humanity and did more for the colored race than any other man." Johnson's opening remarks were followed by a rendition of "John Brown's Body" as well as a number of addresses by Council members and supporters, including John E. Bruce of Albany, James M. Boddy of Troy, and Secretary of State John T. McDonough.[43]

Following these celebrations, many members of the Council began turning their attention to Montgomery Alabama, where white citizens from across the country had converged to attend a conference on the "Negro Problem." Reverend Edgar Gardner Murphy, a local Episcopal minister, had launched the idea of the conference earlier in the year, but had bowed to pressure to exclude blacks from participating. Many African Americans expressed doubt that anything good could come from such an event. As T. Thomas Fortune opined, a conference on the "negro problem" that excluded its subject was like "putting on Hamlet on the stage with Hamlet left out."[44]

The black community's worst fears were realized when the "old bugaboos of Negro domination, marry your daughter to a Negro, and would you sleep with a Negro or permit him to sleep in your chamber" became conference talking points.[45] As Fortune explained in a post-conference editorial, "no single deviation in truthfulness of statement, sanity of argument or fair play and justice in the promises held out for an honest solution of the race question." In addition to the "old bugaboos," Fortune asserted that the ideas dominating the conference pertained to issues such as the failure of African American education and suffrage.[46] He called for members of the race, and black journalists in particular, to publish a full report, including editorials from leading New York papers as well as from representatives of the race as a means to debunk the white supremacist arguments that dominated the Montgomery Conference.

The Afro-American Council, as Fortune surely knew, was already preparing to produce such a document. Before the event, the Council hired George Allen Mebane, former member of the North Carolina legislator and editor of the Raleigh *Banner-Enterprise*, to compile a report on the conference and publish his comments along with criticisms in the northern black and white press. Mebane completed the pamphlet within a month, and the Council widely distributed the document in an attempt to educate the public on the race problem and demonstrate what it believed to be the isolated nature of southern opinion.

One of the most inspired commentaries that appeared in the pamphlet was that of Council member John E. Bruce, who could not believe the audacity of such an event as the Montgomery Conference. Bruce was bowled over by the fact that "the sons of the men who ate sour grapes, and put their children's teeth on edge" now stood in judgment of African Americans. In addition, Bruce expressed enjoyment in thinking about what "Tacitus wrote about the ignorance, stupidity and barbarous manners of the ancestors of these white men of the South and North, whom it took centuries to civilize and refine and make respectable, and who now hold up their hands in holy horror because the negro with only thirty five years of opportunity, isn't a paragon of wisdom, virtue or knowledge." "The orators of the South, in discussing the problem, haven't touched the problem once," he explained. "They have been talking at it, over it, around it, and under it, but none of them have hit the bull's eye (and there are some pretty good marksmen in the South too)." "The South," he concluded, "must confess its faults and begin to make restitution to the Negro for its hell-black crimes covering two and a half centuries. Every one of the men who spoke against us at Montgomery should put his red hand over his mouth and hang his head in shame."[47] Many members of the Afro-American Council certainly concurred with their colleagues' sentiment and hoped that the distribution of Mebane's pamphlet would set the record straight, sway public opinion, and spark renewed interest in the Council.

* * *

During the month following the Montgomery Conference, Council members continued to meet in their local branches.[48] The national leadership also met to outline the program for the Indianapolis convention and discuss the organization's strategy for gaining favorable attention for the concerns of African Americans at the national conventions of both political parties, which were to take place during the coming months.[49]

Around the time of the announcement of the annual convention, however, the organization was also forced to turn its attention toward Booker T. Washington's efforts to create the National Negro Business League, an idea that some took as an attempt to disrupt the work of the Afro-American Council. The genesis of the idea of organizing black businessmen, however, had come from neither Washington nor the halls of Tuskegee. In 1891, T. Thomas Fortune and the *New York Age* endorsed the call of John H. Lewis, a wealthy tailor from Boston, to convene a conference of black businessmen.[50] W. E. B. Du Bois had also touted the idea of African American businessmen coming together following the 1899 Atlanta University conference on "The Negro in Business," and had raised the issue again after becoming the director of the Afro-American Council's Business Bureau at the organization's Chicago meeting during the fall of the same year.[51] Du Bois and the Afro-American Council, however, had failed to act on the idea, and during the early months of 1900, Washington began outlining the development of his own organization.[52]

Members of the Afro-American Council's Executive Committee apparently knew of and endorsed Washington's action. In fact, Du Bois and Washington held conversations regarding the makeup and membership of the new organization.[53] Despite the lack of protest against Washington's proposal by the Council's Executive Committee, several individual Council members cried foul when Washington announced his plans in late spring. In their opinion, Washington was trying to fracture the Council, as his proposed conference was scheduled to meet less than a week before the Council's annual convention in Indianapolis. For example, Ferdinand Barnett, editor of the *Conservator*, accused Washington of stealing the idea from Du Bois and warned of spreading the race's leadership too thin by creating a new organization. He also questioned Washington's motives, arguing that Washington's actions arose out of his inability to control the Council.[54]

However, many did not agree with Barnett's sentiments—at least not openly—and found Washington's proposal to be a logical extension of broader efforts. Edward E. Cooper of the *Colored American* responded to

Barnett's editorial by accusing him of blowing "hot air" and making much ado about nothing. In Cooper's estimation, the race's interest would be "boosted upward both at Indianapolis and Boston" as there was plenty of room for both the Council and the Business League.[55] George Knox of the *Indianapolis Freeman* agreed with his former colleague Cooper, explaining that "Booker T. Washington's latest move, the Colored Men's Business League, is a movement that comes none too soon. . . . Mr. Washington has simply took [sic] up a work that has gone begging for many years. The attention of the race has been called to it time and again, but it has been left to Washington to be the pioneer in the matter."[56] Many Council supporters agreed and continued to work on the political track of the Afro-American Council while lending support to Washington's efforts to strengthen the growth and development of black businesses.

Leaving black business to Washington, the Council focused on the upcoming national political conventions and the necessity of getting both parties to acknowledge and take a stand on lynching and disfranchisement. At the Republican Party's convention held in Philadelphia in June, the Council relied on prominent black Republicans and Council members George H. White and John R. Lynch to introduce resolutions against lynching and disfranchisement. Echoing the Council's 1899 proposals brought before the Census Committee, Lynch's resolution called for the immediate reduction of southern representation as a means of making southern states comply with the Fourteenth Amendment.[57] However, the convention delegates ultimately refused to endorse Lynch's amendment, opting instead to insert a weak commentary that condemned "devises of State governments, whether by statutory or constitutional enactment, to avoid the purpose" of the Fifteenth Amendment.[58]

George H. White, as a representative of the Afro-American Council's Anti-Lynching Bureau, also attempted to get the convention to endorse a strong platform in opposition to lynching and mob violence.[59] Reminiscent of a similar attempt by the National Federation of Colored Men at the 1896 St. Louis Republican Convention, the Republican Party refused to take any position on the issue of lynching other than the weak comments it had made over the past decade.[60] The failure of the Council to get an endorsement at the Republican convention did not bode well for White's bill, which remained hung up in the House Judiciary Committee, due in large measure to the apathy or whims of his congressional colleagues, Republican and Democrat alike.

Afro-American Council leaders pressed forward despite their cold reception in Philadelphia, traveling to Kansas City to call on the Democratic

Party to insert similar planks into its platform. Not surprisingly, the reaction to the organization's request was even colder in Missouri than in Pennsylvania.[61] Some individuals, notably W. Calvin Chase, believed that the Council's call upon the Democratic Party at its convention, or anywhere else, was foolhardy.[62] Chase's sentiment, however, was not universal. Many, especially members of the organization, thought that the Council's plea was a clear and logical demonstration of the group's nonpartisan nature as well as a needed example of its strength as a national Afro-American civil rights organization.

As George Knox of the *Indianapolis Freeman* noted, the Council did the "proper thing in asking the Democratic convention to include in its code of principles a statement condemning" disfranchisement and lynching. Moreover, Knox believed that this action represented a continuation of the abolitionist legacy. Never-ending opposition, he asserted, was the only thing that would create positive sentiment: "The great public has been driven to do the right things. Under the enabling influences of such women as Harriet Beecher Stowe, and such men as William Lloyd Garrison, Wendel Phillips, Lovejoy, Whittier and hundreds of others." "The weight of slavery," Knox noted, "was cleared from the public mind." He continued, "Apathy kills, while activity either for or against quickens. . . . It is left to the race to take advantage of the agitation. It is the time to go on dress parade. The zone of calms had been passed."[63]

Harry Smith of the *Cleveland Gazette* concurred: "Our republican leaders are too busy flirting with southern democrats, even dead Confederate soldiers, and doing everything in their power to subordinate the Afro-American." The reaction of the two conventions provided another example of just how "little difference" existed "between the national democratic and republican parties as far as the Afro-American is concerned." Smith called upon his readers to recognize that fact, cauterize the injury, and act, for the race had to come together on its own and "Do something if the condition is to be changed."[64]

Effecting change was exactly what the Afro-American Council set out to do. Undeterred by the cold reception of its concerns at the political parties' conventions, the organization continued to press forward with its agenda and formalized the program for its "dress parade" at its national convention in Indianapolis. Before the event, however, lynch law reared its all-too-frequent head once more, causing the Anti-Lynching Bureau to step into action once again following the horrific events that occurred in New Orleans during the final days of July.

During an afternoon in mid-July, three policemen confronted Robert Charles and another black youth who had made the mistake of entering a "white" section of town. When the men resisted arrest, a police officer clubbed Charles. In self-defense, Charles drew a gun, wounded one of the officers, and fled the scene. A few hours after the incident, police came to Charles's home to apprehend him. In defiance, Charles shot and killed two police officers and again fled the scene. White New Orleans responded in a "Carnival of Fury," organizing a massive manhunt to rid themselves of Charles and anyone else who stood in the way of white supremacy.[65]

For a number of days, a white mob consisting of police officers and civilians roamed the streets wreaking havoc on the black community as they searched for Charles. On the fourth day, the mob learned of Charles's whereabouts and twenty thousand laid siege to his place of hiding. Refusing to be taken without a fight, Charles killed seven and wounded twenty (eight seriously) of his would-be captors.[66] Finally driven from his place of refuge by fire and smoke, Charles was murdered by the mob. After his slaughter, the *Times-Democrat* reported his body was "shot, kicked, and beaten almost out of semblance of humanity."[67]

The events in New Orleans raised the ire of the black community across the country. The Afro-American Council's Anti-Lynching Bureau was particularly outraged by the incident, and as its representative Ida B. Wells-Barnett immediately began investigating "the Charles affair."[68] The horrendous events in New Orleans, however, were not the only issue on the minds of Council members as they prepared for their annual convention. A few weeks after Charles's stand in defiance of white rule and Jim Crow, members of the Council began reevaluating its position regarding partisan politics.

In the weeks leading up to the Council's annual convention, W. Calvin Chase called on the organization to drop its nonpartisan position and back the Republican ticket. By doing so, Chase believed that it would "be doing its duty toward the party of equal rights and the party that aided in giving the negro freedom"—the one that could enact any change in the future.[69] Edward Cooper, however, maintained the position that the Council had no business "meddling with politics per se." Its mission, he explained, was to "deal in broad principles of citizenship, to devise means for protecting the Negro's legal rights and to enlarge rights and to enlarge our opportunities for moral and material advancement as a people."[70] Julius F. Taylor, editor of the *Chicago Broad Ax*, concurred, but asserted that the issue was a bit more complicated. Believing that a bit of a conspiracy was brewing within the organization, Taylor reported having recently received information that high-ranking officials of the Council would receive a check for ten thousand dollars if the organization publicly endorsed President McKinley.[71]

Whether or not this was true, W. Calvin Chase had created a firestorm by raising the issue of partisan politics once again. His remarks prompted Democrats to respond in the days leading up to the convention, claiming that they would secure a resolution denouncing President McKinley at the Indianapolis meeting. Responding to both sides, many agreed that introducing "simon pure, tenderloin politics into the deliberations" was both wrong and in violation of existing bylaws. The Council's constitution, they pointed out, did not allow it to endorse either party, and the supporters of the organization would not consent such an action.[72] Yet no matter how Council delegates tried to contain it, this reoccurring, divisive political issue would once again rear its ugly head at the Council's national convention.

Around the same time, Booker T. Washington had continued working behind the scenes to aid the organization in its Louisiana test case. It was uncertain whether the Tuskegee principal would attend the Indianapolis meeting, but many within the organization believed that he nonetheless fully supported the Council's platform. Bishop Walters, for example, wrote to Washington a couple of weeks before the convention to extend an invitation for Washington to attend and speak at the gathering. Unsure if he could attend, Washington nevertheless expressed his support, which Walters welcomed:

> Don't think for a moment that I believe you disloyal to our cause. There can be no conflict between the Afro-American Council and yourself. You are contending for the industrial development of the Negro, while we are contending for his civil and political rights. I am with you in your work and I believe you are with us in ours. We understand that you would take the same stand that we are taking but for your school.[73]

Walters's belief that Washington was in accord with the Council's aims may have been correct, especially considering Washington's clandestine activities in aiding the group's Louisiana case. At the same time, the Wizard did not deem the bishop to be the proper man to run the organization—at least not without some sort of regulation. Washington and his cohorts mulled over the proper replacement for Walters as president, but understood Walters would be hard to defeat if he ran for reelection.[74] Similar to the circumstances surrounding the December Executive Committee meeting, Washington entered the Council's convention with the thought that he was going to control the platform of the organization by relying on his associate T. Thomas Fortune, an influential member of the Committee on Resolutions and the speaker that was to give the organization's Address to the Country.[75]

* * *

With these clandestine machinations underway and the press and Council supporters debating the hot-potato issue of partisanship, the members of the organization converged on Indianapolis for their third annual meeting. At the convention, held in the State Senate House, nearly four hundred delegates met, representing ninety-eight councils and affiliated organizations from locations throughout the nation, including New York, Illinois, Maryland, New Jersey, Delaware, Iowa, Ohio, Minnesota, Georgia, Oregon, Kansas, Missouri, Kentucky, Mississippi, North Carolina, Indiana, and Washington, D. C. Additional numbers of concerned African Americans and a few local and state officials joined the convention as well, filling the lower floor and galleries of the Senate House.[76]

Bishop Walters, fresh off his trip to London for the Pan-African Conference, opened his presidential address by proclaiming that blacks "are now face to face with the question of [their] complete civil and political rights" and emphasizing that it was not a "struggle for which [they] dare" retreat. Accusing the government of being derelict in its duty in regards to upholding the U.S. Constitution amendments, Walters called upon the Council to "not be afraid to let the world know that [their] plea is for the complete manhood rights" and act to awaken the consciousness of America to the need to reverse the federal policy of gross neglect. Such sentiment, in Walters's opinion, would be created by agitation, education, and general racial uplift.

On the issue of politics, the Council president hit the heart of the issue, stating that he and the organization had "no sympathy with that class of leaders who are advising" blacks to eschew politics, but encouraged members to become involved, as either a Democrat or Republican, and to hold the parties responsible for their actions. Walters argued that due to their own indifference, African Americans were partly responsible for the apathy toward African American concerns expressed by the major political parties—especially the

Republican Party. Unfailing support of the Republicans since emancipation had led the party to take blacks for granted, ignoring the issues they faced. African Americans, he noted, could no longer present their cause as it had been argued in the past by the likes of Frederick Douglass or John Mercer Langston. Instead, they needed to take a proactive stance by taking their concerns directly to the party and forcing it to respond. If they did not, as he and a number of Council members had emphasized earlier, black voters should seek to hurt the foes of equality at the polls. "Awake from your indifference," he implored his audience, adding "when we became indifferent to our social and political rights so did the Republican party." Make the nation understand, he asserted, that "as freemen and citizens you are struggling for your social, civil, and political rights," and that as representatives of the black community those were the principles for which the Afro-American Council stands.[77]

Even with Walters's clear attempt to put the knotty problem of politics and partisanship to rest, something that the Council and the League had struggled with for more than a decade, the issue would dominate the Indianapolis convention. Only hours after Walters's address, Judson W. Lyons, registrar of the treasury, rose to address the delegation on the issue of "Afro-American Citizenship." Lyons innocuously depicted the disfranchisement amendments of Louisiana and North Carolina as "worse attempts at nullification than that of the Southern states in 1860 and 1861," and reasserted John Lynch's position at the Republican convention by suggesting that the Council go to Republican congressmen to demand that the number of representatives be reduced in the southern states that were ignoring the Fourteenth and Fifteenth Amendments.[78] Lyons's suggestion was, of course, an action that the Council full-heartedly endorsed, but the discussion of political action was enough to launch a firestorm over the issue that had been lingering around the Senate House like an elephant in the room. In response, the Council's proceedings broke into a series of outbursts both glorifying and condemning the two major political parties. The attack against the Democrats was led by individuals such as Nelson Crews of Missouri, Colonel John Lewis of New Orleans, and John P. Green of Ohio. The Democrats found no real defenders, but well-known Democrats such as J. Milton Turner and Frederick McGhee attempted to get the delegation to remember that the Council was a nonpartisan organization. Others including T. Thomas Fortune, George H. White, and Bishop Walters likewise attempted to keep the peace and maintain nonpartisanship.[79]

Despite the efforts of the Council president and his allies, however, the Council closed the day's proceedings with delegates in a full-fledged argument over partisan politics. Alexander Manly scorned the politicians for "dragging dirty peanut politics into the deliberation of the convention." Ida B. Wells-Barnett, in a rare moment sounding strikingly similar to Booker T. Washington, tried to get the delegates to refocus on the agenda at hand: the creation of an organization for the betterment of the race. "Much talk had been expended about citizenship and ballot," Wells noted, but reminded those in attendance "a man with a ballot and without a house would always be a poor addition to the citizenship of any country." "The trouble at hand" she asserted, "had been that the Negroes had never had organization among themselves."[80]

Over the remainder of the convention the political issue continued to lurk under the surface with an occasional protrusion to slow the proceedings and cause the delegation to attempt to mend the problem. In the end however, the Council stayed the course and tried to outline the best plan of action to "reach high beyond the reach of petty politics" and "legislate for the common good of the race."[81] The delegation supported the strong action put forth by the Legislative Bureau and the Resolution Committee, including challenging disfranchisement legislation being passed throughout the South as well as encouraging blacks in the southern states to boycott railroads and streetcar companies that practiced discrimination.[82]

The organization also elected a slate of officers who rose above partisan politics. To the delight of many Council members, Walters sought reelection and easily assumed the presidency for a third term. The organization also elected a number of individuals to the Executive Committee as vice presidents, including editor T. Thomas Fortune and Indianapolis delegate Lillian Thomas Fox. Other elections included that of Ida B. Wells-Barnett to the post of national organizer, and John Mitchell, Frederick McGhee, and W. E. B. Du Bois became directors of the Anti-Lynching, Legislative, and Business Bureau respectively.[83]

To cap off the fractious yet successful Indianapolis convention, Washington delivered the final address of the proceedings entitled "The Afro-American and Industrial Education."[84] Washington was initially going to stay away from the convention, but came in response to charges that he sought to facilitate the Council's demise. A genuine supporter of the Council— at least behind the scenes—Washington attempted to subdue the rumors that his National Negro Business League, which had met the previous week in Boston, was created to compete against the national civil rights organization; he did so by opening his address with a strong assertion that the situation African Americans found themselves in at the turn of the century was not their doing:

> In our case, the world should be constantly reminded that the problems that have grown out of our presence as a race in this country, are not of our seeking or making. White Americans should always bear in mind that their duty toward the American Negro is an unique one. Yea, more than that it is a sacred obligation. The black man was not only brought to this country without his consent, but in the face of his most earnest protest. Every cry, every wail, every moan of anguish of the broken hearted heathen mother, as she saw her child forced aboard the slave ship, every suicide, and every groan and every pleading in the middle passage that marked the journey of the Negro from the shores of Africa to the shores of America, was an earnest plea to the white man not to desecrate the soil of America by engrafting upon it the serious problems which are today demanding solution.[85]

The solution to the problem, Washington argued, rested upon the "intrinsic worth of each individual or group of individuals." "No law can push the individual forward when he is worthless," explained Washington, nor can a law "hold him back when he is worthy." This worth, Washington indicated, would come from industrial education through which the race would gain the foundation necessary to become worthy on its own footing, not a "second or third imitation of someone else." As he had asserted many times before, this emphasis on industrial education for a large majority of the population would not set limitations on the "attainments of the Negro in arts, letters, or statesmanship." Rather, Washington believed the "surest and speediest way to reach these ends, is by laying the foundation in the little things of life that are immediately at our door." "The man who has never learned how to make money to pay his own debts," he warned, "is not the one to be entrusted with the duty of making laws to pay the national debt."[86] Washington ended his address by stressing that he believed, like many members of the Council, that the so-called "Negro Problem" would only be solved once the conscience of America, both white and black, was awakened to the grave situation in which the nation found itself at the dawn of the twentieth century, and when both groups recognized their duty to improve the current state of affairs.

Washington's address was similar to one he had delivered earlier in May 1900 to a Washington, D.C. audience that included a number of Council members.[87] What Washington left out of this speech, however, was a discussion of politics. Many believed that Washington was going to address the Southern attacks on the Reconstruction Amendments, but he failed to utter any words on the issue. Equally important, however, Washington also did not lodge any criticisms against the Council's pro-agitation position. Washington well understood the precarious position that he held as mediator between the races and that he now gingerly walked a tightrope. Such a stance was emphasized when following his Council address he spoke to a white journalist from the *Indianapolis Journal*. When asked whether he would comment on the recent southern legislation, the Wizard informed the reporter, "I would be delighted to give you an interview on that subject if I felt it advisable to talk, but I must decline. I can not see my way clear to giving you anything which I did not utter in my speech to the council."[88]

Unlike Washington himself, William E. Henderson, an Indianapolis attorney, wondered aloud in the local press about Washington's political position. In an interview with the *Indianapolis Sentinel*, Henderson asserted that Washington would have called for the organization to endorse the Republican administration if he had been present during the earlier political wranglings. T. Thomas Fortune took it upon himself to answer Henderson in a letter to the *Sentinel* in which he explained that Washington would not have called for the organization to endorse either political party because Washington understood and respected the constitutional limitations of the group.[89]

Whether that was the actual reason for Washington's apolitical tact in his address is unknown. As has already been noted, Washington usually eschewed political comments in his public appearances, and his address before the Council was consistent with that position. Despite his failure to speak on political issues, his appearance at the convention persuaded many members that he supported the group and helped to quell rumors that he had organized the National Negro Business League to sabotage the Council's work. Many Council supporters thus agreed with Walters's comment to Washington just before the meeting: "There can be no conflict between the Afro-American Council and yourself. You are contending for the industrial development of the Negro, while we are contending for his civil and political rights."[90]

William E. Henderson, however, was determined to continue the political arguments that came to the fore at the Council meeting, promising to produce a signed document of endorsement for President McKinley by Council members as a demonstration of support for the current administration. Henderson's claim surprised many, and they eagerly awaited the publication of the document. Once he released the letter, however, all discovered that only half of the signatures were bona fide members of the Council, and most had been appointed officeholders under the current administration.[91] Expressing the sentiment of the majority of Council members who refused to sign Henderson's statement, Harry Smith of the *Cleveland Gazette* asserted that "those . . . delegates who hastened to sign a statement endorsing the national administration ought to feel like 'three cents'—heartily ashamed of themselves. The Council is a race organization and all members . . . ought to have backbone and manhood enough to endorse its refusal to become a tail of any political party."[92]

* * *

In the wake of the convention, in attempting to distance themselves from partisan politics in an election year, members of the Council simply tried to return to the business at hand. Council delegates returned from Indianapolis, reconnected with their local branches, and continued the protracted, painstaking process of organizing and creating a foundation from which to challenge the growing discrimination and disfranchisement spreading throughout the country. On the both the national and local levels this activity included the preliminary work on the Louisiana test case and the continual propaganda war against lynching and mob violence.

Shortly after the convention, Jesse Lawson wrote to Booker T. Washington regarding the progress of the Louisiana case. The Council, he reported, had retained Arthur A. Birney, former U.S. attorney for the District of Columbia and son of abolitionist James Gillespie Birney, to handle the lawsuit.[93] Lawson wrote to Washington because the Tuskegee principal had recently claimed that he had collected one hundred dollars for the cause during his trip to the North, and Lawson wanted Washington to send the money either to the Council Financial Committee or directly to Birney. In the letter, Lawson also expressed his desire to keep Washington's name out of the press in regards to the Louisiana case: "On the account of the great work you are doing for our people at the South, and the delicate position which you occupy in connection with that work, I think it best for you to keep in the background in matters like the Louisiana case. Your real friends appreciate your position, and will do nothing that is calculated to embarrass you in that work, or jeopardize your standing before the public."[94]

Thus, with the covert assistance of Washington, the Council moved forward on the Louisiana case. Washington in fact was working as vigorously as Lawson and his committee colleagues. Around the same time Lawson wrote to him, Washington was corresponding with Giles B. Jackson, a lawyer and member of the Council from Richmond, Virginia, about Jackson's work on the Louisiana case. Washington was upset with Jackson for not having corresponded with him sooner. Both had been in Boston for the inaugural convention of the Business League and had discussed the matter at some length. According to Washington's letter, Jackson was supposed to work on the legal front as well as assist the Council in raising funds to cover the legal fees. Jackson apologized to Washington for not corresponding sooner, but explained that he was knee-deep in a local legal battle against the City of Richmond's attempt to pass a segregated streetcar ordinance. The local activities, he explained, had prevented him from writing sooner and from collecting any money for the Council's cause. He informed Washington, however, that the local organization had agreed to help raise money to test the constitutionality of the Grandfather Clause as well to as address its own financial needs.

Perhaps most importantly, Jackson discussed his meeting with Albert Pillsbury, the former attorney general of Massachusetts, while Jackson was in Boston. According to Jackson, Pillsbury was not convinced that Louisiana was the proper location for a test case concerning suffrage legislation; he expressed a greater desire for the Council to turn its attention to North Carolina or Mississippi, and strongly believed that the organization would need to institute lawsuits in several states if it hoped to receive a favorable decision from the Supreme Court. Jackson then urged Washington to come to Richmond to discuss Pillsbury's plan in more detail.[95]

Soon after Washington received messages from Jesse Lawson and Bishop Walters thanking him for forwarding the one hundred dollars Washington had collected in the North. Walters also thanked the sage of Tuskegee for his moral and financial support, and expressed his agreement with Washington that the most important work of the Council was "to test the constitutionality of the Louisiana election laws or similar laws in any state."[96] In his letter, Lawson discussed another two hundred dollars that Washington had personally pledged, as well as how this money would be used to secure attorney Birney's services. Contradicting Jackson's prior comments, Lawson remarked that Birney had been in conversation with Pillsbury and that the Boston lawyer had agreed to take the case once it reached the Supreme Court.[97]

In the public record, Edward Cooper used his *Colored American* position to acknowledge the work of Lawson, Walters, and other Council members in their attempt to raise the necessary funds for the Louisiana case.[98] On the local level, the branches met in various locales to prepare for the Executive Committee meeting in late December 1900.[99] Issues on the table for the Executive Committee meeting centered on the activity around the Louisiana case and the recurring question of supporting the reduction of Southern representation in Congress and the electoral college.[100]

Meanwhile, Ida B. Wells-Barnett and the Afro-American Council's Anti-Lynching Bureau continued to garner considerable national publicity. Following the Robert Charles affair, Wells-Barnett had begun an investigation of the events, and within a few months produced the pamphlet *Mob Rule in New Orleans: Robert Charles and His Fight to the Death*.[101] The booklet retold the story of Charles's ordeal from his initial conflict with the police, including the mob role and brutality that followed as he hid, and his dramatic and defiant stand before his slaughter.[102] As historian Patricia Schechter indicates, Wells-Barnett portrayed Charles as a "Christian soldier" and the epitome of "true black manhood": an individual unafraid to stand up against injustices and willing to pick up a gun if necessary.[103] "The white people of this country may charge that he was a desperado," Wells-Barnett asserted, "but to the people of his own race Robert Charles will always be regarded as the hero of New Orleans."[104]

Wells-Barnett continued to prick the conscience of America as she had in her *Arena* article earlier in the year.[105] Toward the end of the pamphlet, she meticulously documented all the instances in which blacks had been brutally burned alive over the course of the past ten years in orgies of violence that became markers of white citizenship and supremacy: "the mobs of this country" have "taken the lives of their victims within the past ten years. In [nearly] every single instance . . . these burnings were witnessed by from two thousand to fifteen thousand people, and no one person in all these crowds throughout the country had the courage to raise his voice and speak out against the awful barbarism of burning human beings to death."[106] To Wells-Barnett, such cowardly, immoral actions by white America were juxtaposed against the heroism and righteousness displayed by Robert Charles as he stood up to the police officers who racially harassed Charles and Leonard Pierce on July 24, 1900. "Men and women of America," Wells-Barnett rhetorically asked her readers, "are you proud of this record which the Anglo-Saxon race has made of itself?" She asserted that their silence demonstrated an endorsement of such heinous acts and that their "see no-evil, hear-no-evil" attitude had only encouraged "a continuance of this sort of horror."[107] Sharing the sentiments of many of her Council colleagues, she encouraged white Americans to recognize the harm that such acts were doing to the moral fiber of the nation and called for them to unite and arouse public sentiment in order to "put a stop to these demonstrations of American barbarism."[108]

In addition to her investigation of the Robert Charles affair and the publication of *Mob Rule*, Wells-Barnett actively protested against a particular local episode of racial injustice.[109] Chicago papers had carried a sensationalized story about the alleged assault of a young white child, Freda Guendal, by Harry Evans, an African American male. In response to the incident, a small mob developed to lynch Evans. The police, however, helped Evans to safety before the mob could get its hands on him.

The following day, Wells-Barnett and physician Belle C. Eskridge went to the Guendal household to investigate the matter further before jumping to conclusions. The anti-lynching crusader reminded the family, "however, ill [Freda] may have been yesterday . . . she was clearly in a state of convalescence to-day," as the victim, on the brink of death the previous evening, was found sitting up in bed entertaining friends the following day. Doctor Eskridge examined the young child and found no evidence of assault, but did believe that she was "a fit subject for the Humane Society" where she could have a good "example and teaching." Wells-Barnett expressed relief that Evans was innocent, but chastised the press for jumping to conclusions and arousing a "spirit of lawlessness."[110]

Shortly after this incident, Wells-Barnett and the Afro-American Council published yearly lynching statistics for 1899. In their report, they calculated that the number of lynchings during the year had totaled 107. Of these individuals, only twenty-seven of the victims had been charged with rape or attempted rape, while twenty-three had been accused of murder, and two had been lynched for merely having bad reputations. These figures once again upheld Well-Barnett's belief that the insidious charge that blacks were lynched due to a proclivity for sexualized violence and rape was both untrue and the root of the actual problem. "From this statistical report," she noted, "it will be seen that the charge that Negroes are lynched only for rape is untrue, that it is a most shameful slander upon the race, and that is a lie out of the whole cloth, the only purpose of which is to silence the criticism and make it easy to continue the work of killing the Negro."[111]

While Wells and the Anti-Lynching Bureau continued their frontal assault against lynch law, the Council made final preparations for its annual Executive Committee meeting. Behind the scenes, Jesse Lawson and Booker T. Washington continued to correspond in regards to the Louisiana case. Lawson discussed the necessity of hiring a local Louisiana lawyer to handle the initial phase of the case, while Albert Pillsbury suggested that the Council procure the services of Armand Romain of New Orleans. The Council agreed and began negotiating to retain Romain.[112] Lawson and Washington also discussed the potential cost of the suit, which Lawson estimated would run the organization roughly $7,500. This estimate included a one thousand dollar retaining fee for Arthur A. Birney, a four thousand dollar fee for Armand Romain's services, and a one hundred dollar fee for Pillsbury to argue the case before the Supreme Court, along with a series of bureaucratic and miscellaneous expenses. Lawson nonetheless expressed optimism that the Council could raise the required amount by the end of 1902.[113]

This encouraging sign was buoyed by movement elsewhere. While the Council slowly built its test case in Louisiana, the group simultaneously continued its lobbying efforts to challenge the steady growth of the Jim Crow system in other areas. During the final month of 1900, the organization received encouraging news regarding its lingering struggle for the reduction of southern representation when Indiana Representative Edgar D. Crumpacker, long a supporter of the idea, introduced a bill to Congress.[114] Calling for the strict enforcement of the Fourteenth Amendment, the Crumpacker Bill sought to reduce the representation in Congress of southern states that had passed disfranchisement legislation. According to Crumpacker's figures, Mississippi had disfranchised over 42 percent of its eligible voters, while South Carolina had stripped over 48 percent of their right to vote. In accordance with the Fourteenth Amendment, Crumpacker argued that both states should lose three congressional representatives, while Virginia, Louisiana, and North Carolina, all of which had passed suffrage-restrictive legislation, should lose one, two, and four congressional representatives respectively.[115]

In late December 1900, during a rare moment of optimism and hope, the Council's Executive Committee met in Washington. As concerns the Louisiana case, Jesse Lawson brought the Committee up-to-date on the group's attempt to select a local lawyer to handle its initial phases. In addition to recapping the year's activities of the group, the Committee voiced its unanimous support for Crumpacker's proposed legislation. At the conclusion of the meeting, members of the Council dispersed to spread the message of the organization and to try to raise funds for its activities. Bishop Walters, in particular, stepped up his Council activities in an attempt to inform the public about the organization's goals, philosophy, and activities. Participating in an Emancipation Day celebration at Faneuil Hall in Boston, Walters invoked the African American tradition of resistance and collective memory by speaking on the glories of African American soldiers and bondsmen freeing themselves during the bloody struggle of the Civil War. The bishop asked the audience to actively support the Council while urging African Americans everywhere to "continue to struggle for their civil and political rights."[116]

While Walters rallied the troops publicly, Booker T. Washington continued to maneuver behind the scenes. During January 1901, Washington and Giles Jackson corresponded about a number of things, including the Council's Louisiana case. Jackson discussed an upcoming meeting between himself and Jesse Lawson regarding the case, but more importantly, Jackson and Washington discussed the Wizard's impending visit to Virginia. Members of the local National Negro Business League had scheduled a public lecture in Richmond featuring the Tuskegee principal. Although the lecture would focus on the Business League and the necessity for building up industrial strength, Jackson and Washington agreed to use a portion of the money collected for admission to aid the Louisiana case. As Jackson cryptically explained, "two thirds" of the money raised would "go to a cause very dear to you and myself and every other Negro in the land, which cause is better known to you and I than to anyone else who will be interested in this lecture."[117]

Elsewhere, many local Councils, particularly those in the Midwest, had their attention directed toward the horrific events that had taken place in Leavenworth, Kansas, on January 15, 1901. Fred Alexander, an African American male accused of assault, had been taken from jail by the local sheriff and hand-delivered to a mob. The mob, in turn, ushered Alexander back to the city of Leavenworth, tied him to a stake, saturated his clothes with oil, and set him afire. "After the human holocaust, the charred remains of the victim were divided between the men, women, and children who had witnessed" the immolation.[118]

As news of Alexander's lynching spread, Afro-American Council supporters in the region began mobilizing. During the final days of January, 150 of these concerned blacks converged in Topeka to strategize about their response. In their deliberations, they confirmed their connection to the Afro-American Council and collectively authored an address to the people of

Kansas. In it, local activists called for citizens of Kansas to insist upon the proper enforcement of all laws and urged the governor, the attorney general, and the Leavenworth county attorney to bring to justice the perpetrators of the Alexander murder. They also called upon all black citizens of Kansas to coordinate their efforts with the Afro-American Council to apply pressure to the state's political machine in order to secure justice and prevent Kansas from becoming another "Georgia."[119] They and the other local groups meeting throughout the state joined in Topeka on February 22, 1901 to solidify a state Council.[120]

Council members meeting in Des Moines, Iowa, to celebrate Abraham Lincoln's birthday also condemned the lynching of Alexander. Charles B. Woods, president of the local Council, called the meeting to order and impressed upon the audience the necessity of uniting to end the so-called race problem. He warned, "you must not expect some other race to solve the question for you, but do it yourself and above all things, let your motto be, 'United we stand; divided we fall.'" Attorney George Woodson also stressed the issue of unity, forcibly impressing upon the audience that only through unity of action within the Afro-American Council would the race be able to gain some method "to stop the burning of our fellow man."[121]

At the national level, the organization held a large meeting in Washington, D.C., at the Second Baptist Lyceum. During the event, dubbed National Afro-American Council Day, Bishop Walters spoke to an overcapacity crowd. Referring to the Alexander lynching, Walters mentioned that all Americans should be ashamed to live in their country, a so-called Christian nation, which had failed to live up to its Christian ideas. Furthering his point, the bishop lamented that outside religious figures from civilizations deemed by whites as uncivilized, such as Wu Ting Fang of China, could come to the United States and understand the problems that plagued the nation far better than most "god-fearing" Americans.[122]

According to Walters, the only route to enlightenment was through the concentration of energy and support for the Afro-American Council. The Council had been formed out of necessity and would only be sustained by the race. Branches, he argued, should be established in every township, and all black societies then in existence should stand with the Council as affiliated bodies. Only once this was achieved could the Council gain more support and realize its broader goals.[123]

Following the bishop's address, George H. White, T. Thomas Fortune, and John H. Hannon all made speeches appealing for material support for the Council and its work in testing the constitutionality of the Louisiana election legislation. A collection followed whereby the organization netted thirty dollars in cash and another thirty in subscriptions for the case.[124]

After Afro-American Council Day, the Executive Committee called a special session to be held on March 5, 1901, in the District of Columbia. According to the Committee's appeal, matters of great importance were at hand. Possibly just as important, however, was the second inauguration of William McKinley. The railroads discounted their fares from all parts of the country for the inauguration, and the Council seized the opportunity to gather the Committee to discuss the activity of the organization.[125]

Prior to this gathering of the Committee, Afro-Americans of Kansas met in Topeka to establish an official state Afro-American Council. William H. Hudson, a physician from Atchison, was appointed president.[126] The one hundred delegates present at the meeting also created an executive committee whose immediate mission was to call upon Kansas Governor William E. Stanley with a request that he post a reward for the arrest and prosecution of the Alexander mob members. The supporters of the state Council also took up a collection for funds to combine with any award that the governor might offer, and was able to secure subscriptions for several hundred dollars. The state committee was able to persuade Governor Stanley to offer a five hundred dollar reward for the apprehension and conviction of Alexander's murderers. With this impressive start, the Kansas Afro-American Council was heartened by its attempts to get for blacks in the state the "same treatment that other races" receive.[127]

A week later, the national Executive Committee converged at the Galbraith AME Church in Washington, D.C., and held one of its most successful meetings. During the session, Jesse Lawson reported on the finances for the Louisiana case, informing those in attendance that the organization had raised $941 dollars. The delegates produced another $161 on the spot, thereby surpassing the thousand-dollar figure necessary to retain attorney Birney to institute the suit.[128] Emboldened by this progress, Committee members were roused further by stirring addresses from Frederick McGhee, Bishop Walters, P. B. S. Pinchback, and Lucy E. Moten. Before adjourning, the Committee created a commission to present President McKinley with "certain facts and requests."[129]

When the group met with the president, it expressed its grave concern about the deteriorating conditions in the South and requested that the president both support the Chandler and Crumpacker bills on congressional representation and take a much stronger stance against racial violence. The group also focused attention on blacks in the military. After recounting the extensive history of black soldiers, it called on the two-term president to give African American soldiers an "increase in representation and regular succession in the line of promotion of commissioned offers."[130]

Following the Executive Committee session, a number of local branches sprang into action and held meetings of their own. The District of Columbia branch asked all citizens of the region to throw their money behind the Council's efforts in Louisiana. Rather than putting their money into "brass bands and frumpery" for an Emancipation Day street parade, the D.C. branch instead asked the community to place its funds in the Council's coffers.[131] Philadelphia's local group held a plenary session at the annual convention with national leaders, which inspired many local activists. According to one local member, Gertrude Mossell, the words of Council members Frederick McGhee, T. Thomas Fortune, and Bishop Walters were so inspiring that the Wesley church raised $1,220.[132]

In addition to the activity in the District and Philadelphia, the Phillipsburg, New Jersey Council instituted a suit against the county of Warren for three thousand dollars in damages on behalf of David Lundy. A mob had attacked Lundy in December because he had married a white woman. During the attack, Lundy's house was demolished and he was beaten so badly that he lost an eye. According to reports, the local Council raised one thousand dollars for the case, in which forty-four arrest warrants were issued.[133]

Meanwhile, in Kansas the new state organization ambitiously called upon its members to raise ten thousand dollars to assist in the apprehension and conviction of the Alexander mob and to bring to "justice any official whose derelection [sic] of duty aided and abetted" the crime.[134] In addition to this activity, Kansas Council president William H. Hudson informed his constituents that eleven cities had formed branches and sent money for the Alexander case. Moreover, the state executive committee had consulted with a lawyer regarding how to proceed, and implied that the suit would include an investigation of the local sheriff's involvement in the lynching.[135]

While this flurry of local activity was taking place, Jesse Lawson and Booker T. Washington continued to converse about the Louisiana case. In a letter to Washington in mid-March, Lawson indicated that the Council had paid the retainer fees for Birney and Romain as well as the filing fee with the Supreme Court. After these expenses, however, only thirty-eight dollars remained in the Council's coffers; an additional six hundred dollars was needed to pay Romain when he filed the suit in Louisiana.[136] Lawson was extremely frustrated with the financial status of the organization. Despite the success that the Council had experienced during recent months, he lamented the continual absence of money and did not believe that his Council colleagues were doing all they could for the cause. Nor did he understand why his Council colleagues were not being more aggressive in their efforts to aid the Louisiana case. He related this frustration to Washington, informing him that he had not received money promised by branches in Rochester, Chicago, New York City, and Jersey City. What was particularly maddening to Lawson was that several hundred dollars in funds promised by T. Thomas Fortune and Bishop Walters for New York City and Jersey City respectively had never materialized.[137]

Despite the Financial Committee's difficulty in raising money for the case, the initial stages of the suit proceeded, albeit with difficulties. The attorneys began outlining a strategic plan, but could not completely agree on the proper course of action. Romain believed that the best strategy was to file suit against the registration laws. Birney and Pillsbury, however, thought the suit should encompass both attempts to register and to vote.[138] In the end, Birney and Pillsbury agreed with Romain. Upon refusal of the registrar to include the prospective plaintiff's name on the rolls, a suit would be instituted in his name.[139]

Once the legal team and the Council agreed upon the proper course of action, the Council left the groundwork of the case, including the selection of a plaintiff, entirely in the hands of Romain. The Council was not always pleased with the speed of preparations for the case or the frequency with which Romain kept it aware of the case's progress. However, the infrequency of reports was only a minor issue in the minds of Jesse Lawson and other members of the Legal Bureau. More important was that the wheels of justice finally appeared to be turning. [140]

* * *

With Romain in control of the legal maneuverings, the Council turned its attention to getting the public and its own members to support the suit. The Council was finding it difficult to keep the community abreast of the activities of the organization. The group's strategy of challenging disfranchisement, the brutality of lynching, and the restriction of African American civil and social rights through legal means was a slow, arduous process, not a glamorous struggle—one that was often falling out of the media headlines and therefore fading in and out of the public consciousness. Lawson and other members of the organization responded by embarking on a public relations campaign. In addition to the protracted nature of the group's activity, central to community apathy toward the activity of the Council was the failure of the black press to publicize the test case on Louisiana voting rights. As Lawson remarked to Washington, the papers failed "to realize the necessity of speaking out," and that they were simply "not pushing the matter."[141] The only paper that continued to discuss the case, according to Lawson, was Alexander Manly's *Washington Daily Record*. The Financial Bureau director speculated to Washington that some of the editors were waiting for some type of subsidy to give publicity to the suit rather than acting in the best interest of the race.[142]

However, the problem with such an explanation was that a large number of the Council members, and especially those on the Executive Committee, were editors of the race's papers. Why should they await payment for publicizing the activities of the organization they supported? Were they really holding out solely for money? A more central problem, it appears, was a conundrum similar to the one the Afro-American League found itself in during its brief tenure: the failure to properly disseminate information. With no national organizer, the Council relied on various individuals, especially its secretary and president, to disseminate news. There is no record of that information having reached the various newspapers throughout the country. Therefore, individuals had to pick up the slack and either collect or publish information on their own.[143]

During May 1901, both Ida B. Wells-Barnett and Jesse Lawson attempted to fill this void. Wells-Barnett's article, "National Afro-American Council," published in *Howard's American Magazine*, provided a concise history of the organization.[144] She expressed optimism for the group's future and believed that one of the Council's greatest accomplishments was its ability to bring into its membership so many representative African Americans from all religious denominations and many of the fraternal orders. According to Wells-Barnett, all that was needed was for "indifferent and unbelieving" individuals to join "their forces with those of the men and women who are striving with might and main to complete a solid foundation upon which shall rest the fabric for Negro weal or woe in this country."[145] She stressed the need for people to become more familiar with the activity of the Council's bureaus, because that was where the work of the organization really resided. Finally,

Wells-Barnett briefly mentioned the work of the Council in the Louisiana case and stressed the need for better financial and moral support if the organization's Legal Bureau was to be successful.[146]

Taking a more direct route, Financial Bureau chief Jesse Lawson published an extensive article on the Louisiana case in the *Washington Post*.[147] Lawson condemned the Grandfather Clause in the voting law and outlined the steps that the Afro-American Council was taking to prove that the clause was unconstitutional. Professor Lawson quoted extensively from an article by Louisiana Senator Samuel Douglass McEnery that had appeared in the *New Orleans Times Democrat* in 1898, in which McEnery had warned that the Grandfather Clause, if passed, would cause the state to lose representation. Lawson believed that using McEnery's own words would gain the Council's arguments some traction as the article circulated throughout the nation.[148] Following the article's publication, Lawson sent 150 copies to Booker T. Washington to help him raise funds for the Council's case.[149]

While Lawson and Wells-Barnett were trying to get the attention of the nation directed toward the Louisiana suit, William H. Hudson and the Kansas Council were moving forward with its case concerning the murder of Fred Alexander. As the *Topeka Plaindealer* explained in mid-May, "several lawyers have been seen [and] sworn depositions have been taken in the city which gloats of burning a live 'nigger' like fiends of hell to a heart-rendering death. . . . [And] the details of procedure have been carefully planned." Now, the editors assured their readers, the Council was "ready to take the next step in the open."[150]

A few weeks later, the editors again discussed the case, this time centering on its focus. J. H. Childers, chief editor of the *Topeka Plaindealer* and Council member, informed his readers that the Kansas Afro-American Council was laboring to "visit retribution upon the head of the cowardly sheriff of Leavenworth county, whose complicity in the recent outrageous crime . . . is conspicuous." Childers further noted that the Council was compiling evidence to prove that the sheriff was actually "a party to this dastardly crime." Childers and the Council asked their Kansas constituents to send donations for the legal case as well as to aid the Council's efforts to prod the State of Kansas into pass anti-lynching legislation.[151]

While the Kansas organization was calling on its supporters to aid in the local struggle, the national Council issued the call for the fourth annual convention to be held in Philadelphia on August 7 through August 9, 1901. In his call, Bishop Walters made special reference to the Louisiana case. Having recently received notice from attorney Arthur A. Birney that the case was progressing "satisfactorily," Walters informed Council members and sympathizers that more money was necessary for the suit. He acknowledged that the organization had raised one thousand dollars, but noted that another five hundred was immediately due, and that another one thousand would be necessary when the Supreme Court rendered its final decision.[152] He assured the black community that the Council was making progress and demonstrating to the nation that African Americans were "interested in [their] civil and political rights."[153] For that reason, if nothing else, Walters believed that the forthcoming convention in Philadelphia was the most important of all, and urged every "Negro church, college, benevolent society, and other race organizations" to send representatives and pay the annual dues of five dollars.[154]

Following the call, many Councils began preparations for the annual convention. In the District of Columbia, for instance, the local organization held a large meeting and fund-raiser at the Nineteenth Street Baptist Church. During this proceeding, Jesse Lawson informed those present about the progress of the Louisiana suit. Other speakers included Reverend Walter H. Brooks, George H. White, and Lillian Clayton Jewett. At the end of the meeting, attendees agreed to create a separate Council branch that would send delegates and annual dues directly to the Philadelphia convention.[155]

Local Councils met in New York City and Hartford, Connecticut, as well.[156] In both locations, the necessity of financially supporting the organization was the central topic of the meetings. In New York, members called on all groups to support the efforts of the Council and to send delegates to Philadelphia.[157] In Hartford, the monetary situation of the organization posed a challenge to local Council members and all race organizations. "What is Connecticut going to give toward the $2,000 needed to test the Louisiana case . . . ?" the *Colored American*'s Hartford correspondent asked. "We cannot afford to close our ears to this matter." The writer then issued a challenge to Council supporters as well as members of the various churches and societies of the city to send as many dues-paying delegates as possible to Philadelphia, or to at least send money to support the test case fund. The correspondent pleaded with his readers to show their "loyalty to [their] race in some way."[158]

In Kansas, the state organization prepared for the convention while keeping its members apprised of the progress of the Alexander suit. During July 1901, the Council, working in conjunction with the Ministerial Union—a group of ministers created around the same time as the state Afro-American Council—met with Kansas Attorney General Godard to demand the removal from office of Leavenworth Sheriff Everhardy. When they had made a similar request to the attorney general back in February, the group had been told that they needed to collect the necessary evidence for the attorney general to consider such action. After five months of gathering affidavits, the group presented the attorney general with twenty sworn statements accusing the sheriff of "neglect of duty and malfeasance in office."[159] Upon receiving the evidence, Godard told the group that he would survey the material and take appropriate action. Unwilling to passively await the attorney general's response, the group took its case to the press. Both the *Topeka Plaindealer* and the *Kansas City Journal* responded by publishing the evidence.[160]

* * *

Several weeks prior to the annual convention, the organization finally officially filed suit in Louisiana. Armand Romain had chosen David J. Ryanes as the plaintiff. Ryanes had lived in New Orleans since March 1860 and, despite his illiteracy, had voted in Louisiana for a number of years before the state passed its new constitutional amendment.[161] On July 10, 1901, Ryanes attempted to register to vote, but Jeremiah M. Gleason, supervisor of registration for the New Orleans parish, refused Ryanes's registration based on Article 197 of the Louisiana constitution.[162]

Romain on behalf of the Council responded by immediately initiating a suit in the name of Ryanes to test the constitutionality of Louisiana's "grandfather's clause." In the brief filed by the Council's legal team, the plaintiff alleged that Gleason's refusal to register Ryanes was illegal and without constitutional authority, and was equivalent to the complete denial of Ryanes's right to vote. Therefore, the brief argued, Gleason's action was in violation of the Fifteenth Amendment. The legal team contended, moreover, that Article 197 of the Louisiana constitution constituted an unlawful plan to disqualify Ryanes because of race, color, and previous condition of servitude. The clause therefore constituted a denial of equal protection of the laws and a violation of the Fourteenth Amendment.[163]

As the convention approached and the Louisiana suit got underway, Bishop Walters and the rest of the Council's Executive Committee moved to finalize its plans. In late June, Walters had written Booker T. Washington asking him if he were going to be present at the Philadelphia convention. To the bishop's disappointment, the Wizard responded that he would be unable to attend.[164] Walters believed that Washington's absence would be a mistake.

He understood that the Tuskegee principal was working behind the scenes with the Council, but at the same time, considered it important that Washington show some public connection to the Council—even if in the form of expressed opposition to the organization's open endorsement of political agitation. As Walters explained:

> I am sorry that you are not to be at the Philadelphia meeting. I am afraid that the enemy will test it against us. On my part, they will think that I don't want you to be present. And on your part, that you are a cowardly leader, afraid to come. It would be better for all concerned if you could come in on the last day and make a real conservative speech. It would defeat those who will make capital out of your absence. . . . A conservative speech will save you and keep hold on all the people.[165]

Regardless of Walters' pleading, Washington refused to attend the Philadelphia meeting.

Despite this setback, the Council pressed forward with preparations for the convention. On the eve of the meeting, Gertrude Mossell published a publicity piece in the *Colored American Magazine.* Mossell's article, "The National Afro-American Council," briefly outlined the creation and activity of both the national organization and the Philadelphia branch.[166] Urging all race-loving individuals to give their support to the group, she affirmed that the Council was the organization that was going to gain world recognition as well as social and political rights for black Americans: "We have come upon the world's stage of action at a propitious movement," stated Mossell. "The Council," she asserted, "is similar to all other like efforts, in that it sets forth our grievance to the world and aims at the betterment of the condition of the Afro-Americans of the United States." However, "it differs from all others in that it seems to have been born with the breath of life in it. It has stepped from its swaddling clothes, and it is the earnest, sincere desire of every thinking Afro-American, whether 'unuttered or expressed,' that it may continue to live and grow in strength and usefulness."

Shortly after Mossell's supportive comments, nearly 135 delegates from thirty-one states assembled in Philadelphia's Odd Fellow Temple on August 7, 1901, for the organization's fourth annual national convention.[167] The afternoon session opened with Walters's presidential address. Keeping with the theme of the organization's activities over the past year, disfranchisement was the central focus of the president's speech. "The disfranchisement scheme is wrong in principle and unwise in policy," Walters proclaimed. "We propose to prove it. . . . We have instituted a test case at New Orleans [and] we believe that the election laws of Louisiana, Mississippi, South Carolina, and North Carolina are unconstitutional."[168]

Leaving the discussion of the Louisiana case for Jesse Lawson, Walters directed his attention to the Crumpacker Bill and the necessity for the reduction of Southern representation in Congress. "The only thing that will stop the South in its nefarious business of disfranchisement is to reduce its representation," Waters affirmed. Attempting to quell those protesters who believed that such action might cause suffering for African Americans in various regions, he declared that, although some suffering might occur in the short term, the long-range effect would be liberation from "political serfdom."

The following day, the convention's attention turned toward the issue of mob violence. Reading a speech penned by his absent wife, Ida B. Wells-Barnett, Ferdinand Barnett sparked a discussion that became one of the most enthusiastic of the session. Barnett noted that the country's obsession with lynching demonstrated its uncivilized nature. "This country is the only one in the world that has lynching," asserted Barnett. "Even barbarous Africa and the Kaffir lands of the Transvaal are free from its curses."[169] Like many who discussed the topic before him, the *Chicago Conservator* editor dismissed the widespread belief that lynchings were provoked mainly by outrages against white women. Out of ninety-one known lynchings that had occurred in 1901, only twelve were the result of such accusations, and the veracity of these claims was speculative at best.[170]

George H. White, who had lost his congressional seat in the past election, agreed that something had to be done, but was pessimistic. Legislation he introduced had been filibustered by Congress and never saw the light of day during the remainder of his tenure. Yet despite White's doubt, most of the delegates agreed with Walter H. Brooks of Washington, D.C., who stated that it was the Council's duty to protest against all odds. "We are robbed and outraged every day in the South," he noted, "and it is our duty to protest. We have been compelled to see certain privileges taken away and the signs of the times point to still greater losses in the future. We can stop this," so long as members of the race take it to the politicians and demand change.[171] The Council, in turn, agreed to once again ask that the president and Congress support and pass anti-lynching legislation.[172] Jesse Lawson later presented a report on the work being done on the Louisiana suit. After the session, the

Council collected another $325 for the treasury—a far cry from the thousand dollars it hoped to collect, but enough to keep the suit moving forward.

Closing the meeting, the group held elections; Walters again defeated George H. White for president. Fortune and White were elected vice presidents, Frederick McGhee as director of the Legal Bureau, and Ida B. Wells-Barnett as head of the Anti-Lynching Bureau. A slight shift in the organization was caused by the absence of W. E. B. Du Bois, who was replaced as head of the group's Business Bureau by Booker T. Washington's secretary, Emmett Scott. The Council hoped that Scott's appointment would lead to better relations between the National Negro Business League and the Council as well as stronger political and financial support for the Council's efforts.[173]

* * *

Council members left Philadelphia excited that the organization was gaining a foothold in the community and was making progress with its legal challenge in Louisiana. Successful in publicizing its opposition to the disfranchisement legislation, the group demonstrated that it was not willing to sit idly by as the southern governments stripped blacks of their citizenship rights. Long-time critic W. Calvin Chase, however, once again derided the organization by labeling the meeting a "farce," chastising the group for hiring white lawyers, and characterizing its membership as "buffoons."[174] However, the group continued to ignore its greatest detractor, focusing instead on national and local activities already at hand.

A week after the Philadelphia convention, the Ryanes case was taken up by the Division D Civil District Court of New Orleans. As the hearing opened, Attorney-General Guion filed an exception on the part of the State of Louisiana on the basis that the court did not have jurisdiction over the case. Guion argued that the issue was a political one, and that Ryanes's petition had demonstrated no valid cause for the court to take action.[175] In the event the judge overruled these exceptions, Guion had filed another motion asking the court to dismiss the suit upon trial, arguing that such action was necessary because the registrar had refused to register Ryanes due to his lack of qualifications, not because of his skin color.[176]

In the afternoon session, both sides submitted their arguments. Guion argued that Ryanes did not possess the qualifications to vote and that the registrar was carrying out his duty by not allowing the plaintiff to register.

Attorney Romain, arguing for the Council, countered by asserting that Ryanes had a constitutional right to vote that was protected by the Fifteenth Amendment and therefore had the right to register in Louisiana and exercise his federal right to the franchise.[177] The session ended with Judge Sommerville's agreeing to deliberate on the case in the coming days.

On August 19, 1901, Sommerville called the District Court into session and dismissed the suit. According to Judge Sommerville, his decision was rendered in accordance with a number of factors. First, the judge denied that the Fifteenth Amendment gave individuals the right to vote. He further argued that the U.S. Constitution recognized the right of states to regulate suffrage.[178] He also argued that the "grandfather clause" of the suffrage clause (section five) required voters to have registered before August 31, 1898. Since Ryanes admitted that he did not possess the literacy or property qualifications, the plaintiff, in Somerville's opinion, had waited too long to qualify under section five of the Louisiana Constitution. The judge also based this decision on the fact that Ryanes had failed to allege that anyone had been registered under section five or that he had been injured in any way by that provision of the constitution, which the judge felt somehow disqualified the complaint. "It may be that discrimination against him was intended under that section," Sommerville noted, "but intention is insufficient to entitle him to relief in a court of justice."[179] Having pointed out that Ryanes did not meet the literacy and property requirements and that he had failed to register during the time of operation of section five, Judge Sommerville dismissed the case on the grounds that Ryanes's petition failed to show cause, which was needed for the court to issue a writ of mandamus.[180]

Upon dismissal of the suit, the Council's Legal Bureau appealed the case to the Louisiana Supreme Court.[181] What is particularly curious, however, is that the black press did not cover the Council's appeal or afford any space to the initial case. Once again it appears that the Council failed to inform the public of its activities, and therefore may have undermined its own efforts to elicit greater support from the community. The organization was preparing to continue to push its case through the court system, and in doing so it was actively fighting for the community's rights, but it still needed to keep people appraised of its activity.

Shortly after Judge Sommerville dismissed the Ryanes suit, the Afro-American Council received another blow to its legal strategy. The Kansas Council received word from Attorney General Aretaf A. Goddard that he had found the evidence presented to him to be insufficient to warrant Sheriff Peter Everhardy's removal from office. Many in the organization believed that the attorney general was acting out of political ambition, noting that he had "the supreme court judgeship bee buzzing in his political Stetson." Regardless of his rationale, his refusal still constituted a setback. Following the attorney general's decision, the group referred its case to Governor Stanley, who had earlier supported the activities of the organization by offering a reward for the apprehension of murderous ruffians. The governor's support however, did not include the removal of a public official. As the editors of the *Topeka Plaindealer* pointed out, Stanley was "ambituous [sic] to be [a] United States Senator."[182]

While the Kansas Council awaited Governor Stanley's response to its request, the national organization's Legal and Legislative Bureau moved forward with its own legal struggles. Despite the setback in the Louisiana suit, the organization widened its attack on the suffrage provisions of the southern constitutions. This time, the organization focused its attack on Booker T. Washington's home state, Alabama.

In late 1900, Alabama politicians had announced their intention to hold a constitutional convention during the following year. The Afro-American Council, seeing the writing on the wall, became immediately alarmed and put its Legal and Legislative Bureau into action. Jesse Lawson and Washington discussed the ramifications of the convention, fearing that the delegates would enact a new suffrage provision disfranchising a large number of black Alabamians.[183] While the convention was taking place in June 1901, Lawson wrote to William C. Oates, former governor and ex-congressional representative from Montgomery, who was one of the convention delegates.[184] Lawson attempted to persuade Oates, reputed to have liberal views on the suffrage question, to persuade his colleagues to vote against the inclusion of a grandfather clause. As Lawson explained, many constitutional lawyers agreed that inclusion of such a clause in the Louisiana and North Carolina constitutions conflicted with the federal constitution and would eventually be declared unconstitutional. The Council representative also suggested to Oates that if he could persuade his fellow delegates to accept this view, then Alabama would avert any reduction of representation in Congress and the electoral college in the event that Crumpacker's bill should pass through Congress.[185]

To the delight of the Afro-American Council and Washington, Oates argued against the inclusion of the grandfather clause—and against any disfranchisement legislation for that matter. In a speech before the convention, he warned that the purpose of the proceedings was not the disfranchisement of African Americans. According to Oates, the convention was called to "redeem our beloved State from a condition into which she had fallen by dishonest elections." Blacks, he continued, "are too large a part of our population to be excluded as a mass. They should be admitted to a share in the government."[186] Yet despite these efforts, the convention agreed upon new suffrage provisions that systematically eliminated the African American voting public.[187]

Once the Alabama constitutional convention passed the new provisions, Washington became concerned as to how they would affect African Americans and decided to promote a campaign encouraging black Alabamians to register to vote. In late December 1901, Washington wrote to Jesse Lawson asking the Afro-American Council to become involved in the Alabama situation, requesting that the Legal and Legislative Bureau prepare a circular to educate voters about their rights while encouraging them to register. He also called upon the organization to prepare a suit to test the Alabama laws. Lawson enthusiastically responded to Washington's request, assuring him that the Bureau would draw up the circular as soon as it received the registration laws, and further noted that the treasury currently had one hundred dollars that might be used to institute a test case in Alabama.[188]

Thus as the second year of the century came to a close, the Afro-American Council was preparing its second constitutional suit. Though it had suffered a number of setbacks on the national level, at the state level in the Louisiana case, and at the local level in the Kansas-led Fred Alexander suit, the organization continued on with its legal strategy. Building on the vision of T. Thomas Fortune and the Afro-American League, the Council was educating the public on the problems African Americans and the nation faced and was appealing to the country's court system to "force from demagogues and fanatics all the just rights which the Constitution" guaranteed them.[189] The strategy was neither glamorous nor quick; rather, it was an arduous war of attrition that would take the determination of many persistent activists over a number of years. The Afro-American Council found itself in the early stages of this battle fighting against the iniquitous discriminatory legislation as it was being created and seeping into the consciousness of America. Members of the Council, like those of the League before them, were laying the groundwork for activists and organizations that would develop in the coming years, most directly the Committee of Twelve, the Niagara Movement, and the National Association for the Advancement of Colored People. In the meantime, at the end of its third full year of existence, the Council stood on the brink of yet another year in its sole position as the only nationwide protest organization struggling to awaken the conscience of America on the immorality of the situation and to end the continued deteriorating social and political condition of the African American population.

Chapter 6

Invasion of the Tuskegee Machine

> Let us turn a deaf ear to criticism, ridicule and slander, and push forward to the goal.
>
> —Alexander Walters

> Afro-Americans of all men have nothing of manhood and nothing of right and justice to surrender in these times which try men's souls. . . . Our motive should be always first for the race, at all times and under all circumstances
>
> —*Cleveland Gazette*

Surpassing the lifespan of its predecessor, the Afro-American Council entered its fourth year of existence in 1902. The organization had successfully instituted national and local suits aimed at protecting the rights of African Americans, but as with the Afro-American League, it struggled for financial security as it sought to gain a larger mass following. Despite this situation the organization continued to push forward, focusing on its legal and legislative agenda. Such action was increasingly vital as states and local municipalities continued to pass and strengthen segregation laws, including the increasing number of cities passing legislation creating Jim Crow cars on their streetcar systems. Moreover, more southern states continued to find ways to systematically remove African Americans from the electorate. In this context, the Afro-American Council understood the importance of its legal strategy.

The Council and the Afro-American League had been at the forefront of the struggle against southern disfranchisement and the rise of Jim Crow since 1890, and despite the continued proliferation of both, the efforts of these organizations show a continued attempt on the part of a certain cadre of African Americans to stop the spread of white supremacy. It is in the unremitting toil of organizing and activism within these groups throughout the late nineteenth and early twentieth centuries that we can see African Americans struggling to stop the growth of the Jim Crow system. In 1902, the members of the Council were trying through any means to push forward their legal and legislative strategy. They scrapped together whatever meager resources they could to lobby Congress to reverse the proliferation of segregation as well as to create test cases that challenged the spread of disfranchisement.

In the early months of 1902, the Council chose to focus its attack on the issue of suffrage. Since the creation of the organization, four southern states—Alabama, Louisiana, North Carolina, and Texas—had created or strengthened disfranchisement legislation, bringing the total to nine states that had instituted some type of disfranchisement law since Mississippi issued its plan in 1890. Considering such rapid expansion, the Council understood the magnitude of its Louisiana case and knew it was imperative that the group begin expanding its fight against the southern states' attempts to eliminate the black electorate.

Throughout January and February, Booker T. Washington worked with Jesse Lawson and the Legal and Legislative Bureau on these important issues, focusing particularly on the idea of instituting a test case regarding the Alabama constitution. Early in January, Lawson received a copy of the Alabama registration laws from Washington after which he immediately drafted a circular. The following month, black Alabamians on a list supplied by Washington began receiving the Council's circular urging that they stand against the new suffrage legislation. It asked them to read the new constitution, pay their poll tax, and make certain that they registered to vote at the proper time. The pamphlet also stressed the importance of voting intelligently and presented a detailed analysis of the suffrage provisions of the Alabama constitution.[1]

The initial response to the circular was favorable. In early February, Lawson wrote to Washington informing him that many individuals had written back with requests for more circulars or specifying other individuals who should receive the document. In addition, some of the recipients had requested more information about the work of the Council and asked how to get involved.[2]

While Washington and the Council were laying the seeds for a test case in Alabama, the organization also continued to work on its Louisiana suit and concurrently maintained its general fight against the continuous onset of

Jim Crow. In early February, Jesse Lawson spoke to the Bethel and Literary and Historical Association at the Metropolitan AME Church urging the audience to support the Council and its Louisiana suit. He also discussed his enthusiasm about the Crumpacker Bill and Pennsylvania Representative Edward Morrell's proposed bill that would make segregated railroad cars illegal. According to Lawson, both pieces of legislation were encouraging, and he explained that the Council's Legal and Legislative Bureau was working to publically demonstrate the Council's support for the bills.

The following month, the District of Columbia branch of the Council held a meeting. Initially that meeting focused on the progress of the Louisiana case, then the discussion turned toward the expansion of railroad segregation throughout the South and Edward Morrell's proposed bill. Following a number of speeches on the matter, the group passed a series of resolutions expressing frustration with the "Jim Crow car law now in vogue in several of the Southern States [which] is aimed at the civil rights of . . . colored people."[3] Noting that Morrell's bill was a just measure, the group called on all "patriotic and fair-minded citizens" to join the organization in petitioning Congress to pass the legislation immediately.[4] Directly after the session, Jesse Lawson and George H. White published a broadside containing the Council's resolution, attached it to a petition, and sent it to various supporters throughout the country.

With all this activity occurring, Frederick McGhee, a long-time supporter of the League and the Council and a member of the Legal Bureau, began organizing the group's annual convention scheduled to take place in his hometown of St. Paul, Minnesota. In March, McGhee began conversing with Tuskegee in an attempt to assure Booker T. Washington's participation. McGhee considered the Wizard's presence at the meeting to be essential. In his initial correspondence with Washington's secretary, Emmett Scott, McGhee urged him to make sure that Washington attended the convention as "our people will feel bad if we do not get him."[5] A week later, McGhee wrote to Washington directly, "expressing deep anxiety concerning [his] coming to the meeting."[6] The Council needed to organize a sound and "defined course," McGhee informed Washington, and "it is not a flattery when I say that we can't safely adopt that policy without your judgment and advise."[7]

* * *

While McGhee and his colleagues in Minnesota were coordinating the St. Paul convention, his associates in the Council's Legal and Legislative Bureau continued its demanding yet continuous multipronged process of lobbying the federal government in the hopes of gaining favorable legislation to end the discriminatory actions of the southern states. In Washington, D.C., for instance, the Council met at the Nineteenth Street Baptist Church. Speakers at the event included the Reverends Walter H. Brooks of the Nineteenth Street Baptist and George Lee of the Vermont Ave. Baptist Church and Jesse Lawson, who in an address entitled "Southern Disenfranchisement and Jim Crow Cars" told his audience that a number of people from throughout the country had returned petitions urging Congress to pass Edward Morrell's bill.[8] Additionally, he announced that he and other members of the Council had been asked to appear before the House Committee on Labor's hearing to discuss Harvey I. Irwin's Bill no. 12940.[9]

For several months, Lawson and a group of his colleagues had been urging Congress to create a commission to inquire into the condition of African Americans throughout the United States. After a series of meetings with various congressmen, the Council activists had succeeded in persuading Kentucky Representative Harvey I. Irwin to introduce a bill creating a commission. Under the proposed bill, the U.S. president would create a five-member Freedmen's Inquiry Commission, the purpose of which was "to make a comprehensive investigation of the people of the Negro race in the United States, their educational progress, and the best means of promoting harmony between the races."[10] The commission would have the power to call on persons and request papers as well as hold hearings.

Shortly after the bill had been introduced and referred to the House Committee on Labor, Jesse Lawson was called before the committee to speak for the Council and its support for the legislation.[11] While Lawson was testifying before the committee, other members of the organization were discussing the matter with the executive branch of the government. Sometime during Lawson's days on Capitol Hill, AME bishop Abraham Grant, Daniel Murray, and other Council members called on President Roosevelt to discuss the Irwin Bill and garner his support for signing it if it passed through Congress.[12]

With this multipronged lobby effort, the Council was using any means possible to try to gain passage of favorable legislation to end the discriminatory acts of the southern states. This activity gave members of the Council, especially in the District of Columbia, the sense that the organization was on the verge of achieving success to back up its rhetoric. The Washington, D.C. branch hoped to energize the community at the group's monthly meeting with the story of its lobbying activity. At the gathering, Bishop Grant and Jesse Lawson informed the audience of their recent activities and called for the community to "rally as one man against the infamous discrimination that are sapping the life-blood of the race's citizenship." Grant forcibly argued that African Americans had to "agitate, educate, and cooperate until every right guaranteed [them] is accorded and that what we have shall be safe-guarded as a precious treasure." Furthermore, he warned the government of the danger of selling out the nation's principles for gold. Following Grant and Lawson's addresses, Reverend Walter H. Brooks echoed many of his colleague's sentiments as he spoke and then lifted a collection of over fifty dollars for the Council's legal activities.[13]

The week after the D.C. meeting, Lawson returned to Capitol Hill and presented additional arguments for the Irwin Bill. At the second hearing, Lawson once more reiterated the necessity for the passage of the legislation to end racial friction. He believed that racial antagonism, at its highest since the Civil War, was caused by ignorance on both sides of the color line, and that the facts presented by such a commission would enable the American people to adopt a different attitude toward one another.

Lawson also began to be a bit more forceful with the House Committee on Labor. He argued that despite African Americans being tax-paying citizens, they no longer had a representative in Congress or anywhere in the federal government. According to Lawson, the commission was necessary because it would accord the black population some sort of voice in shaping national policies.[14]

Several weeks after Lawson's second testimony, Ohio Representative William Robert Warnock, chairman of the Committee, submitted a report in favor of the measure.[15] Days later, however, a number of congressmen submitted a minority report opposing the Irwin Bill on basic principles. They did not believe that a special commission was necessary since the inquiry "into the educational, moral, and industrial development of the race [was] now being carried on by at least three bureaus of Government—the Census Office, the Bureau of Education, and the Bureau of Labor." Moreover, they saw no reason for a special commission "to investigate the general condition of the negro race any more than that such a commission should be created for the purpose of investigating the general condition of every other race of people who are citizens of the Republic." Finally, the congressmen did not think that the black population should get any exclusive commission to give them special footing. African Americans, in the eyes of the dissenting congressmen, needed to work out their destiny without the aid of the federal government.[16]

The real fear of the Democratic congressmen had little to do with the spending of federal funds for an unnecessary commission. Rather, the representatives believed that the inquiry by such a commission might be used in justifying Indiana Representative Edgar D. Crumpacker's measure, which was still stuck in Congress. They argued it was their belief "that the commission would spend more of its time making the investigations which Mr. Crumpacker desired to impose on a committee of this House than it would investigate any other subject which it might consider under the broad terms of the bill." The Democratic congressmen further claimed that the supporters of the bill meant to promote harmony between the races by "turning over to the domination of Negroes the governments of every county, city, and State in the United States in which they are numerically in the majority." Therefore, they concluded, "the logical and inevitable effect of the passage of this bill will be to weaken the powers of the several states, and will lead to an unwarranted interference in their affairs by the federal government."[17]

The Democratic congressmen seemed to have been most persuasive in their argument. Despite the testimony by Lawson and the support of a number of Committee members, no action was taken when the bill was referred back to the House. Notwithstanding the lack of congressional action, the Council persisted in its efforts to lobby for the passage of positive legislation as well as to promote the legal activities of the organization. While his Legal Bureau colleague was testifying before the House Committee on Labor, Frederick McGhee was on a fund-raising tour of the Midwest. At his various engagements he spoke of the group's legal challenges against suffrage laws sweeping the South and outlined the arguments the legal team would present before the Supreme Court once the case was brought before it.[18]

With the momentum experienced by Lawson's testimony and McGhee's speaking tour, Council members sought to quickly push forward onto other lobbying efforts and legal activities. First on the docket was another trip to Capital Hill for Lawson and a few of his D.C. colleagues, this time to testify before the House Committee on Interstate and Foreign Commerce.[19] In preparation for the hearings, Daniel Murray drew up an amendment to the Interstate Commerce Law that would have made discrimination related to interstate travel a crime.[20] Murray and other Council supporters wanted the Committee to pass the Morrell Bill, but since that seemed unlikely, the Congressional

Librarian drew up a strong amendment that would virtually accomplish a similar purpose as the proposed bill. According to the Murray amendment, a person who violated the "rights, privileges and immunities of passengers traveling on . . . any mode of convenyance [sic], engaged in Interstate communication or commerce" could be fined up to five thousand dollars or be imprisoned for up to six years.[21] Armed with this amendment, Lawson and three Council colleagues appeared before the committee on May 9. 1902.

Jesse Lawson was the first to testify. He explained to the committee that he and his colleagues represented about nine million citizens of the country: citizens whose rights were becoming more of a farce every day, which was the reality while the "friends" of black people were in control of the government.[22] He asserted that there was great interest in the Morrell Bill throughout the nation as demonstrated by the large number of petitions that had been returned to the Council and forwarded to the House, and he proposed that the House pass the measure. Additionally, he urged the committee to consider the proposed Murray amendment to the Interstate Commerce Law.[23]

After reading the amendment into the record, Lawson stepped down to allow ex-North Carolina representative George H. White to enter his own testimony to his former colleagues. White, a bit more forceful than Lawson, called on the committee to pass the legislation and amend the existing law. The discriminatory practices of the South, he argued, were a violation of the rights of African American citizens and existed for no reason other than as a "badge of caste, of degradation, of humiliation."[24] Furthermore, he opined, the committee and Congress had to step in because the federal and state courts practically excluded blacks from justice when they asserted their rights and protested Jim Crow discrimination.[25]

Next to address the committee was Reverend Walter H. Brooks, whose testimony injected a strong degree of sarcasm into the hearings. Reverend Brooks carefully made clear to the committee that he understood why whites had set up the Jim Crow car system. As he explained, the Jim Crow car was "always nearest to the engine of all the passenger coaches, so that in case of any serious accident the black man, who is the best prepared to meet his God, will be the first to reach heaven, or if he survives the last to extricate himself from the debris of the wreck."[26] On a more serious note, Brooks explained to the congressmen that the laws were unjust because blacks purchased the same price ticket as their white neighbors, yet failed to secure like accommodations. As did White, Brooks commented on the degradation associated with segregation of interstate travel and warned the committee that whatever degraded blacks "in the long run [would] degrade" the nation as a whole.[27]

Following Reverend Brooks came the testimony of the final Council member to speak before the committee, Cyrus Fields Adams, Council secretary and brother of the St. Paul *Appeal* editor John Quincy Adams. In his remarks, Adams argued that the Jim Crow laws did not work because there were a number of African Americans who slipped through the cracks and passed for white. To support his position, he cited South Carolina Senator Benjamin Tillman's comment that if his state had made the designation of a white person stronger than "one-eighth Negro blood" he would lose "400 families in his district who claimed to be white people."[28]

Adams's remarks hit the committee like a ton of bricks as the members could not fathom their system of racial apartheid being circumvented with such ease. In disbelief, the committee chairman asked Adams, "Do you claim that anywhere in the South a man who has negro blood in him is classed as a white man?"[29] Adams replied in the affirmative, but when asked to name individuals, he became reluctant. However, after Jesse Lawson piped in and named former Louisiana senator Randall L. Gibson and former secretary of state of the Confederacy, Judah P. Benjamin as examples of individuals he had heard were of mixed descent, the Council secretary gained confidence and dropped the bomb by claiming that Alexander Hamilton was a black man who passed for white—according to the nation's definition. This remark sent the committee members into hysterics, but Adams's comment stood and his point was made. The congressmen then asked numerous questions of the Council members as they tried to grasp the concept that there were African Americans walking around in the white world on a daily basis.

Once Adams completed his testimony, Lawson rose again and closed the hearings by urging the committee to amend the current interstate commerce law. He then for a second time offered the Murray amendment and insisted that any change not only insist "upon an equivalent of right, equal accommodation, but . . . upon identical accommodations and identical rights as American citizens."[30] Adams quickly reiterated Lawson's point, stating that the Council "will not accept any bill that speaks of separate and equal accommodations!"[31]

The testimony of Lawson and his colleagues before the House Committee on Interstate and Foreign Commerce is an excellent example of how the Council used multiple angles to try to accomplish one of its goals: the end of discriminatory segregation laws. For months, Council representatives throughout the country gave a number of addresses on the issue to try to inform the community about the important legislation. In conjunction with this activity, the organization collected signatures on petitions in support of Morrell's bill, and by the time of the hearings twenty-five petitions with more than 1,500 signatures had been submitted to the Committee. Then the Council's Legal and Legislative Bureau made sure that Council members had a voice in the hearings to present their argument about the unjust separate coach laws spreading throughout the nation's rail system. Thus, the Council was operating on multiple fronts to try to compel the federal government to pass legislation that would end or at least curtail the spread of Jim Crow.

* * *

Following the hearings there was such a buzz about the Council members' testimony that Edward Cooper republished the Murray amendment and called on supporters to read it and write their congressmen urging for it to be incorporated in the pending batch of revisions to the Interstate Commerce law.[32] Bishop Walters also seized the moment to go on a speaking tour to drum up support for the Council and its upcoming convention and to highlight the activities of his colleagues on Capitol Hill as well as some local activities of the organization.

The local activities that Walters was prompting included the actions of the Rochester, New York branch, who had become involved in a regional civil rights case. George W. Burkes had sued a local white bootblack for refusing to shine Burkes's shoes. In the initial trial, Burkes secured a positive verdict and received $113.40 in damages. The defendant, however, appealed the case and gained a reversal of the verdict in a higher court on the basis that a shoe-polishing stand maintained on public property did not constitute a place of public accommodation. Upon the decision of the high court, the local Council jumped into the case and began working on an appeal.[33]

The action by the Council in the Burke case and before the congressional committees along with its work on the Louisiana and Alabama cases was keeping the organization in the original vision of Fortune's Afro-American League. The Council was a national civil rights organization, based in local and state branches throughout the country, contesting discrimination in the local, state, and federal courts as well as the hall of Congress and the office of the U.S. president. The activities of the organization were laying the foundation for the style of African American legal activism that would continue to be central to the struggle for civil and political equality throughout the twentieth century.

While the organization was engaging in all of this positive activity and momentum however, many throughout the nation were still not aware of the organization's activities. As had plagued the group since its inception, the black press failed to give it any extensive coverage. Things had not improved since Jesse Lawson complained to Booker T. Washington in 1900. For example, outside Washington, D.C., no major paper reported on the activities of the Council's Legal and Legislative Bureau activities in early 1902.

To make matters worse, some members of the Council, as well as a number of people outside the organization who were aware of the actions of the Council, believed that the group was not militant enough, and that in some way Washington was the reason for its "conservatism." Since the last national convention, a growing anti-Washington camp had begun to materialize throughout the nation. In the years since Washington's Atlanta address and his ascendancy to the position of chief mediator between North and South, black and white, the racial situation had not improved. Since 1895, African Americans had made progress in industrial and higher education and had continued to accumulate property, but at the same time their overall condition in America had stagnated or even deteriorated. Lynchings continued to average nearly one hundred yearly, southern states continued to strip blacks of their franchise, and states and communities throughout the country expanded the process of both de facto and de jure segregation.[34]

During this period, Washington continued to articulate a public position of extreme conservatism. The Tuskegeean often portrayed members of his race as criminals and upheld the stereotypical characteristics of blacks as being stupid, lazy, and immoral. Furthermore, he espoused the idea that African Americans were childlike, inferior human beings who were unfit for higher civilization and should be grateful for scraps tossed their way by whites.[35] Especially problematic was that many whites began employing Washington's rhetoric as the rationale for their own anti-black positions.[36]

In addition to Washington's public position of accommodation, many in the black community were becoming frustrated with his lack of criticism of President Theodore Roosevelt. Shortly after an assassin's bullet struck William McKinley and Roosevelt became president, the new executive officer invited Washington to dinner at the White House. Many in the community believed that relations with the new president would be better than they had been under McKinley. Despite the initial hopes, however, Roosevelt quickly showed that he was not a true friend of the community especially where southern politics were concerned. He rapidly began replacing African American officeholders with lily-white southerners, and showed no indication that he would step in to prevent the South from removing blacks from politics by disfranchisement.[37] Moreover, in his first national address he failed to mention and condemn the continuation of mob law.

Many within the community blamed Washington for Roosevelt's failures. Leading this crowd were the editors of the *Boston Guardian*, William Monroe Trotter and George W. Forbes.[38] Trotter, born in 1872, was the son of James Monroe Trotter, a veteran of the 55th Massachusetts regiment. He graduated from Harvard in 1895 and was the institution's first black elected to Phi Beta Kappa. After graduation he briefly worked in real estate in the Boston region, but as he was frustrated with the continued deterioration of race relations throughout the county, he became increasingly engaged in civil rights activities and finally started the *Guardian* in 1901. As the newspaper was founded on a platform of embracing civil rights and opposing segregation under any circumstances, the *Guardian*'s editors believed that Washington's policies and influence were an "unmitigated evil sapping the will" of blacks "and their white friends to resist second-class status."[39] As the editors proclaimed in the paper's inaugural issue, "We have come to protest forever against being proscribed or shut off in any caste from equal rights with other citizens, and shall remain forever on the firing line at any and all times in defense of such rights."[40]

In the spring of 1902, in addition to their articles in the *Guardian*, Trotter and Forbes began leading discussion groups, which debated the issues of political rights, the necessity of higher education, and the policies of Washington.[41] Additionally, a number of black newspapers— especially the *Chicago Broad Ax* and the *Washington Bee*—began echoing the sentiments of the *Guardian* and republished many of the Boston paper's articles and editorials within their own pages. With this spread of anti-Washington sentiment, Trotter felt strong enough to bring a challenge to the Tuskegee Wizard before the Afro-American Council, the nation's only black civil rights organization and a group that had for its entire existence attempted to balance itself between the "conservative" position of Washington and the necessity of legal and political agitation for equality.

As the Council's fourth annual convention approached, the stage was thereby set for a dramatic event. Since it was still uncertain whether Washington would actually attend the meeting, many individuals wrote to the

Tuskegee principal alerting him as to what was about to take place in the Twin Cities. Writing to Washington in late June, Frederick McGhee warned that "there will probably be some effort made to have some expression go forth from the Council with respect to your position as given in your speeches and lectures."[42] More directly, Peter J. Smith, a Boston confidant of Washington, informed him that the *Guardian* "folks are going to use every effort to have the Afro-American Council denounce you . . . and from what Bishop Walters says they have their plans pretty well in hand and propose to capture the convention."[43] With this information in hand, Washington decided to appear at the convention—even though his name no longer appeared on the program.[44]

In 1902, the Afro-American Council was the only national civil rights organization fighting to stop the growth of the Jim Crow system and to bring an end to the reign of racial terror that permeated the South. As the organization convened for its fourth annual convention, however, it was clear that despite the Council's best efforts to establish itself as a group that was openly agitating for black rights no matter who belonged to the organization, pressure was building within the group, and many were going to use the Council as the setting to fight out larger ideological struggles. Opening the convention, Bishop Walters attempted to put those issues to rest as he outlined the group's recent activities: the testimony of the Legal and Legislative Bureau before the House Committees in support of the Irwin and Morrell Bills and the action of the group in the Louisiana and Alabama suffrage test cases.[45] These activities, according to Walters, demonstrated that the Council was standing firm in demanding the rights guaranteed to African Americans as citizens of the country, and that all race-loving individuals should throw their weight behind the organization.

Following Walters the two firebrands T. Thomas Fortune and William Pledger echoed the president's argument, but were also more assertive in their tone and the acknowledgement of the necessity of Afro-America to protect itself, especially the women of the community. The Afro-American's "first duty," said Fortune, "is to protect himself and his . . . sisters from scoundrels like Benjamin R. Tillman." Pledger, a bit more forceful, declared that no man who fails to look after his family and see that they are cared for "can expect to hold the respect of the community. . . . If the colored man wants the white man to respect colored womanhood, he must be ready to defend, with his life if necessary, the woman under his own roof."[46]

With the Council's leadership asserting the central position of the organization in the fight for civil rights and the general well-being of the African American community, the remainder of the speakers over the next couple of days, including among others Josephine Silone Yates, W. E. B. Du Bois, James H. Guy, Isaiah B. Scott, and Josephine St. Pierre Ruffin, outlined the diverse activities of the organization for the moral, economic, and political development of the community. On these issues there was no disagreement from the delegates on the approach or activity of the Council.[47] The issue that concerned many was who was going to lead the struggle, or more important, who was going to be the face of the organization.

This issue came to the forefront when William Pledger called for the Nominating Committee to make its report on the second day of the convention. Since the report was actually scheduled for the following day, the change in procedure caused confusion on the floor—all the more so since as many were unaware of the change in schedule, not all of the delegates were present.[48] Moving forward however, the committee recommended that T. Thomas Fortune, who was the Executive Committee director, and President Bishop Alexander Walters switch posts, and that Cyrus Field Adams, Fannie B. Williams, Frederick McGhee, Martha Webster, and Richard W. Thompson assume the posts of secretary, corresponding secretary, financial secretary, assistant secretary, and treasurer respectively.[49] The delegates present approved the report, but apparently did not believe that its implementation would take place until the full delegation voted again the following day during the official time slot for the Nominating Committee's report. This, however, did not occur. With the delegates' approval of the report, Fortune became president of the Council.[50]

The turning over of the gavel to Fortune set off a firestorm of protest. Many were concerned about Fortune's role as the leader of the organization due to his independent nature. Furthermore, despite his tremendous talent, Fortune had suffered a number of setbacks in recent years both in his health and pocketbook. Some believed he would use his position as Council president to promote his own advancement. Additionally, despite the occasional disagreements between Fortune and Washington, they remained close confidants, and many thought Washington would essentially run the organization.[51]

Despite the fact that his colleague Frederick McGhee in some ways had called for this very maneuver, Harry Shepard of St. Paul launched the first attack. He did not think that Fortune was fit to lead the organization because his knack for alienating people was "driving our friends from us."[52] Moreover, he believed that the move to elect Fortune and the other officers was illegal, and to place them in their seats without a full vote "means the extermination of the Council as a body."[53] In addition to Shepard, a number of delegates, including Ida B. Wells-Barnett, expressed anger over the election, but the appointments remained unchanged.[54]

After this initial salvo of protests, the convention continued as delegates heard a number of addresses, including an elegant speech, "The Undoing of the Fourteenth and Fifteenth Amendments," delivered by attorney James H. Guy of Topeka, Kansas; Jesse Lawson's report on the Legal and Legislative Bureau's activity; and finally that of Booker T. Washington, who had been placed on the program after George H. White for personal reasons had failed to arrive in St. Paul.[55] Relying on his typical themes, the Tuskegeean discussed the great progress that the race had made since emancipation, emphasizing the importance of coalitions with white allies in the North and South and dispelling the notion of there being any great strain between the races. Washington did not mention the elections, but in a possible attempt to dispel some of the doubts expressed at the convention, did try to assure the audience that the Council was the organization demonstrating an ability to work for the betterment of the race from multiple fronts. He was "glad to see in this Council so many evidences of the fact that we can sink the individual preferences and differences and unite in the one direction of uplifting the race."[56]

With a slap at his critics he declared that

> such organizations as this should bear in mind that we cannot by ourselves help forward the race in any large degree by fault-finding, condemning or criticizing . . . We must bear in mind that destruction is easy, construction is difficult; but it is by construction that the ability of a race is measured rather than by destruction or fault-finding. The object lesson of the negro succeeding in every committee as a wealthy prosperous farmer, or as a contractor, or as a banker or as a cotton-mill owner, worth scores of mere abstract speeches.[57]

Washington told his audience that they must not become discouraged, but assured them that he did not "underestimate the seriousness of the tremendous problem that [was] before the race."[58]

However, Washington's address did nothing to suppress the anger that many Council members felt surrounding the elections. The following morning,

Frederick McGhee, the man who had asked Washington to come to St. Paul and take control of the organization and one of the individuals who had warned him about the pending move to censure by the *Guardian* crowd, opened the final day's session with a legal challenge of the election. After much heated discussion, McGhee's challenge was dismissed. But Nelson Crews, a court clerk in Kansas City and the Council's director of the Immigration Bureau, reignited the embers of the debate when he announced that he would accept the election of the "alleged Council president" as long as the Council elected officers fairly in the future.[59]

After a lively discussion initiated by Crews's comment concerning Fortune's "alleged" status, Crews demanded that the new officers resign so that the group could hold new elections.[60] The delegates voted against the motion, but passed an amendment to the Council's constitution. Designed by Isaiah B. Scott, editor of the *Southwestern Christian Advocate*, the amendment called for the organization to hold its elections by vote on the second day of the annual convention.[61] Though this solution provided a clear process for future conventions, some were frustrated with the Council's unwillingness to address the actions that had already taken place, and both Nelson Crews and Ida B. Wells-Barnett resigned from their positions on the Immigration and Anti-Lynching Bureaus respectively.[62]

Even with all the frustration concerning the election of officers and the resignation of Crews and Wells-Barnett, the Council concluded its convention with a strong Address to the Nation. In many ways it was of the general sort that people had come to expect from the organization, and one that few of the delegates would have a problem fully endorsing. It discussed the general condition of the race, emphasized the industrial and higher educational progress of the community, denounced lynching and mob violence, and vowed to continue to struggle against the growing disfranchisement legislation. Finally, the Address harshly criticized Congress, which the Council saw as refusing to exercise its power under the U.S. Constitution to enact new legislation to end suffrage abuses and vigilante violence. As a whole, the Address stated the purpose of the Council and outlined its central position in agitating for black rights.[63]

* * *

Despite the strength of the Council's Address to the Nation and the general sentiment that the group was an organization that was fighting for the rights of African Americans, many of the delegates left the Twin Cities with mixed feelings about what had occurred during the meeting. Ultimately, what was evident was that the Council, as the main vehicle for African American protest, would continue to be the battleground for both personality and ideological struggles. A vast majority of the delegates left St. Paul vowing to put frustrations aside and press forward with the policies and activities set forth by the organization. Others, however, were not ready to so be silent concerning the actions of the Council, and began to air their disappointments and opinions in the nation's black press.

William Monroe Trotter, who never made it to St. Paul for the convention, was the first to openly criticize the organization. According to the *Guardian* editor, the election of T. Thomas Fortune to the presidency of the Council was "as bad a calamity as could have befallen the organization."[64] Trotter did not see Fortune as the independent person that he had been even five years previously. The *Age* editor, according to Trotter, was "a politician . . . a perpetual office seeker," and his presidency "marks the overt entrance of the Council into the business of office seeking" and politics. The editor railed President Roosevelt for replacing "colored Republicans with white Democrats" and the Council for remaining passive to "the elimination of the Negro from Southern politics." Trotter further charged that the Council discredited itself by "springing Booker T. Washington on the convention," and believed that the Tuskegee principal was in reality the president of the organization in "everything except name." Finally, the voice of the *Guardian* asserted that individuals such as W. E. B. Du Bois were no longer to be trusted since they failed to act against Washington's coup. Trotter asserted, "we might have expected Prof. Du Bois to have stood in the breach here, but like all the others who are trying to get into the band wagon of the Tuskegeean, he is no longer to be relied upon."[65]

A number of African American newspapers republished Trotter's comments with favorable editorial remarks of their own. Julius Taylor of the *Chicago Broad Ax* concurred with Trotter's assessment, but added that Fortune, although a prominent voice in the past, had more recently "spent much of his time endeavoring to drink up all the cheap fighting whiskey in the United States."[66] W. Calvin Chase in his *Washington Bee* dubbed the fourth annual convention "a measly failure." He believed that the Council "may be able to do something for the race," but he did not think that it would accomplish anything in "its present organized capacity and while under the spell of its present manipulator."[67]

Furthermore, Edward Cooper of the *Colored American*, previously a great advocate of the organization, dubbed the St. Paul meeting "a roaring farce." Cooper noted that, among others, Walters, Fortune, Pledger, White, and Lawson "deserved the thanks of the race for their laudable efforts to build up a powerful instrument for racial protection." He asserted, however, that "candid observers must admit that the outlook for one reason and another, does not seem promising for finite results under the aegis of the Afro-American Council."[68] Cooper then asked his readers to suggest where the race should go from there.

Although an unquestionable undercurrent of frustration existed with the Council and its activities, there were still many within the community and the organization who supported the work of the group. As *Richmond Planet* editor John Mitchell noted, "The recent meeting of the National Afro-American Council seems to have been anything but a success if we judge by the unfavorable reports,"[69] but such reports were very unfortunate at this time, since the race is "in the midst of anarchistic conditions." Mitchell came to the defense of his old friend as he asserted that T. Thomas Fortune thoroughly understood the situation and that the "machinery of the organization [was] not in untried or inexperienced hands." He urged the community to come together under the Council, the only national organization working to turn the tide of oppression. "Let us hope that peace will prevail and harmony reign in the camps of our oppressed and down-trodden people," Mitchell asserted. "Let us be for ourselves and then others will be for us."[70] Harry Smith of the *Cleveland Gazette* concurred: "T. Thomas Fortune can make an acceptable president [and] we stand ready to do all in our power to help him."[71]

Amid the convention fallout, Washington, Fortune, and their allies moved to secure leadership of the organization and push forth the Council's agenda. In a letter to Washington, Emmett Scott noted "it is not hard for you to understand that we control the Council."[72] Fortune impressed upon Washington the importance of the group moving quickly and asserting its prominence in the community. "The race everywhere is discontented and ready to respond to political action more than any sort," he noted. The task was to harness this discontent and create a "political machine."[73]

Not all of Washington's allies, however, were pleased with the events in St. Paul. As noted above, Frederick McGhee, who requested that Washington come and take over the organization, led the opposition on the final day of the meeting. McGhee's colleague on the Council's Legal Bureau Jesse Lawson also expressed in his August 6, 1902 correspondence to the Tuskegee principal his disappointment with the manner with which the elections had taken place. "Corruption wins not more than honesty," he wrote, "and the Afro-American Council will never gain the confidence, and co-operation of the people until it abandons its corrupt methods of doing things." Central to Lawson's aggravation was people being unaware of Washington's true involvement in the Council's activity. Despite this frustration, however, the tireless Council activist hoped that the group would accomplish something in the near future that would achieve harmony within the race. Lawson then turned his attention to the Louisiana case and told Washington that he was sending him the latest details as reported by attorneys Romain and Birney.[74]

As the smoke was clearing after the St. Paul convention, John Mitchell, Jr., again addressed the issues that concerned many. After reflecting on the meeting, he published a well- thought out piece, "Shall the Wheels of Race Agitation Be Stopped?." In his essay, he tried to put the agitation to rest by focusing the community's attention on the pertinent issues.[75] Mitchell was dismayed that the leaders of the race were "fiddling while Rome is burning," but stated that the elections having been held on any other day than publicized was just a mistake, not a crime.[76] The loss of Ida B. Wells-Barnett was a great blow to the organization, he believed, but emphasized once more that Fortune was an "able and brilliant agitator." That fact, combined with Walters's leadership of the Executive Committee, assured Mitchell that the organization was in "safe hands."[77] Since "the men who created [the Council] are still in charge," he asserted, "we cannot believe that its power for good has disappeared or its mission ended." The "wheels of agitation," he argued, could not stop as long as "men are being burned at the stake," nor as long as "this race-agitation had done much good in imbuing a few Afro-Americans with manhood."[78]

Mitchell assured his readers that the Council was still alive and was moving forward toward its goals of ensuring African Americans their rights under the Constitution. Whether Mitchell's article succeeded in soothing the nerves of Council members is unknown. But he made a persuasive argument that until there was evidence that the organization was working contrary to its stated objectives, African Americans should continue to support the group.

Following the convention and its fallout, the Council tried to set the quarrels aside and return to its core objective: the struggle for the social, civil, and political rights of the African American community. The main focus at this time was the Councils continued work in Louisiana and Alabama as well as its federal lobbying efforts. Of particular interest for a number of members of the organization was the lack of attention President Roosevelt was paying the southern "lily-white" movement. Many Council members, particularly those in the District of Columbia branch, believed that the organization needed to take the initiative in getting Roosevelt to make his position on the issue public. The leaders of the branch wrote to Bishop Walters suggesting a meeting with the president. The bishop agreed and wrote to Roosevelt requesting a conference. Walters and the Council wanted reassurances from the president that he would lend the power of his office to bring the lily-whites to a halt.[79] Though Roosevelt was not keen on the idea, he conceded to an interview after Booker T. Washington encouraged the meeting.[80] After a short meeting in October, the Council delegation felt confident that they had convinced the president to unequivocally state that he was against lily-whitism and that he would take action on the issue.[81] Despite their success, however, Walters and his committee did receive some criticism from the black community for their action.

Curiously, Council president T. Thomas Fortune was frustrated with Walters for having called on Roosevelt. He claimed that because the organization had not convened an Executive Committee meeting to endorse the action, the three individuals did not have the right to appear before the president as Council representatives. In an open letter, Fortune claimed that Walters's visit had "muddled waters" and created bad publicity for the Council.[82] Fortune's comments are peculiar given that the Washington branch of the Council had always acted as a lobbying group for the organization,. As a general rule, the local branch was supposed to observe the government and act whenever necessary.

Expressing an understanding of the history of the District of Columbia's Council branch, Edward Cooper of the *Colored American* responded to Fortune's criticism. In an editorial he accused Fortune of splitting hairs and argued that Walters, like any citizen black or white, had a right to call on the president. Furthermore, given the bishop's current and past status on the Council, the editor believed Walters had acted within his rights. Finally, in the light of the recent events of the St. Paul convention, Cooper asserted that the Council had a magnificent opportunity to do great things for the race, but warned that if it continued to "quarrel over trifles while the vessel is between the awful rocks of Scylla and Charybdis," the group would fail.[83]

The internal quarrels, however, continued. Walters and Fortune were both frustrated with the work of George White and Jesse Lawson in the Legal Bureau and were finding it "utterly impossible to work harmoniously." Walters wrote to Washington urging him to assist in creating a "steering committee" that would give a hand to the Bureau in directing its activities.[84] To make matters pricklier, as the year came to a close Fortune was accorded the political appointment that so many in St. Paul believed was chief among his objectives. His new assignment as Special Immigrant Agent of the Treasury Department was to study race, labor, and trade conditions in Hawaii and the Philippines.[85] Though pleased with Fortune's personal success, many called upon him to relinquish the Council presidency. As Harry Smith of the *Cleveland Gazette* asserted, "if our friend, T. Thomas Fortune, is the man we think he is, he will promptly resign from the presidency of the organization."[86]

Fortune did not resign, but instead put the ball in the court of Council supporters. On the eve of his departure he published a call to all members of the Council to stand up and push ahead with the organization's agenda. "My last thought" before he departed for the "far East," he proclaimed, "is the Afro-American Council and its future well-being, as the one organization of the race whose primal objective is the preservation and proper defense of the civil and political rights of the Afro-American people." The Council's greatest failure, he asserted, was that it had no substantial organization. Like the Afro-American League, "the masses of the people do not belong to it or support it with their sympathy and money." Moreover, Fortune explained, the Council's annual conventions were "composed of fraternal delegates and delegates representing business and professional interests." From the "adjournment of one annual convention to the assembling of another," the Council was little more than the Executive Committee.[87]

In light of the situation, Fortune authorized an amendment to the constitution allowing the formation of local Councils with only ten members. He believed that this alteration would allow five hundred branches to report to the Louisville convention in July 1903. Fortune also specifically called upon women to organize their separate branches. He especially believed that the women would come together in branches for the betterment of the race and push the organization closer to his goal of five hundred branches.[88] In addition to the publication of this call, Fortune hired secretary Cyrus Field Adams to compile the minutes of the Council's annual conventions and publish them in pamphlet form along with a reprint of Fortune's call so as to stimulate interest in the organization's activities.[89]

As Fortune was issuing his call, the Council was beginning to expand its activities challenging the disfranchisement of black voters in the South. In particular, Bishop Walters was invited to speak on behalf of the Council in Richmond, Virginia, in support of a local challenge to that state's new constitution. Similar to actions taken in the Carolinas, Alabama, and Louisiana,

Virginia with the endorsement of a "popularly" elected convention had rewritten its constitution to disfranchise its African American citizens. With the support of local attorney and Council member James H. Hayes, and white New York lawyer John S. Wise, Richmond blacks organized the Virginia Industrial League and initiated a suit challenging the state constitution.[90]

While speaking in Richmond, Walters took the opportunity to firmly assert the position of the Council as an organization standing up for black rights. "We are contending under God for legal rights, every one of them, and we should boldly say so," Walters declared to a large audience. "The duty of the hour was to press this fight, and every Negro who has a drop of manly blood in his veins will come up to the colors." "God removed President McKinley," he asserted, adding "God was displeased and called him home." Walters called for African Americans to "stand together" and fight, focusing on the long-standing goal of insisting that "southern representation in congress [be] cut down." Finally he told the audience to pressure President Roosevelt. Despite lack of support from the Republican Party and some actions of the sitting president, Walters believed that God had raised Roosevelt up to replace McKinley and improve the situation.[91]

Keeping up the pressure and rhetoric, the Council's Executive Committee gathered for its annual meeting at the Lincoln Congregational Church in Washington, D.C., on January 26, 1903. Bishop Walters and William A. Pledger, the Council's first vice president, who was placed in charge of the organization in Fortune's absence, led the charge calling for the Council to forcefully defend the rights of the community. Following their addresses, the Committee heard a series of lectures by individuals such as Reverend George Lee, John C. Dancy, P. B. S. Pinchback, and James H. Hayes on the actions that African Americans and the Council needed to take in order to gain full political and civil rights. In addition, the group confirmed Louisville as the location of the upcoming annual convention and announced that disfranchisement would be the central theme of the discussion. Finally, the Committee called on Congress to act on the measures already the subject of congressional debate, especially the Irwin Bill.[92]

When they returned from D.C. feeling invigorated following the energetic and motivational meeting, especially in the light of the manner in which the St. Paul meeting had been concluded, many of the committee members were surprised by the press the Council was receiving. At the Monday evening session, James H. Hayes delivered an address on "The Disfranchisement of the Afro-Americans of Virginia and What They Have Done to Resist It."[93] "I am not an anarchist," Hayes affirmed, "I do not believe in killing anybody, yet if necessary stand up for your rights and be killed for standing up. But the oppressing, shooting, murdering, burning, lynching, jim crowing, and disenfranchising of the Negro will breed a race of Nat Turners, and the sword and torch will devastate and dissolve the South."[94] The white press construed Hayes's comment as an endorsement of violence, claiming that he had called for African Americans to resist the new constitutions with "sword and torch in hand."[95]

While such a comment was not too far removed from Hayes's embrace of a self-defense strategy, violence was not what he was calling for. Actively pushing the cause of his Virginian colleagues through the state courts, Hayes viewed the legal process as the current path for African Americans to pursue. However, in spite of his belief in legal strategies, he refused to retract any of his comments.

After the *Post* published its version of the proceedings, a number of African Americans moved to denounce Hayes's remarks, calling them unfortunate. Cooper of the *Colored American* believed that Hayes was now "discredited and despised as a senseless agitator" and predicted that he had destroyed his "utility" in the Virginia suits.[96] Bishop Charles S. Smith of Louisiana added that advising "the Negro to have recourse to the torch and the sword to right fancied wrongs inflicted by whites upon them is but ravings of a crank or a manic."[97]

In response, members of the Council's Executive Committee tried to introduce a bit of damage control. Cyrus Fields Adams, assistant register of the treasury and Council secretary, distanced himself from Hayes's comments by claiming that he was not in attendance during the lecture. At the same time, however, he assured the readers of his open letter that the attorney's comments were exaggerated and taken out of context.[98] Bishop Walters and William Pledger issued a statement claiming that the "public press of the country contained inaccurate and misleading reports," and called for the northern press to publish the resolutions and statements.[99]

At the other end of the spectrum, a handful in the African American community fully defended Hayes's remarks and called for black America to stand behind his sentiments. Persistent critic of the Council William Calvin Chase praised the organization and Hayes, claiming that the Council had "at last concluded that it is best to have men connected with it." He further noted that "there was not a dissenting voice at the conclusion of Mr. Hayes' speech," asserting that the "big cowards" came out when a few whites spoke out against the meeting.[100] John E. Bruce, the ardent nationalist and free-lance journalist, also supported Hayes, claiming that his comments were no more "incendiary or revolutionary than Patrick Henry's impassioned 'Give me liberty or give me death.'" Hayes's fellow Virginian John Mitchell, Jr., a passionate journalist who was never afraid of a fight, likewise came to Hayes's defense, affirming that he stood beside Hayes and was willing to go to the other world with him if the "bullies and braggarts" came after the fighter.[101]

While all this public maneuvering was taking place, Hayes himself was drawn into the fight by a group of white Louisianans. Shortly after his "infamous" Council speech, he received a letter from the New Orleans Coliseum Club stating that "The Coliseum Club will give Nigger Hayes $3,000 and transportation if he will deliver in our hall his speech verbatim as delivered before the Afro-American Council in Washington on the 26th."[102] Hayes responded that he would go to New Orleans any time the Coliseum Club designated, at his own expense, and deliver the same speech.[103]

In the midst of the Hayes controversy, the national office of the Council issued its first call for the Louisville convention in July, reiterating that the convention would focus on disfranchisement issues and that the group was raising funds for the legal struggles in which it was currently involved.[104] In addition, Cyrus Field Adams, the group's secretary, published an article, "The Afro-American Council: The Story of its Organization—What It Stands For—Its Personnel," in the *Colored American Magazine*.[105] Besides providing an overview of the Council's creation, listing the existing membership, and reprinting the Executive Committee's recent address to the country, Adams continued to distance himself from Hayes's Washington, D.C. speech. Asserting the position and objective of the Council, Adams attempted to connect the organization and its plight to that of the fading moral-suasion tradition of the abolitionist movement rather than the "John Brownism" of Hayes.

"There is a battle to be fought," Adams explained, "not with swords and guns on bloody fields, but in the arena of public opinion. The combat must be fiercely contested with skill, courage and intelligence, and must be persistently waged until a healthy public sentiment is created which will accord to every race his God-given rights." To accomplish this goal, Adams affirmed that the Council needed to have "the cordial and cheerful support and encouragement of every manly Afro-American who has faith in the power of numbers and efficacy of intelligent organization, and who has pride in his race and the courage 'to do all that doth become a man' to give it character [and] respectability."[106]

Despite Adams's assurance that the Council was not interested in the "sword and the torch," James Hayes's remarks continued to exact support from other Council members and supporters. A short time after the publication of Adams's article, Hayes was invited by Albany, New York Council members to speak on the organization and his fight in Virginia. At the event, the audience raised a collection to aid Hayes in the Virginia legal struggle.[107]

* * *

The Hayes incident, while in many ways blown out of proportion, continued to highlight the small fractures that persistently expanded in the months after the Council's St. Paul convention. The Council continued to be the only national organization fighting for the rights of the black community, but its umbrella was becoming too small to cover all its members and their ideologies. This reality would become even more apparent as the year progressed.

While the Council was dealing with the fallout from the Hayes incident and also preparing for its annual convention, W. E. B. Du Bois, who was a member of the Council but one who was beginning to look beyond the organization, published his famous *The Souls of Black Folk.* William Edward Burghardt Du Bois was born in Great Barrington, Massachusetts, in 1868. His mother, Mary Silvina Burghardt Du Bois, and her relatives raised him in this small western Massachusetts town "by a golden river and in the shadow of two great hills."[108] He received a college preparatory education in the local schools, and at the age of thirteen began writing articles for T. Thomas Fortune's *New York Globe.* After graduation, in 1884, he attended Fisk University where he earned his first degree in 1888. During the same year, Du Bois enrolled in Harvard where he earned his second degree in philosophy, then studied as a graduate in Berlin before becoming the first African American to earn a doctorate (in history) from Harvard in 1895. After receiving his degrees, the young scholar took a position at Wilberforce, the a research position at the University of Pennsylvania, and later settled in Atlanta, Georgia, at Atlanta University to teach sociology and direct a series of empirical studies of the social, economic, cultural, and institutional lives of southern African Americans. While in Atlanta, Du Bois became involved in the activities of the Afro-American Council and quickly made a name for himself through a series of publications as a keen scholar of America's "race problem."

Souls, a collection of poignant essays on race, labor, and culture, had nothing directly to do with the Council, but would have ramifications within the organization. During the first few years of the century, Du Bois's racial philosophy had been in transition. It was during this period that he placed increased emphasis on the importance of higher education, the "Talented Tenth," and the franchise.[109] By the time *The Souls of Black Folk* was published, Du Bois's position had been transformed to the degree that he found it necessary to differentiate between Booker T. Washington's racial philosophy and the path he and a growing "radical" core of black intellectuals sought to travel.

Most black leaders of the period agreed with the ideology of self-help and racial solidarity and on the need for economic and moral development. A wedge, however, was growing between them regarding the immediate importance of the ballot and the relative emphasis placed on industrial and higher education. Such differences had been evident in the ideological struggles taking place within the Afro-American Council since the beginning of the new century, but it was Du Bois's publication of *Souls*, and in particular the essay, "Of Booker T. Washington and Others," that gave the confrontation legs.

In that essay, the Atlanta professor first paid tribute to Washington, especially his ability to bring about a compromise between northern, southern, and African American interests. In doing so, however, Du Bois warned that Washington might have sold short the interests of blacks. Washington's "programme," noted Du Bois, practically accepted the "alleged inferiority of the Negro race," allowed economic factors "completely to overshadow the higher aims of life," and preached a "submission of prejudice."[110] Du Bois furthermore claimed that Washington's speeches were filled with "dangerous half-truth[s] that the South" used to justify its present attitudes toward African Americans—for example, the position that the future of black Americans depended primarily on their own efforts rather than fair treatment by white Americans.[111]

The two intellectuals drew inspiration for their varying beliefs from two opposing New England models. Du Bois was attracted to the educational philosophy of the New England school system, the apex being his alma mater, Harvard. Washington, on the other hand, looked to another model: one symbolized by business-minded craftiness of the northern capitalists. Du Bois noted, however, that Washington's position evoked a triple paradox. First, Washington wished to make the mass of black folk property owners, but publicly downplayed the need for rights, without which property could not be depended upon. Washington also advocated the development of black self-respect through augmentation of skills, but his advice that black folk submit to injustice undermined self-respect by such means. Third, the Wizard's advocacy of common and industrial schooling while depreciating higher education contradicted the reality that blacks who taught in the common and industrial schools would have to receive their own training at institutions of higher learning.[112] In addition to this paradox, Du Bois noted that while not a "direct result of Mr. Washington's teachings," disfranchisement, greater segregation, increased lynchings, and the withdrawal of aid for black higher education had all followed his ascendancy to power.[113]

Du Bois's criticism of Washington's model of leadership constituted a warning shot. It demonstrated frustration, but not full-blown contention. Du Bois himself was displeased with Washington's course of action, but he had not come to the point of parting ways with the Wizard of Tuskegee. The community acknowledged the great significance of the publication of *Souls*. Many recognized, as did the *Indianapolis World* and the *Chicago Broad Ax*, that Washington had been praised as well as condemned by the Atlanta professor. But rather than predicting the arrival of a great apocalyptic moment between the two growing schools of thought, the community believed that *Souls* would educate the public and lead to a greater, more successful approach—a hybrid strategy, perhaps—to solving the race problem. As Julius Taylor of the *Chicago Broad Ax* explained, *Souls* "should find its way into every home black and white, throughout this land for ultimately it will revolutionize public sentiment on the 'Race Problem,' and spur the Negro on to greater or more heroic efforts to come into the full possession of his civil and his political rights."[114]

At the time of the publication of Du Bois's collection of essays, the Alabama suffrage case for which Washington and the Council had laid the groundwork some sixteen months prior had reached the Supreme Court. Few who praised Du Bois's criticism of Washington's public position of franchise restriction could have possibly imagined that the Tuskegeean was so involved in the suit. As Washington and Jesse Lawson had feared in early 1902, African Americans were denied the right to register in Alabama. They were generally told to come back after January 1903, which disqualified them from voting.

In 1902, the group had instituted a suit on behalf of Jackson W. Giles of Montgomery, Alabama, and the Colored Men's Suffrage Association of Alabama. Giles, an educated man who worked as a janitor in the Montgomery post office, was chosen as the one to attempt to register in the Middle District. After being twice denied, the group took the case to court. Unlike the Louisiana suit, however, an African American lawyer became chief counsel in the case. In his report to the Financial Committee of the organization,

Frederick McGhee had accused Washington of having "too much faith in white men" and proclaimed that the Council would no longer support the case unless African American lawyers were brought on to handle the proceedings.[115] Despite his being the major contributor to the suit, and possibly in response to mounting criticisms of his actions at the St. Paul convention, Washington acceded to the Council's demand and retained New York lawyer Wilford Smith.[116] The case was brought before the Supreme Court on appeal after the circuit court failed to render a positive verdict. Smith based the case on the guaranties of the Fifteenth Amendment and Section 1979 of the revised statutes of the United States. The Reconstruction Amendment guaranteed Giles the right to vote regardless of his skin color, and the statute protected citizens from restrictions being placed on their rights and held those responsible for such restrictions liable to the party injured.[117]

At the hearing the plaintiff's legal team labeled the Alabama election law a "fraud" and asked the Supreme Court to declare it so. It also requested that the Court force the board to register Giles as a voter. The court, in a cunning move, asked why, if the law was fraudulent, they should add yet another name to its fraudulent list. The jurists claimed that it was "impractical" to order a state to inscribe African Americans on its voting rolls: "If the conspiracy and intent exist, a name on a piece of paper will not defeat them." Finally, the Court ruled that it had no jurisdiction in the suit, claiming instead that it was a political issue and therefore belonged before Congress, which under the House could reduce the representation of those states that practiced disfranchisement.[118]

As Harry Smith of the *Cleveland Gazette* observed, the "ghost of [Justice] Rodger B. Taney" must have turned "green with envy" in the face of the Court's shrewd move to once again place African Americans outside the law's protection.[119] Despite the devastating blow, however, no one associated with the case or the Council folded his or her tent regarding pursuit of the legal strategy. In his coverage of the decision, Smith noted that the Council's suit testing the constitutionality of the Louisiana suffrage amendment was pending before the Court and that the Council-supported case in Virginia was on its way. Moreover, Giles and his supporters, including Washington, vowed to continue their fight against the Alabama legislation.[120]

Indeed, the anti-suffrage laws were looming as the overshadowing issue of the upcoming Louisville convention. As Council national organizer George W. Clinton remarked in an interview with the *Colored American* in late April 1903, suffrage was expected to dominate the discussions as individuals who had hitherto taken an indifferent approach were now aroused, especially in the light of the Supreme Court's decision in the Alabama case. Clinton believed that the Council would cry out for a "cool-headed" yet "aggressive" effort that would "awaken public sentiment against the wrongs that are being done the Negro by the suffrage laws in the South." He did not foresee Congress agreeing to reduce the representation of those states that disfranchised their African American population. He believed that the only way to change the sentiment of congressional representatives was that a large turnout take place in Louisville and that the Afro-American Council, the country's only national civil rights organization, continued to grow. In contribution to this idea, Clinton had recently spoken in Mobile, Alabama; Pensacola, Florida; and Charlotte, North Carolina, to promote the Council's activities.[121]

Reverend Clinton and his Council colleagues were correct to focus on the issue of the franchise. As the Council's Louisville convention approached, the suffrage issue dominated discussion throughout the black community. In early spring, Boston lawyer Archibald Grimké, William Monroe Trotter, and others called for a suffrage conference to meet in the Northeast. On April 4, 1903, thirty-five African Americans from six New England states met in Boston's Parker Memorial Hall to discuss the history and importance of the franchise for African Americans.[122] Two months later the New England group joined forces with like-minded individuals and convened at the Bridge Street AME Church in Brooklyn, New York, for the first National Negro Suffrage Convention.[123]

At the convention two hundred delegates drawn from New England, New York, New Jersey, and Virginia attempted to outline an agenda that would agitate for the African American's social and political rights. William Monroe Trotter led the charge to institute resolutions condemning Booker T. Washington and the Republican Party. James H. Hayes, leader of the Virginia delegation, led the defeat of Trotter's condemnation of Washington. In the end, the convention passed a series of resolutions echoing the agenda of the Afro-American Council. The group also agreed on a slate of delegates—which included Trotter—to attend the Council's Louisville convention. The delegates pledged to bring before the Council questions of suffrage, higher education, civil rights, and methods of protest.[124]

The suffrage convention was a sign of what was happening throughout the country, particularly in the Northeast. During the first half of the year, anti-Washington sentiment had gathered steam. An increased number of individuals, including Trotter, Archibald Grimké, and Ida B. Wells-Barnett, began escalating their criticism of the Tuskegeean's public statements on political activities and his close relations with the Roosevelt administration. Several newspapers including the *Washington Bee*, the *Chicago Conservator*, the *Chicago Broad Ax*, and the *Cleveland Gazette* joined these critical voices as they too sharpened their attacks on the Wizard.[125]

Washington had tried to subvert both concerns with the publication of his position on suffrage in the *North American* magazine. Washington explained that he was for "universal, free suffrage," but believed that conditions in the South called for equally applied restrictions upon the franchise for a period of time. He asserted that laws that restricted the vote from one race and not the other were unjust and would ultimately retard the region as it encouraged blacks to "secure education and property" while at the same time encouraging whites to "remain in ignorance and poverty."[126]

The Tuskegee principal's statement did not quell the criticism. Although he had cleared up his position on the suffrage, an issue that he and others believed W. E. B. Du Bois had "badly misconstrued" in *Souls*, he did not demonstrate to the growing "radical" group that he was emphatically against restrictions placed upon black suffrage. Washington, always the politician, attempted to placate both sides, but succeeded mainly in assuring whites that he was not demanding the immediate franchise for African Americans throughout the South.[127] To make matters worse, Du Bois published an article in *Booklovers Magazine* where he implicitly labeled the Tuskegeean a political boss. Furthermore, the Atlanta professor took a few steps closer to the Trotterites as he, like increasing numbers among the anti-Washington crowd, strengthened his criticism of Washington and blamed him for the growing negative attitudes of whites in regard to the African American population.[128]

Not one to act whimsically, Washington did not hedge all of his bets on pacifying the Trotterites with his double-talk. As the Louisville convention approached, the Wizard acted in some ways exactly as Du Bois had pictured him as he finagled behind the scenes attempting to get his ducks in a row for the meeting. With T. Thomas Fortune in transit, secretary Cyrus Field Adams took the lead role in ensuring that Fortune would be reelected and that a sizable pro-Washington faction would be present at the convention.[129] Adams negotiated with individuals, encouraging them to attend, and tried to dissuade any and all who might seek the presidency—especially Bishop Walters and William Pledger—from challenging Fortune.[130]

At the same time, in an attempt to rally the troops behind the Council, Bishop Walters published a long detailed article in the *AME Church Review* concerning the issue of disfranchisement and the way to combat the continued passings throughout the South of unconstitutional legislation. As Walters noted, the Afro-American Council was formed to resist "disfranchisement to the bitter end." He averred that all African Americans should throw their weight and purse strings behind the group's work in the Louisiana and Alabama suffrage cases. Calling for the race to "put aside braggadocio and bitterness, and push [its] cause with prudence," he stressed that "In this struggle the watchword must be "NO SURRENDER."[131]

* * *

The stage was thereby set for the Louisville convention. Washington and his supporters had prepared themselves for the worst. The expanding group of Eastern "radicals" had organized a sizable delegation to attend the meeting under the auspices of the National Negro Suffrage League. On July 1, 1903, these forces as well as other more independent supporters of the Council met at the Odd Fellows Hall in Louisville for the organization's fifth annual conference.

The fireworks began almost immediately. According to reports, there arose some discrepancy over the seating of the delegates. From the beginning of the Council, an annual membership fee of five dollars had been levied on any delegate who wished to speak or vote at the convention. Members of the National Negro Suffrage League questioned the policy and called for some of its delegates to be seated without the full membership fee being paid. Representatives from both organizations moved their discussion off-site and negotiated an agreement, which included the possible appointment of the National Negro Suffrage League's leader, James H. Hayes, as national organizer of the Council.[132]

While the negotiations over the seating of delegates were being concluded, the Council's proceedings continued with speeches by, among others, Pratt Ennis of the Easter school and Bishop Walters. Walters attempted to direct the attention of the delegates to the task at hand. In his address, he recalled the origins of the organization, focusing on the burning of Sam Hose as the incident that led him to appeal to Fortune for the revival of the Afro-American League. Furthermore, he stressed that the reasons for calling for the revival of the League had not become any less pressing than they were in 1898. He pressed upon the audience the necessity to continue fighting the South's attempts to strip the black population of its citizenship rights and strengthen segregation. Finally, Walters asserted that the Council was the only national organization fighting these actions, and called on everyone to put aside their differences and lend their support to the civil rights group.

Despite his best efforts however, tempers still raged, and a few hours after the bishop spoke, a slight disagreement surfaced concerning the issue of the election of officers. Frederick McGhee, who had become increasingly anti-Washington since the St. Paul convention, questioned the choice of time slot allocated for the election of officers. In McGhee's opinion, the election of officers should have taken place at once, but the organization had scheduled the elections for the following day. Fearing a duplication of the previous year's election irregularities, McGhee demanded an explanation.

Attempting to explain the basis for the decision to hold elections on the second day of the convention, Secretary Cyrus Adams read the provision of the Council's constitution describing the election procedures. After the fallout from the election catastrophe of the St. Paul convention, the group had adopted the Scott amendment calling for the organization to hold its elections by vote on the second day of the annual convention.[133] Despite the fact that the group was adhering to its constitutional provisions, McGhee was not satisfied and tried to filibuster the proceedings. The conference chairman ruled the St. Paul delegate off the floor and proceeded with the session, which included president Fortune's address to the organization.[134] Overall the remainder of the day's proceedings stayed calm with the delegates selecting committees and later hearing addresses from, among others, Wilford Smith, who informed the audience of the progress of the Alabama case.[135]

Tensions however would not remain in check for long; in fact, the following day's sessions were the most explosive of the Council's existence. The "radical" faction, led by William Monroe Trotter and William Ferris, had been bruised in the fight over the seating of the delegates and suffered further tattering in debates carried on in the Committee on Resolutions. At the committee meeting, Trotter, Ferris, and their Boston compatriot George Forbes had tried to secure the passage of a number of resolutions that the committee subsequently vetoed. The first of these advocated the position that agitation was the only path to securing civil and political rights. Both the second and the third resolutions condemned the southern states for their disfranchising of the black population and drastically reducing funding for African American education. Despite the vetoes concerning the wording of these resolutions, the Boston delegation did manage to secure a resolution calling on President Roosevelt to urge the reduction of southern representation.[136] Notwithstanding the passage of these particular resolutions, the Boston contingent attributed the vetoes to the manipulation of Booker T. Washington, and held that only his public racial philosophy was going to be supported by the organization.

With these actions on their minds, the delegates came to the convention on Thursday, July 2 and found a picture of Washington and his school on display on the stage. When Fortune rose to introduce the local artist who had painted the portrait, William Ferris stood to protest the display and was not mollified until a picture of an individual representing higher education and manhood rights was given similar recognition on the stage. After a four-minute speech, which "turned the convention upside down," the angered delegates calmed down when a picture of the late Reverend Joseph C. Price, the first president of the Afro-American League, was placed on the stage opposite to Washington.[137]

The bedlam did not subside for long, however. When it came time for the Committee on Nominations to make its report for the Council officers, there was an attempt by a number of older members, including Frederick McGhee and the representatives of the National Negro Suffrage League, to prevent the organization from electing the same slate of officers as the previous year. Many of these delegates, however, had lost their vote since they had failed to pay the full five-dollar membership fee. Therefore, despite an able fight on the part of a number of "radicals," the Committee's nominations stood and T. Thomas Fortune was again elected president of the Council. William Pledger assumed the post of first vice president, Cyrus Adams of secretary, and Bishop Walters as head of the Executive Committee. That Committee included William Monroe Trotter as the Massachusetts representative.[138]

Still steaming, the delegates met again later that evening at McCauley Theater for what could have been another boisterous session. Tempers were kept in check however, and over three thousand calm people heard addresses by Walters, William H. Lewis, Fortune, and Washington. For his part, Washington called for interracial cooperation and for African Americans to remain calm. The time period, he indicated, required the "ripest thought and sober judgment," not extreme actions and the creation of a mob. He insisted, however, that he was not "asking that the Negro act the coward" for "we are not cowards."[139] In addition to the duties of the African American population, he called on the nation to stand up for its principles and to administer justice for all: "there should be meted out equal justice to the black man and the white man whether it relates to citizenship, the protection of property, the right to labor, or the protection of human life. Whenever the nation forgets or is tempted to forget, this basic principle, the whole fabric of government for both the white and the black man is weakened."[140]

Though Washington's speech was well received and none of the delegates tried to speak out against the Tuskegee principal during the session, tempers were still running high as the delegates assembled for their final session on Friday morning. Following addresses by, among others, William M. Farmer of St. Louis and C. H. Phillips of Tennessee, the Committee of Resolutions presented its report and provided the spark that ignited yet another firestorm. The resolutions dealt with topics familiar to Council supporters—mob law, suffrage, and unfair judgment of the race by its "criminal class"—but there was no strong pressure on Roosevelt to provide assistance. William Monroe Trotter, who had requested such a resolution in the meeting of the Committee, protested; in a long speech he put the conference on notice that he and his northern colleagues were "not going to sit supinely by and let the whites put their feet on our necks."[141] In addition to the call for a resolution urging Roosevelt to encourage Congress to restrict southern representation, Trotter also insisted that the other resolutions he had advocated for during the Committee meeting be adopted. Following the ruckus, the delegation agreed to add the resolution on Roosevelt, but declined to add any of the other Trotter decrees.[142]

After again putting out a bushfire started by Trotter, the Council concluded its combative fifth annual convention with the reading and publication of its much less controversial Address to the Nation. Echoing Washington's speech the previous evening, the address appealed to the nation's sense of justice. The Council felt that the great majority of the country believed in the "spirit of freedom and exact justice to all," and speaking as representatives of "10,000,000 American citizens of African descent," the group presented its case to the American people. African Americans had not come to America of their own choosing, the Council noted, but since they were here, they demanded to be treated fairly and with equal justice. The organization asked the nation to judge African Americans on an individual basis—not as one monolithic group. It would not be fair to judge the white race "by those of their number who have assassinated Presidents or been guilty of treason or have betrayed and murdered innocent women."[143] Furthermore, the address spoke out against the continuation of mob violence and called on President Roosevelt to act on that issue as well as the continued disfranchisement of black citizens in the South. Finally, the group's address emphasized the necessity to organize protests on the issue of the franchise, since those "who first started in ostensibly to disenfranchise the ignorant Negro had been broadened and strengthened. Their purpose now includes almost all Negroes."[144]

Despite the confrontational nature of the convention, the Afro-American Council concluded its fifth national meeting still as *the* major national organization fighting the South's attempts to strip the African American population of its citizenship and to strengthen segregation. In the wake of the convention, however, the attention was not placed on this fact or on the actions of the organization in its various civil rights activities. Instead, the reaction of the press to the meeting focused on the dissent expressed by the Boston and Northeastern crowd and the manner in which Booker T. Washington's forces controlled the proceedings. As John Thompson of the *Iowa State Bystander* noted, "the difference arose over a factional fight between the industrial, the higher education and the political divisions in the gathering, but the industrials won out."[145] The *Washington Bee*, edited by the Council's constant critic W. Calvin Chase, was much harsher, calling the meeting a "fraud." Chase, furthermore, appealed to the Council to step aside and allow a new force to assemble: "let this apologist for a council be abolished and let New England make a move to organize a council of the people, by the people and for the people."[146] Confirming the sentiments of Chase, William Monroe Trotter remarked, "nothing is clearer than that all agitating for the Negro's political rights must be carried on by northern men in the north."[147]

Not everyone agreed with the sentiments voiced by the two newspapers. John E. Bruce, for instance, believed that the Council's joining forces with the National Negro Suffrage Association and its naming of James H. Hayes as National Organizer demonstrated its commitment to agitating for the rights of African Americans. He concluded that "the marriage of these two organizations will result beneficially to all and it is sincerely hoped that the sticklers and kickers and the fault finders will make way for the MAN of action, who has been selected to recruit the mass of the race into an effective and potent organization which shall represent the Negroes highest ideals and conceptions of good and useful citizenship."[148]

The "kickers and fault finders" as well as supporters shared equal blame as far as one letter writer to the *Colored American* was concerned. Many problems encountered at the Louisville convention, according to Selah, the author of the letter, centered on egos. It is "a sad fact that too many of our so-called leaders have developed the 'cerebral elephantiasis,'" he argued, "and like

Andrew Johnson, the unlamented, they probably entered the Council chamber each chanting:"

Sing, oh my muse, the lofty theme,
Sing I and Mine and Me!
We are lofty individuals now,
Way down in Tennessee.[149]

Egos or not, the obvious victors of the Council convention were Washington and his lieutenants. Trotter concluded "there was never a clearer case of being dominated by one man."[150] Washington's triumph, however, was not the problem. The few who knew of his work behind the scenes did not believe that the Council's activities would come to a halt. The Washington-"controlled" organization had lent full support to the Louisiana, Alabama, and Virginia suits over the preceding year, and there was no direct evidence that such support would be withdrawn anytime soon. But a basic and enduring problem, of course, was lack of funds. Ironically because Trotter and a large contingent of the National Negro Suffrage Association had declined to pay the full membership fee at the conference, they had actually placed the organization in a more precarious situation than had the Tuskegeean over the previous year.

* * *

What was apparent in the fallout from the Louisville convention was that the coalition, which had been carefully cultivated by the Afro-American Council over the first five years of its existence, was quickly rotting. The failure of the organization to secure any legal victories had disappointed many. Supporters both within and without the organization were calling for more sweeping agitation. An ongoing weakness was the Council's lack of publication of its efforts. Nowhere, for example, had the organization commented on its support for the Jackson Giles cases.[151] Moreover, the group's willingness to allow Washington to so publicly dominate the 1902 and 1903 conventions allowed anti-Washington factions to unfairly depict the organization as little more than a puppet representing Washington's unpopular southern strategy. These lapses led to fissures within the coalition. Many had become disillusioned with Washington's strategy and disturbed by the recent court decisions, and they became more focused on direct agitation to achieve their goals. The seriousness of the situation became apparent right after the Louisville convention as pro-and anti-Washington forces prepared for a fight.

Prior to the Council convention, Washington had agreed to speak to the Boston branch of the National Negro Business League in late July 1903. As this came only a few weeks after the bumpy convention, tensions remained high. After having returned to their homes following the Council meeting, William Monroe Trotter and his colleagues kept the criticisms flowing. With Washington's scheduled appearance in "freedom's birthplace" now confirmed, Trotter and his forces planned to seek revenge for their setbacks at Louisville and force the Tuskegee principal to respond to his critics.[152]

In anticipation of a spectacular event, the AME Zion Church on Columbus Avenue was overflowing on the night of the Business League meeting. William H. Lewis, assistant district attorney of Boston, presided over the event, and after a brief prayer by Reverend James H. McMullen, he opened the meeting with a short speech and the introduction of T. Thomas Fortune. In his introductory remarks, Lewis made a cursory reference to Washington, prompting a series of hisses and catcalls from the audience. Lewis then warned the audience not to disrupt the proceedings.[153]

When the audience calmed down, Fortune rose to address the assembly. After a few opening remarks, the *Age* editor made a comment concerning the behavior of the Boston delegates at the Council convention and drew an immediate round of hisses, heckles, and hoots. Following a long pause, Fortune continued, but was disrupted by Granville Martin, a close associate of Trotter and the *Guardian*, who had been accused by Fortune and others of leading the opening round of catcalls. After some disturbance, including the removal of Martin and the dispersal of pepper powder, Fortune, coughing and wheezing, concluded his address. The performance of Harry Burleigh, a noted New York singer, followed.[154]

The audience was calmed by Burleigh's singing, and warmed to an address by local lawyer and early Council supporter Edward Everett Brown. But this proved to be the proverbial calm before the storm. After Brown's speech and a brief collection, Lewis rose to introduce Washington. In his introduction, Lewis urged the audience to keep the peace and hear the Tuskegeean out. Trouble immediately began, however, as Washington chose to begin his address with an "old mule" tale. This questionable beginning instantly caused the Trotterites to curl their lips and shout down the Sage of Tuskegee. Leading the charge, Martin rose and shouted a series of questions at the speaker. Washington's failure to address Martin's concerns drew even more criticism from the audience. Lewis, desperate to regain order, called for the police to again remove Martin from the floor.

With order finally restored after nearly fifteen minutes, Washington returned to the podium. Upon resuming his address, he was again interrupted by a series of questions from Trotter and Moses Newsome. William Lewis again tried to restore order and called upon the police not only to remove Trotter but to arrest him. After the removal of Trotter and a few of his cohorts, the meeting, much of which had moved out into the streets, reconvened and Washington concluded his address.[155]

After what became known as the Boston Riot, blame was cast from all sides. Supporters of Washington criticized the Trotterites while the growing community of radicals assailed Washington and his Tuskegee Machine. The white community expressed astonishment that any group of African Americans would so significantly disagree with Washington's philosophy.

The truth, of course, was that Washington's racial philosophy had now come under serious attack, with the Boston Riot offering but a single example of the growing post-Louisville criticism. Around the time of the Boston events, for example, attorney and state representative Edward H. Morris of Chicago appeared before an Odd Fellows meeting shortly after John Metcalf was lynched by a mob in Danville, Illinois. Similar to criticisms waged by Du Bois and others, Morris accused Washington of being responsible for much of the racial violence in the country. In an interview with the *Chicago Inter Ocean*, the former League and Council member repeated his claims: "Booker T. Washington is largely responsible for the lynching in this country." "The learned doctor," asserted Morris, "teaches the colored people that they are only fit to fill menial positions . . . by the same pernicious doctrine whites come to regard the colored people as inferiors." As a result, when an African American is accused of a crime, whites think that there ought to be some different system to try him. And if "he is lynched they think, Oh, he's only a Negro. It doesn't count much. There is even a rag-time tune," Morris proclaimed, "Mr. Coon, you're all right in your place."[156]

Morris was not the only one to step up the criticism of Washington's public portrayal of African Americans. In seeking to explain one of the underlying reasons for the Boston Riot, Reverend John Hagin of Fall River, Massachusetts, asserted "through [Washington's] influence the predominant sentiment in the United States is against higher education for the Negro." Reverend Hagin further stated that there was "growing sentiment in favor of disenfranchisement in the country" and increased belief "that the Negro is little above an animal." "Mr. Washington's incessant criticisms, slurs, and jokes about the race," argued Hagin "have gotten such wide publicity that a stereotype is formed." He then asserted that "all" of these actions by Washington was "to get money for Tuskegee."[157]

With such sentiment growing throughout the country, the Afro-American Council found itself in a difficult position. While the leadership of the organization believed that Washington was in accordance with the group's legal strategy, in order to maintain its credibility in the community the Council needed to push its agenda forward and attempt to demonstrate that the accommodating stance with which Washington was publicly identified was not the philosophy that guided the organization. Such a move was especially needed as the Suffrage League gained a foothold on the East Coast.

Even though the National Negro Suffrage League had merged with the Council at the national level, the League's local branches remained autonomous. In the post-Boston Riot era, the New England Suffrage League attracted an onrush of interest. Viewed as martyrs, Trotter and his colleagues seized the moment at the group's first meeting following the Boston affair. In early September 1903, the League met in Boston at Trotter's home on Sawyer Avenue. With approximately fifty individuals in attendance, the group made plans to issue strong repudiations of Washington and his leadership. In its deliberations, the participants asserted their commitment to suffrage as the only remedy to the race problem. They criticized the Republican Party for its failure to stand against the actions of southern Democrats. Lastly, they called upon Roosevelt to "dispense of Booker T. Washington" as the race's "political spokesman," declaring that the president had caused "irreparable harm to our race by acknowledging Booker T. Washington as the dictator of the American Negroes."[158]

The growth of the Suffrage League posed a threat to the influence of the Afro-American Council, but, as some observers suggested, only in the sense that the group was organizing those opposed to Washington's participation in the Council. William T. Menard noted that the new organization was gaining a numerical advantage in some cities because of its adverse position to Washington's methods. But the Suffrage League's actual success was impossible to predict due to its philosophy being similar to that of other kindred institutions. The mission of the group, according to Menard, was to protect the rights of African Americans and to pressure the political parties to provide a guarantee of these rights. This was, as Menard explained, "the identical mission of the Afro-American Council."[159] Shortly after the Boston Suffrage League meeting, the Council's Legal and Legislative Bureau moved to demonstrate that the new groups were, as Menard argued, alternative formations based on the same principles.

In early September the Council's legal team—J. Madison Vance, director; Frederick McGhee, vice director; and Jesse Lawson, financial secretary—announced that they were taking on the case of Reverend Henry Theodore Johnson, editor of the *Christian Recorder*. Johnson had sued the Pullman Company for refusing to serve him breakfast in one of the company's dining cars. The initial case was tried in the federal courts of New Jersey without Council support. At the conclusion of the trial, the jury returned a verdict in favor of the plaintiff. Despite the jury's decision, however, the judge set aside the verdict and awarded judgment to the Pullman Company.

A few months after the ruling, the Council intervened and began forging plans to carry the case on appeal to the U.S. Supreme Court. The Council's legal team believed it had three solid points upon which it could argue the case. First, the Fourteenth Amendment clearly indicated that African Americans had rights equal to those of whites, especially in all matters of interstate commerce. Second, the Supreme Court ruling against the Civil Rights Act of 1875 dealt with acts in several states, not interstate commerce. Finally, the "Common Law of England" was still "the law of this country so as not altered or emended by the statutes or decisions of the courts" so that it could not be denied that a "public caterer of refreshments," for example, would be "bound by common law to treat all citizens alike without discrimination so long as they are willing and able to pay." In assuming the burden of carrying the case to the Supreme Court, the Council wished to ensure that the judge's initial ruling would not stand as the rule of the land, leaving African Americans with no recourse to securing justice.

Bureau leaders also assured their readers that they had not "relaxed one fractional part of [their] zeal and effort to bring before the Supreme Court . . . the cases involving the suffrage question and that the decision in the Giles' case" had not weakened their resolve. The Council, the legal team asserted, was pushing forward with the Louisiana case, and believed that when it reached the Supreme Court the Council would receive a favorable decision. Plans were also afoot to secure legislation from the Fifty-Eighth Congress that would ensure enforcement of all aspects of the Fourteenth Amendment. Finally, Council lawyers appealed to their "brothers throughout the country" to assist in securing the necessary funds to carry these cases through the courts, warning that a "failure to respond now may mean a prolonged disregard of both our political and civil rights."[160]

Meanwhile, work on the Giles case in Alabama was temporarily shelved when attorney Wilford Smith's attention was drawn to another legal matter. Following the Boston affair, Washington had retained the New York-based lawyer to prepare a case against Trotter and his associates. In early October 1903, Trotter and Granville Martin were found guilty of disturbing the peace and sentenced to thirty days in jail.[161]

Washington's vindictiveness angered many within the community and led to further polarization. Trotter and Martin had become martyrs in the eyes of many race men and women. After the two men were released from jail, nearly two hundred people attended a liberation day celebration in Boston.[162] Washington, understanding that trouble was afoot, moved quickly to cut off his critics and set to work on other issues that would hopefully head off criticism of his racial philosophy and the activities of the Afro-American Council.

First on the list was the Alabama suffrage case. Directly after the Boston trial, attorney Smith returned to work on the second Jackson Giles case. In mid-October he filed a motion to advance the hearing of the case by the Supreme Court. He also attempted to combine the Giles case with that of Dan Rogers—a suit challenging the exclusion of African Americans from juries.[163] Montgomery County officials resisted the joinder of the suits. The Supreme Court agreed with the county and also declined another Smith motion to have the hearing date moved forward.[164]

Despite his failure to persuade the Court to reschedule the hearing, Smith received praise for his legal work in Alabama. Few were aware, however, that the Giles case was associated with Washington or the Council. Hence, the Alabama cases did little to nothing to stem the criticism of either the man or the organization. To make matters worse, the National Negro Suffrage League continued to obtain converts. In Washington, D.C., the organization was gaining strength under the leadership of Reverend Sylvester L. Corruthers and W. Calvin Chase.[165] The group, moreover, was preparing to hold a national convention in the District in mid-December 1903.[166] Understanding the threat, Washington wrote to Fortune in early November warning that they would have to "watch all these movements carefully during the next year in order to keep control of the Afro-American Council."[167]

However, the Suffrage League's actual threat to the Afro-American Council may have been more imaginary than real. Many individuals including, among others, Bishop Walters, Reverend Corruthers, and James H. Hayes held memberships in both organizations. The organizations were also linked at the national level with Hayes being the president of the Suffrage League and the national director of the Council. Furthermore, the major strategies of the groups were virtually the same. Such facts, however, were of little solace to Fortune and Washington; both believed that the Suffrage League might provide Trotter and his cohorts a national platform to challenge the Council and Washington's racial leadership.

In a move to consolidate its political clout and attempt to head off any steam the National Negro Suffrage League might gain from its upcoming convention, at its Washington, D.C. meeting on December 10, 1903, the Council's Executive Committee sought to make some drastic changes. At Bishop Walters's suggestion, the Committee moved to strike the long-standing nonpartisan clause from the organization's constitution.[168] In an election year, the Committee believed that the involvement in partisan political activity would be helpful in pressuring the Republican Party to stand against the growing Jim Crow system.[169]

In his address, Walters avowed that the race had a friend in Roosevelt. He was also convinced, however, that the Republican Party as a whole required nudging when it came to supporting African Americans. In his earlier *Church Review* article, the bishop had pointed out that the black population could count significant numbers of Republican voters in certain states. If used correctly, such power could pressure the party to stand by the rights of African Americans. For instance, Walters noted that in Republican Pennsylvania there were 51,688 black voters; in Massachusetts, 10,456; in New Jersey, 21,474; in New York, 31, 425; and in Ohio, 31,425.[170] Given the strength of these numbers, Walters demanded that the black voters force the Grand Old Party to wake up.

Members of the Council's Executive Committee agreed, and moved to make the Council a more partisan organization. The Committee offered three reasons for striking out the clause that had undermined the group up to that moment. First, it believed that partisan action would be necessary to rid the country of "Jim Crow, the convict-lease system, and unfair election laws, all enacted by the Democratic party of the South." Second, Committee members believed it was their duty to secure the nomination and reelection of Theodore Roosevelt, whom they regarded in a cautiously optimistic light: the president had recently spoken out against lynching and had pushed for the confirmation of William Crum in South Carolina, two issues that the Council had been supporting. They in no way assumed that the president was a racial equalitarian, but he was taking steps that his predecessors had failed to do. In the turbulent world of early twentieth-century America, the Council believed that it could not afford any other candidate to take office. Finally, the Executive Committee believed that it could influence the Republican Party's platform and candidates through "united action." Such action and influence would come from the Council if it were to transform its status from a nonpartisan to a partisan organization.[171]

T. Thomas Fortune believed that the Council's new political stand would "revolutionize the personnel of the organization while strengthening the objects of the organization."[172] Many members hoped the Council's becoming a more politically active organization would subvert the calls for the development of a new civil rights organization.

In the shadow of the Council's meeting, the National Negro Suffrage League converged on Washington, D.C. for its national convention. Calling upon every African American who owned a home or an acre of land to attend the convention, Suffrage League president James H. Hayes vowed to "make a death effort to see if we [could] use the political power we hold, and which fast passing from us, to save our people."[173] The League's strength lay in New England, Virginia, New Jersey, Pennsylvania, and Washington, D.C. Like the Afro-American Council conventions, however, representatives from nearly every state of the Union attended the meeting, which had nearly 250 delegates.

When the delegates met at the Metropolitan Baptist Church, the rhetoric was at times forceful—especially when it came to the issue of deciding whether to endorse President Roosevelt. In the end, the new civil rights organization did not endorse the president's reelection, but instead (as the Council had done numerous times) appealed to the Roosevelt Administration to use its power to introduce legislation supportive to the African American struggle. Also, like the Council, the Suffrage League asked its members to cast their votes "in Congressional districts in the North . . . as a means of enforcing recognition of their rights of the race." Finally, it called suffragists to reconvene in Chicago the day before the National Republican Convention in order to endorse a plank demanding full black suffrage everywhere and ask that Republicans insert it into their platform.[174]

In the end the National Negro Suffrage League, at this point, was little more than a mirror image of the Afro-American Council. The resolutions of the new civil rights organization echoed those of the Council. Moreover, the New England delegation, led by Trotter, was unable to put an anti-Washington stamp on the group. The Suffrage League's presence, however, challenged the Council as the Suffrage League was an alternative race organization striving for the social and political rights of African Americans.

As the Council concluded its fifth year of existence, it faced greater challenges than before, but was considering significant adjustments in order to remain viable. The group continued to press forward with its legal strategy, with some within the organization believing that its new, partisan activity would aid in that struggle. The group, however, had to gain more support and show some results for its years of activity if it was going to remain the nation's leading civil rights organization. Moreover, in light of growing anti-Washington, anti-Tuskegee sentiments within the African American community, the group was pressed to demonstrate that the pervasive influence of the Tuskegee Machine had not eroded either its militancy or principles.

Chapter 7

An Army of Mice or an Army of Lions?

> We must cease us from our forming
> Each his little worthless band,
> And it leading to destroy
> The very things that ought to stand—
> And must stand all linked together
> Not a single one left out,
> If we'd power have to battle
> Things which we should put to rout.
> —Clarence Emery Allen

Members of the Afro-American Council were determined that the tempests of 1903 would not become the hurricane of 1904. Despite the fact that the organization had been successful in instituting national and local suits aimed at protecting the rights of African Americans, the failure to achieve quick or significant victories in those cases prevented the group from gaining the respect and backing of a large segment of the community. Furthermore, the public presence of Booker T. Washington among the Council's ranks had made a great number of activists uneasy. These issues plagued the Council in late 1903 and early 1904 and would soon lead to the creation of other national civil rights organizations that would compete with the Council for the community support and resources it so desperately needed. In fact, during 1904 and 1905, the African American community would see the development of three new national civil rights organizations: the Committee of Twelve, the Constitution League, and the Niagara Movement. All of these organizations in some shape or form were an outgrowth of the Afro-American Council.

Indeed, it was the personality and ideological struggles that began to surface in 1902 at the Council's St. Paul convention and continued to germinate throughout 1903 that gave life to these new organizations. At the same time, however, the very core of the new developing groups differed little from the Council or its predecessor the Afro-American League.

This period of African American organizational and social and political history is extremely important. Twenty years after T. Thomas Fortune originally called for the creation of a national civil rights organization to challenge the federal, state, and local backpedaling from the Reconstruction Amendments and the onset of the Jim Crow system, many within the community's leadership were becoming frustrated and impatient. During the previous two years of Council activity, the organization continued its slow and arduous process of building test cases and lobbying the federal government to gain favorable legislation to counter the disfranchising and discriminatory actions of the southern states. But its failure to raise sufficient funds or calibrate its message to properly inform the membership and the community of its actions and agenda allowed individuals within and without of the group to continue to criticize and increasingly look for alternative venues of agitation.

Confronting this situation head-on, the leaders of the Council sought to demonstrate that the Council was the one association that could unify the cadre of individuals seeking to protect blacks from the continued growth of white supremacy sweeping the nation. They did so by continuing the Council's work on the ground, in the courts, and on Capitol Hill. The pressing matter, however, was to try to bring the African American activist community back under the tent of the Council, or at least to quiet the criticism and gain cooperation with the burgeoning dissenting voices.

* * *

In an effort at damage control and an attempt to set the tone for the year, Council president T. Thomas Fortune wrote a letter to the editor of the *New York Evening Post* upholding the organization's status as the nation's only civil rights organization. He also attempted to explain away the commotion and confusion of 1903. A group of malcontents, he asserted, had unsuccessfully tried to seize control at the Council's last national convention. Some of these individuals, he added, had also tried to gain control of the recently formed National Negro Suffrage League, which had combined forces with the Council. Their activities, Fortune assured his readers, were unsuccessful, and he encouraged all in such a climate of confusion and treachery to turn their attention and resources to the Council, a proven organization.[1]

With all of this choreography occurring, Fortune and a number of race leaders prepared to meet at Carnegie Hall for a secret conference. The meeting, nearly a year in preparation, had been proposed by Booker T. Washington in February 1903 to unite divergent race leaders. Over the course of the year, Washington had been in contact with W. E. B. Du Bois and a number of other individuals trying to solidify the list of participants. Initially around fifteen individuals were to be included, but as both Du Bois and Washington maneuvered to ensure that an adequate number of supporters would be present to espouse their respective schools of thought, the list grew to include nearly thirty.[2]

As the conference approached, the Tuskegee principal and the Atlanta professor each lined up support for his respective position among the named participants. Du Bois sent a memorandum to Francis Grimké, Clement Morgan, Frederick McGhee, and Kelly Miller warning all of the tactics that Washington might employ at the conference, with such measures including "conciliation and compromise, irritation, and browbeating, [and] silent shutting off of discussion."[3] Du Bois also arranged the participants into categories according to their leanings toward the Wizard—for example, "anti-Washington," "Uncertain, leaning toward Washington," and "unscrupulously for Washington." He concluded the memo by calling for all participants to "bring every speech or letter or record of Washington so that he can face his record in print."[4]

In this atmosphere of mistrust punctuated by a few "leaks" made to the press on the eve of the meeting, the conferees convened in Carnegie Hall on January 6, 1904.[5] After the remarks of a few white supporters, who had been invited by Washington, the Tuskegee principal officially opened the proceedings with an address asking for the delegation to understand the precarious situation within which he lived in the South. Du Bois followed the Wizard by stating that there could be no compromise on African Americans' civil and political rights, higher education, and public accommodation. The Atlanta professor insisted, furthermore, that Washington cease and desist with public comments that made blacks the butt of humor and ridicule.[6]

What followed was three days of heated discussion and persuasive closing addresses by both Du Bois and Washington. Afterwards the delegation agreed on a program containing eight resolutions covering migration, suffrage, segregation, lynching, education, and race relations, in general, as well as specifically southern conditions and the dissemination of information to the general public.[7] The group also endorsed the necessity of spreading "knowledge of the truth in regard to all matters affecting the race." Finally, it called for the creation of a "Committee of Safety with twelve members" [Committee of Twelve] to serve as a bureau of information and to "seek to unify and bring into cooperation the action of the various organizations" throughout the nation.[8]

After the meeting, with both factions claiming victory, conferees dispersed throughout the nation ready to work with their respective organizations and uphold the principles set forth by the delegation. For the Afro-American Council, the conference at Carnegie Hall confirmed the leaders' belief that they were on the correct path. The resolutions passed by the group mirrored those the Council had been espousing since its inception in 1898. Moreover, many of the members of the conference were past or present supporters of the national civil rights organization. Consequently, many Council members believed that when the soon-to-be Committee of Twelve set out to coordinate the activities of the various race organizations, the Council itself would be the prime beneficiary. Such sentiment was reflected in a letter sent to Washington by Council member Frederick McGhee: "I take this liberty to extend to you a personal compliment for your conference," he purred, "and beg to assure you . . . that all differences are at an end, and that the support you shall now receive will be a wholly united and full faith support."[9]

T. Thomas Fortune also viewed the conference in a positive light, and moved to capitalize on the goodwill that had been generated. He immediately embarked on a lecture tour through the North, West, and South to encourage the development of local Councils and to raise money for the national organization. Fortune, however, quickly became disillusioned with the trip. Although pleased with the turnout and the response he was getting from the audience, he became angry when he realized how little the race was willing to financially support the activities of a national civil rights organization. "They come out to applaud, to echo, but put pennies in the cause," he complained. Such results were leading him to believe that "the effort to get the race interested in the preservation of its rights as men is a fool's errand."[10]

Fortune was not alone with his assessment of the situation. After the Supreme Court ruled again on the Jackson Giles cases, which constituted the

Council's Alabama disfranchisement challenge, many would echo the Council president's opinions. In early January 1904, prior to the Carnegie conference, Wilford Smith had again argued the Giles case before the Supreme Court. Smith scorned the new Alabama constitution, asserting that it had been passed via fraudulent schemes to circumvent the federal constitution and deny black citizens of Alabama the right to suffrage. He concluded that the Giles case was simply a call for fair and equal treatment based on the Fourteenth and Fifteenth Amendments of the U.S. Constitution.

The defense, led by state attorney William A. Gunter, Jr., contended that the action of the registrars constituted judicial action, and that under Alabama law registrars were exempt from actions for damages. The cases, he argued, were not really a matter for the Court to hear since Giles's never actually tried to vote. Gunter claimed that if the plaintiff had gone to the polls and demanded his right to vote, then his case might fall within the jurisdiction of the federal courts. Furthermore, Gunter contended, the Alabama courts had already ruled that the case was not a federal constitutional matter.[11]

On February 23, 1904, the Supreme Court ruled that it indeed lacked jurisdiction in cases where a state court had previously rendered a decision on non-Constitutional grounds.[12] Giles, therefore, had no basis to bring his suit to the Supreme Court.

William Monroe Trotter of the *Guardian*, possibly still stinging from Smith's role in his recent legal matters, argued that the adverse decision was due to the inability of the race to secure the work of a more eminent counsel. Although it might be flattering to black pride to know that an African American attorney had argued the case, it would have made greater sense, he reasoned, for the community to have engaged the support of an attorney with superior weight in the profession so as to make a more favorable impression on the country and the courts. Then uncharacteristically, he called on the race to support the Council's Louisiana case—which, after three years was finally moving through the state courts. At the same time, however, Trotter feared the ramifications of an accumulation of adverse legal decisions. If the Council could not raise enough money to push its case through the courts, he argued, the organization should step aside and allow another race organization to form and take control of this important issue.[13]

The problem of securing sufficient funds for the race to challenge the growing Jim Crow system was angering many within the community. John Quincy Adams, editor of the *St. Paul Appeal* and member of the local Council, was especially appalled in light of the fact that Japanese immigrants throughout America had pooled their resources to aid in their native country's fight against Russia. As he noted in one of three editorials devoted to the subject, "The Japanese in the United States will raise a fund of $5,000,000 to aid their country in the war between Russia and Japan. The Afro-Americans in this country have more wealth than the few thousand Japanese who live here and with a $5,000,000 fund they could settle the race problem."[14] Moreover, Adams proclaimed, twelve Japanese in Orange, New Jersey, "raised a fund of one thousand dollars for their country in one night." "Why can not," he pleaded, "10,000,000 Afro-Americans raise a large fund to defend the rights of their race?"[15]

The call for the establishment of a defense fund had been an issue for members of the Afro-American Council since the inception of the organization, but many were becoming pessimistic about the fund actually coming into being. The legal strategy approach was, however, still viewed by supporters of the organization as the only path to gain their manhood rights. The Council's Legal and Legislative Bureau, with whatever money it could scrap together, continued to push forward with the Louisiana case as well as the transportation segregation case of Henry T. Johnson against the Pullman Company that its members had added to their challenges the previous September.

The importance of a legal strategy was also highlighted by the Committee of Twelve's first public document. Even before the Committee had been officially selected, Washington, Du Bois, and Hugh M. Browne—former head of the physics department of Hampton Insitutute and then-current leader of the Institute for Colored Youth in Philadelphia—solicited Wilford Smith to prepare a pamphlet explaining to the community ways in which to qualify the juries. They also discussed the importance of creating a leaflet detailing voting requirements for the various southern states.[16] This move was in direct response to Washington and Smith's success in getting a favorable ruling in the *Rogers v. Alabama* case on January 18, 1904.[17] In early March, an appeal was issued by Washington, Du Bois, and Browne calling for all blacks to find their voice and become active members of the court system (that is, jurists) and the lawmaking process.[18]

Around the same time, the three met to finalize the list of the Committee of Twelve. The full membership included Du Bois, Washington, Browne, Archibald Grimké, Dr. Charles E. Bentley, Bishop George Clinton, Bishop

Alexander Walters, Kelly Miller, T. Thomas Fortune, Frederick McGhee, Charles Chesnutt, and Charles W. Anderson.[19] After the Committee was set, the group agreed to meet in the near future to solidify the organizational plans and begin its own race work and the coordination of the various race organizations.

* * *

As the Committee of Twelve was getting under way, the leadership of the Afro-American Council was experiencing dramatic changes. Despite the apparent success by those present at the Carnegie meeting in bringing together a fragile alliance of the diverging groups of activists from within the community, the tensions, frustrations, and infighting would continue within the Committee of Twelve, the Afro-American Council, and the community at large. Compounding this situation was the pressure so many activists were feeling as they fought to stop the spread of white supremacy. The laborious, time-consuming struggle, with meager funds and minimal support, had taken its toll on many believers. Several looked to get out of the fight, blame others, or search for new angles. This battle over personality, ideology, and leadership would continually cause causalities in the struggle and would often threaten the universal agenda of the activists by dividing the resources and energy to fight for the enforcement of the Fourteenth and Fifteenth Amendments as well as to bring an end to racial violence.

During the early spring of 1904, the internal and external fights continued to strain the tenuous coalition holding the Council together as clashes were played out within the organization and in the national press. In late March, for instance, T. Thomas Fortune quarreled with Booker T. Washington. Among other issues, Washington heard that Fortune in some way had disclosed the principal's involvement in the Alabama suffrage cases. After some discussion with Washington, Fortune wrote to Emmett Scott saying that he had decided to resign from the presidency of the Afro-American Council. "I want to cut loose from the whole situation of selfishness and throat-cutting and pursue my own purposes, and to damn and praise, as the situation warrants, unhampered in any direction," Fortune declared.[20]

Fortune also wrote William H. Steward, first vice president of the Afro-American Council, informing him of his decision. He indicated that he was leaving the organization, and that, according to the group's bylaws, Steward would succeed him as president. As for the reasons behind his departure,

Fortune declared that from the beginning the organization had been kept in existence "with small response from the masses of the race, to stem the fearful tide of civil and political and material degradation of the race to a condition of pariahs in the citizenship of the Republic." He explained that he had "grown old and impoverished in the long struggle," and "must now take heed" of his "age and precarious health and devote . . . time and energies to repairing [his] personal fortunes in the interest of [his] immediate family."[21]

Though Fortune's resignation may have surprised many, in actuality it had been in the works since the Louisville convention. The backbiting among race leaders and the failure of the masses to give any substantial support to the organization had always bothered him. By the spring of 1904 he had had enough. This did not mean, however, that the old, fearless agitator had given up on African Americans gaining their full civil and political rights. He believed that victory would be theirs and that, if he had the strength and the finances, he would continue the struggle despite the "the deadly apathy of the mass of the race and the malignant antagonism and vituperation of many thoughtful men of the race."[22]

The Council would continue, even though Steward, editor of the *American Baptist*, lacked Fortune's political strength and organizational skills. Steward's tenure as Council president was further complicated by the fact that shortly after Fortune's resignation, it appeared the fragile alliance created by the "radicals" and "conservatives" in the forming of the Committee of Twelve was about to rupture as the "radicals" were gaining some strength. In early April 1904, for instance, the National Negro Suffrage League held a large successful mass meeting in Cambridge, Massachusetts, which attracted delegates from Chicago, New England, the District of Columbia, and Virginia.[23] Moreover, that same month, *The World To-Day* published five articles on the race problem, which were authored by Booker T. Washington, Kelly Miller, Jesse Lawson, Ida B. Wells-Barnett, and W. E. B. Du Bois. The essays penned by the latter two contained what were quite possibly the severest attacks on the Tuskegeean to date.[24]

In his essay, "The Tuskegee Idea," Washington espoused the general philosophy of solving the race problem that he had been pushing publicly since he had arrived in Alabama. What is needed? he asked, then answered, "Education undoubtedly, the rational education of the sons and daughters of these black men. Teachers and teachers of teachers are needed, for these people are ignorant; preachers are needed to supply sanctions for moral conduct; doctors are needed to battle with disease." "But we must remember," Tuskegee's principal asserted, that "civilization rests upon economic foundations; industrial efficiency must gradually be developed in these black men."[25]

While Washington used his article to promote his leadership and "Tuskegee Idea," Ida B. Wells-Barnett used her space to criticize the principal. In particular, she directed her ire toward the negative stereotypes that Washington continued to perpetuate. In fighting an image war with the nation, many African Americans were engaged in efforts challenging the notion of black inferiority. However, Washington, the most prominent black leader in the country, actively disseminated such images before white audiences as a fund-raising tool. Washington's complicity in perpetuating negative stereotypes of blacks had been a subject of discussion at the Carnegie Conference, and for a few months thereafter, Washington had laid low. But given that white audiences had come to expect the Tuskegee principal's "darky" stories at his lectures, Washington was only able to contain himself for so long.[26]

In March, Washington spoke to the Chicago Women's Club, opening his speech with an account of African Americans being hog thieves. Unfortunately for Washington, Wells-Barnett was in the audience and, though she did not speak out at the meeting, she did use her article to reiterate the story and highlight the damage that the Tuskegeean was doing with his stories and racial philosophy. As Wells-Barnett noted, African Americans were aware that Washington had "the ear of the American nation as no other Negro of our day, and he is therefore molding public sentiment. . . . They [also] know that the white South has labored ever since reconstruction to establish and maintain throughout the country a color line in politics, in civil rights and in education, and they feel that with Mr. Washington's aid the South has largely succeeded in her aim." She and her "class of Negroes" called for Washington to "use his great abilities and influence to speak of and demand for the rights withheld when discussing the Negro question"—or to simply refrain from speaking on the issue as in her mind, his rhetoric was doing more damage to their cause.[27]

Despite the severity of Wells-Barnett's critique, W. E. B. Du Bois's article contained the most damaging criticism of Washington. Moreover, the essay constituted more of a signal break with Washington then had Du Bois's 1903 *Souls*' essay, "Of Booker T. Washington and Others," as the title, "The Parting of the Ways," clearly indicated.[28] Juxtaposing Washington's leadership and racial philosophy with that of the great black leaders of the past, the Atlanta professor now concluded that the Tuskegee principal stood in historical as well as moral opposition to older leaders such as Bishop Daniel Payne, Alexander Crummell, T. Thomas Fortune, and Frederick Douglass. According to Du Bois, none of these individuals could have supported Washington's position as they had "fought for the highest education available," and they understood that it was "impossible for free workingmen without the ballot to compete with free workingmen who have the ballot."[29] Moreover, these leaders of the past understood that blacks would only become free if they had "the courage and persistence to demand the rights and treatment of men and to cease to toady and apologize and belittle themselves." Du Bois therefore called on African Americans to "refuse to kiss the hand that smites us," and to "insist on striving by all civilized methods to keep wide educational opportunity, to keep the right to vote, to insist on equal civil rights and to gain every right and privilege open to a free American citizen."[30]

Directly following the publication of Du Bois's article, Fortune echoed identical sentiments. In response to recent violence in Saint Charles, Arkansas, where thirteen African Americans were murdered over the course of a week, the former Council president published an editorial in the *Age* that called upon the race to assert its manhood. The editor lamented that the "commercialism of the North, which controls the newspapers . . . [,] has joined hands with the commercialism of the South to rob the Negro of his civil and political rights and to degrade him to a peon, a slave, while the mass of the American people . . . are ignorant of the facts."[31]

However, the real problem, according to Fortune—echoing the frustrations he had vocalized when he resigned from the Council—lay in the inaction of the African American community. Through it all, he noted, "the Negro slumbers, indifferent, in so far as helping himself through existing organizations is concerned, refusing to contribute in enthusiasm and money to contend for his rights in the courts, allowing himself to be shot like a dog, instead of being shot like a man, while in the desperate act of shooting." In conclusion, the editor asserted, "we do not like the hand that smites us. It is ignominious. We need manhood, and we need it at once."[32]

Fortune's former organization concurred with his assessment and issued yet another call for the race to aid the Council in its legal struggles. In mid-April, Frederick McGhee, vice-director of the group's Legal Bureau, published a circular pleading for funds to support its work in the Henry T. Johnson suit. McGhee, in highlighting the importance of this case and others like it, called attention to the fact that the "women of our race, our mothers, wives, sisters, and daughters" were preparing to attend the meeting of the National

Association of Colored Women's Clubs in St. Louis and were raising money to secure special Pullman cars at extra expense to prevent the humiliation of riding in Jim Crow cars. The St. Paul attorney expressed all honor to the women of the race, but declared it a shame that they were compelled to resort to such means "in order to have decent accommodations on a public carrier. *The women of no other race will be thus compelled to do.*"[33] To "provide against just this condition," he noted, for eight months the Council had "spent some effort to collect funds to test the right of the Pullman Company to refuse such accommodations."[34]

McGhee called on the race to submit funds to support the group's efforts in the Johnson case to prevent such action. The case, he asserted, would have been dropped had the organization not dipped into its reserve funds. Now it was in serious need of money to prosecute the appeal through the final determination. All it would take, he noted, was a dollar from everyone who felt enough interest in this vital race matter. Finally in a possible attempt to spur the race's churches into action, McGhee, a devout Catholic, noted that a number of priests had extended him invitations to speak before "their parishioners and receive contributions to the fund." He felt, however, that such funds should "come wholly from the race," and therefore challenged African American pastors to make the same offer to help the cause.[35]

When publishing McGhee's call in the *Chicago Broad Ax*, editor Julius Taylor appended a comment affirming the "duty of the preachers through their churches and those belonging to the societies and so on, to contribute money to the sums ever so small, for the purpose of assisting to test the right in the highest court in the land, of the Pullman Palace Car Company to force the best women of the race to ride 'Jim Crow cars;' now is the time to strike while the iron is hot."[36] John Quincy Adams of the *Appeal* concurred and called on the people to send as much "as they feel able to subscribe to this cause, in which every Afro-American in this country is vitally interested."[37]

But as the Council pushed forward with its legal strategy, scratching together whatever resources it could, the group suffered yet another blow to that very approach. On April 25, 1904, after years of discussion and strategizing, the group saw its effort to challenge disfranchisement thwarted again in Louisiana. The state supreme court had dismissed the Ryanes case on the curious basis that the plaintiff had neither "proven nor alleged that the matter in dispute exceeded $2,000"; consequently it lacked jurisdiction.[38]

Following this deflating defeat, the Council fell into a somber and unenthusiastic mood. After years of struggle, slow legal maneuvering, and snail-like financial growth, many Council members had become completely disillusioned with the legal strategy. Despite some support for the Johnson case, the departure of Fortune combined with the defeat in Louisiana had led many to feel that the Council was on its last legs.

To compound matters, the infighting within the organization and among the cadre of activists loosely supporting the group continued. Behind the scenes, for instance, instead of accepting the coalition that James Hayes had announced at the Council's Louisville convention, Washington, Steward, and others in the Council were moving to suppress the National Negro Suffrage League and force Hayes back into the fold of the organization. Making matters increasingly worse, "bad blood" was continuing to grow between the pro-and anti-Washington factions. Additionally—and dividing the activists even more—yet another civil rights organization threw its hat into the ring.

Initiated in late 1903, the Constitution League, an interracial civil rights organization, gained strength throughout the early months of 1904. The group was the brainchild of New York businessman John Milholland, who had made a large profit from his pneumatic tube business. Milholland had long been an advocate of black rights and a supporter of the Council, and had contributed financial support to that group's Alabama suffrage cases.[39] As early as 1900 he had expressed to Booker T. Washington the need for an interracial civil rights organization and assured the Tuskegeean that those supporting such an effort for "equal rights, common sense and imperative Justice" would not have to worry about funds if Milholland were successful in some of his business ventures.[40] Given the turmoil taking place within the Afro-American Council throughout 1903, Milholland sensed that the time was opportune to launch his organization for the protection of African America's political rights.[41]

The Constitution League's initial activity centered on the upcoming presidential election and an attempt to get the Republican Party to place some sort of antidisfranchisement plank into its platform. In the wake of the recent decision in Louisiana and the Supreme Court's decisions in the Alabama cases, such action aligned the League with the other civil rights organizations and many of the leaders of the African American community. The Afro-American Council and the Negro Suffrage League had already discussed the necessity of having their voices heard at the upcoming Republican National Convention in Chicago.

In the light of the recent rulings, both organizations wanted to step outside of the courts and push for the Republican Party to support reduction of congressional representatives for the states that disfranchised black voters. This however was a controversial move: not all supporters of the two groups were in agreement on how to approach the issue of disfranchisement, and the idea of reduction would become an issue that would further strain the ideological coalition holding together the Afro-American Council and the Negro Suffrage League. Nonetheless, with their tenuous alliances in tow, the organizations prepared for the Republican Party convention.

* * *

The Constitution League was no less eager to put its plan into action. League secretary Albert Humphrey wrote to President Theodore Roosevelt indicating that "friends of the Administration" in the newly formed League hoped that the Party would insert "an emphatic Constitutional Suffrage Plank" in its national platform. He noted that since the organization's inception, they had worked earnestly "to aid in arousing public sentiment in this direction" and had already gained the endorsement of "over twenty states" for their position advocating "the enforcement of the Constitutional Amendments." Despite this support, however, Humphrey informed the president that he believed many states were waiting for the national party to sound the keynote. He believed public sentiment, when properly aroused, would favor the reduction of representation in Congress and the electoral college in cases where states had disfranchised their citizens.[42]

While the Constitution League was maneuvering to obtain presidential support for a strong suffrage plank, representatives of the Council and the National Negro Suffrage League met in Chicago to draft a plank of their own to present to the Republican Party's committee on resolutions. The meetings between the groups, however, became embroiled in semantic arguments. Some participants suspected that Booker T. Washington was orchestrating the resistance of Council members to statements suggested by Hayes and his Suffrage League colleagues. Particularly contentious was the wording regarding positions advocating the reduction of southern representation, a policy that Washington and President Roosevelt were known to oppose.[43] At the time, some Council members questioned whether it was wise in the wake of the recent adverse decisions in the Louisiana and Alabama suffrage cases to demand reduction of congressional representation. This was an action that some, including Washington, believed could only bring about more negative sentiment toward their cause and might unintentionally sanction disfranchisement.

Unbeknownst to the participants in the joint meeting of the Council and the Suffrage League, however, Washington was corresponding with Humphrey about aiding the Constitution League's attempt to introduce its planks to the Resolution Committee.[44] The Constitution League's planks were just as militant as that either of the other two organizations were suggesting. Washington did not openly endorse the League's planks, but he did suggest to Humphrey that he should contact Henry Cabot Lodge to see if they could be placed into the Republican Party's platform at the convention.[45] It is unknown why Washington would assist the Constitution League's actions but not openly aid the Council or the Suffrage League, especially when both Washington and Fortune had consistently spoken out against the reduction strategy. Washington may have believed that the plank would have more weight coming from an interracial organization. He may have also been trying to demonstrate to Millholland and Humphrey that he was sympathetic to their cause in order to keep the Constitution League and Milholland's purse strings in his orbit.

In the end, none of the organizations was able to persuade the Republican Party to insert its planks into the platform. The struggle between the Council and the Suffrage League over the reduction of representation offered just a highlight of the trouble waiting on the horizon. Washington's reluctance to support the issue continued to anger more radical race men and women, and many believed that he was using his connections to persuade the Roosevelt Administration to stand against such action.

Moreover, the issue of reducing southern representation had gained some steam in recent months due to the Platt Bill—a bill introduced by New York senator Thomas C. Platt to reduce the membership of the House of Representatives, a reduction that would come from removing nineteen seats from the eleven southern states that had disfranchised African Americans. The Constitution League fully supported the Platt Bill as did the National Negro Suffrage League. Many Council members also supported the bill, but as had been the case regarding previous reduction proposals such as the one introduced by Indiana Congressman Edgar Dean Crumpaker, not everyone believed that such action would gain African Americans sympathy for their cause. Washington particularly adhered to this view, consistently refusing to publicly support reduction of congressional representation. His failure to fully explain the rationale behind his opinion, especially in the light of the failed legal suits against disfranchisement and the feeling that a new path was necessary, angered critics and some supporters alike. Moreover, since Washington's true participation in the Louisiana and Alabama cases was not public knowledge, his critics were able to seize onto his resistance to antidisfranchisement action and paint the Tuskegee principal as a man who stood against their cause to uphold the Fourteenth and Fifteenth Amendments. Indeed, Washington's position on the issue of the franchise and how and when African Americans should fight for that "badge of political equality, the insignia of one's citizenship" was placing him outside of the circle of activists as well as an increasing number within the African American community.[46] As a matter of fact, there was a growing sense that fighting against disfranchisement and for the reduction of southern representation was becoming an issue that many of Washington's enemies within the Council, the Constitution League, and the National Negro Suffrage League could use to form a more concrete alliance against the Tuskegeean.

The franchise issue even sent ripples into Washington's developing Committee of Twelve. The opinion on what line of attack the Committee should take on the franchise was among those that were being hotly contested by the group as it was solidifying its positions. Indeed, a number of the members, including W. E. B. Du Bois and Archibald Grimké, stood against the Tuskegee principal on the issue, and ultimately this became one of the reasons for the resignation of Du Bois from the organization before its steering committee meeting.

The Committee was to hold its first meeting in July in St. Louis. Du Bois did not respond to the initial call for the conference, but his wife, Nina, later sent Washington a telegram explaining that Du Bois was ill and would not be able to attend the meeting.[47] Du Bois's illness prompted Washington to postpone the gathering to the following week in New York, but Du Bois again failed to respond. This time the meeting went forward without the Atlanta professor, and lacking opposition, the Committee adopted all recommendations proposed by the Wizard.[48] After the gathering, however, the Tuskegeean did write Archibald Grimké to explain that he had reconsidered Grimké's proposal of having the secretary of the group work directly on the franchise, impressing upon the community the importance of registering and voting in all elections as well as promptly paying all taxes relating to suffrage.[49]

Such a move kept Grimké on the Committee, but came too late for Du Bois. Angered by the moderate goals of the Committee and the fact that it had convened without him, he announced his resignation from the new civil rights organization.[50] As Du Bois explained to Grimké in mid-August, he was leaving the Committee to assemble a stronger "body of fearless people" who would stand up to the Wizard and fight for the civil rights of African Americans.[51] Such a move was surely predictable following publication of Du Bois's "The Parting of the Ways" back in April, but many had hoped that the fragile coalition would hold together for the betterment of the race.

With his exit from the Committee of Twelve, Du Bois again made himself more attractive to the burgeoning "radical" anti-Washington forces, who had once more placed their focus on capturing the Afro-American Council. With William Steward at the helm of the Council instead of the more capable T. Thomas Fortune, they now believed that they had a legitimate chance of gaining control. In their eyes, Steward was a weak leader who lacked the negotiating and political skills of the two previous presidents. Bishop Walters, moreover, had expressed little to no interest in recapturing the presidency of the organization. The anti-Washingtonists were also encouraged by the fact that the National Negro Suffrage League had again agreed to hold a joint convention with the Council, which in their minds gave them more strength and numbers.

The Council was ready, however, for such a move, and attempted to assert to the public its preeminence as the nation's civil rights organization. When Steward issued the call for the meeting to be held in August 1904, he declared that the St. Louis convention was of the utmost importance. As he explained, "in the view of the legislation against us as citizens, not only against our civil rights, but against our suffrage, no one should question the necessity for an organization of this character, and every Afro-American, without regard to his views on other subjects, should be willing to unite in an organized effort to improve these conditions."[52] More important, Steward, subtly affirming that the Council was not controlled by Washington, reiterated that disfranchisement was the paramount issue of the meeting and that all positions on the issue would be discussed.[53]

Such declarations were not assuring to everyone. The Council's constant critic, W. Calvin Chase, responded to Steward's call to gather the clans by questioning his attempt to raise "a dead corpse."[54] Chase claimed that the organization had been born "deformed" and had "ever since to walk on crutches."[55]

The truth was that under Steward's leadership, the Council had shown little new activity, and the president himself rarely traveled to promote either the group or its lingering legal activities. Moreover, given the recent Louisiana decision, the organization was certainly in a somber mood, but many still firmly believed in the Council's overall mission and were optimistic that the group would recover from its recent problems.

With optimism and a certain sense of defensiveness, therefore, members of the Afro-American Council congregated in St. Louis on Tuesday, September 6, 1904, for the group's seventh annual convention. According to press coverage, the St. Louis meeting was the most harmonious in the Council's existence.[56] In addition to the amicable feeling, the gathering appears to have been the group's most conservative one as well.

The press noted that the organization's Bureaus had reported a "decided increase in the work of the Council," but none of the coverage elaborated upon what type of work was on the rise. One could assume that Legal Bureau director J. Madison Vance discussed the recent defeat in Louisiana and promoted the Bureau's work on the Henry T. Johnson case, but there was no discussion of that report in the press. Moreover, there was no news concerning the Council's plans to prevent the continued disfranchisement of blacks in the southern states.[57]

In the end, the organization elected the most passive, Tuskegee-orientated leadership to date. William Steward was reelected president, John Quincy Adams of the *St. Paul Appeal* was named a vice president; his brother, Cyrus Field Adams, the secretary; and James H. Guy of Topeka, Kansas, the national organizer. The directors of the Bureaus included J. R. Morris, Education; Emmett J. Scott, Business; Fannie Barrier Williams, Literary; J. Madison Vance, Legal; and George L. Knox, Anti-lynching.[58] Bishop Walters was reelected director of the Executive Committee, but his reelection was not enough to reassure the growing chorus of radicals that the Council was the organization prepared to fight against repeal of the African American community's civil rights, suffrage, or general well-being as Steward had suggested prior to the convention.

Even the group's national Address, which always contained some reference to the group's struggle for civil rights and its defense of suffrage, was devoid of the militancy traditionally expressed by T. Thomas Fortune and Bishop Walters. The appeal was solely cast in terms of moral suasion. The only reference to the Council's struggle for black America's civil rights or suffrage was the following:

> In the face of the organic law of the nation, and in bitter opposition to the enforcement of the 13th, 14th, and 15th amendments, to which all of these states have pledged allegiance, written in the constitution by the blood of thousands of our countrymen and the expenditure of billions of treasure, in the face of the righteousness of a just cause and by the power of might, almost an entire race in one portion of our country is denuded of every right by unjust laws of disfranchisement.[59]

At the end of this statement, the Council returned to its moral suasion argument and asserted that it is "essentially true of a nation as of an individual that true greatness and enduring success rests on righteousness." Moreover, the Council noted that "no one can wrong his brother without injuring himself, and a community in which the moral sentiment of the people is not strong enough to restrain or organized lawlessness is endangered of being engulfed." The Council therefore appealed to "all patriotic and fair-minded citizens of all creeds and nationalities to give [its] cause a fair unprejudiced and patient hearing."[60] Absent was any appeal to the U.S. president or Congress to act; justice was left to "the people."

The moderate racial position publicly promoted by Tuskegee now clearly dominated the workings of the Afro-American Council. It is curious why, at such a crucial stage given the growth of the radical circle and the development of alternative civil rights organizations, Washington would alter the course of the group in such a way. Despite assertions that he had controlled the group over the preceding few years, it had always advanced a more diverse public position. At the close of the seventh annual convention, the delicate balance was gone between the moderate and radical racial philosophies.

One of the probable reasons for the weakening of the Council may have had to do with the development of the Committee of Twelve. Washington undoubtedly wanted the group that he visibly controlled to become the country's main civil rights organization. With a diluted Council that possibility became more probable. Moreover, at that moment Washington was beginning to throw support to the interracial Constitution League, which he may have seen as a more viable way to appeal to the country for African American civil rights. Such a position would explain the basis for his endorsing the Constitution League's efforts to press the Republican Party's adoption of a strong suffrage plank rather than supporting similar plans proposed by the Afro-American Council and the National Negro Suffrage League.[61]

Whatever the reasons for the Council embracing a moderate stance at its seventh annual convention, some members of the group immediately began to press the issues that had formed the foundation of the organization. Directly following the St. Louis convention, the Legal Bureau published and distributed a circular advertising its activities and called for contributions to a fund to support Reverend Henry T. Johnson's suit against the Pullman Company.[62] Signed by J. Madison Vance and Frederick McGhee of the Legal Bureau and Jesse Lawson, financial secretary of the Council, the circular provided the details of the case and reiterated the Council's argument from earlier in the year that it could only move forward with assistance from the "people."[63] Specifically the members of the Bureau asked for "ONE DOLLAR from each person who feels enough interest in this vital race matter."[64]

Despite the efforts of the Council's Legal Bureau to assert the organization's activist side by highlighting its work in the Johnson case, more critics of the group, and particularly of Washington, attempted to seize the moment and create their own civil rights organizations. One such instance occurred directly on the heels of the appeal by the Council's Legal Bureau. Ever since its September meeting, held in conjunction with the Council, the National Negro Suffrage League had been fading into the background. In its wake, the group's core membership formed the New England Suffrage League.[65] At the new organization's inaugural convention held in Providence, Rhode Island, a series of five resolutions was passed outlining the group's general philosophy. Resolved to petition Congress to provide one hundred and twenty million dollars per year for the next twenty years to subsidize black education in the South, the group also took a strong stand against lynching and urged the government to pass anti-lynching legislation. The delegates also called on the government to pass the Morrell and Crumpacker Bills and to enact legislation that would enforce the Fifteenth Amendment.[66]

Members of the Afro-American Council could have easily endorsed all of the objectives of the new organization. Moreover, every resolution of the New England Suffrage League, except for the annual petition for one hundred and twenty million dollars, had been given material support by the Council during its seven years of existence. With the exception of the Crumpacker Bill, moreover, Washington would have agreed with all of the resolutions. The question as always was how the group's objectives would be implemented.

The New England Suffrage League sought to become an organization known for promoting its objectives through agitation and propaganda. However, while publicly assuming that the good people of both races would acknowledge the problem and solve it together, Washington advocated patience. At least this was Washington's public stance, for as has been observed, he was continually involved behind-the-scenes in orchestrating agitation and legal challenges. But the Council had been on the front lines for many years and appeared to be suffering from shell shock. Although its legal initiatives continued, many believed that the organization had lost momentum.

* * *

Amid the confusion caused by the proliferation of seemingly similar civil rights organizations, many of the familiar faces attempted to clarify where they stood on the issue of civil and political rights. Booker T. Washington, for example, moved to make it clear at a gathering in Cambridge, Massachusetts, in October 1904 that he stood firmly for black civil and political rights. "I do not believe in the Negro giving up anything that is guaranteed by the constitution of the United States," he affirmed. "[A]ny subterfuge or makeshift that gives the ignorant white man of the south the right to express his choice at the ballot box and withholds that same right for the colored man is an injustice to both races."[67]

Whether his critics would have taken such an assertion seriously is unlikely, but by giving this type of speech in Boston, Washington was clearly trying to subdue the rising dissention in the Northeast. More important, by quelling dissent he wished to demonstrate to whites that he remained *the* black leader with whom to consult. By manifesting agreement with other blacks concerning the issue of black rights, Washington hoped to show that the complaints of Trotter and others were unmistakably personal rather than ideological.

W. E. B. Du Bois, after making a more concrete break with Washington with his recent publications and exit from the Committee of Twelve, was also asserting his voice in the public debate. The Atlanta professor actually distinctively pushed his opinion and status on the issues as he called out to the community and asked it to respond using the call-and-response tradition of the African American church. In October 1904 he published his "Credo" in the pages of the *Independent*, affirming his belief in God, humanity, and civil rights, and calling upon the community and the nation as a whole to adopt this manifesto.[68]

At the same time as Du Bois and Washington were beginning their battle over leadership of the African American community, and in the absence of any authority shown by Council president William Steward, Bishop Walters began to assert himself once again. Most important, as he had previously done with his 1903 *Church Review* article on disfranchisement, Walters distanced himself from Washington and his political views. In an article appearing in the *Washington Bee* shortly after the Council's St. Louis convention, Walters informed Chase that he did not share Washington's political philosophy and methods and had for years refused to speak at Tuskegee in order to prevent the public from misconstruing his cooperation with Washington as any endorsement of the Wizard and his racial philosophy.[69]

Distancing himself even further from the Tuskegee principal, Walters also began to speak out more strongly against President Roosevelt and his administration. Whereas earlier the bishop had held out hope that the Republican leader was going to be more sympathetic to issues raised by African Americans, by the end of Roosevelt's first term, Walters realized that the native New Yorker was just another politician. Though Roosevelt had made some— essentially symbolic—black appointments, he offered nothing new to the government's dealings with the race problem. Moreover, in his annual address to Congress in December, he again remained silent on the need for federal action to enforce the Fourteenth and Fifteenth Amendments and/or end lynching and mob violence.[70]

In light of this situation, Walters admonished Council members and the black community in general for remaining silent.[71] White southerners, Walters asserted, were winning the battle in persuading the Roosevelt Administration to adopt a virtually hands-off policy regarding black rights in the South, and were increasingly successful in cultivating general apathy about that issue nationally.[72] To end this situation and give the community a voice, Walters called on members of the race to unite and stand for their rights and support the Council in its struggle. Moreover, as he understood the confusion created by the recent plethora of organizations, the bishop asked for the race leaders and organizations to collaborate rather than fight against the Council in an effort to devise an effective policy to counter expanding implementations of segregation and the spread of disfranchisement.[73]

As the year came to a close, therefore, the Afro-American Council and its leadership seemed to be regaining its footing. The resurgence of Walters represented a reawakening of the Council from its lethargic state under Steward's tutelage. Moreover, the organization's Legal and Legislative Bureau, under the helm of J. Madison Vance, Frederick McGhee, and Jesse Lawson, continued its attempts to raise money for the Johnson legal case.[74] Despite such efforts, however, the organization actually suffered its worst year in its seven-year history. The Council had attempted to create a national civil rights organization, but had continued to be baffled by the lack of mass support. Furthermore, throughout 1904 the organization continued to suffer from its affiliation with Washington and his perceived control over its activities. With those difficulties came competition for the organization's status as *the* national civil rights organization from groups such as the Committee of Twelve and the Constitution League. Moreover, the organization's setback in the Louisiana suffrage suit—the group's most publicized legal activity—and the lack of steady leadership provided by Steward, the Council's current president, caused many to believe that the Afro-American Council had run its course.

In an attempt to counter that feeling and to follow up his end-of-the-year call for the various factions of the race to unite, Bishop Walters called for a meeting of the minds. On January 18, 1905, a group of individuals belonging to the Committee of Twelve, the Council, and the New England Suffrage League met in the *Guardian* office for the purpose of outlining a broad race policy to present to President Roosevelt. The areas of discussion were delineated by Walters and were crafted around issues upon which all participants could agree. They demanded first that the U.S. attorney general uphold the Fifteenth Amendment; second, that the Administration carry out the provisions of the Fourteenth Amendment so as to eliminate discrimination on railroad cars; and third, that the government provide educational aid to schools in the "most needy states," meaning the South.[75]

While many of these positions mirrored those of the Afro-American Council and the new civil rights organizations, Walters made certain that there were no political office seekers or officeholders as participants in the meeting. After a year of moving the Council to become a more partisan organization, the bishop realized that the partisan position had not gained the Council anything, and in some ways it may have contributed to the frustration of individuals who were creating the rival groups. This was especially true in regards to Washington's role with the Council and his position of being Roosevelt's black political advisor.[76]

At the conclusion of the meeting, the group issued a letter to like-minded individuals outlining the three positions that the participants deemed necessary to discuss. Shortly afterward they made their gathering public and published an open letter announcing that a number of individuals had been asked to meet in conference at Kelly Miller's home in March 1905. The organizers explained that they would use the proposed meeting to coordinate the activities of the various organizations to which they belonged and would form a committee to meet with Roosevelt.[77]

* * *

While this activity was taking place, yet another civil rights organization was sprouting into existence. Since Atlanta University professor W. E. B. Du Bois had resigned from the Committee of Twelve, he had been undertaking a more central position within the leadership of the race. Indeed, having aligned himself with the anti-Washington contingent of the Northeast, by the early months of 1905 many viewed him as the leader of the "Trotterites"—the growing anti-Washington faction lead by William Monroe Trotter, but not comprised of activists solely from the Northeast.[78]

In late February 1905, the Atlanta professor ventured to St. Paul, Minnesota, to give an address at the House of Hope Church and to meet with Frederick McGhee, an increasingly important ally and member of the Afro-American Council's Legal Bureau. Though McGhee was still a member of the Council—as late as December 1904, one of the local papers, the *Appeal*, had carried a circular bearing his name that requested monetary support for Reverend Henry T. Johnson's case—he was becoming increasingly frustrated with the group's inability to gain a significant legal victory. During Du Bois's stay in St. Paul as a guest of McGhee, the two race men undoubtedly discussed the necessity of creating an alternative organization to the Council.[79]

Meanwhile, the racial climate of the country was worsening. In the South, decades of weak-to-miserable agricultural conditions had given way to the development of populist aid organizations whose laudable goals turned toward racist and nativist explanations for the decline. Tacked onto their original ideals was a steadfast commitment to control the African American population. The rise of such sentiment led to increased incidents of whitecapping and the melding of populist ideals with the aspiration of Democratic office seekers, which contributed to an ever-greater climate of hatred directed against the black population and provided a clear path for further disfranchisement and segregation.[80]

There was little-to-no movement on the part of the federal government to protect African Americans from the rising crescendo of terror in the South. Moreover, the anti-black sentiment of the South acquired a foothold throughout the nation as many northern liberals as well as the national government acquiesced to the mounting tide of racist thought. Stemming largely from the intellectual minds of those educated at white southern universities, much of this racial philosophy found a growing audience in northern journals such as *Forum*, *North American Review*, *Arena*, *Harper's Weekly*, *Nation*, *Atlantic Monthly*, *Popular Science Monthly*, and *Outlook*. Such sentiment was bolstered by the popularity of a number of larger studies and novels such as Charles Carroll's *The Negro a Beast*; William P. Calhoun's *The Caucasian and The Negro in the United States. They Must Separate. If Not, Then Extermination. A Proposed Solution: Colonization*; and Thomas Dixon's *The Leopard Spots* and recently published *The Clansman*.[81]

Since its incarnation, the Afro-American Council had stood steadfastly against the swelling anti-black sentiment, rising Jim Crow system, and racial violence, but with the upsurge of civil rights groups coupled with the organization's weak showing in 1904 and the negative image of Booker T. Washington's presence within the group, many within the Council sought to reconfirm its preeminent role as the nation's leading civil right organization. In early June 1905, with Bishop Walters again at the visual forefront of the Council, the group issued the call for its eighth annual convention to be held three months later in Detroit, Michigan.[82] As the call was put forth, local and state Councils met for their annual meetings and made plans for the national convention.[83]

Despite this activity, skeptics remained. For instance, Harry Smith of the *Cleveland Gazette* wondered what had happened to the Council's suit in Louisiana. Apparently unmindful of the negative decision rendered by the Louisiana court the previous year, Smith claimed that "before the [Council] was Booker T. Washingtonized . . . it was sustaining a case . . . to test the constitutionality of the disfranchisement amendment to the constitution of Louisiana . . . what has become of it?"[84] Smith had failed to carry any news concerning the state court's decision in the case, and nearly a year later the skeptics were asking what had happened to the suit. The Council had once again failed itself as it was unable to properly disseminate information about its own activities, leaving the community to wonder about those activities and the validity of the organization itself.

To make matters worse, as the group was broadcasting the call for its eighth annual meeting, a major challenge to its status as the preeminent national civil rights organization was about to be announced. The growing group of radicals sensed that the time was right for the launching of a new national organization and used the announcement of the Council's convention to unveil their plan. During the same month as the Council's advertisement,

Du Bois sent a circular proposing a meeting of a few dozen race leaders. "The time seems," he asserted, "more than ripe for organized, determined and aggressive action on the part of men who believe in Negro freedom and growth." He called on those receiving the circular to meet during the summer for the following proposes:

1. To oppose firmly the present methods of strangling honest criticism, manipulating public opinion and centralizing political power by means of the improper and corrupt use of money and influence.
2. To organize thoroughly the intelligent and honest Negroes throughout the United States for the purpose of insisting on manhood rights, industrial opportunity and spiritual freedom.
3. To establish proper organs of news and public opinion.[85]

Although the call went out under Du Bois's name, the creation of the new group was a collaborative effort. As the Atlanta professor himself noted, "The honor of founding the organization belongs to F. L. McGhee, who first suggested it; C. E. Bentley, who planned the method of organization and W. M. Trotter, who put the backbone into the platform."[86] Approximately a month after the letter was distributed, twenty-nine race men converged on Buffalo, New York, and Fort Erie, Ontario, on the Canadian side of Niagara Falls to discuss the proposed organization.

During the four-day event the participants quibbled over the wording of the new group's "Declaration of Principles," but they all agreed that they had traveled to the Niagara region to create an organization that thoroughly stood for the manhood rights of African Americans. Though many of the delegates openly opposed Washington's racial philosophy, Du Bois made it clear that opposition to the Wizard was not the reason he had called the delegation to the site. According to J. Max Barber, a delegate from Atlanta and editor of the *Voice of the Negro*, Du Bois insisted that "We have gathered to discuss principles not men. If Mr. Washington can subscribe to the principles he will be welcomed as a member of the Niagara Movement. If he cannot, that is his business."[87]

As Barber explained, the new movement sought "to reinstitute ideals in human behavior for the white man as well as the black." Those in the Niagara Movement believed, he asserted, "that it is better for the Negro to be a man with a man's spirit and a man's intellectual and moral stature than that he should be a coward with any amount of thrift and energy."[88] The delegates concurred with Barber's enunciation of the philosophy of the new movement, and after three full days of discussion agreed upon the structure of the new organization and its basic principles.

The platform, written in sharp tones by William Monroe Trotter and W. E. B. Du Bois, consisted of eight basic demands setting forth the position of the new civil rights group. The members of the Niagara Movement demanded:

> freedom of speech and criticism, an unfettered and unsubsidized press, full manhood suffrage, abolition of segregation, recognition of human brotherhood as a practical present creed, recognition of the highest and best education as the monopoly of no race or class, belief in the dignity of labor, and united effort to realize these ideals under wise and courageous leadership.[89]

There was nothing, however, new in these demands. The Niagara Movement's core principles echoed the grievances listed by a young T. Thomas Fortune as the reasons for the creation of the Afro-American League in 1887 and reflected the objectives of the Afro-American Council in 1898.[90] The real departure from the previous organizations and that of Booker T. Washington's position was the pledge to cooperate with labor unions—and possibly the militant tone surrounding its Declaration of Principles. On the other hand, both the Council and the League had used strong language such as *demand*, *urge*, and *repudiate* in their past national addresses as well.[91]

After approving the Declaration of Principles, the delegation agreed upon a constitution for the new group based on an outline drafted for the Committee of Twelve by Du Bois and submitted to Washington in early 1904. The Niagara Movement's general organizational structure was also reminiscent of its Afro-American League and Council counterparts.[92] The basic structure of the organization consisted of state associations: sixteen states plus the District of Columbia at its inception. The chairmen of the state associations comprised the group's Executive Committee and were led by the General Secretary (Du Bois was the first to hold the position).[93] Finally, the following committees were established: Finance, Interstate Conditions and Needs, Organization, Civil and Political Rights, Legal Defense, Crime, Rescue and Reform, Economic Opportunity, Health, Education, Press, and Public Opinion.[94]

Following the opening meeting of the Niagara Movement, Washington attempted to limit the flow of publicity concerning the new civil rights organization. In seeking to gather as much information about the movement prior to its inception, the Wizard had unsuccessfully tried to spy on the conference proceedings.[95] Washington clearly viewed the movement as a threat and sought to isolate the group by encouraging a media blackout of its proceedings.[96]

At the meeting, despite Du Bois's efforts during the proceedings to suppress criticisms of Washington, the Niagara Movement's very existence provided an implicit critique of the Wizard's program as well as introducing an alternative path. The Niagara Movement's membership was essentially made up of the Trotterites who had sought to challenge Washington since 1902. Moreover, sentiments expressing the Movement's Declaration of Principles—for example, that the race needs "leadership and is given cowardice and apology"—could only be read as a direct challenge to Washington's leadership.[97]

John H. Murphy, Sr., of the *Baltimore Afro-American Ledger* was not pleased. Editorials appearing during July 1905 addressed criticisms that the Tuskegee principal had not been "radical" enough regarding the "suffrage matter and the civil rights of the Negro." According to Murphy, Washington's decision not to publicly express himself to the full limit regarding political and civil rights was a pragmatic one: anyone who "enjoys a personal acquaintance of Dr. Washington must know that he believes that the Negro ought to have every right, both civil and political, which any other man enjoys." Washington had merely chosen to cultivate those "things within our power, which will cause the least amount of friction."[98]

Murphy saw nothing wrong with such a position, and believed that there was no reason for strife between those in the race. As he explained, Washington was dwelling on the phase of the "problem" that had a more "direct and immediate benefit to the great masses," and there was no reason another group could not emphasize agitation. As Murphy asserted, "both phases need emphasis, and certainly we ought to be able to do it without seeking to belittle the most illustrious member of the Negro race in the world."[99]

Such sentiment had been demonstrated with Washington's public and private association with the Afro-American League and Council. The problem appears to have been that the disagreements between the two growing camps had become based on personalities, and in Washington's mind the increased amount of attacks on him and his policies would lead to more friction with white philanthropists and a possible drop in financial support. Such a situation would decrease the amount of financial support he would be able to provide for both his public and private causes.[100]

While this may have been Washington's theory, what contributed to the current state of affairs was the Afro-American Council's failure to gain any significant victories. In its tenure as the leading civil rights organization, it did not raise sufficient funds or calibrate its message to properly inform the membership and the community of its actions and agenda. This allowed many of Washington's critics to blame the failure of the Council on his policies, despite the fact that until the 1904 convention, even with his comrade T. Thomas Fortune at the helm, the organization had continually pushed its strong agenda, using a multipronged approach to bring challenges for the rights of African Americans on the local and national levels through propaganda, the courts, the halls of Congress, and the office of the U.S. president. Moreover, Washington supported all this activity, though often only privately, by encouragement, resources, and money. Despite the history of the Council, however, many had become impatient and used Washington and his public positions as the means to argue for a new in name (but not in desire or method) organization outside of the Tuskegee principal's orbit.

* * *

In the wake of the creation of the Niagara Movement and the growing anxiety of Washingtonians, Bishop Alexander Walters rose once again to reassert the supremacy of the Afro-American League/Council strategy. The strategy T. Thomas Fortune had outlined more than twenty years before had become the prototype all the developing civil rights groups were using as their model—a permanent organization that did not ask, but demanded that justice be done, a national civil rights association that met annually in convention, but was based in local and state branches throughout the country, whose purpose was to fight not only racism in general but to contest discrimination and mob violence via the local, state, and federal courts and governments. Walters was an individual who could not be strictly placed in any camp. The bishop continuously worked with whomever he could for the betterment of the race, and he used his acknowledged standing as a rightful individual to defend the Afro-American Council in a time of strife. Prior to the gathering of the Niagara Movement at Fort Erie, Walters had issued the call for the eighth annual convention of the organization to assemble in Detroit beginning in late August. With the birth of the Niagara Movement, Walters now openly campaigned for a return to the presidency of the organization, and issued a call for the return also of the "old guard" to the ranks of the Afro-American Council.

Directly following his call, Walters published an open letter written generally to all race men and women, but specifically to seventy-seven individuals—including, among others, T. Thomas Fortune, Booker T. Washington, Frederick McGhee, Ida B. Wells-Barnett, Henry McNeal Turner, Archibald and Francis Grimké, Mrs. Jerome Jeffery, Gertrude Mossell, John Mitchell, Jesse Lawson, Daniel Murray, and Reverend William H. Brooks. There he set forth "clearly and forcibly the necessity for the continued existence of the National Afro-American Council" and the participation of a number of individuals across the political spectrum. As if in response to the creation of the Niagara Movement, Walters warned that the recent racial violence in New York; the lynching of seven African Americans in Watkinsville, Georgia; the venomous racial rants of the Mississippi Governor James K. Vardaman; and the continued proliferation of "Jim Crow" practices necessitated an amplified call to the "derelict members of the Afro-American Council . . . to do something to check this onslaught upon their civil and political rights."[101]

In response to the accusations that the Council had not accomplished anything during its tenure, the bishop cited the numerous addresses made by organization leaders, committee member meetings with individuals from both the McKinley and Roosevelt Administrations, testimony before various government committees, and institution of legal test cases, including a challenge to the Louisiana suffrage legislation. All this, he believed, spoke effectively for the organization's involvement with its membership and the financial support the Council had received since its inception in 1898. Finally, speaking directly to the creation of the Niagara Movement, Walters noted that "we have waited and given others time to organize . . . I am of opinion that the men who gave the Council such unselfish support, should take hold again."[102]

A week later, William Steward, Walters, and Cyrus Field Adams issued the official call for the Council's Detroit convention. Reprinting much of Walters's letter, the call outlined the reasons to support the Council and stressed the necessity for large numbers of people to return in order that a comprehensive plan of attack could be enacted with respect to the paramount issue affecting the race: disfranchisement.[103]

Amidst this resurgence of energy and direction, the Afro-American Council's Legal Bureau won a victory in Florida. In April 1905, white state representative John Campbell Avery of Pensacola introduced a streetcar segregation bill into the state legislature. Despite a flurry of protests by black Floridians, the Avery Bill was passed on May 12 and was set to take effect on July 1.[104] Boycotts of the streetcars began in Pensacola almost immediately after Avery proposed the bill and they spread to other cities—including Jacksonville—once it went into effect.[105]

In Jacksonville, blacks moved to test the constitutionality of the Jim Crow legislation. On July 8, 1905, James E. Cashin, a black bartender, was arrested for refusing to sit in the colored section of the streetcar. Immediately after the arrest, local attorney J. Douglas Wetmore, a member of the Afro-American Council's Legal and Legislative Bureau, filed suit in Duval County court.[106] The tactic backfired when county solicitor W. J. Bryan refused to prosecute Cashin on the grounds that the company had not properly installed signs designating the separate sections of the car.[107]

Despite this legal setback, the boycott continued, and behind the scenes Wetmore continued his plan to initiate a legal test case. Several weeks following the first attempt—after the company had installed a one-foot-high sign demarcating the white and colored sections—he arranged for Andrew Patterson to board the North Jacksonville line and occupy a seat designated for white passengers. At the end of the line, Patterson was arrested. Wetmore went before Circuit Judge R. M. Call to file a writ of habeas corpus, claiming the separate coach law to be unconstitutional on a number of grounds.[108] On July 25, Judge Call held that the Avery Law was indeed unconstitutional—but on the basis that it was "class legislation" because it allowed black domestics to sit in the white compartments.[109] W. J. Bryan and state attorney general W. H. Ellis appealed the decision to the Florida Supreme Court. In quick action, the court confirmed Judge Call's decision and declared the Avery law unconstitutional.[110] After this favorable ruling, the local Council and the leaders of the boycotts in Pensacola and Jacksonville celebrated their victory and called off the boycotts.[111]

With this legal victory and Walters's call for the rejuvenation of the organization, a number of individuals weighed in on the wisdom of supporting the group. In the pages of the *Age*, T. Thomas Fortune praised the call for the return of the old guard and believed that with their return the Council would be raised to the position of strength he had visualized in 1887.[112] Endorser of the Niagara Movement Harry Smith of the *Cleveland Gazette* also expressed support for Walters's return to the Council presidency. He believed that

Walters's departure from that position had allowed the group to become "Booker T. Washingtonized" and let the Louisiana test case die.[113] Smith felt that the return of Walters to the presidency would radicalize the Council and encourage the "old guard" to return to the organization.

Despite support such as this, not all were certain that a return of Walters to the Council's leadership was the correct course of action. Initially, Washington and his secretary Emmett Scott were skeptical about Walters's regaining control of the Council. Though Walters had worked well with Washington in the past, he was not exactly in the Tuskegee orbit. Moreover, over the past year he had distanced himself from the Wizard's policies. Such independence worried Scott. Walters, however, had been in contact with Richard W. Thompson, head of the National Negro Press Bureau and longtime supporter of Washington as well as the Council, explaining that his desire to return to the presidency was not for the purpose of undermining Washington. He wanted a return to the original policy of the Council advocating for civil and political equality while allowing the Wizard to maintain his adherence to a conservative line—thereby retaining white support and clandestinely aiding the Council's cause.[114] Above all, the revitalization of the Council would counter and destroy the Niagara Movement's growing momentum.[115] Though still somewhat skeptical, Washington supported Walters's move to regain the control of the organization.

Walters, however, was unable to easily sway others within the community. Shortly after returning from the inaugural conference of the Niagara Movement, Frederick McGhee penned a long, angry, and open response to the bishop, which was published in the *Washington Bee*.[116] McGhee questioned the validity of reviving the Council at a time when people had lost confidence in the organization. He stated that Fortune—the initiator of the movement—had abandoned the group, and those who controlled the Council over the past few years had allowed it to dwindle in its effectiveness. Moreover, the former member of the Council's Legal and Legislative Bureau asked why Walters was calling on the old guard to return when it was he who could have saved the group, "but instead calmly acquiesced for harmony's sake" to the "injurious and death-dealing" methods that caused its demise.[117] Little would be gained by reviving a dead organization, reasoned McGhee, but its members joining and strengthening the Niagara Movement could allow continued pursuit of the Council's ideas and goals.

Such sentiments had already been expressed a week earlier by the editors of the *St. Louis Advance*: "the Niagara Movement comes in the fullness of time. The old apologetic Afro-American council is dying of inanity, the Booker T. Washington 'lay low and keep dark' policy has nauseated the manly Negro, and the lack of proper leadership was falling like a pall upon the race."[118] The *Advance* recommended that everyone leave the Council behind and "stand up with Du Bois for manhood suffrage, for the abolition of class distinctions."[119] Ida B. Wells-Barnett, although not a member of the Niagara Movement, published her own strong letter attacking the bishop and the Council.[120]

With such opinions about the Council and its value as an organization, Walters and the supporters of the nation's oldest civil rights organization had their work cut out for them. They were not, however, willing to simply close the doors of the Council and fold up its work. Walters and a number of the "old guard," mixed with some new blood and energy, pressed forward with the agenda and activity of the Council and sought to cooperate with the new developing organizations whenever possible.

Actually, this is what many within the community were calling for in the wake of the proliferation of organizations. As individuals began to declare their loyalties to one side or the other, some within the community were calling for a unification of the two groups. First to push such an agenda was Alexander Manning of the *Indianapolis World*. He encouraged the Council to create a "union that [would] stick," one with the support of all interests within the community. "Then when the world strikes at our rights," he argued, the Council with the full backing of the community could "hunt out the offender and see him at the polls."[121]

The possibility of a union of the Council and the Niagara Movement, however, seemed remote at the time. As the Council convention approached, Niagarites were seeing some success in their organizing efforts. Movement leaders claimed that the membership had increased from twenty-nine branches in July to forty-four by the time the Council convention opened in late August.[122] Moreover, local branches of the Movement had become active. In late August, for example, the New York branch of the organization met at the Brooklyn residence of Dr. Owen M. Waller, a recent migrant to the city from Washington, D.C., where he was rector of St. Luke's Protestant Episcopal Council. Those present heard from a number of speakers, including a visiting native of Baltimore, Maryland, Reverend Garnett R. Waller, who informed the gathering of the Baltimore Niagarites' struggle against disfranchisement in their city.[123]

In the midst of the Niagara Movement activity and the discussion of a merger between the Council and Niagara, Council supporters converged on

Detroit. Walters's call, and surely the competition posed by the Niagara Movement, had brought out the old guard, with the result being a large, successful convention. Seventy-five delegates from twenty-one different states were in attendance.[124] Walters was reelected president while Steward swapped positions with the bishop and became chairman of the Executive Committee.[125]

According to press coverage, the event displayed the harmonious tone of the St. Louis convention: "there was absolutely no political sideplay, no impugning of motives, no disposition to 'hog things.'"[126] Unlike the St. Louis proceedings, however, harmonious did not mean conservative. The organization reaffirmed its nonpartisan character and raised nearly three hundred dollars to fund its activities of testing Jim Crow legislation.[127]

One of the highlights of the convention was the battle plan presented to the delegation by William H. Lewis, assistant district attorney of Boston. His address, "The Legal Status of the American Negro," which was declared "a masterpiece" by Mary Church Terrell and many others in the audience, was delivered to a large enthusiastic delegation at the Bethel AME Church on the second day of the meeting. Beginning by citing the late Massachusetts Senator George F. Hoar's declaration that the "Negro is the football of American politics," Lewis outlined the past and current legal status of the black community, carefully describing the ways in which African Americans had been stripped of their civil and political rights and how the community throughout much of the country currently stood as "a perfect nondescript, an alien in the land of his birth, a land watered and nourished by the sweat, blood and tears of his fathers."[128]

Citing Cicero, Lewis than rhetorically asked the audience, "Since these things are so, how are we to obtain these rights desired?" He believed the focus should begin with the franchise and set forth a three-layered attack. First, he called on the Council to hire the best legal talent in the country to bring cases "squarely before the Supreme Court." Second, foreshadowing tactics by the NAACP and later the Student Nonviolent Coordinating Committee, Lewis encouraged the Council to organize schools throughout the South to train the male population "under forty" to read and prepare them to qualify to vote under the revised constitutions. Finally, he called on the organization to assail the state legislatures and businesses with petitions to make it clear that the African American community will never "surrender the precious heritage of American citizenship."[129] The Boston assistant attorney general, echoing Bishop Walters, believed that if the Council took these more activist positions, it would be successful and would one day realize Alfred Lord Tennyson's dream:

Of knowledge fusing class with class,
Of civic hate no more to be,
Of love to leaven all the mass,
Till every soul be free.[130]

Lewis concluded his address to tremendous applause from a determined delegation willing to follow his lead. J. Douglas Wetmore, the fighting lawyer from Florida who had just been elected director of the Legal and Legislative Bureau, rose and commended his colleague and seconded his call for the top legal minds to examine disfranchisement legislation and "fight them in the highest courts of the country."[131] Wetmore also vowed to continue to apply pressure in his own legal struggles in Florida.

With the delegation asserting its activist side, it was obvious the organization was not taking the creation of the Niagara Movement lightly. Although the group's Address to the Nation failed to acknowledge the existence of the new civil rights organization, it did attempt to legitimize the Council's national preeminence regarding civil rights issues. The Address noted that "for seven years, through mistakes, bickerings, and internal as well as external attacks, the Council [had] haltingly, but without abatement of its high purpose, gone forward."[132] The nine propositions that the group had adopted at its founding convention in 1898 were reiterated, including the investigation of lynchings, the challenging of the constitutionality of Jim Crow legislation, the promotion of legislation guaranteeing the Fourteenth and Fifteenth Amendments, the continued efforts at prison reform, the promotion of migration from terror-ridden sections of the country, the encouragement of both industrial and higher education, the promotion of business enterprises, and the encouragement of moral elevation and social uplift.[133]

In addition, the Address affirmed that the Council had been successful in accomplishing some of its "high purpose[s]." It argued that lynchings had decreased in number, largely through the efforts of the Council's Anti-Lynching Bureau under the successful leadership of Ida B. Wells-Barnett, John Mitchell, Jr., and now Mary Church Terrell. Finally, the Address ended with another assertion that the Council, though not completely successful, was the only national organization actively testing the growing Jim Crow legislation, and it encouraged the community to "organize and contribute of their means" for the continuation of such action.[134]

* * *

Following the Detroit convention, there were calls from other circles for the two national civil rights organizations to unify their efforts. One example was a poem written by Clarence Emery Allen, published in the *Washington Bee* the day after the convention. In one stanza Allen cried out for unity:

> We must stick, must stick together—
> As one mighty force must stand,
> If we'd withstand the mighty siege
> Being waged on every hand.
> We cannot single-handed live—
> 'Tis only folly for to try!
> We must stand and stick together,
> Or lose the fight and die.[135]

Archibald Grimké echoed the poetic appeal in a thoughtful article, "Right Afro-American Leadership," published by the *New York Age* in mid-September 1905. There he put forth a call for an alliance among the three groups—industrial education, higher education, and political rights—who he saw "going by separate ways, or apparently separate ways, to the same destination . . . race freedom and progress."[136] Grimké proposed that the three groups, represented by members of the Council, the Niagara Movement, the Tuskegee sphere, the American Negro Academy, and the Committee of Twelve, put their petty bickering aside and form one grand army.

As he described this new army, it resembled the original model of the Afro-American Council. The group would be formed with the political rights supporters forming the center and the education advocates the powerful wings. But the leadership of the new, unified organization he counseled would not fall to an individual who sought division, but rather to one "who is a healer of differences within the race; to the man who is big enough and broad and wise enough to include all that is so to bring about the union in one mighty organization."[137]

In retrospect, Grimké was calling for the same type of leadership proposed by Bishop Walters in his address before the very first Council convention held in Washington, D.C., in late 1898. Many suspected that Grimké's article, though thought provoking, was a Washingtonian trick. W. Calvin Chase of the *Washington Bee* quickly responded to the article, asserting that it came "from a quarter which has brought disaster upon every movement."[138] Furthermore, Chase asserted that there could be "no peace, no union, no harmony, until truth and righteousness [had] won a single and complete victory over falsehood, error, and corruption."[139]

Disregarding the call for immediate unity, the *AME Church Review* simply asked for harmony and definitiveness in aim, and noted that the Niagara Movement Declaration of Principles was "bold and broad." However, the editors asserted that if these were "reduced to essentials," they were "strikingly like the declarations that the Afro-American Council has put forth, and ought to establish friendly co-operation with ultimate combination. But still," they argued "such organic union can come of its own accord," and therefore for the moment they urged each group to "pursue its own methods for the general good and hasten by generous rivalry the strength of the effort to arouse the American conscience."[140]

The editors acknowledged that the Council had decided to focus on the issue of southern disfranchisement and the Jim Crow car laws. They called on the Niagara Movement to concentrate on these issues as well, or others of its choosing, but to agitate for African American rights without fighting with other organizations pursuing the same general goals.

Agitation was the watchword of both organizations, and while the discussion over unity was taking place in editorial columns, the Council and the Niagara Movement pressed forward. The Council was particularly eager to get to work and demonstrate that it was an organization that was fighting for the rights of African Americans, not one that was advocating a "lay low" policy.[141] Shortly after the Council's national convention the newly elected legal director J. Douglas Wetmore wrote Washington asking for suggestions as to where the Legal Bureau should devote its energy. Washington urged Wetmore and the Council to look into challenging the elimination of Negro militias. According to Washington, Georgia had recently passed a bill abolishing the state's black militia, and in his opinion the bill was unconstitutional since the state still received federal funds for its national guard.[142] In addition to his correspondence with Wetmore, Washington wrote to Bishop

Walters to congratulate him on his presidency and to urge him to focus on creating local councils "North and South."[143]

While Wetmore looked into the feasibility of challenging the validity of Georgia's legislation, the Council continued working to halt the geographical spread of separate coach laws. The organization's corresponding secretary, Lewis G. Jordan, who was a Baptist minister, missionary, and businessman from Louisville, Kentucky, took the lead in this arena. As he was concerned not only with the growth of Jim Crow legislation, Jordan concentrated on the customary practices of the railroad companies. He noticed that incoming cars from states where separate car laws operated were not removing their signs in states that were free of such legislation. Fearful that custom unchallenged would become law, he decided to nip the practice in the bud, and in September launched a letter-writing campaign focusing on the practices of the Baltimore and Ohio Southwestern Railroad Company (B&O).[144]

Reverend Jordan concentrated his complaint on Illinois Central cars being delivered to the B&O in St. Louis, Missouri. He protested that the signs "For Whites Only" and "For Colored Passengers" were not removed when the cars traveled through Missouri, Illinois, Indiana, and Ohio—all states without separate coach legislation. Initially, the representatives of the B&O attempted to dismiss the complaint by stating that the signs were non-removable and were not in violation of any law. However, as Jordan and the Afro-American continued to press the issue, they succeeded by mid-October in persuading the railroad to remove the separate car signs from passenger cars traveling from St. Louis through Ohio.

In the light of Jordan's successful challenge, the Council began urging other railroad companies to end the customary practices of maintaining segregated seating signs in states such as Pennsylvania and Delaware. The group also protested the actions of a conductor on the Chesapeake & Ohio Railroad who had forced a group of African American women to sit in a segregated section of the train in a state that did not have Jim Crow legislation. Due to the Council's protest, the conductor received a reprimand from his employer.[145] In addition to his petition and letter-writing campaign, Jordan worked with J. Douglas Wetmore, Hightower T. Kealing, and George W. Clinton to actively organize several local Councils throughout the country.

However, as the Council pressed forward much in the way it had since its inception with its agitation and lobbying activities, the Niagara Movement was continuing to organize and expand its presence throughout the nation. In particular, the Movement was preparing to hold a series of

Thanksgiving memorial services to honor a tradition of protest and to spread the Niagara principles. This year the group planned to honor the lives and services of Frederick Douglass, William Lloyd Garrison, and Albion W. Tourgée.[146] According to J. Max Barber, editor of the *Voice of the Negro*, the event was wholly successful: it was "safe to estimate that 10,000 Negroes assembled to keep green the memory of these great men."[147]

As the Niagara Movement was developing the Council continued to expand its legal challenges to separate council legislation. Blacks in Pensacola and Jacksonville, Florida, led by J. Douglas Wetmore, were preparing to challenge separate coach municipal ordinances put into place shortly after the state Supreme Court had ruled the Avery Bill unconstitutional in *Florida v. Patterson*.[148] In mid-October 1905, Reverend L. B. Croom of Pensacola agreed to get himself arrested for sitting in the white section of a car—a crime for which he was promptly sentenced to a thirty-day jail term. Wetmore and Isaac L. Purcell, an attorney from Pensacola who aided in the Patterson case, swiftly instituted a habeas corpus suit. While the Croom case was pending in the courts, Andrew Patterson, following arrangements made by Wetmore, challenged the Jacksonville ordinance. Ten days later, on November 24, the court rendered a decision against Croom, thus upholding the Pensacola ordinance. Wetmore appealed the decision, but on December 6 the circuit court upheld the ruling of the lower court. The following day, Judge Call, the local judge who had declared the Avery Law unconstitutional in July, ruled against Patterson and Wetmore in the Jacksonville test case.[149]

Despite these defeats and the changing sentiment of the Florida courts, Wetmore agreed to appeal both cases to the state supreme court. To publicize this activity as well as other work carried out by the Afro-American Council, Lewis G. Jordan sent out a circular letter to Afro-American newspapers throughout the country. Jordan explained that the "Council has a specific object" to unite all people who believed that it was worth laboring for "the civil and political rights of the Afro-American people . . . by [the] legal process."[150] To demonstrate the work that the Council had accomplished or was currently engaged in, the coordinating secretary gave details of some of the organization's previous legal efforts—including the Louisiana Grandfather Clause suit and the Alabama suffrage cases. He also explained that the organization was currently involved in an attempt to wipe out the separate coach laws of Florida. Finally, Jordan published a number of his pieces of correspondence with the management of the B&O urging the railroad to end its segregation policies in states that did not have separate coach laws.[151]

In publishing this information, Jordan hoped to demonstrate to the people that "whatever may have been charged as a mistake in the past, the Council [had] purged itself and declared that it would forever stand on its original platform." It had begun "anew the defense for the civil and political rights of the race." Moreover, he desired that African Americans acknowledge the work of the organization and begin funding the group due to the fact that "the legal bureau [was] handicapped for want of funds to test cases constantly put into our hands." Furthermore, like the Niagara Movement, Jordan and the Council laid claim to the legacy of William Lloyd Garrison during the centennial of his birth. Garrison, Jordan declared, "fully expressed the determination of the Afro-American Council in the present fight for [the race's] political and civil rights when he—echoing Fortune's 1890 League address—declared, 'I am in earnest—I will not equivocate—I will not excuse—I will not retreat a single inch—AND I WILL BE HEARD.'"[152] Jordan urged the community to be heard through its funding of Council legal and legislative activities.

Despite Jordan's strong demonstration of work carried out by the Council, not everyone saw the validity of supporting the organization. Only the *New York Age* and the *Washington Bee* published Jordan's circular. The *Baltimore Afro-American Ledger* acknowledged the letter as well as the recent work of the Council, but John Murphy did not see reason enough for the community to support the organization. He believed that it was better to allow multiple individuals and organizations to agitate for Afro-American rights rather than placing all confidence and monies with one organization.[153]

W. Calvin Chase expressed similar sentiments. While willing to publish the circular in his *Washington Bee* and acknowledging the merit of the Council's work, he believed that local communities should fund themselves rather than pass "their hats to those who have troubles and burdens of their own."[154] He did not, for example, see the validity of the citizens of the District of Columbia funding a case in Florida when segregated trains entered those citizens' own city daily despite the absence of separate coach legislation.

Chase and Murphy were not the only ones with a limited understanding of how a concentration of energy and funds elsewhere might have an effect on their own local situation. Other editors failed as well to consider that a victory in Florida might set a precedent that could strike down separate coach legislation throughout the nation. Council supporters understood the importance of their work and continued to struggle with or without the financial support of the community. J. Douglas Wetmore, for example, pressed forward with the Crooms and Patterson appeals, and by the end of the year he had secured a hearing by the state supreme court for early 1906.[155] Lewis G. Jordan and J. Douglas Wetmore also listened to Chase's concerns and began planning a challenge to the customary practice of segregating cars that entered the District of Columbia.[156]

As the year came to a close, local Councils on both coasts were also active. In California, the Los Angeles Council, led by James Alexander, the recently elected president of the state organization, came to the assistance of Levy F. Mallory. Mallory, a porter on the Southern Pacific Railroad, was arrested by two Los Angeles police officers on November 20, 1905 under the suspicion that he was responsible for the murder of an El Paso, Texas policeman. On February 17, 1900, Newton Stewart had been shot and killed when the El Paso police raided the barracks of the black soldiers of the Twenty-Fifth Infantry stationed at Fort Bliss after they had tried to free a fellow soldier who was arrested for "creating a disturbance." Though a number of suspects had been questioned over the years, no individual had been charged with the murder.[157]

Mallory immediately proclaimed his innocence and the local Afro-American Council began trying to gain his release. Upon securing the facts of the case, James Alexander wrote to California Governor George Pardee appealing to him to "save an innocent man." In his letter, Alexander noted that Mallory had not been in the Twenty-Fifth Infantry nor was he stationed at Fort Bliss in February 1900. He was, instead a member of the Twenty-Fourth Infantry and was stationed at Fort Wingate, New Mexico. Alexander believed that the mix-up had been caused by the incompetence and discriminatory action of the Los Angeles police department and called upon the governor to right the wrong. After reviewing the evidence, Governor Pardee quickly sent a telegram demanding Mallory's release and called for the charges to be dropped.[158]

Demonstrating how the Council used any means possible as well as a multipronged, various-angled attack on the continued broadening of segregation, discrimination, and general racial prejudice, while the California Afro-American organization was involved in the Mallory incident, members of the New York City and Jersey City branches joined with New York City's Colored Citizens Protective League to stop the theatrical production of Thomas Dixon's *The Clansman*. Having toured the country for a number of months, the production in nearly every instance had sparked some sort of racial hostility.[159] Following the voicing of community concerns, the two groups formed a committee— which included local Council supporters T. Thomas Fortune and Dr. William H. Brooks—to call upon New York City Mayor George B. McClellan. The committee argued that the play be cancelled on the "grounds of its immortality and its tendency to embitter racial feeling and antagonism, if not directly leading to more riots."[160]

With this action as well as the activity of Reverend Lewis G. Jordan and the local branches in California and Florida, the Afro-American Council closed out the year with momentum and a renewed sense of purpose. The organization had righted its ship and sailed ahead with its demanding yet continuous multipronged process of propaganda campaigns, legal suits, and lobbying efforts in the hopes of gaining some favorable legislation to end the discriminatory actions of the southern states and get the federal government to uphold the Fourteenth and Fifteenth Amendments. Any deficiencies that individuals had accused the Council of having at the beginning of the year had been cast aside. In the wake of the creation of the Niagara Movement, among other factors, Walters and other leaders within the organization had been successful in purging the group of its deadweight and again setting the Council on the course of battling for the interests of the African American community. At the 1905 convention, the new leaders had vowed to concentrate their energies on the struggle against disfranchisement and the spread of separate coach legislation, and in the months following the convention they had succeeded. Walters, Jordan, Wetmore, and the remaining leaders were once more on their way to demonstrating that the organization of nearly ten years represented the voice of the people and could lay claim to the ideals set forward in 1890 at the formation of the Afro-American League and again in 1898 at the creation of the Council.

Such was the situation as viewed by all. Even W. E. B. Du Bois acknowledged the existence of a new breath blown into the Council. In an article published at the beginning of 1906, he and the Niagara Movement took credit for pumping "new life into all the older Negro organizations" and "welcomed the renewed activity of the Afro-American Council."[161] At the same time, however, Du Bois assured his readers that the Movement was not "considering any proposition for merger or self-effacement."[162] And yet questions remained: Could the organizations sustain the momentum of 1905? Moreover, could they do so while competing for already limited resources? Nonetheless, as

1906 unfolded, the community had a rejuvenated Afro-American Council and an organizing Niagara Movement vowing to fight for African America's civil and political rights. Among the leadership of both organizations the future seemed bright, but only time would tell whether they were to be an "an army of mice" or an "army of lions."

Chapter 8

"It Is Strike Now or Never"

> Let us no longer allow ourselves to be amenable to the just reproach that though we have the strength of a giant we use it like a child.
>
> —T. Thomas Fortune

> Courage brothers! The battle for humanity is not lost or losing. . . . The Slav is moving in his might, the yellow minions are testing liberty, the black Africans are writhing toward the light, and everywhere the laborer, with ballot in his hand, is opening the gates of Opportunity and Peace.
>
> —W. E. B. Du Bois

Building on the momentum of the final months of 1905, the Afro-American Council entered 1906 full of energy and primed to have a successful year. The Constitution League and the Niagara Movement also entered the New Year focused and ready to organize. Such determination and concentration was necessary for, despite the best efforts of these organizations, it seemed they were only slowing the steamroller of white supremacy. Whites continued to violate and rewrite the rights of African Americans with impunity. Moreover, racial tensions, which often lead to violence, continued to increase with the proliferation of sensationalized scare stories about black crime, rampant black sexuality, and "negro domination." At the beginning of 1906 such a situation was epitomized by the popularity of Thomas Dixon's best-selling novel *The Clansman*, the theatrical adaption of which was traveling throughout the country to rave reviews. In this climate each organization understood the importance of its individual existence, but over the course of the year unforeseen events would pull the three groups closer together and lay the groundwork for a unified interracial organization that would stand for black rights on the same basic principles outlined by T. Thomas Fortune nearly twenty years before.

Indeed, though historians have paid scant attention, the immediate years preceding the creation of the National Association for the Advancement of Colored People (NAACP) in 1909 were active ones for all of the nation's civil rights organizations. It was not just the Niagara Movement that was pushing Fortune's 1884 vision of a national civil rights organization: a permanent organization that demanded equality; a national association that came together annually in convention, but was based in local and state branches throughout the country; an organized effort to fight not only racism in general, but to contest discrimination and mob violence by using the local, state, and federal courts and governments. The Afro-American Council and the interracial Constitution League, as well as the Committee of Twelve, were also vigorously working during this period—building test cases, lobbying the federal government, creating petitions, and publishing propaganda to counter the disfranchising and discriminatory actions of the southern states that were becoming increasingly accepted or at least tolerated throughout the nation. The efforts of all these organizations lay the foundation for what would become the NAACP as the groups worked both independently and collectively to demand that the nation uphold the Fourteenth and Fifteenth Amendments and bring an end to the spread of white supremacy and racial violence.

* * *

Both the Niagara Movement and the Afro-American Council sought to communicate to the nation that they were alive and well and moving forward with their various agendas. In January 1906, as previously noted, W. E. B. Du Bois, general secretary of the Niagara Movement, published a piece in the *Voice of the Negro* concerning the progress of his organization—now seventeen branches strong—and promoted the group's proposed November convention.[1] The Afro-American Council sent Bishop Walters, Lewis G. Jordan, and J. Douglas Wetmore on speaking tours throughout the country.[2] Additionally, the Council's legal team laid out its plans of attack against the continuing efforts to extend Virginia's Jim Crow law into the District of Columbia.[3]

While moving forward with their own plans, both the Council and the Niagara Movement were also beginning to cooperate with the Constitution

League. During the final months of 1905, John Milholland began organizing a mass meeting on the issue of black rights to be held at Cooper Union in New York City. The purpose of the gathering was "to protest against the way in which the Coloured Citizens [were] treated in the South" and to mark the opening of the League's Southern Suffrage Campaign.[4] On January 22, 1906, Milholland and the League sent out a circular announcing the meeting and outlining the need for a protest strategy against the unlawful situation in the South in regards to suffrage.[5]

Less than two weeks after the distribution of the circular, three thousand people assembled at Cooper Union to participate in one of "the most significant [events] in American politics . . . the beginning of the end of the shameless conditions in the South whereby the Constitution of the United States had been defied, nullified, trodden under foot by the forces that sought to destroy this government."[6] Both blacks and whites were in attendance, and all of the major civil rights organizations were represented. Participants included W. E. B. Du Bois of the Niagara Movement, Mary Church Terrell and J. Douglas Wetmore of the Afro-American Council, and Archibald Grimké and Kelly Miller of the Committee of Twelve.[7]

In his opening address, Milholland spoke in harmonizing tones, calling for a united front in the fight against injustices committed in the South and by the federal government. He also called for multifaceted remedies to the race problem including legal suits, protests to the Roosevelt Administration and Congress, and educational measures. In his discussion of education as a remedy, Milholland outlined the League's desire for the immediate passage of a comprehensive federal education bill. At the same time, however, he distanced himself from Booker T. Washington. While the League recognized the "potential forces for uplifting of the colored people" in institutions such as Tuskegee, Atlanta, Fisk, Hampton, and others, Milholland averred, "We say without hesitation that education, will never alone be sufficient to bring about a satisfactory solution of the problem." He asserted that "All the Negro schools and colleges of the Southern States have never been able to prevent the enactment of one disfranchisement statute nor prevented the steady curtailment of the Afro-American's rights and privileges. 'Jim Crow' legislation has kept pace with the beneficent results of the Slater and the Peabody funds."[8]

Following Milholland were a number of speakers, including Mary Church Terrell, director of the Afro-American Council's Anti-Lynching Bureau. Putting the struggle in wider context, Terrell contrasted with biting irony the recent mass protest in Washington against the massacres of Russian Jews with the nation's indifference to the "butcheries of Afro-Americans in the South."[9] She called on African Americans and white northerners to wake from their lethargic, apathetic state and breathe some moral justice into the South. She asked, "when one section of the country reverts to barbaric, antediluvian practices, shall we let the rash and wicked brother toboggan to his ruin?" Terrell also labeled the act of disfranchisement as treason and contrary to the basic principles upon which the government was founded.[10]

Du Bois, who spoke next, also addressed the subject of disfranchisement. The Atlanta professor and Niagara member, similar to Washington and Fortune, believed that reduction of southern representation was not the solution to the problem. According to Du Bois, those struggling for the rights of African Americans needed to focus on the upholding of the Fifteenth Amendment. Following Du Bois's paper came addresses from Archibald Grimké (Committee of Twelve), William Sinclair (Constitution League and Afro-American Council), Clement Morgan (Niagara Movement), and finally J. Douglas Wetmore (Afro-American Council), who spoke about his legal suits in Jacksonville and Pensacola, Florida.[11]

The proceedings at Cooper Union demonstrate that while tensions, frustrations, and infighting may have continued within the band of African American activists, these individuals were also beginning to find some space for a fusion of their missions. Absent from the meeting was the bitter personality fights of the Afro-American Council's Louisville convention or the public censures of one organization or the other. The activists were converging on a shared agenda—the enforcement of the Fourteenth and Fifteenth Amendments as well as an end to racial violence—and while each organization worked on its own suits, lobbying efforts, and development, the groups and their leaders were willing to cooperate in the laborious, time-consuming struggle.

With the unifying energy of the successful Cooper Union event driving them, the Constitution League immediately began lobbying Congress for support of the organization's constitutional and political remedy to the race problem. Andrew B. Humphrey, the organization's secretary, was sent to Washington to drum up support for the group.[12] In this congressional election year, Milholland and Humphreys sought to organize support among congressional Republicans for the group's program—steps toward proper constitutional representation "and a restoration in all States which shall insure a righteous liberty of political action without distinction of race or color."[13] Moreover, come November, the Constitution League planned to organize against congressional representatives whom they identified as standing against black rights. Additionally, several weeks following the Cooper Union meeting, the Constitution League joined with the Niagara Movement to hold equally impressive organizational gatherings in Philadelphia and Washington.[14]

As for the Afro-American Council, following the Cooper Union meeting the organization also proceeded with its program of focusing on disfranchisement and Jim Crow laws. Wetmore returned to Florida to argue his cases before the state supreme court. Unfortunately, the court upheld the constitutionality of both Pensacola and Jacksonville's segregation ordinances.[15] The decision, however, did not deflate the enthusiasm of Wetmore or the Council. Indeed, a week after the decision Wetmore was in a Washington, D.C. meeting with Lewis G. Jordan, the Louisville, Kentucky-based Baptist minister and Council corresponding secretary, to outline a plan of attack against the segregation of railroad cars entering the District.[16] Jordan also sent out circulars to the black press concerning the Council's activity and called on supporters of the cause to each send in one dollar to create a million-dollar defense fund.[17] In addition to Jordan's work, he, Wetmore, and Bishop Walters lectured throughout the South to promote the Council's activities as well as the need for a legal defense fund.[18]

Individuals immediately began sending money in support of the Council's activities. Among the contributors was Washington, who sent Walters a personal check for twenty-five dollars.[19] Washington reiterated his support for the Council's activity and hoped that others would contribute to the cause. In addition, he corresponded with Walters and Wetmore throughout the month of March regarding other Council activities—including his support for the Council's attempt to create a larger test case against southern railroad segregation legislation.[20]

Some of this discussion and interest in segregated railways centered on activity taking place in Virginia. African Americans in the state had a long history of challenging Jim Crow cars in both railroad and streetcar transportation.[21] Since 1904, many black communities in Virginia had had on-again, off-again boycotts and protests against local ordinances, but in January 1906 the General Assembly enacted separate coach legislation, which went into effect the following June. Immediately following the Assembly's passage of the legislation, communities sprang into action. Boycotts were begun in Richmond, Newport News, Danville, Lynchburg, Portsmouth, Berkley, and Norfolk.[22] Many subscribed to the ideas expressed in a poem published in Council supporter John Mitchell, Jr.'s *Richmond Planet*:

. . . rain may fall and wind may blow,
I'll not take the "Jim Crow" car . . .
'Twould you your right debar,
Go, cringe and crawl and grin and then
Ride on the "Jim Crow" car.[23]

The Council, having directed much of its attention over the past year toward Jim Crow cars, immediately lent its support to many of the boycotts. The group especially became interested in the work of the Newport News community. Beginning in late March, the organization ordered five thousand buttons with the inscription "I Will Walk" and sent them to Newport News for community members to wear as they boycotted the streetcars.[24]

Over the next few months the group focused its attention on the Virginia boycotts, organizing local Councils and securing the cooperation of "a chain of literary and other societies." According to one report, the Council organizers sent out "30,000 tracts and pamphlets and 8,000 letters to the leaders of the race" explaining the history and activity of the organization.[25]

In addition to this organizing activity, the Council's legal team sought to work with the protests in Virginia and institute legal test cases against the separate coach legislation. Council lawyers also laid plans to continue with their suits in Florida and Louisiana.[26] To coordinate support for this growth of legal activity, Jordan announced in late June that the Council had selected the One Cent Savings Bank of James C. Napier—a Council member from Nashville Tennessee—as the repository for the group's defense fund, and called on the race to focus on raising one hundred thousand dollars "to fight the disenfranchisement laws of the South."[27] Jordan ambitiously hoped that the organization could raise "at least $10,000" by the group's national convention in September.

In an effort to accomplish this goal, Jordan sent out a circular to a number of individuals and the black press. "Does the Negro know the value of the ballot?," the appeal read. "Will the Negro ever rise in defense of his manhood rights or will he simply sit 'whining' and see himself stripped of the last vestige, the highest boon to American citizenship and himself beaten and riddled with bullets?" It continued with a claim to the Council's history and determination: "The Afro-American Council is sending this letter to you with the hope that you will think upon these things and act with us along the lines indicated. For ten years the Council has steadily fought the disfranchising and 'Jim Crow' laws, so humiliating to self-respecting men and women. . . . The results may not be very gratifying, but we have kept at it."[28] The recipient was than encouraged to send monetary support to the Council's legal defense fund to enable the organization to press forward and fight disfranchisement and the spread of the Jim Crow system.

Additionally, in building on the unifying impulse sparked by the Cooper Union event, the Council began working in conjunction with the Constitution League to rally African American voters in every congressional district for the November elections. Both organizations were determined to "have one or more men in the next congress who will fight the battles of all the people."[29] To aid in this effort Jordan mailed out ten thousand copies of a chapter culled from William Sinclair's *Aftermath of Slavery* that was printed as a pamphlet entitled "Negro and the Law." Every Republican member of Congress received a copy.[30]

Sinclair, a member of the Council and the Constitution League, had published *Aftermath of Slavery* the previous year. His work discussed the process of slavery's demise and the postbellum world in which African Americans had found themselves. Sinclair outlined the development of the "Apartheid South," discussing economic exploitation, imprisonment and peonage, Jim Crow legislation, disfranchisement, and lynching and mob violence, as well as the accomplishments of black Americans despite all the handicaps they were forced to overcome. Hightower T. Kealing, managing editor of the *AME Church Review* and Council supporter, proclaimed in a review of the book that Sinclair had furnished "the sledge hammer demolition of the fallacious and mendacious arguments of those who have well nigh convinced the world that Negro suffrage was a mistake."[31]

In the chapter circulated by the Council, Sinclair focused on the failure of the law to protect African American citizens. He discussed how blacks were often stripped of their citizenship rights by state and municipal legislation that trumped federal law, as well as by the brutal acts that occurred under the nose of the legal system—lynchings, mob violence, and the workings of the southern penal system.[32] To accompany the pamphlet, Jordan attached a letter stating: "We implore you as one representing the party of Sumner, of

Lincoln, of Grant, and a long list of champions of human liberty and manhood rights, to take up our cause. . . . When a question involving the rights of our people comes up, will you open your mouth and speak for the absent? We have no man of color in either house to plead our cause."[33]

Jordan was pleased with the response that he was receiving from a number of congressional representatives and senators, including many who pledged their support and encouraged the organization to contact individual representatives if it felt that a particular piece of legislation would improve the race's condition.[34] Such reaction, combined with the limited but promising funds coming to the One Cent Savings Bank, gave the coordinating secretary hope that momentum was building. Moreover, the collaborative ventures with the Constitution League continued to provide a sense that the Council was gaining assistance and cooperation in the struggle it had been fighting alone for nearly a decade.

* * *

While the Afro-American Council and the Constitution League were pushing forward with their agendas both independently and in tandem, the Niagara Movement was also on the move. In late June, W. E. B. Du Bois sent out an appeal for the community to support the organization financially. Like the Council, for much of its life the Niagara Movement was struggling to push its agenda without mass support. As Du Bois noted, "The point to-day is, Can't we squeeze five dollars more?"

For the cause that lacks assistance
For the wrong that needs resistance
For the future in the distance
And the good that we can do?[35]

Over the past few months the Movement had focused on organizing. It held joint sessions with the Constitution League in Philadelphia and Washington, D.C. In its first year of existence the group had also sent out thousands of pamphlets and leaflets promoting itself, including reprints of the group's Declaration of Principles, Constitution, and By-Laws, and Du Bois's plea for five dollars.[36] In response to this activity the organization was now 170 members strong with branches in thirty-four states—up from the seventeen branches at the beginning of the year.[37] But financial support continued to be precarious.

In addition to this organizing work, members of the Movement directed their attention to three issues. First, the Niagarites lobbied against the anniversary celebrations scheduled to take place at the upcoming Jamestown Exposition commemorating the tercentennial of the settlement because of a proposed segregation policy at the event.[38] Second, they called on members and supporters alike to protest remarks made by Reverend T. Nelson Baker of Pittsfield, Massachusetts, who in an editorial appearing in the *Congregationalist* had chastised black female delegates of the Student Volunteer Convention for complaining about segregated seating.[39] Du Bois drafted a leaflet and sent out 250 copies to representatives of the race calling for an appropriate response in defense of black womanhood to both Baker and the editor of the *Congregationalist* for printing such an attack.[40]

Finally, the Movement joined with members of the other national civil rights organizations to protest the enactment of the Warner-Foraker amendment. In May, Ohio senator Joseph Foraker had introduced an amendment to the Interstate Commerce Commission's Rate Bill affirming that "good service and accommodations" had to be provided to all passengers "paying the same compensation."[41] Many within the community were not pleased with the amendment for its provisions seemed to ratify separation and uphold the 1896 separate but equal doctrine. Members of the Niagara Movement, the Constitution League, the Afro-American Council, and the Committee of Twelve, including Archibald Grimké, William Sinclair, George H. White, Hightower T. Kealing, William Monroe Trotter, and Clement Morgan, all tried to influence as many congressmen as possible to rescind the measure. With such widespread outcry and concerted effort, the amendment died in committee in deference to the protest of all the major national civil rights groups.[42]

Shortly after this collective victory, Du Bois sent out another circular—this one announcing the second annual national convention of the Niagara Movement. The Niagarites planned to meet in mid-August at Harper's Ferry, West Virginia, the site of John Brown's raid, which was therefore symbolic for having sounded the death knell of slavery. Du Bois and his colleagues certainly wanted to tap into this symbolism as the Council had done in 1899 when it held celebrations in honor of John Brown's centennial. In the appeal, Du Bois recapped the activity of the organization during the past year and called on all to come and show their support for the emerging civil rights organization.[43]

The Afro-American Council also used publicity of the collective victory against the Warner-Foraker amendment as an opportune time to announce its annual convention in New York City in October 1906. Encouraged by recent comments of Secretary of War William Taft, who remarked that the "grandfather clause" would not withstand a Fifteenth Amendment test, and of Associate Chief Justice David J. Brewer of the U.S. Supreme Court, who asserted that a properly argued case challenging revised southern constitutions would force the Court to find them unconstitutional, in its call the Council proposed to focus on the issue of suffrage and the creation of test cases to carry to the Court challenging disfranchisement. The rallying cry, according to Walters, was "Remember the Disfranchised!"[44]

Hearing the call, a number of groups and individuals began to express their support for the Council and its activity. Walters received a unanimous endorsement from the AME Church supporting the Council in its attempt to raise money to carry suffrage cases before the Supreme Court. Lewis G. Jordan, too, had recently received an endorsement from the New England Baptist Convention, where he spoke about Council activities and the necessity of "raising a million dollars for a defense fund."[45] Moreover, the Council let it be known that it had gained the cooperation of John Milholland and Oswald Garrison Villard—civil rights activist, editor of the *New York Evening Post*, and grandson of William Lloyd Garrison—both of whom were scheduled to attend and address the Council at its ninth annual convention.[46]

With all this momentum and support, former president T. Thomas Fortune picked up the pen to champion the Council and its call for the legal defense fund. In an editorial entitled "A Chance to Help Ourselves," he praised Walters and the Council for promoting such an idea and urged members of the race to contribute. As he had done for over twenty years, Fortune expressed the need for the community to carry a case to the Supreme Court, proclaiming that the "courts are open to use, from Alabama up to Washington." Moreover, as John Quincy Adams, editor of the St. Paul *Appeal*, had done previously, Fortune compared black America's unwillingness or inability to raise the funds to that of immigrants' readiness to collect funds to support their own struggles. "The despised Chinamen," Fortune observed, "raised $300,000 in thirty days to fight the Alien laws of the Pacific coast; to bring our suit we need only one tenth as much. If we can't do one tenth of what the Chinamen easily did—well, we richly deserve to be disfranchised."[47]

While the voices of the national leadership of the civil rights activist community were calling for action, chapters of the Council and branches of the Niagara Movement continued to form throughout the nation. The

Afro-American Council in particular experienced a rush of activity leading up to its fall convention. Appointed the group's southern organizer in February, George King published a lengthy letter outlining his success in strengthening the Council's presence in the South. According to King, local councils were being created throughout the region especially in the rural districts.[48] Branches met in, among other locations, Des Moines, Iowa; Asbury Park, New Jersey; Providence, Rhode Island; San Antonio, Texas; Riverside, California; and Brooklyn and Rochester, New York, to prepare for the annual convention.[49] Questions of strategy and the Council's overall program were chief topics of discussion at all of the meetings. In California, James Alexander, state president of the Council, encouraged members of the organization to become active in the local elections. "What President Roosevelt may say in praise of us at the nation's capital, or what Ben Tillman of South Carolina, or Gov. Vardaman of Mississippi, may say in abuse of us, does not effect like local conditions . . . let us not unwisely jeopardize our well being," urged Alexander in asking members to use their votes wisely.[50] In San Antonio, schoolteacher and local Council leader Joseph R. Morris encouraged the national organization to make plans to come south in the future, hold a convention, and speak "manly" from the heart of the region.[51] All the locals expressed their support for the Council's development of a legal defense fund and the group's decision to focus on railroad and streetcar segregation as well as the ballot.

The issue of disfranchisement became a particular focus for the organization after Walters's proclamation to "Remember the Disfranchised!," which served as the rallying cry for the Council's convention. Moreover, the cry aided the Council in gaining the cooperation of Milholland and the Constitution League as they too were focusing on the franchise during the election year. The Council also gained more interracial support as the editors of the white *Philadelphia Press* announced its support for the organization's program. According to the *Press*, the Council had "for its first task the preparation and requisite financial support of a case to test the Grandfather Clause so directly that the Federal Supreme Court cannot evade it. Nothing can be more important!"[52]

Through these efforts activists continued to find consensus. "Remember the Disfranchised!" became a rallying cry for unification of agenda and action among the organizations, the members of which found common cause with the Council's focus on segregated transportation. This was particularly the case with the Niagara Movement, which was becoming involved in a Virginia-based test case as its supporters met for the group's first full convention.

* * *

In late August 1906, forty-five Niagarites met at Storer College in Harper's Ferry. The proceedings were drenched with symbolism as the event opened with the delegates singing the "Battle Hymn of the Republic" and "John Brown's Body." A day was devoted to the honor of John Brown, with a lengthy tributary address by Reverend Reverdy Ransom, who was accompanied on stage by, among others, Lewis Douglass, son of Frederick Douglass; Mrs. Evans the aunt of John Copeland, who was hanged with Brown; and William Monroe Trotter, who presented the delegation with a piece of wood from Brown's Springfield, Massachusetts home, which he had collected on his trip from Boston.[53]

In his address, Ransom used the memory of Brown to urge the audience to follow in the martyr's footsteps and fight for the rights of African Americans, a struggle that Ransom saw as divinely ordained. He connected Brown to David and Moses, and in doing so asserted that Brown was commissioned by God to face the mighty slave power. He averred that the struggle today was equally as important, and that Brown's spirit called upon the nation to rise out of its silence and inactivity. "Like the ghost of Hamlet's father," Ransom proclaimed, "the spirit of John Brown beckons us to arise and seek the recovery of our rights, which our enemy 'with witchcraft of his wit, with traitorous gifts' has sought for ever to destroy." The "gage of battle has been thrown down," continued Ransom. "The lines are clearly drawn; the supremacy of the Constitution has been challenged. In fighting for his rights the Negro defends the nation. His weapons are more powerful than picks and Sharp's rifles which John Brown sought to place in his hands at Harper's Ferry."[54] The new weapons were the Constitution, the ballot, the courts, and organization, as well as the desire to protest and resist—and Ransom urged the Niagarites to go out and use them. Ransom's address was met with tremendous applause and approval. Du Bois later recalled "that speech more than any single other event stirred the great meeting."[55]

The audience certainly felt that the fires of the great abolitionist struggle for justice had been rekindled and that as Ransom asserted, the soul of John Brown was marching on through them. Over the remainder of the convention the speakers outlined the diverse activity of the organization for the moral, economic, educational, and political development of the community. Speakers included Frederick McGhee, who addressed the "status of the Negro's civil rights in certain states."[56] In concluding his address, the Niagara legal director condemned "mere lip service, and called upon Niagara members to show their sincerity by sacrifice." According to McGhee, it was "unworthy for the colored people to be slothful in contending for these principles for which John Brown gave his life at Harper's Ferry."[57] Speaking later, William Monroe Trotter concurred with his midwestern colleague and called on the Movement to demonstrate its conviction by supporting the recent case of Barbara Pope.[58]

Apropos, and adding further inspiration to the proceedings, Pope was in attendance by request. Two weeks before she had been arrested in Virginia for violating the separate coach laws. Pope had purchased a first-class ticket in Washington, D.C., and had refused to move to a Jim Crow car when the train crossed the Virginia state line. She was arrested, found guilty, and fined ten dollars plus costs.[59] In light of the case of Niagaraite and Howard law professor William H. H. Hart in Maryland, where the state court questioned whether the Supreme Court would uphold a lower court's decision that interstate travel could be segregated in the same way that intrastate travel had been in *Plessy v. Ferguson*, Niagarites believed that they could gain a victory with Pope's case. [60] All agreed and the Movement's Committee of Legal Defense began at the Harper's Ferry meeting to strategize about its first legal suit.

As the meeting came to a close the delegates heard the Address to the Nation, penned by Du Bois, who was again elected general secretary of the Movement. In the Address, Du Bois asserted a greater degree of militancy than had been shown in his public declaration the previous year. Indeed in many respects it matched the sharpness, tone, and content of Fortune's 1890 inaugural Afro-American League speech. "[W]e will not be satisfied to take one jot or tittle less than our full manhood rights," Du Bois affirmed. "We claim for ourselves every single right that belongs to a freeborn American, political, civil and social; and until we get these rights we will never cease to protest and assail the ears of America."[61] He claimed that the grievances that he and all Niagarites strove to correct would be redressed through the ballot and "persistent, unceasing agitation." He continued, "we do not believe in violence . . . but we do believe in John Brown, in that incarnate spirit of justice, that hatred of a lie, that willingness to sacrifice money, reputation, and life itself on the altar of right."[62] The Address ended with a plea for equity. Was it possible that "a nation that has absorbed ten million foreigners into its political life without catastrophe [can] absorb ten million Negro Americans into that same political life at less cost than their unjust and illegal exclusion will involve?"[63] With the conviction that the morning was breaking "over blood-stained hills," Niagara Movement members left their convention to claim their rights.[64]

It was apparent following the Movement's first full convention that the civil rights organizations were clearly operating on parallel tracks. Members of the Afro-American Council could easily endorse all the objectives and actions of the Niagara Movement. Moreover, the Niagara Movement's support and action in the Barbara Pope case put it in line with the Council's activity in pushing for a larger test case against southern segregation legislation. Finally, the Niagara Movement's firm stance on suffrage displayed at the Cooper Union event and as the second doctrine on the organization's Declaration of Principles placed the group in concert with the Council and the Constitution League on the issue of disfranchisement.

Recognizing this sense of common purpose, and to generally seize upon the momentum following the successful Niagara convention, the Afro-American Council stepped up its own activities. A number of individuals continued to press for the creation of a legal defense fund.[65] For his part, Bishop Walters published an article in the *Colored American Magazine* outlining the Council's work and history. Asked at that moment what the most important thing the race could do to secure its rights, he answered without hesitation, "Go into the courts and fight it out."[66]

Affirming the organization's primacy in the area of legal action, the bishop noted that the Council was "not only the first in the field to test in the courts, the discriminatory laws of Southern States, but [was] also first to stimulate those Afro-Americans who, outside of the Council, have carried their cases to the Supreme Court."[67] Countering speculation about the past and future effectiveness of the organization, Walters traced some of the activities of the group, highlighting the Louisiana test cases, which he saw as encouraging others to take their grievances to the courts. He then concluded by questioning whether the Council was "not doing something definite now in creating favorable sentiment by agitation and by collecting funds to continue the struggle against" discriminatory laws.[68]

Meanwhile, there had been an upsurge in the number of individuals calling for a merger of the various civil rights and social uplift organizations.

During the summer prior to the two groups' conventions, W. Calvin Chase urged a union of the National Negro Business League and the Niagara Movement. After some consideration and possibly some criticism, the editor of the *Bee* decided that the Business League should remain independent, but suggested a merger of the Niagara Movement and the Afro-American Council. A few months later, T. Thomas Fortune endorsed the idea of unification, believing that the interests of the race would be served better by one unified national civil rights organization.[69] In the spirit of this discussion, the Afro-American Council extended an invitation to the Niagara Movement to send representatives to its October convention.[70]

Though a merger was doubtful at this time, events occurring just prior to the Afro-American Council's national convention did bring the two organizations closer together. On the night of August 13, 1906, a group of armed men "shot up" the town of Brownsville, Texas. During the disturbance one person was killed and two others were wounded. A local military investigation concluded that black soldiers, members of the Twenty-Fifth Infantry, were the culprits, even though the identities of the gunmen were never established. [71]

A couple of weeks after the incident, the Council's Committee of One Hundred, a group organized in late July to coordinate the activities of the Council as the national convention neared, met at the Metropolitan Union AME Church in New York and temporarily set aside the issue of the convention in order to discuss the fate of the Brownsville soldiers.[72] The committee determined that the surrender of the "Afro-American soldiers would mean their abandonment and certain death." Hence, Council members led by J. Douglas Wetmore established a committee "on the ways and means to prevent the sacrifice to race prejudice of the soldiers of the 25th Infantry." The group, which solicited the assistance of Niagara Movement members, met at Wetmore's office and drafted a "strong" letter to Secretary William Loeb "requesting information as to the plans of the War Department." Furthermore, representing both national civil rights organizations, the group called for an interview with President Roosevelt.[73]

* * *

A few short weeks after Brownsville, the streets of the South's golden hope ran with blood. Atlanta, Georgia, the southern city that many believed to be the model for the New South, became the site of a deadly riot in late summer 1906. The simultaneous sounding of the fire alarm, riot call, and militia muster shattered the calm Saturday evening. Racial tensions had been on the rise in the city for a number of months, spurred by the Hoke Smith disfranchisement gubernatorial campaign, allegations of African American criminal activity, and recent theatrical production of Thomas Dixon's *The Clansman.* Tensions continued to escalate until they could no longer be contained and they ferociously exploded upon the city.[74]

On Saturday evening, mobs struck out at any African American who unfortunately happened upon their path, killing a number of innocent blacks. Sunday was ominously quiet and the pall that hung in the air exploded the following day. Occasionally reinforced by police, the mobs focused their renewed energy on the southeastern portion of the city. Much of the anger was directed toward schools, businesses, and homes of law-abiding citizens of the community. Shots were exchanged between the mobs and African Americans choosing to protect themselves and their property. In the end, thousands of dollars of property was damaged, with ten African Americans dead and sixty hospitalized.[75]

Du Bois was out of town doing research, but he immediately returned to Atlanta. Fear for his family and images of the town that he had praised three years earlier in his essay "Of the Wings of Atlanta," published in *The Souls of Black Folk*, mixed in his head. Perhaps he recalled the lines of John Greenleaf Whittier's poem "Howard at Atlanta" that he had used for the epigraph of that essay:

> O black boy of Atlanta!
> But Half was spoken;
> The slave's chains and the master's
> Alike are broken
> The one curse of the races
> Held both in tether;
> They are rising—all are rising—
> The black and the white together.[76]

The Atlanta professor wondered what had gone wrong, and in response composed the "Litany of Atlanta":

> Listen to us, Thy children; our faces dark with doubt, are made a mockery in Thy sanctuary. With uplifted hands we front Thy heaven, O God, crying: *we beseech Thee to hear us, good Lord!* . . . Surely, Thou

> too art not white, O Lord a pale, bloodless, heartless, thing? . . . But whisper—speak—call, great God, for Thy silence is white terror to our hearts![77]

After five days of on-again, off-again violence, the flaring racial embers cooled a bit. *Voice of the Negro* editor Max Barber declared, "Behold! We have peace—No, not peace, but a wilderness called peace. Sixty or seventy colored people are in jail for killing one policeman, while sixteen whites are in jail for the whole riot which resulted in the murdering and maiming of more than a hundred people."[78]

Booker T. Washington, visiting New York at the time of the riot, wrote an editorial to the *New York World* urging the "best white people and the best colored people to come together . . . to stop the present disorder."[79] Once the violence subsided, the Wizard traveled to Atlanta to pledge his support for the "reconstruction" of the city and the restoration of order.[80] In public, Washington advanced a cautious, nonconfrontational position. He also sought to control the way that the community responded to the horrid events. He advised one of his agents in New York, Charles Anderson, to "not let the Afro-American Council condemn the riots."[81] Behind the scenes, however, he hired a detective agency to investigate the violence and requested that President Roosevelt send troops to the city.[82]

Washington's typically differing private and public responses did not serve him well. The horrendous violence in the perceived progressive city of Atlanta was, in many people's eyes, a symbol that racial violence had completely permeated American society. Roosevelt's failure to respond made many more African Americans skeptical of the Republican Party. Moreover, the failure to generate any concerted outcry in the northern white community caused many African Americans to believe that they had no place to turn. It was truly the nadir.

Washington's limited response added to this feeling. In some ways it was only fitting that the beginning of the end of Washington's leadership followed the Atlanta riots. His ascendancy to power had begun in the city ten years before. But it was now clear that the city that best represented his public philosophy of interracial cooperation and ascending economic and educational prosperity had failed African Americans. Destiny or not, the events in Atlanta resulted in a decisive shift in the way Washington's public position of accommodation was perceived by others.

Thunderstruck by the blood and violence of Atlanta, the civil rights organizations attempted to find the correct response. The bloodshed combined with Washington's response pushed each group closer together as the civil rights leaders sought to combine their efforts, or at least coordinate them more directly. Moreover, in wake of Atlanta, all the organizations—the Afro-American Council, the Niagara Movement, and the Constitution League—adopted a more aggressive attitude and feeling of urgency in their messages.

The first sign of a significant shift in attitude was seen in the Afro-American Council. A week before the organization was to meet for the convention in New York, the group's Committee of One Hundred met at the Abyssinian Baptist Church where Dr. Matthew W. Gilbert, minister of the Mt. Olivet Baptist Church, denounced John Temple Graves and Hoke Smith for fanning the "hot flame of persecution of defenseless and law abiding Afro-Americans." Two days later three hundred people met under the auspices of the Brooklyn Afro-American Council at the Concord Baptist Church. During the proceedings the master of ceremony, Reverend William R. Lawton, outlined the objects and aims of the Council and claimed that the group was the only organization that had formed for the "self-defense" of the race. Following Lawton was Dr. William L. Hunter, a Brooklyn physician and the author of the popular pamphlet *Jesus Christ Had Negro Blood in His Veins.* According to reports, the audience "held its breath" as if "expecting an explosion." Dr. Hunter did not disappoint. Continuing along the same lines as Reverend Lawton, he urged the organization to continue to prepare for "self-defense"—"not with brickbats and fire sticks but with hot lead," adding "Die outside of jail and do not go by yourself."[83]

Such comments were certainly not what Washington had in mind when he urged Anderson to control the Council's response to the riots. Two weeks later the Afro-American Council met for its ninth annual convention. The necessity of a strong organization to respond to issues such as Atlanta and the spread of disfranchisement was a central theme of the proceedings. Lewis G. Jordan set the tone as he opened the first session with a report of the organization's activities throughout the year and a plan detailing where the Council needed to put its energy— including the petitioning of Congress, the carrying out of letter-writing campaigns against the segregation practices of various railroads, the filing of legal suits against segregation in Florida and Washington, D.C., and the conducting of a propaganda campaign.[84]

Additionally, the corresponding secretary, possibly directly given the recent events and the need for the Council and all the organizations to remember why they had formed, echoed T. Thomas Fortune's 1890 inaugural League address in sharpness and tone when he impressed upon the delegation the importance of protesting both customs and laws. Jordan declared resoundingly, as the League architect had nearly twenty years before, "We who know our rights . . . must contend for them." More important, he asserted, "we are not cowards nor are we guilty of one-third of the crimes laid at our door. We have suffered in silence hoping that our enemies would become conscience smitten and give up. But since they show themselves more aggressive, we will rise in our own defense." Essential to this defense were contributions to the Council's legal defense fund, and Jordan, again channeling Fortune, called on the example of Irish Americans to urge his colleagues as the Irish had just raised one hundred thousand dollars to push the cause of Home Rule.[85]

Following Jordan were a number of speakers equaling his passion and endorsing his plan. Those who spoke included Council president Bishop Alexander Walters. Despairing at the current racial climate in America, the Council leader asserted that when the organization was founded in 1898, the delegates had created a national civil rights organization with the motto "Our plea for equal rights for all, regardless of race, color, creed or previous condition of servitude." In his mind, the Council had not wavered from its founding principles. Despite its efforts for more than eight years, however, there had been little improvement. The bishop insisted that "the object of our enemies is to make us serfs and they are going to continue to do everything in their power to obtain their object; hence, it is nonsense for us to cry peace!," adding "When there is no peace, and there never will be peace until the negro is accorded the rights given to other citizens of the commonwealth." Certainly fired up with all that had happened in recent months, the bishop stated, "it is generally understood that our struggle is for equal rights." "We may use diplomatic language and all kinds of subterfuge," he acknowledged, "but the fact remains that the enemy is trying to keep us down and that we are determined to rise or die in the attempt."[86]

Walters declared that it was time for the people to rise up and put some strength in the civil rights organization. Conditions demanded that the Afro-American community raise the funds for a fight that was going to take some time to win. The Council's desire to create a legal defense fund, which Jordan had already emphasized, was central to the struggle against the rising tide of discrimination and disfranchisement in the courts. Walters commended all efforts of the Council's Legal Bureau in this area, as well as similar work carried out by groups such as the Niagara Movement and the Constitution League.[87]

Over the next two days members of the Council and other affiliated organizations presented papers following the general themes outlined by Jordan and Walters. Among the speakers were a number of whites, including John Milholland of the Constitution League, who spoke of the need for a strong civil rights organization and cooperation between existing groups. He also reproached President Roosevelt for failing to adequately address the race problem. Milholland believed that the president's lack of action was placing him in the bracket with "Andrew Jackson or with James Buchanan."[88]

In his address, Reverend George Lee of the Vermont Ave. Baptist Church in Washington, D.C., brought all of the resentment of recent events to the fore. "I preached peace after the Atlanta riots," he explained, "but don't misunderstand me. It was prudence, not my religion. If I had the power to stop that kind of thing, even by force, I'd use it."[89] "In the South," he continued, "they are scheming all the time to keep the negro down, but I tell you he is bound to rise. Just so certain as they keep this thing up in the South something is going to happen. The trouble is all one-sided now." But, Lee asserted, "trouble never stays one-sided for long. There is going to be trouble on the other side soon." In conclusion, Reverend Lee wondered whether America would prevent violence from spreading and demanded to know "how much longer the American people are going to scatter to the four winds that section of the Constitution which calls for equal rights for all, regardless of color, race, or previous condition."[90]

Other addresses included those of Nannie Helen Burroughs, Fannie Barrier Williams, Mary Church Terrell, J. Douglas Wetmore, T. Thomas Fortune, and William S. Scarbrorough.[91] In addition, Oswald Garrison Villard, as had Jordan, Walters, and Milholland, spoke to the convention regarding the issue of creating and supporting a strong organization. He tendered an eloquent speech on the Council's aims and emphatically endorsed the organization's legal efforts.

> The Afro American Council asks for a fund to carry to the Supreme Court the question of the ballot in the South. It ought to have a national defense fund reaching into the hundreds of thousands of

> dollars for a hundred different purposes. . . . It should be able to fight in the courts every unjust discrimination, to protect and aid threatened or injured colored schools, and to generally supervise the welfare of the race.[92]

Finally, on the last night of the convention, Washington spoke to the delegation. He discussed the need for calm, tempered action in light of the recent Atlanta events, noting "our victories in the past have come to us through our ability to be calm and patient, often while enduring great wrong."[93] Like the other speakers, Washington also spoke of the need for organizations such as the Council. At the same time, however, as always speaking as a man who lived in the South, he warned those in the North "before giving advice to the Negro in the South, the Negro in the North should be very sure that what he advices is that which he himself is willing to go into the heart of the South and put into practice. Be careful not to assist in lighting a fire which you will have no ability to put out."[94]

Washington's sentiments failed to reign in the Council. Following the meeting, the press praised both the event and the direction in which the organization was heading. There were no significant references to a "Booker T. Washingtonized" Council—in fact W. Calvin Chase, the Council's longest and harshest critic, praised Bishop Walters's leadership.[95] The white press of New York, moreover, virtually ignored Washington's plea for calm. It focused instead on the words of Walters, Reverend George Lee, and John Milholland, who called for action both by the Afro-American community and the Roosevelt Administration lest the nation be forced to reap what it had sown. Such coverage was punctuated by the incendiary title assigned to the *New York Times*' article on Bishop Walters's address: "Talk of War on Whites at Negro Conference."[96]

Following the convention, Washington's attempts to suppress the ire of Council members became ever more awkward—almost to the point of backfiring. Following Milholland's address, the organization passed a series of resolutions attacking Roosevelt for his inaction and called on him to create a committee to investigate the southern situation upon which federal action might be taken. Andrew B. Humphrey subsequently sent Roosevelt a copy of the resolutions as a joint demand of the Afro-American Council and the Constitution League, with Washington's name as one of the endorsers.[97] Washington immediately moved to smooth things over with Roosevelt and tried to move against the independent tendencies of the Constitution League and the Afro-American Council.[98]

Emerging from its convention with a stronger sense of purpose, the Council looked forward to a possible continued cooperation with Milholland's Constitution League. The Council leadership also found promise in the goodwill shown by the presence of the Niagara Movement's Lafayette M. Hershaw at the meeting.[99] With this demonstration of cooperation there arose once again a discussion in favor of the unification of the national black organizations. In an insightful article entitled "Co-operation vs. Antagonism," Charles Alexander of *Alexander's Magazine* argued that the three black groups—the National Negro Business League, the Afro-American Council, and the Niagara Movement—needed to unify. Alexander believed that what separated the three organizations were merely petty differences. Although they approached the Negro Problem from different angles—the NNBL focusing on "material gain," the Afro-American Council emphasizing "conservative agitation backed by financial aid," and the Niagarites believing in "moral suasion and radical agitation"—their respective goals were the same: to gain "recognition of the Negro as an American citizen with equal rights and privileges."[100] Alexander believed that this goal would continue to elude the organizations as long as they remained antagonistic; they needed to unify into one organization cooperating and attacking the problem on all fronts.

Despite the solidarity demonstrated at the Council's convention and a seemingly greater sense of cohesion of agenda and thought in the wake of Atlanta, unification remained elusive. Maintaining their separate efforts, both the Council and the Constitution League turned their attention toward the upcoming congressional elections. As reported by Lewis G. Jordan, the Council tried to coordinate voters in favorable congressional districts to put into office a friendly voice. For its part, the Constitution League focused on Republicans in the South. Milholland also sent Gilchrist Stewart, a young New York attorney, Tuskegee graduate, and son of Afro-American League activist T. McCants Stewart, to Washington, D.C., to read a "riot act" to every Republican congressman from whom he could obtain a hearing.[101] In addition, the Constitution League worked to suppress a production of *The Clansman* in Philadelphia.[102]

During this period the Niagara Movement's legal team focused on its test-case strategy and made preparations for the Barbara Pope appeal in Virginia. The Council's Legal Bureau was also at work in this regard. Lewis G.

Jordan continued his letter-writing campaign to railroads that customarily segregated passengers in states free of Jim Crow legislation. J. Douglas Wetmore instituted a legal suit against the Theatrical Syndicate of New York for refusing orchestra seats to African American patrons. In addition, Wetmore was looking to institute a test case against segregated transportation, but much of his time—as well as that of his Council, Niagara, and Constitution League associates—in the closing months of the year was caught up with investigating the Brownsville affair.

* * *

In the aftermath of Atlanta and the heated Council convention, President Roosevelt announced that he was discharging "without honor from the Army" the African American soldiers in the Twenty-Fifth Infantry and "forever disbarring them from re-enlisting in the Army or Navy of the United States as well from employment in any civil capacity under the Government."[103] The black community and many of its white allies reacted to the dismissal with unprecedented bitterness. Many looked to Washington for a reaction, but the Wizard, who had been consulted by the president regarding the dismissal and had privately failed to persuade him to reconsider, once again took a conciliatory approach. Afraid of what his public condemnation of Roosevelt would do to his relations with the president's administration and northern white philanthropists, Washington chose instead to "swallow the bitter pill and . . . minimize the importance of the decision."[104]

Washington's calm, conciliatory approach in the aftermath of Roosevelt's decree once again damaged his reputation in the eyes of many race leaders and those of many rank-and-file African Americans. Thousands within the community felt betrayed by the president's decision. T. Thomas Fortune spoke for many when he characterized the dismissal of the soldiers as lynch law by executive order. The editor and activist believed that the decision was a continuation of Roosevelt's acquiescence to southern racial attitudes. He claimed that the president's position was "carrying into the Federal Government the demand of the Southern white devils that innocent and law-abiding black men shall help the legal authorities spy out and deliver practically to the mob black men alleged to have committed some sort of crime." "The principle involved," Fortune argued, was "not only vicious and contrary to the spirit of the Constitution, but it [was] an outrage upon the rights of citizens who are entitled in civil life to trial by jury and in military life to trial by court martial."[105]

Shortly after Roosevelt's order, Bishop Walters instructed the Afro-American Council's legal director J. Douglas Wetmore to investigate the facts in the case and to enlist a white attorney, if necessary, to represent the discharged soldiers.[106] The Constitution League also sent its own investigator, Gilchrist Stewart, down to Brownsville.[107] In addition, Milholland contacted Mary Church Terrell, director of the Afro-American Council's Anti-Lynching Bureau and former president of the National Association of Colored Women's Clubs, to meet with Secretary of War William Taft and see if he could suspend the order until further investigation.[108] By the end of the month, Stewart, along with Richard Stokes, a Council member who was working with Stewart in his investigation, had written to Roosevelt declaring that they had found no evidence that any of the soldiers was guilty. All were accounted for on the roll call and gun shells supplied for evidence could have been collected by anyone on the firing rage, while whites in the region had previously expressed hostility toward the new black soldiers and may have staged the raid to insure their removal.[109] A few days later, Senator Joseph B. Foraker, of Ohio, submitted a resolution directing the Secretary of War to provide the Senate with all details of the case. Shortly thereafter, the Constitution League sent Stewart's completed report on Brownsville to Foraker, who then submitted it to the Committee on Military Affairs.[110]

In this increasingly hostile atmosphere, President Roosevelt delivered his annual address to Congress. Angered by black enmity toward his lack of action in Atlanta along with the dismissal of the Brownsville soldiers and his general attitude toward the race problem, the president lashed out. He remarked that lynching was a pardonable and necessary evil in response to black men's propensity for rape—"the most abominable in all the category of crimes even worse than murder."[111] The president also struck a Washingtonian stance by urging blacks to uplift themselves and focus on industrial education.[112]

Indeed, the president's address in many ways was an attempt to use Washington's public message for Roosevelt's own purposes, and in doing so he weakened both his and Washington's status in the black community. Washington's failure to speak out forcefully on either of the traumatic events of 1906, followed by a racist, backward address delivered from a president whom he advised, destroyed any vestige of creditability the Tuskegee principal had enjoyed with the growing civil rights organizations. In turn

Washington's weakening position in the black community brought the civil rights organizations closer together, and the calls for a more unified group were once again heard within the community.

The Afro-American Council ended the year 1906 on just such a conciliatory note. Calling on local Councils throughout the country to hold Emancipation Celebrations, Bishop Walters asked the branches to coordinate their activities with other organizations. He wanted them to turn the "birthday of their freedom" into not only a celebration, but a protest against the wrongs that had been committed against black Americans over the previous forty-two years. He also appealed to all societies, churches, and organizations to give to the Council's defense fund.[113]

In connection with the Council's Emancipation Celebrations in Washington, D.C., the group's Executive Committee met together with Niagara Movement members in the District to hear J. Douglas Wetmore's report on Brownsville.[114] This example of organizational collaboration again offered hope of the unified effort for which many had yearned.[115] The groups subsequently passed a series of resolutions condemning Roosevelt and commending Senator Foraker for their respective actions. They also agreed to raise money for the cause of defending the soldiers.[116] The Committee appointed a group to call on Foraker and express its appreciation of his efforts on behalf of the troops.[117] The next day many of the members of the Executive Committee addressed a mass meeting on the Brownsville Affair.[118]

With the Council and the Constitution League keeping the pressure on, the Senate unanimously agreed to authorize an investigation into the dismissal of the Brownsville soldiers.[119] In the wake of the decision, Lewis G. Jordan quickly published a circular calling for Council members and like-minded individuals and organizations to "not delay, but act, and act at once." He encouraged members to contribute five dollars to one of the repositories of the Council's Legal Defense Fund, noting "the investigation has been ordered," and "now if the Negro is called to trial and is not ready, all we have fought for . . . will be lost." It was time for the race to demonstrate its strength. The soldiers of the Twenty-Fifth Infantry "would be honored today by the American Government as Captain Dreyfus is by the French, if the Negro had stood by them like the Jews stood by Dreyfus." The race must show, he exclaimed, "that we are interested in the soldiers, and more than that in the principle of justice."[120]

As to the issue of justice, Jordan also took the opportunity to discuss cases that the Council hoped to initiate—if it could raise the necessary funds. The Council Coordinating Secretary brought to the public's attention the legislature's intentions in the new state of Oklahoma to pass Jim Crow clauses into its constitution. Arkansas, Jordan remarked, had also recently passed a servants' bill, which, according to one black citizen of Arkansas was "pure and simple peonage." The Arkansas legislature was also preparing to pass a bill to segregate public schools.[121]

In light of these incidents and more, Jordan pleaded with African Americans to set aside the differences of the past and "in this hour of our racial death—grapple with the most outrageous wrong ever done ten million people."[122] For Jordan and many within the Council, the response was simple: "It is strike NOW or NEVER."[123]

* * *

During early 1907 all the organizations kept up the pressure both through independent action and ever increasingly through coordinated efforts. The Afro-American Council and the Constitution League kept the Brownsville issue alive. While the Constitution League worked directly with Foraker in the Senate hearings, the actions of Bishop Walters and the Afro-American Council also "kept the pot boiling" over Brownsville in the public eye.[124] Walters, Jordan, and Wetmore called on Senator Foraker in January to assure him of the Council's support. Moreover, Jordan sent out an appeal for funds to aid Foraker in the spring.[125] The Niagara Movement also continued with its legal activities with particular focus on the Barbara Pope case.

In January, the Niagara Movement's legal team led by Frederick McGhee persuaded the Virginia Supreme Court to void the initial ruling against Pope and remand the case for a new trial.[126] As McGhee biographer Paul Nelson noted, the appeal probably never went to trial because the "state of Virginia simply conceded the case on the sensible ground that the statute in question did not provide for criminal penalties to passengers who refused to change rail cars."[127] This meant that thirty-nine years before *Henderson v. United States* and forty-seven years before *Brown v. Board of Education*, the Movement had aided in establishing, according to Du Bois, "that under the present statute Virginia cannot fine an interstate passenger who refuses to be Jim Crowed."[128] This was a small victory, however, since no ruling on the actual practice of segregation had occurred, but it was a victory nonetheless. The case also represented a symbolic victory as it meant that African Americans traveling to "Jamestown to the exposition cannot be Jim Crowed on the railroads."[129]

Shortly thereafter, members of the Niagara Movement met with the Afro-American Council in Baltimore for the latter's annual convention. Walters had invited Washington to attend, but he declined while professing support for the Council and its activities.[130] The Wizard's planned absence was undoubtedly a wise decision as the pendulum had swung decisively against him. No matter what he might do behind the scenes to aid the Council's efforts, he would be deemed a hindrance to the cause if he could not speak openly.

While Walters's strong call no doubt contributed to Washington's reluctance to attend the convention, it was an important factor in attracting many Niagara Movement members and at least some members of the Constitution League to the conference. In the call Walters enumerated a list of grievances:

> The increasing energy of those bent on the creation of a public sentiment adverse to the Afro-Americans. The open advocacy by Senator Tillman, Governor Vardaman, John Temple Graves, and others, of the repeal of the Fourteenth and Fifteenth Amendments to the Federal Constitution, thus reducing the Afro-Americans of the South to serfdom; the timid and uncertain stand of those who assay to befriend us, even to President Roosevelt, who has said so much about "fair play" and the "Door of Hope" but who has dealt us a severe blow in the dismissal of the colored soldiers of the Twenty-Fifth Infantry without an adequate trial the bold and defiant assaults of those satisfied with nothing short of our absolute undoing, certainly necessitates the meeting of the leaders of the race in an advisory way.[131]

Such sentiment certainly would have tipped Washington off that there would be very little support for him or his public philosophy at the Baltimore meeting.

When the nearly two hundred delegates arrived in Baltimore, they were not disappointed. Walters's Council address, which opened the proceedings, was just as strong as his call: "The story of the year for colored people in America has been but a repetition of the old story of their struggles and wrongs. . . . Denied nearly everywhere in the South the rights of American citizens . . . in the North the race has been knocking at the door of opportunity, open to all races in the republic, but . . . it alone . . . because it is black, darker than other races."[132] Discrimination, Walters argued, must be "fought to the death."[133] He counseled that "lynching would not end with blacks sitting idly by, but by constant agitation, citizen education, and the assistance of the federal government."[134]

Possibly with a nod to the Niagaraites and the Constitution League, the Council president further argued that the group was here to stay and would continue to fight for the rights of African Americans. The organization would not be "silent or patient at the bidding of such unworthy counselors, regardless of their high official position or their race or color."[135] This obvious attack on Washington was commensurate with the critical situation in which African Americans now found themselves. Representing the voice of the people, the Council would refuse to "cry peace as long as the separate coach is in existence. It is a disgrace to our civilization and we must ever fight it. There must not be any let up until the last Jim Crow car has passed into oblivion. The ballot was the badge of political equality, it indicated citizenship and should be sought and obtained by all men, black or white."[136]

Walters also harshly condemned Roosevelt for his dismissal of the Brownsville soldiers as well as the anti-black statements contained in his annual address. He warned the president that the Council would not allow him to put the incident "under the rug" and vowed that the group would punish its "enemies and seek their destruction at the polls, regardless of any ill consequences to party or self." In contrast, he praised the work of Senator Foraker and pledged the organization's support to "the noblest Roman of them all." Finally, the Council president reasserted a principle dear to the Council throughout its history but often lost while the cloak of Washington still hung over the organization: "we are unalterably opposed to any special educational brand as a badge to racial inferiority." Envoys from all the civil rights groups followed Walters's with equally enthusiastic speeches. Among them were Lewis G. Jordan (Afro-American Council), Sylvester L. Corrothers and Lafayette M. Hershaw (Niagara Movement), Archibald Grimké (Committee of Twelve), and William Sinclair (Constitution League).[137]

Supporters of Washington and the conciliatory approach were not absent from the conference, however. Present were Washington's agent, Melvin Chisum, who had infiltrated the Brooklyn branch of the Niagara Movement, and recorder of deeds for the District of Columbia, John C. Dancy, both of whom remained within the Tuskegee sphere of influence.[138] But when Dancy spoke up against the Council's reprimanding of Roosevelt, he was told "it would be best for him to board the train and return to Washington."

W. Calvin Chase, for his part, acknowledged in his *Washington Bee* the presence of the "two apologists" at the conference, but considered them harmless and noninfluential given that their "speeches fell flat."[139]

Ultimately the conference delegates resolved to support Senator Foraker in his struggle for the Brownsville soldiers. The Council also pledged its support to the Niagara Movement and acknowledged its success in the struggle to abolish Jim Crow cars. Additionally, the group formally condemned President Roosevelt. Some delegates went so far as to label Washington a "Judas to his race" for his alliance with the president.[140]

Although a handful of Washington's supporters still retained official Council positions, the general makeup of the elected leadership of the organization signaled a changing of the guard. Walters was again elected president, while Lewis G. Jordan was reaffirmed to the position of coordinating secretary. Sylvester L. Corrothers of the Niagara Movement and William Sinclair of the Constitution League were elected vice presidents, and Archibald Grimké of the Committee of Twelve and Niagaraite Lafayette M. Hershaw were chosen to direct the Council's Literary and Newspaper Bureaus respectively. In addition, William Hart, a Niagararite who had gained victory in his 1905 segregation case against the state of Maryland, was after some heated debate led by W. Calvin Chase tapped as the successor to J. Douglas Wetmore as the head of the Legal Bureau.[141] Finally, among the remaining offices, Mary Church Terrell again assumed the head of the organization's Anti-Lynching Bureau and Fannie Barrier Williams accepted the position of assistant secretary.[142] The forging of a unified race organization had begun.

* * *

It was clear that the Council had rebounded and freed itself from the grip of Booker T. Washington whether he was willing to support the organization behind the scenes or not. Many within the black community quickly acknowledged the shift. The new organ of the Niagara Movement, the *Horizon*, declared that the Council had "unhorsed Booker T. Washington, repudiated his doctrines, and fairly spat upon him."[143] Harry Smith of the *Cleveland Gazette* also praised the strong sentiments emanating from the Baltimore convention and asked that the group never again lower its standards.[144] Finally, W. Calvin Chase of the *Washington Bee*, traditionally the Council's harshest critic but just elected to the group's Legal Bureau, proclaimed the convention a great victory for the race. As Chase observed, "the colored Americans ought to feel themselves highly congratulated because for once in their history their representatives declared for their freedom and independence."[145]

What was obvious in the wake of the Baltimore convention was that the old coalition between Washington and the Council was dead. In the aftermath of the horrendous events of 1906, the Council could no longer affiliate with the Tuskegee principal. His inability to speak out on issues had finally become too much for the Council leadership to weather no matter how much financial support he had given the organization. Walters no longer believed that Washington and the Council were moving in the same direction. Rather, they were approaching the same problem from different angles, one pushing industry and thrift, the other civil and political rights.

Shortly after the Council convention the Niagara Movement met in Boston for its third annual meeting. Like the Council, the Niagarites expressed anger with the Roosevelt Administration and other political leaders who failed to stand up for the rights and defense of black Americans. Focusing on Georgia, its Address to the Nation began:

> For the third time the Niagara Movement in annual meeting appeals to the world and America. This has been a year of wrong and discrimination. There sits today in the governor's chair of a sovereign southern commonwealth a man stained with blood of innocent black workingmen who fell in the Atlanta massacre, and whose unavenged death cries to God for justice.[146]

In addition to this attack on Georgia's political leadership, Du Bois and his colleagues, not unlike the Council, called for "the 500,000 free black voters of the North: Use your ballots to defeat Theodore Roosevelt, William Taft, or any man named by the present dictatorship." It was better to "vote for avowed enemies than for false friends."[147] The delegates also discussed the necessity to challenge Jim Crow cars, offered their support to the Brownsville soldiers, and demanded that the nation stand up for its stated ideals.

Niagara Movement members also discussed the various ways it could fight for the rights of the Afro-American community, including cooperation with other organizations, creating voting blocks, initiating legal test cases against Jim Crow Cars, and petitioning state governments.[148] Similar to the Council, of great importance to the delegates was the attack on separate coach legislation. The Interstate Commerce Commission had just affirmed that separate coaches was not an area that it was willing to regulate, which in many ways limited the Niagara Movement's victory in the Pope case to Virginia.[149]

Despite the strong sentiments expressed in Faneuil Hall, however, the Niagara Movement was struggling for its existence. Reverend John M. Waldron, pastor of Shiloh Baptist Church in Washington who had relocated from Jacksonville, Florida—where he had worked with J. Douglass Wetmore and the local Afro-American Council in its struggle against the segregated streetcars—was concerned about the Movement's failure to attract the masses, and urged the group to cooperate with the country's growing Socialist organizations and working-class whites.[150] Du Bois favored this approach as well, realizing that "less momentum" existed at the third gathering. The attacks by Washington combined with internal conflicts were taking their toll.[151]

The internal strains no doubt concerned Du Bois more than anything else. William Monroe Trotter was the source of much of the discord, but Du Bois and other members of the Movement were not always the easiest individuals with whom to get along.[152] Moreover, the organization, like the Council, was in dire financial straits.[153] Notwithstanding this situation, the Niagara delegates remained determined. "[W]e are not discouraged," Du Bois affirmed in his annual address. "Help us, brothers, for the victory which lingers, must and shall prevail."[154]

In the months following the two conventions, both the Niagara Movement and the Afro-American Council focused considerable attention on the 1908 elections. In February, for instance, they collaborated on a letter to the "leading colored politicians" of the South prior to the Republican convention regarding lily-whites throughout the region. J. Milton Waldron wrote Du Bois to explain that he, Archibald Grimké, and Judson W. Lyons had drafted the letter and that "Bishop Walters and other prominent members of the Afro-American Council" had decided to add their signatures. Because of this collaboration, the committee agreed to send the letter out in the name of both organizations.[155]

As the presidential campaign heated up, so did the fragmentation within the African American community. Washington was aligning himself with Secretary of War William H. Taft, who stood with Roosevelt in the dismissal of the Brownsville soldiers, while many within the community were leaning toward supporting the candidacy of Democrat William Jennings Bryan.[156] In

July 1908, Du Bois clearly stated the choices that he and many in the Niagara Movement believed existed: "If between the two parties who stand on identically the same platform you can prefer the party who perpetuated Brownsville, well and good! But I shall vote for Bryan."[157]

Du Bois and the Niagara Movement were not alone in wondering how the community could support Taft after Brownsville. Bishop Walters and many within the Council also took a similar stance. The Council president actually confronted Secretary Taft during a stump speech at the Cooper Union in late January. The bishop asked him to justify the president's actions and questioned whether Taft was willing to go before the country and justify the soldiers' discharge. The secretary refused to answer Walters's question, but the bishop continually appeared at regional Taft events making similar queries. Each time the secretary refused to answer, he further alienated himself from black voters.[158]

In this climate of rising support for Bryan's candidacy, and possibly because of his increased frustration with his lack of control inside the Niagara Movement, William Monroe Trotter called for a meeting at the Zion Baptist Church in Philadelphia in early April. Trotter did not want Du Bois present nor did the Niagara leader want to attend as he believed that nothing good could come from the meeting. Du Bois was through with Trotter and had actually contemplated resigning his post in the Niagara Movement in late 1907 because of the recalcitrant *Guardian* editor.[159] Despite the Atlanta University professor's apprehensions, many members of the Niagara Movement, the Afro-American Council, the New England Suffrage League, and the American Negro Academy did attend the meeting and agreed to establish yet another organization—the National Negro American Political League—electing Niagaraite J. Milton Waldron president and Bishop Walters to the executive committee.[160]

The new organization, seemingly doomed from the start due to pending personality conflicts, declared that its main purpose was to prevent the nomination of both Roosevelt and Taft. In other areas, the organization mirrored the stances of the Afro-American Council and the Niagara Movement with its platform of fighting for African American civil and political rights and its position and fighting against the spread of Jim Crow legislation. Moreover, Trotter actually called for the Afro-American Council, the New England Suffrage League, the Niagara Movement, and the American Negro Academy, all of whom had representatives in the new group, to unify under the National Negro American Political League.[161]

While not agreeing to a complete merger, Walters consented to have the Council change its annual meeting date and location so as to join the new organization and any others in Chicago prior to the Republican national convention. Du Bois did not, however, agree to alter the meeting place of the Niagara Movement's convention, contending that the new group had not set the stage for a merger, but had created a new organization in an already crowded arena.[162]

Du Bois's disaffection was due not only to Trotter's involvement in the new group but to the general state of all the civil rights organizations in the spring of 1908. Neither Niagara nor the Council was able to build on the momentum created by their flurry of activity in the aftermath of the Atlanta riots and the Brownsville affair. Neither initiated additional legal test cases challenging either disfranchisement or separate coach legislation.[163] Moreover, both suffered from dwindling numbers, financial debt, and an inability to garner consistent support on the part of either their leaders or the masses.

Yet despite these failings, neither the Council nor Niagara Movement faithful were discouraged. Both organizations continued to prepare for their respective conventions, and in some regions, local branches of both groups held regular meetings. Moreover, during March and April 1908, Bishop Walters and W. E. B. Du Bois discussed the possibility of uniting the two organizations to better serve the race.[164] It seems that the two leaders understood that the small cadre of individuals willing to organize for the race was disjointed and overorganized.

In an effort to make a gesture toward unification, Bishop Walters, while still president of the Afro-American Council, joined the Washington, D.C. branch of the Niagara Movement in April.[165] At the same time, Du Bois and Niagara Movement members created a formal committee to coordinate its activities with the Constitution League, of which Du Bois became a director.[166] Finally, as the Afro-American Council and the Niagara Movement were preparing once again for their annual conventions, Du Bois made a public call for a unification of the Niagara Movement, the Council, the American Negro Academy, and the new National Negro American Political League. He claimed that each of the associations "had its raison d'etre," but that everyone now needed to recognize the groups' shared objectives by incorporating their memberships into a united organization.[167]

The primary difficultly faced by all the groups, as Du Bois explained, was financial. The combined annual dues were fourteen dollars, "a prohibitive fee for the masses," and a wasted sum accumulated by the limited membership of the groups because of duplication of work. Unification of the organizations would bring together money and energy, the general secretary reasoned, and he urged the leaders of all the groups to bring their members to the Niagara Movement's meeting in Oberlin, Ohio, in late August. To avert suspicion of his motives and possibly to bring the varying personalities into the fold, Du Bois vowed to "accept no office in the gift of the united organizations."[168]

Despite the efforts of Du Bois and Walters, unification never arrived, and their two groups limped along for the next couple of years. Before either organization completely died off, however, they as well as a number of members of their respective groups lent their support, energy, and experience to the creation of a new civil rights organization. In August 1908. a bloody race riot occurred in Springfield, Illinois. Disturbed by the acts of violence in the "land of Lincoln," southern-born journalist and socialist William English Walling graphically described the two days of racial violence in an article published in the *Independent*. Walling lamented that there was no group prepared to respond to crises faced by the black population. "Either the spirit of the abolitionists, of Lincoln and of Lovejoy, must be revived and we must come to treat the Negro on a plane of absolute political and social equality," he argued "or Vardaman and Tillman will soon have transformed the Race War to the North." Yet, "who," Walling questioned, "realizes the seriousness of the situation and what large and powerful body of citizens is ready to come to their aid?"[169]

This call likely sparked resentment in the minds of Walters and Du Bois, both of whom had been requesting assistance for a number of years. Nonetheless, egos were set aside and both agreed to participate in the National Negro Conference, held from May 30 to June 1, 1909. This conference led to the creation of the National Association for the Advancement of Colored People (NAACP).[170]

Resolutions passed by the new civil rights organization—which included members from the Afro-American Council, the Niagara Movement, and the Constitution League, as well as the Committee of Twelve—were reminiscent of principles embraced by both the Afro-American Council and the Niagara Movement. More important, like those organizations, the new group's resolutions recalled Fortune's original 1887 and 1890 calls for the formation of the Afro-American League.[171] The NAACP demanded that the Fourteenth and

Fifteenth Amendments be strictly enforced and that educational funds be equally distributed irrespective of the racial makeup of a given school's student population.[172] The group proposed carrying out much of its work through agitation, propaganda, and the court system.[173] The NAACP was thus a new incarnation of Fortune's dream. It was an organization created by individuals, both black and white, willing to stand their "ground on this civil rights business."[174]

Epilogue

> [T]o break down color bars, . . . [to obtain] for the Afro-American an equal chance with others in the avocations of life, and to . . . [secure] the full privileges of citizenship.
>
> —Constitution of the Afro-American League, January 1890

> We were welding the weapons, breasting the blows, and preparing the membership for the larger stronger organization.
>
> —W. E. B. Du Bois

Immediately following T. Thomas Fortune's death in 1928, the *Amsterdam News* published an extensive obituary praising the fiery journalist and civil rights activist for his long career and tireless devotion to the race, social uplift, and equal rights. The tribute to his life and work acknowledged his pioneering efforts in organizing the Afro-American League, an organization that the *Amsterdam News* editors referred to as "the parent of the Niagara Movement, the National Association for the Advancement of Colored People, and all similar organizations since."[1] Eight years later, W. E. B. Du Bois acknowledged Fortune and his Afro-American League for laying the groundwork for the NAACP's utilization of both agitation and a legal defense strategy.[2]

The *Amsterdam News* and Du Bois each recognized that the NAACP and the tactics it utilized had not developed in a vacuum. As *An Army of Lions* demonstrates, the League and the organizations that developed in its wake provided the ideological and tactical template upon which the NAACP was formed. The methods of agitation, legal redress, and moral suasion used by these early activists and organizations became the prototype for many of the better-known civil rights organizations of the twentieth century. The creation of the NAACP, therefore, represented a realignment or an adjustment rather than the failure of Fortune's League idea. Indeed, the formation of the NAACP effectively marked the implementation of the merger that Bishop Alexander Walters and W. E. B. Du Bois had called for in 1908. As a result, the NAACP brought together members of the Afro-American Council, the Niagara Movement, the National Negro Independent Political League, the American Negro Academy, the Constitution League, and the Committee of Twelve rather than superseding those organizations.

The NAACP centennial has come and gone. While it was a moment that many within and outside the organization privately may have wished had never had to occur—the organization should have put itself out of business long before its centennial, achieving its goals of securing full citizenship and equal rights for African Americans as protected by the Fourteenth and Fifteenth Amendments of the Constitution—the reality is that it is still needed to protest against injustice and abridgment of rights and has survived to continue to fight this lingering and historic battle. While it is certainly important to recognize the accomplishments of the "oldest and badest civil rights organization around," it should be remembered that the origins and achievements of the organization rest, in part, on the thought, labor, and activism of preceding generations.[3]

As *An Army of Lions* reveals, a rich tradition of activism, debate, and struggle predated the NAACP. And while there are a multitude of issues that plagued the pre-NAACP civil rights organizations, these groups nonetheless fashioned a rich and multifaceted legacy of struggle as well as networks of activists that later converged to help form the NAACP. Advancing and defending black citizenship while also seeking to foster greater economic and educational opportunities for African Americans during the late nineteenth and early twentieth centuries was not an easy undertaking. Because of the rising tide of racial discrimination, disfranchisement, and mob violence, traditional modes of political redress were limited in effectiveness. Therefore, activists involved in these pre-NAACP organizations attempted to redefine black politics after the fall of Reconstruction and the rise of white supremacy. A certain cadre of activists came together and sought to demand their rights outside of the older model of party politics and inaction of the black convention movement. During the period from the creation of the Afro-American League to the call for the NAACP, African Americans increasingly lost nearly all traces of their brief Reconstruction era influence as a political constituency. (During the late nineteenth century both political parties, but particularly the Republican Party, turned away from black voters. Additionally, the rapid growth of disfranchisement weakened the black voting block and eliminated the black officeholders.) In this political climate, through debate and contestation, individuals in the League and other organizations searched for how to proceed politically. In the end they created a multilayered protest strategy that used propaganda, moral suasion, lobbying, boycotting, petitioning, voter education, and calls for self-defense while attempting to curb or eliminate discrimination, lynching, and disfranchisement. What became central to this multifaceted approach however was litigation—a test-case strategy. The nation's judicial system became the primary venue and the courtrooms turned into the fundamental location for their ambitious struggle to get the nation to uphold and stand by the Fourteenth and Fifteenth Amendments and bring about an end to racial violence.

The utilization of this legal strategy is the most enduring and significant legacy that carried forward to the NAACP. T. Thomas Fortune and T. McCants Stewart formulated this strategy when the Afro-American League was being formed in the late 1880s, and Fortune, Stewart, Frederick McGhee, Madison Vance, Jesse Lawson, Ida B. Wells-Barnett, J. D. Wetmore, Booker T. Washington, Elizabeth Carter, Wilford Smith, Mary Church Terrell, and George H. White, among others, carried it forward as the various groups attacked the rise of Jim Crow. Moorfield Storey, Arthur Spingarn, Clarence Darrow, Charles Hamilton Houston, and Thurgood Marshall thus picked up and expanded upon the rallying cry of Afro-American Council leader Bishop Walters, who in 1906 admonished the leaders of the race to "go into the courts and fight it out."[4]

The pre-NAACP organizations not only provided tactics that reemerged with the foundation of the new civil rights organization, but they also furnished battle-tested activists. Nine of the original signers of the Call, for example, had been or were still associated with the Afro-American Council, the Niagara Movement, the Committee of Twelve, the National Negro American Political League, or the Constitution League. Moreover, fourteen members of the Committee of Forty and sixteen members of the first group of officers and committee members were associated with these organizations. More specifically, the leaders of every organization except the Committee of Twelve had signed the Call, had spoken at the National Negro Conference, had been named members of the Committee of Forty, and had become members of the original list of officers nominated to the first executive or general committees of the NAACP.

These individuals had demonstrated their will for decades to challenge Jim Crow and racial violence. When William E. Walling published his editorial and Oswald Garrison Villard issued "The Call," these hardened activists answered with a resounding yes, bringing their expertise and energy to a new, concerted effort. In fact, the new organization was neither new nor unforeseeable. Rather, for many it was the organization for which they had been calling for years: one Villard had outlined at the 1906 Afro-American Council convention, one Du Bois and Walters had urged in 1908, and one Villard and Walters had described at the National Negro Conference in the summer of 1909.

That new organization, in turn, picked up the precedent set by T. Thomas Fortune's Afro-American League and amplified the same claims, attempting to ensure the establishment and enforcement of the constitutional guarantees provided within the Reconstruction Amendments. In 1883, following the Supreme Court's ruling on the civil rights cases, Fortune had urged his readers to "stand their ground on this civil rights business." The individuals who came together in 1909 heeded the same call. They believed, as Fortune had, that African Americans needed to assert their "rights, and if they have to die in defending them, or bankrupt themselves, better a dead man or a pauper who dared to assert his manhood than a living slink who prized his miserable life and money above the right to live as a man."[5] The road would not be easy, but in many ways it had already been paved by women and men who, in the face of seemingly insurmountable odds, fought against rising racial discrimination and violence to let the nation know that African Americans knew their rights "and had the courage to defend them."[6]

Abbreviations

The following abbreviations are used throughout the notes.

AMECR	*AME Church Review*
AC	*American Citizen*
Guardian	*Boston Guardian*
BAAL	*Baltimore Afro-American Ledger*
BTWPLC	The Papers of Booker T. Washington, Manuscript Division, Library of Congress, Washington, D.C.
BTWPH	*The Booker T. Washington Papers*, ed. Louis R. Harlan et al. (Urbana: University of Illinois Press, 1972–1989)
BTWPT	Booker T. Washington Papers, Tuskegee University, Tuskegee, Alabama
CBA	*Chicago Broad-Ax*
CG	*Cleveland Gazette*
CT	*Chicago Tribune*
DP	*Detroit Plaindealer*
IF	*Indianapolis Freeman*
IW	*Indianapolis World*
ISB	*Iowa State Bystander*
LAT	*Los Angeles Times*
NYA	*New York Age*
NYF	*New York Freeman*
NYG	*New York Globe*
NYT	*New York Times*
Appeal	*St. Paul Appeal*
TP	*Topeka Plaindealer*
VN	*The Voice of the Negro*
WB	*Washington Bee*
CA	*Washington Colored American*
WP	*Washington Post*
WS	*Wichita Searchlight*

Notes

PREFACE

Epigraph. Ida B. Wells *DP*, September 18, 1889.

1. *NYA*, September 21, 1889; *IF*, September 28, 1889; and *IF*, October 5, 1889.

2. C. Vann Woodward, *Origins of the New South, 1877–1913* (Baton Rouge: Louisiana State University Press, 1951); C. Vann Woodward, *The Strange Career of Jim Crow* (New York: Oxford University Press, 1966); Edward L. Ayers, *The Promise of the New South: Life After Reconstruction* (New York: Oxford University Press, 1992); Michael Perman, *Struggle for Mastery: Disfranchisement in the South, 1888–1908* (Chapel Hill: University of North Carolina Press, 2001); August Meier, *Negro Thought in America, 1880–1915: Racial Ideologies in the Age of Booker T. Washington* (Ann Arbor: University of Michigan Press, 1963); Robert L. Factor, *The Black Response to America: Men, Ideals, and Organization, from Frederick Douglass to the NAACP* (Reading, Mass.: Addison-Wesley, 1970); Leslie H. Fishel, Jr., "The North and the Negro, 1865–1900" (PhD diss., Harvard University, 1953); Heather Cox Richardson, *The Death of Reconstruction: Race, Labor, and Politics in the Post-Civil War North, 1865–1901* (Cambridge, Mass.: Harvard University Press, 2001); Emma Lou Thornbrough, "The National Afro-American League, 1887–1908," *Journal of Southern History* 27, no. 4 (1961): 494–512; Emma Lou Thornbrough, *T. Thomas Fortune: Militant Journalist* (Chicago: University of Chicago Press, 1972); Benjamin R. Justesen, *Broken Brotherhood: The Rise and the Fall of the National Afro-American Council* (Carbondale: Southern Illinois University Press, 2008); and James M. McPherson, *The Abolitionist Legacy: From Reconstruction to the NAACP* (Princeton, N.J.: Princeton University Press, 1975).

3. *DP*, October 18, 1889.

4. W. E. B. Du Bois, "Social Planning for the Negro, Past and Present," *Journal of Negro Education* 5 (January 1936): 110–25, 118; and Herbert Aptheker, *Afro-American History: The Modern Era* (New York: Citadel Press, 1971), 127–58, 158. See, e.g., David Levering Lewis, *W. E. B. Du Bois: Biography of a Race, 1868–1919* (New York: Holt, 1993); Patricia Sullivan, *Lift Every Voice: The NAACP and the Making of the Civil Rights Movement* (New York: New Press, 2009); and Gilbert Jonas, *Freedom's Sword: The NAACP and the Struggle Against Racism in America, 1909–1969* (New York: Routledge, 2005). The one recent example of a change in the scholarship is Benjamin Justesen's *Broken Brotherhood.* Justesen gives a detailed account of the Afro-American Council's national conventions

and leadership, paying no attention to local activity, and sees the Council as a precursor of the NAACP, but he makes no connection back to the Afro-American League. In fact, other than brief mention, Justesen gives no details of the Afro-American League activities or of its being the origin of the Council and its legal strategy. Instead, he sees the League and the Council as two distinct organizations or ideas.

5. W. E. B. Du Bois, "Growth of the Niagara Movement," *VN* 3 (January 1906): 44–45, 45. See Meier, *Negro Thought in America*; Factor, *The Black Response to America*; Louis R. Harlan, *Booker T. Washington: The Making of a Black Leader, 1856–1901* (New York: Oxford University Press, 1972); Louis R. Harlan, *Booker T. Washington: The Wizard of Tuskegee, 1901–1915* (New York: Oxford University Press, 1983); Justesen, *Broken Brotherhood*; McPherson, *The Abolitionist Legacy*; Thornbrough, "The National Afro-American League, 1887–1908"; and Thornbrough, *T. Thomas Fortune.*

6. See Meier, *Negro Thought in America*; Factor, *The Black Response to America*; Harlan, *Booker T. Washington: The Making of a Black Leader*; Harlan, *Booker T. Washington: The Wizard of Tuskegee*; McPherson, *The Abolitionist Legacy*; Thornbrough. "The National Afro-American League, 1887–1908"; and Thornbrough, *T. Thomas Fortune.*

7. August Meier, "Towards a Reinterpretation of Booker T. Washington," *Journal of Southern History* 23, 2 (1957): 220–27, 227.

8. Jacquelyn Hall Dowd, "The Long Civil Rights Movement and the Political Uses of the Past," *Journal of American History* 91, no. 4 (March 2005): 1233–63; and Sundiata Keita Cha-Jua and Clarence Lang, "The Long Movement as a Vampire: Temporal and Spatial Fallacies in Recent Black Freedom Studies," *Journal of African American History* 92, no. 2 (2007): 265–88.

9. *NYF*, June 18, 1887; Thornbrough, *T. Thomas Fortune*, 108; and *NYF*, July 9, 1887. See also *BTWPH* 2, 357.

10. *NYA*, October 19,1907.

11. Sullivan, *Lift Every Voice*, 22.

12. Fifth session, sixth annual meeting of the NAACP, Baltimore, May 5, 1914, 9, *NAACP Papers*, cited in Sullivan, *Lift Every Voice*, 22.

13. *Colored American Magazine* 7 (July 1904): 611–15.

14. Harold Cruse, *Plural but Equal: A Critical Study of Blacks and Minorities and America's Plural Society*, (New York: William Morrow, 1987), 11.

15. *NYA*, January 25, 1890.

16. Alexander Walters, "The Afro-American Council and Its Work," *Colored American Magazine* 11 (September 1906): 207

17. *DP*, October 25, 1889; emphasis in original.

CHAPTER 1. ACELDAMA AND THE BLACK RESPONSE

Epigraph. Henry McNeal Turner, "The Conflict for Civil Rights. A Poem. By Rev. H. M. Turner" (Washington, D.C.: Judd & Detweiler, 1881).

1. Herbert Shapiro, *White Violence and Black Response: From Reconstruction to Montgomery* (Amherst: University of Massachusetts Press, 1988), 24. See also Jane Dailey, "Deference and Violence in the Postbellum Urban South: Manners and Massacres in Danville, Virginia," *Journal of Southern History* 63, no. 3 (1997): 553–90 and Jane Dailey, *Before Jim Crow: The Politics of Race in Postemancipation Virginia* (Chapel Hill: University of North Carolina Press, 2000).

2. Charles E. Waynes, *Race Relations in Virginia, 1870–1902* (Totowa, N.J.: Rowman and Littlefield, 1971), 30.

3. La Wanda Cox and John H. Cox, eds., *Reconstruction, the Negro, and the New South* (Columbia: University of South Carolina Press, 1973), 258.

4. Ibid., 261.

5. Ibid., 262.

6. Waynes, *Race Relations in Virginia, 1870–1902*, 31; and Shapiro, *White Violence and Black Response*, 24–25.

7. Shapiro, *White Violence and Black Response*, 25. See also Dailey, "Deference and Violence in the Postbellum Urban South" and Dailey, *Before Jim Crow*.

8. Rayford Whittingham Logan, *The Betrayal of the Negro: From Rutherford B. Hayes to Woodrow Wilson* (1965; rpr. New York: Da Capo, 1997).

9. Edward L. Ayers, *The Promise of the New South: Life After Reconstruction*, 157.

10. *NYF*, December 6, 1884; emphasis in original. For a full look at racial violence in the Reconstruction period, see Joint Select Committee to Inquire into the Condition of Affairs in the Late Insurrectionary, *Report of the Joint Select Committee to Inquire into the Condition of Affairs in the Late Insurrectionary States: Made to the Two Houses of Congress February 19, 1872*, vol. 13 (Washington, D.C.: U.S. Government, 1872).

11. See *Thirty Years of Lynching in the United States 1889–1919* (New York: NAACP, 1919); Edward L. Ayers, *The Promise of the New South: Life After Reconstruction*, 301–4, 435–37; W. Fitzhugh Brundage, *Lynching in the New South: Georgia and Virginia, 1880–1930* (Urbana: University of Illinois Press, 1993); Philip Dray, *At the Hands of Persons Unknown: The Lynching of Black America* (New York: Random House, 2002); and Michael J. Pfeifer, *Rough Justice: Lynching and American Society, 1874–1947* (Urbana: University of Illinois Press, 2004).

12. C. Vann Woodward, *The Strange Career of Jim Crow*.

13. Valeria W. Weaver, "The Failure of Civil Rights 1875–1883 and Its Repercussions," *Journal of Negro History* 54 (October 1969): 368.

14. John E. Bruce, "Reasons Why the Colored American Should Go to Africa," in *The Voice of Black America: Major Speeches by Negroes in the United States, 1797–1971*, ed. Philip S. Foner (New York: Simon and Schuster, 1972), 489–91.

15. Gilbert Thomas Stephenson, *Race Distinctions in American Law* (New York: D. Appleton, 1910), 110.

16. See Emma Lou Thornbrough, *T. Thomas Fortune: Militant Journalist* and T. Thomas Fortune, *T. Thomas Fortune the Afro-American Agitator: A Collection of Writings, 1880–1928*, ed. Shawn Leigh Alexander (Gainesville: University Press of Florida, 2008).

17. Leslie H. Fishel, Jr., "Repercussions of Reconstruction: The Northern Negro 1870–1883," *Civil War History* 14 (1968): 343.

18. Ibid., 334.

19. V. P. Franklin, *Black Self-Determination: A Cultural History of the Faith of the Fathers* (Westport, Conn.: L. Hill, 1984), 179. See also I. Garland Penn, *The Afro-American Press and Its Editors* (1891; rpr.. New York: Arno Press, 1969) and Martin E. Dann, ed., *The Black Press, 1827–1890: The Quest for National Identity* (New York: Capricorn, 1972).

20. T. Thomas Fortune, "Whose Problem Is This?" *AMECR* 11 (October 1894): 253.

21. Stephenson, *Race Distinctions in American Law*, 109–11; Weaver, "The Failure of Civil Rights 1875–1883 and Its Repercussions"; and *Civil Rights Cases*, 109 U.S. 3 (1883). See also Michael Perman, *Struggle for Mastery: Disfranchisement in the South, 1888–1908.*

22. Bruce, "Reasons Why the Colored American Should Go to Africa," 489–91.

23. *NYG*, October 20, 1883.

24. Henry McNeal Turner, *Respect Black: The Writings and Speeches of Henry McNeal Turner*, ed. Edwin S. Redkey (New York: Arno Press, 1971), 60.

25. Ralph L. Crowder, "Race, Politics, and Patronage: John Edward Bruce and the Republican Party," 83; John Edward Bruce, *The Selected Writings of John Edward Bruce: Militant Black Journalist*, ed. Peter Gilbert (New York: Arno Press, 1971), 23–26.

26. Crowder, "Race, Politics, and Patronage," 83; and Bruce, *The Selected Writings of John Edward Bruce*, 26.

27. *NYG*, October 20, 1883; emphasis in original.

28. *NYF*, December 6, 1884; emphasis in original. (Fortune's *Globe* folded and became the *Freeman* in 1884.)

29. *Hartford Telegram*, reprinted in *New York Globe*, January 19, 1884; emphasis in original. See also Thornbrough, *T. Thomas Fortune*, 106; Robert L. Factor, *The Black Response to America: Men, Ideals, and Organization, from Frederick Douglass to the NAACP* (Reading, Mass.: Addison-Wesley, 1970), 117–20; and August Meier, *Negro Thought in America, 1880–1915: Racial Ideologies in the Age of Booker T. Washington.*

30. *NYF*, December 6, 1884.

31. See Howard Holman Bell, *A Survey of the Negro Convention Movement, 1830–1861* (New York: Arno Press, 1969) and Meier, *Negro Thought in America.*

32. *NYF*, June 4, 1887.

33. Ibid.

34. *NYF*, May 28, 1887.

35. *NYF*, August 20, 1887. See also Robert J. Swan, "Thomas McCants Stewart and the Failure of the Mission of the Talented Tenth in Black America, 1880–1923" (PhD diss., New York University, 1990), 144–45; and Albert S. Broussard, *African-American Odyssey: The Stewarts, 1853–1963* (Lawrence: University Press of Kansas, 1998). Swan claims that Stewart was the one who provided the theoretical foundation of the League. While this may be true, Swan never supplies sufficient evidence of such.

36. *NYF*, May 28, 1887.

37. Ibid. See also Eric Foner, "Class, Ethnicity, and Radicalism in the Gilded Age: The Land League and Irish America," in *Politics and Ideology in the Age of the Civil War* (New York: Oxford University Press, 1980). At its peak, the Land League in America boasted more than nine hundred branches, which together raised more than $500,000 to support the struggle in Ireland.

38. Kerby A. Miller, *Emigrants and Exiles: Ireland and the Irish Exodus to North America* (New York: Oxford University Press, 1985), 442.

39. Ibid., 444; and Theodore W. Moody, *Davitt and Irish Revolution 1846–82* (Oxford: Oxford University Press, 1982), 543. For more on Henry George and the Land League, see Edward T. O'Donnell, "'Though Not an Irishman': Henry George and the American Irish," *American Journal of Economics and Sociology* 56, no. 4 (October 1997): 407–19.

40. *NYF*, January 2, 1886.

41. O'Donnell, "'Though Not an Irishman'"; Foner, "Class, Ethnicity, and Radicalism in the Gilded Age"; and Thomas N. Brown, *Irish-American Nationalism, 1870–1890* (New York: Lippincott, 1966).

42. *NYF*, May 28, 1887.

43. *The Pilot*, June 11, 1887; and *NYF*, June 18, 1887. It is important to note that less than a month before the Afro-American League met for its first national convention, O'Reilly featured an article entitled "Good Effects of a Threat: A Lesson for Southern Negroes From Irish Laborers," in which the author calls for an organization much like the Afro-American League to organize and fight against the increasing discrimination in the South. Phineas, "Good Effects of a Threat: A Lesson for Southern Negroes from Irish Laborers," *The Pilot* 18 (1890). For a discussion of O'Reilly and African Americans, see John R. Betts, "The Negro and the New England Conscience in the Days of John Boyle O'Reilly," *Journal of Negro History* 51 (October 1966): 246–61; and Mark R. Schneider, *Boston Confronts Jim Crow, 1890–1920* (Boston: Northeastern University Press, 1997).

44. *NYF*, June 4, 1887; Thornbrough, *T. Thomas Fortune*, 107; Emma Lou Thornbrough, "Afro-American League," *Journal of Southern History* 27, no. 4 (November 1961): 496; and Factor, *The Black Response to America*, 120.

45. *NYF*, June 4, 1887; Thornbrough, *T. Thomas Fortune*, 107; and Thornbrough, "Afro-American League," 496.

46. *NYF*, June 18, 1887.

47. *NYF*, June 18, 1887; Thornbrough, *T. Thomas Fortune*, 108; and *NYF*, July 9, 1887. See also *BTWPH* 2: 357.

48. *NWF*, July 9, 1887.

49. For the fullest description of the career of John Mitchell, Jr., see Ann F. Alexander, "Black Protest in the New South: John Mitchell, Jr. and the Richmond Planet." (PhD dissertation, Duke University, 1973). It is important to note, however, that Alexander does not mention Mitchell's association with the Afro-American League or the Afro-American Council.

50. *NYF*, July 9, 1887.

51. *NYF*, September 17, 1887.

52. *NYF*, September 10, 1887.

53. Ibid. See also *Southwestern Christian Advocate*, September 1, 1887.

54. *NYF*, September 10, 1887. Robert Factor sees the election of Harrison and the hopes of his presidency as a possible reason for the apathy toward the Afro-American League.

55. Ibid.

56. *NYF*, September 10, 1887.

57. Ibid.; and Thornbrough, *T. Thomas Fortune*, 109.

58. *NYF*, September 10, 1887; *NYF*, September 17, 1887.

59. *NYF*, October 8, 1887.

60. Bess Beatty, *A Revolution Gone Backward: Black Response to National Politics, 1876–1896* (New York: Greenwood Press, 1987), 93–132; and Logan, *The Betrayal of the Negro*, 52–78.

61. Beatty, *A Revolution Gone Backward*, 105.

62. Ibid., 105–6.

63. *Western Appeal*, December 22, 1888.

64. Beatty, *A Revolution Gone Backward*, 109.

65. *Western Appeal*, December 22, 1888.

66. Ralph L. Crowder, "Race, Politics, and Patronage: John Edward Bruce and the Republican Party," *Afro-Americans in New York Life and History* 26 (January 2002): 75–111. See also *NYA*, January 14, 21, and 28, 1888.

67. *NYA*, January 5, 1889. See also *NYT*, December 18, 1888.

68. Factor, *Black Response to America*, 120–21. See also Penn, *The Afro-American Press and Its Editor*, 526; T. Thomas Fortune, "The Afro-American League," *AMECR* 7 (July 1890): 2–6; and *DP*, October 11, 1889. On William Matthews, see William J. Simmons, *Men of Mark: Eminent, Progressive and Rising* (1887; rpr. New York: Arno Press, 1968), 246–51.

69. Factor, *Black Response to America*, 120–21.

70. *DP*, October 18, 1889; and *DP*, October 25, 1889. The circular was sent to such as individuals as John R. Lynch, James M. Henderson, W. S. Scarborough, Augustus Straker, John P. Green, Ida B. Wells, Albion W. Tourgée, Henry McNeal Turner, Booker T. Washington, and J. C. Price.

71. *NYA*, October 19, 1889.

72. Meier, *Negro Thought in America*, 129.

73. *NYA*, November 9, 1889.

74. *DP*, November 8, 1889.

75. *NYA*, November 9, 1889.

76. Ibid.; and *Washington Post*, November 5, 1889.

77. *NYA*, November 16, 1889. See also *DP*, November 8, 1889.

78. *WB*, November 16, 1889; and *IF*, November 16, 1889.

79. *WB*, November 16, 1889. It is important to note that Chase and a number of other prominent African Americans in the D.C. area organized an Afro-American League in the region and announced its formation in the same issue of the paper. The branch included the following elected officials: Thomas T. Symmons, Thomas L. Jones, Travis Glascoe, John Edward Bruce, A. G. Davis, C. H. Watson, Rev. W. B. Johnson, J. Coles, William Johnson, N. J. Johnson, Rev. A. A. Lott, Mrs. M. A. D. Hood, and W. Calvin Chase.

80. *CG*, November 30, 1889.

81. *CG*, May 28, 1887

82. *NYG*, June 2, 1883.

83. *NYA*, November 9, 1889.

84. T. Thomas Fortune to George Washington Cable, 6 December 1889, *George Washington Cable Papers*. Howard T. Hon. Memorial Library, Tulane University, New Orleans, LA.

85. *NYA*, October 5, 1889 and *DP*, October 25, 1889. John Mercer Langston's biographer does not mention either the letter from Matthews or anything about Langston's brief agreement to head the Afro-American League. See William Francis Cheek, "Forgotten Prophet: The Life of John Mercer Langston" (PhD dissertation, University of Virginia, 1961).

86. *NYA*, October 5, 1889.

87. *NYA*, October 26, 1889.

88. *NYA*, October 5, 1889.

89. *CG*, November 9, 1889. In October, Reverend William H. Heard had written to Fortune expressing similar sentiments. See *NYA*, October 26, 1889. For yet another similar commentary from the Philadelphia League, see *IF*, October 19, 1889.

90. *NYA*, October 26, 1889.

91. Stephenson, *Race Distinctions in American Law*, 110.

92. *NYA*, November 30, 1889.

93. Ibid., and *Atlanta Constitution*, July 27, 1889.

94. *NYA*, November 30, 1889; *CG*, November 30, 1889; *WB*, November 30, 1889; *DP*, November 29, 1889; and *IF*, December 7, 1889.

95. Ibid. It is important to note that only the *New York Age* lists William Heard as a signer.

96. *NYA*, December 21, 1889; and Thornbrough, *T. Thomas Fortune*, 110–11. See also T. Thomas Fortune, "The Race Problem: The Negro Will Solve It," *Belford's Magazine* 5 (September 1890): 489–95.

97. *NYA*, December 21, 1889.

98. Ibid.; emphasis in original.

99. *NYF*, December 6, 1884.

CHAPTER 2. "STAND THEIR GROUND ON THIS CIVIL RIGHTS BUSINESS"

Epigraph. Howard L. Smith, *NYF*, July 2, 1887; W. H. Bonaparte, *NYF* July 9, 1887.

1. *NYA*, January 4, 1890.

2. *NYA*, January 11, 1890.

3. *NYA*, January 4, 1890.

4. *AMECR* 6 (January 1890): 377–78; I. Garland Penn, *The Afro-American Press and Its Editors* (1891; repr. New York: Arno Press, 1969), 531–32.

5. *NYA*, November 16, 1889; *CG*, November 30, 1889. This was changed from Fortune's initial decision that there would be three delegates for every one hundred members of the League. See *NYA*, November 9, 1889 and January 25, 1890. According to the account of Bishop Walters, who was not present at the national meeting, there were 141 delegates from twenty-one states. Alexander Walters, *My Life and Work* (New York: Fleming H. Revell, 1917), 135. According to Emma Lou Thornbrough, there were 135 delegates from twenty-three states. Emma Lou Thornbrough, *T. Thomas Fortune: Militant Journalist* (Chicago, University of Chicago Press, 1972), 112. According to the *Cleveland Gazette*, the *Detroit Plaindealer*, and the *Washington Bee*'s accounts of the convention, there were two hundred delegates. See *CG*, January 25, 1890; *DP*, January 17, 1890; and *WB*, January 18, 1890. *Official Compilation of Proceedings of the Afro-American League National Convention, January 15, 16, 17, 1890* (Chicago: Battles and Cabbell, 1890), 19–20; and *NYA*, January 25, 1890. For different tabulations, see Thornbrough, *T. Thomas Fortune*, 112. The credentials committee reported that 141 delegates from twenty-one states attended the convention, the majority coming from regions close to Chicago, including thirteen from Indiana, forty-four from Illinois, nine from Michigan, twenty from Ohio, four from Iowa, three from Minnesota, five from Nebraska, and three from Wisconsin. The South was well represented with eight delegates from Georgia; one each from North Carolina, South Carolina, Texas, Tennessee, and West Virginia; two each from Kansas and Kentucky; and seven from Missouri. The Northeast was also adequately represented with one delegate from Massachusetts, four from Pennsylvania, and seven from New York.

6. The term *middle class* is used loosely here to designate those in the African American community who had acquired a certain level of livelihood that set them apart from the rest of the African American population of freemen and women and freedmen and women who were primarily agricultural workers. For more information on the class structure of the African American population during this period, see Sidney Kronus, "Some Neglected Aspects of Negro Class Comparison," *Phylon* 31 (Winter 1970): 359–71; and August Meier, "Negro Class Structure and Ideology in the Age of Booker T. Washington," *Phylon* 23 (Fall 1962): 258–66.

7. Meier, "Negro Class Structure," 260.

8. T. Thomas Fortune believed that unless "the women of the race take hold of the Afro-American League it will never be the power it should be." See *NYA*, November 23, 1889.

9. African American women did participate on the local and state levels, and in some locations they actively aided in the creation of the state organizations.

10. *Official Compilation of Proceedings*, 4–8, 8; *NYA*, January 25, 1890; *CG*, January 25, 1890; and *New York Age*, February 1, 1890.

11. *Official Compilation of Proceedings*, 8.

12. Ibid., 8–9.

13. Ibid., 9.

14. Ibid., 9 and 12.

15. Ibid., 18.

16. Ibid., 19.

17. Ibid., 27–28.

18. Ibid., 28.

19. Ibid. The *Detroit Plaindealer* made reference to this resolution being sent off to Congress by telegram during the proceedings. See *DP*, February 14, 1890.

20. *Official Compilation of Proceedings*, 28.

21. Ibid., 36–40.

22. Ibid.; Thornbrough, *T. Thomas Fortune*, 112; and Robert L. Factor, *The Black Response to America: Men, Ideals, and Organization, from Frederick Douglass to the NAACP* (Reading, Mass.: Addison-Wesley, 1970), 120. See also Thornbrough, *T. Thomas Fortune*, 114–15; and August Meier, *Negro Thought in America, 1880–1915: Racial Ideologies in the Age of Booker T. Washington* (Ann Arbor: University of Michigan Press, 1963), 129.

23. *Official Compilation of Proceedings*, 41–42; Thornbrough, *T. Thomas Fortune*, 115; I. Garland Penn, *The Afro-American Press and Its Editors*, 532. For more information on J. C. Price, see William Joseph Walls, *Joseph Charles Price: Educator and Race Leader* (Boston: Christopher Publishing House, 1943); and August Meier, "Negro Racial Thought in the Age of Booker T. Washington, Circa 1880–1915" (PhD diss., Columbia University, 1957), 234–41. Price did not arrive at the Chicago convention until the second day of the proceedings; therefore he was not seated with the North Carolina delegation but rather as a delegate at large. See *Official Compilation of Proceedings*, 8 and 21.

24. *NYA*, February 8, 1890.

25. Thornbrough, *T. Thomas Fortune*, 116. For coverage by the *Chicago Tribune*, see January 16, 17, and 18, 1890.

26. *The Nation* 50, February 13, 1890; and *The Appeal*, February 22, 1890. See also Thornbrough, *T. Thomas Fortune*, 116.

27. *The Appeal*, February 22, 1890; *The Nation* 50, February 13, 1890; and *The Appeal*, February 22, 1890.

28. *Official Compilation of Proceedings*.

29. *DP*, May 9, 1890; *CG*, November 9, 1889; and Leslie H. Fishel, Jr., "The Genesis of the First Wisconsin Civil Rights Act," *Wisconsin Magazine of History* 49 (1966): 327.

30. Fishel, Jr., "Genesis of the First Wisconsin Civil Rights Act," 327.

31. *DP*, February 21, 1890; *DP*, April 11, 1890; May 9, 1890.

32. *DP*, May 9, 1890. On the Barnwell Massacre, see George B. Tindall, *South Carolina Negroes, 1877–1900* (Baton Rouge: Louisiana State University Press, 1952).

33. *DP*, May 9, 1890.

34. Ibid. For more on William T. Green, see Leslie H. Fishel, Jr., "William Thomas Green: Black Milwaukee's Lawyer-Leader, 1887–1911," *Milwaukee History* 19 (1996): 85–94.

35. *DP*, May 30, July 4, and September 26, 1890. For more information on Jacob Litt, see Larry Widen, "Jacob Litt: Milwaukee's Forgotten Showman," *Milwaukee History* 19 (1996): 2–13.

36. *DP*, May 30 and July 4, 1890. See also Fishel, "Genesis of the First Wisconsin Civil Rights Act," 327.

37. *DP*, July 11, 1890.

38. *DP*, September 26, 1890.

39. Ibid.

40. *CG*, January 25, 1890.

41. *CG*, March 8, 1890.

42. Ibid.; *DP*, March 22 and 29, 1890.

43. *DP*, March 8 and 29, 1890.

44. *DP*, March 22 and 29, 1890; emphasis in original.

45. *DP*, March 22 and 29, 1890.

46. *DP*, March 22, 1890. Another such petition was sent from Scioto County. *CG*, March 29, 1890.

47. *CG*, March 22 and 29, April 12 and 19, and May 3 and 17, 1890.

48. *CG*, April 26, 1890; emphasis in original.

49. Ibid., May 24, 1890.

50. Ibid., May 31, 1890.

51. Ibid., October 11, 1890.

52. *DP*, February 7 and 14, 1890; and *NYA*, February 15, 1890. See also Meier, *Negro Thought in America*, 70–71; and Thornbrough, *T. Thomas Fortune*, 116–17.

53. *DP*, February 7 and 14, 1890; and *NYA*, February 15, 1890.

54. John Edward Bruce, *The Selected Writings of John Edward Bruce: Militant Black Journalist*, ed. Peter Gilbert (New York: Arno Press, 1971), 33.

55. Ibid., 41 and 39.

56. Ibid., 38–39.

57. Ibid., 41.

58. Ibid., 42.

59. Ibid., 39.

60. *DP*, March 7, 1890. See also Dorothy Drinkard Hawkshawe, "David Augustus Straker: Black Lawyer and Reconstruction Politician, 1842–1908." (PhD diss., Catholic University of America, 1974), 109–29.

61. *DP*, March 7, 1890.

62. Ibid., March 14, 1890.

63. Ibid., April 11, 1890.

64. Ibid., May 16, 1890.

65. Ibid., May 23, 1890.

66. Richard R. Wright, Jr., ed., *Centennial Encyclopedia of the African Methodist Episcopal Church* (Philadelphia, 1916), 96–97; and David Graham Du Bois, "Mission and Ministry in America and Africa: Reflections on David and Etta Graham," *AMECR* 117 (Oct.–Dec. 2001), 41–44.

67. *DP*, July 11, 1890.

68. Ibid., October 24, 1890. Reverend Graham would relocate to Minnesota, where he became the pastor of St. Peter's Church in Minneapolis, and assisted in the creation of the state organization in Minnesota.

69. *DP*, October 17 and 24, 1890; and Hawkshawe, "David Augustus Straker," 120–22.

70. Robert J. Swan, "Thomas McCants Stewart and the Failure of the Mission of the Talented Tenth in Black America, 1880–1923" (PhD diss., New York University, 1990), 149.

71. Ibid., 151; *NYA*, April 26 and May 17 and 31, 1890. This would ultimately become the Chase-Ward Bill.

72. *NYA*, May 31, 1890.

73. Ibid.

74. *NYA*, July 5, 1890.

75. Ibid., June 7, 1890.

76. Ibid.; Swan, "Thomas McCants Stewart," 153.

77. *NYA*, June 14, 1890.

78. Ibid., July 5, 1890.

79. Ibid., June 14, 1890; and Thornbrough, *T. Thomas Fortune*, 118.

80. *NYA*, June 21, 1890.

81. Ibid.; and Thornbrough, *T. Thomas Fortune*, 118.

82. *NYA*, June 21, 1890.

83. *NYA*, October 11, 1890; and *CG*, October 11, 1890. Besides the state leagues that have already been mentioned, groups were formed in Michigan and Nebraska. See *CG*, March 19, 1890 and May 17, 1890.

84. *NYA*, October 11, 1890; *CG*, October 11, 1890.

85. *NYA*, October 11, 1890; *CG*, October 11, 1890.

86. *CG*, October 11, 1890.

87. *NYA*, December 6, 1890.

88. T. Thomas Fortune, "The Afro-American League," *AMECR* 7 (July 1890): 4.

89. David Vassar Taylor, "Pilgrim's Progress: Black St. Paul and the Making of an Urban Ghetto, 1870–1930" (PhD diss., University of Minnesota, 1977).

90. *WP*, May 21, 1887.

91. Hazel v. Foley (Foley Brothers), Judgment of October 17, 1887, 25515 Civil Court of the Second Judicial District (Minn.).

92. Hazel v. Foley (Foley Brothers), Appeal of October 22, 1887 from the Judgment of October 17, 1887, 25515 Civil Court of the Second Judicial District (Minn.).

93. David V. Taylor, "John Adams and the Western Appeal: Advocates of the Protest Tradition" (master's thesis, University of Nebraska at Omaha, 1971), 36–37; see also David V. Taylor, "John Quincy Adams: St. Paul Editor and Black Leader," *Minnesota History* 43 (Winter 1973): 292–93. See also *Western Appeal*, November 12 and 26 and December 31, 1887.

94. Taylor, "John Adams and the Western Appeal," 42–44; see also Taylor, "John Quincy Adams," 292–93. See also Paul D. Nelson, *Frederick L. McGhee: A Life on the Color Line, 1861–1912* (Minneapolis: Minnesota Historical Society Press, 2002), 26–27. It is important to note that because McGhee did not move to the city until just before the formation of the Afro-American League, Nelson does not mention the Minnesota Protective and Industrial League. It is also important to note that the instigator for the creation of the Minnesota Protective and Industrial League, John Quincy Adams, praised Fortune's League idea in an editorial on June 11, 1887. *WP*, June 11, 1887.

95. *WP*, November 29 and December 13, 1890; and Nelson, *Frederick L. McGhee*, 29–31.

96. *WP*, December 20, 1890; and Nelson, *Frederick L. McGhee*, 29.

97. *Appeal*, January 3, 1891; and Nelson, *Frederick L. McGhee*, 29. It should be noted that the *Western Appeal* became the *Appeal* in 1891.

98. *Appeal*, January 31, 1891.

99. Ibid. The phrase "Perfect Freedom" was the name of the speech delivered by Frederick McGhee at the Emancipation Day demonstration.

100. *Appeal*, April 11 and 18, 1891. It is important to note, however, that the Delicatessen Restaurant had obviously not learned its lesson when it came to the Hazel family: Rosa, William's wife, brought suit against the establishment three years later. See Nelson, *Frederick L. McGhee*, 171.

101. *Appeal*, May 16 and 23, 1891; *NYA*, May 6, 1891.

102. *DP*, January 30, 1891.

103. Ibid.; *DP*, February 27 and March 20, 1891; and Fishel, "Genesis of the First Wisconsin Civil Rights Act," 329.

104. *DP*, March 20, 1891.

105. *DP*, April 10, 1891; and Fishel, "Genesis of the First Wisconsin Civil Rights Act," 329 and 330.

106. *NYA*, March 28, 1891; Swan "Thomas McCants Stewart," 151, Thornbrough, *T. Thomas Fortune*, 120.

107. *NYA*, March 28, 1891.

108. *DP*, January 2, 1891; and *IF*, March 1, May 24, June 14 and June 21, and September 2, 6, and 27, 1890.

109. For a text of the act, see *DP*, September 18, 1891.

110. *Appeal*, June 20 and 27, 1891; and *IF*, July 11, 1891.

111. *Appeal*, June 27, 1891.

112. *DP*, July 24, 1891.

113. *NYA*, July 11, 1891. The Wisconsin League also discussed the problems in gathering enough funds to send their delegate to the national convention. See *DP*, June 5, 1891.

114. It is important to note that though they were not members, John Mercer Langston and B. K. Bruce publicly supported T. Thomas Fortune's case against the Trainer Hotel. Langston lent his legal assistance, and Bruce was one of the first to donate money to the defense fund. See also *NYA*, July 11 and 25, 1891; and *DP*, May 19, 1891.

115. *NYA*, July 25, 1891.

116. Ibid. According to William H. Anderson of the *Detroit Plaindealer*, it was Wells who "captured the house" in her address to the convention. See *DP*, July 24, 1891.

117. *NYA*, July 25, 1891.

118. Ibid.; and *DP*, July 24, 1891.

119. *NYA*, July 25, 1891 and *DP*, July 24, 1891.

120. *NYA*, July 25, 1891.

121. *CG*, August 1, 1891. See also Linda O. McMurry, *To Keep the Waters Troubled: The Life of Ida B. Wells* (New York: Oxford University Press, 1998), 122–23.

122. *DP*, July 24, 1891.

123. *NYA*, August 8, 1891; and Thornbrough, *T. Thomas Fortune*, 121. Ida B. Wells had already challenged the Jim Crow seating arrangement nearly a decade before; see Ida B. Wells, *Crusade for Justice: The Autobiography of Ida B. Wells* (Chicago: University of Chicago Press, 1970), 18–20.

124. *NYA*, September 5, 1891; and Factor, *The Black Response to America*, 127. It is important to note that Fortune supported William Heard's actions in an earlier case against discrimination on the railway. In December 1887 before the League became a national movement, Fortune applauded the actions of Heard and William H. Council, who had both appealed to the legal system to challenge their treatment on the rails. Fortune stated that he believed their course of action was the type that the League needed to encourage and support. See *NYA*, December 17, 1887.

125. *IF*, August 8, 1891.

126. *NYA*, August 22 and 29, 1891.

127. *NYA*, August 29, 1891.

128. *NYA*, August 22, 1891.

129. *Atlanta Constitution*, September 3, 1891.

130. *A Brief History of the Afro-American League of San Francisco with Some Reference to Its Objectives and What It Has Accomplished* (San Francisco, 1895),; *Souvenir Programme of the Afro-American League of San Francisco* (San Francisco, 1902), 1–5; and James A. Fisher, "A History of the Political and Social Development of the Black Community in California, 1850–1950. (PhD diss., State University of New York at Stony Brook, 1971), 160–61.

131. *Appeal*, August 29, 1891; *DP*, September 4, 1891; and *IF*, August 8, 1891.

132. *Appeal*, August 29, 1891.

133. *NYA*, September 5, 1891; and *DP*, September 11, 1891.

134. *NYA*, September 5, 1891. Many prominent politicians and Washington, D.C. residents congratulated Fortune and the League on their victory, but it is neither clear if they offered any support financially nor whether they were now willing to put their shoulders behind the wheel of the Afro-American League. The signers of the letter included John Mercer Langston, P. B. S. Pinchback, T. H. Greene, H. H. Williams, Thomas E. Miller, E. L. Thornton, James T. Bradford, William E. Matthews, and Robert H. Terrell. *NYA*, September 19, 1891; and *DP*, September 25, 1891. J. C. Price, the former president of the League, offered his congratulations to Fortune and the League, and questioned why the masses did not support the organization on a larger scale, but offered only his subscription for the *Age* as a symbol of his support of the group. See *NYA*, October 3, 1891.

135. *NYA*, September 19, 1891.

136. *DP*, September 25, 1891.

137. *Appeal*, September 12, 1891.

138. *DP*, September 18, 1891.

139. Ibid. The *Cleveland Gazette* would echo this sentiment two months later; see *CG*, November 14, 1891.

140. *Appeal*, August 29 and September 12, 1891; and *DP*, September 4, 1891.

141. *Appeal*, September 12, 1891. For a full discussion of the Minnesota Civil Rights Committee and the Samuel Hardy suit, see Nelson, *Frederick McGhee*, 32–35.

142. *Appeal*, August 29, 1891. It is important to note that Paul Nelson, who was the biographer of Frederick McGhee (the lawyer and chairman for the Minnesota Civil Rights Committee, and a member of the League's Legislative Bureau), claims that the Afro-American League had abdicated the Heard case, which set the stage for the St. Paul branch to set itself apart. However, this is not true. As has been demonstrated, at the same time that the St. Paul members created the Minnesota Civil Rights Committee, Fortune was pleading with the local Leagues to pay their dues so the Heard case could be fought. Nelson, *Frederick McGhee*, 32. See also *NYA*, September 19 and October 3, 10, and 24, 1891.

143. *NYA*, October 10, 1891.

144. Ibid. It is important to note that Fortune makes a mistake in referring to the Hardy case, calling it the "case of Mr. Wallace."

145. *NYA*, October 10, 1891.

146. *Appeal*, October 17, 1891.

147. *Appeal*, October 17, 24, and 31 and November 7 and 14, 1891.

148. *Appeal*, November 14, 1891.

149. *Appeal*, September 26 and November 21, 1891.

150. *Appeal*, September 12, 1891.

151. *NYA*, November 14, 1891; *CG*, November 14, 1891; and Thornbrough, *T. Thomas Fortune*, 119.

152. *NYA*, November 14, 1891; and Swan, "Thomas McCants Stewart," 155.

153. *NYA*, November 14, 1891.

154. Ibid.; Thornbrough, *T. Thomas Fortune*, 119; and Swan, "Thomas McCants Stewart," 156. Trainer's lawyers immediately filed an appeal; the legal battle dragged on for another two years, but in the end Fortune still emerged victorious.

155. *NYA*, November 14, 1891; and Swan, "Thomas McCants Stewart," 156.

156. *NYA*, November 14, 1891.

157. *NYA*, November 21, 1891.

158. *DP*, October 6, November 6,and December 18, 1891.

159. *DP*, December 18, 1891.

160. *DP*, September 4, 11, 18, and 23, and October 1 and 6, 1891.

161. *DP*, October 6, 1891.

162. Otto H. Olsen, *Carpetbagger's Crusade: The Life of Albion Winegar Tourgée* (Baltimore: Johns Hopkins, 1965), 312–31; see also Mark Elliott. *Color-Blind Justice: Albion Tourgée and the Quest for Racial Equality from the Civil War to* Plessy v. Ferguson (New York: Oxford University Press, 2006); and Mark Elliott, "Race, Color Blindness, and the Democratic Public: Albion W. Tourgée's Radical Principles in *Plessy v. Ferguson*," *Journal of Southern History* 67 (May 2001): 287–330.

163. *Official Compilation of Proceedings*, 29–33.

164. Quoted in Olsen, *Carpetbagger's Crusade*, 307.

165. See ibid., 312–31.

166. Ibid. *DP*, October 31, 1891.

167. *DP*, January 8, 1892.

168. *DP*, February 12, 1892.

169. Ibid., February 19 and March 4, 1892.

170. Ibid., February 19 and March 4 and 18, 1892.

171. *IF*, July 2, 1892.

172. Edward L. Ayers, *Vengeance and Justice: Crime and Punishment in the 19th-Century American South* (New York: Oxford University Press, 1984), 238.

173. *DP*, April 8 and 22, 1892. Some of the signers of the appeal were Peter H. Clark, Reverend Daniel Payne, Reverend Benjamin Tanner, Reverend Henry McNeal Turner, Booker T. Washington, and Frederick Douglass.

174. *DP*, May 6, 1892.

175. *DP*, May 20, 1892.

176. Ibid., June 3, 1892.

177. *Appeal*, June 4, 1892.

178. *DP*, September 2, 1892.

179. *IF*, July 22, 1893. See also Fisher, "Political and Social Development of the Black Community in California," 161.

180. *IF*, July 22, 1893.

181. Ibid., July 29 and October 14, 1893.

182. Thornbrough, *T. Thomas Fortune*, 122; and *IW*, August 26, 1893.

183. *IF*, July 22, 1893.

184. *IF*, July 14, 1894; and *Woman's Era* 1 (August 1894), 6 and 8.

185. On the Memphis lynching, see McMurry, *To Keep the Waters Troubled*; Wells-Barnett, *Crusade for Justice*; Mildred Thompson, *Ida B. Wells-Barnett: An Exploratory Study of an American Black Woman, 1893–1930* (Brooklyn: Carlson, 1990); and Patricia A. Schechter, *Ida B. Wells-Barnett & American Reform, 1880–1930* (Chapel Hill: University of North Carolina Press, 2001).

186. Quoted in McMurry, *To Keep the Waters Troubled*, 146–47.

187. Schechter, *Ida B. Wells-Barnett & American Reform*, 85. At the exposition, the Afro-American League of Tennessee, led by Benjamin Arnett in conjunction with T. Thomas Fortune and the National Executive Committee, presented Representative James M. Ashley with a collection of his speeches for his position against slavery and his strong advocacy for the rights of African Americans during Reconstruction. Frederick Douglass composed the introduction to the collection. This is the only reference to Douglass working in conjunction with the Afro-American League. See James Monroe Ashley, *Duplicate Copy of the Souvenir from the Afro-American League of Tennessee to Hon. James M. Ashley, of Ohio*, ed. Benjamin W. Arnett (Philadelphia: A. M. E. Church, 1894).

188. *IF*, July 14, 1894; *LAT*, July 30, 1894.

189. *IF*, July 14, 1894; *LAT*, July 30, 1894.

190. *Woman's Era* 1 (August 1894), 6 and 8; and *IF*, August 25, 1894. It is also during 1894 that Fortune had his judgment against the Trainer Hotel affirmed in an appellate court, but no League-supported newspaper viewed the victory as a success for the organization. It is as if the origins of the case were forgotten.

191. *NYA*, October 29, 1887.

192. *DP*, October 18, 1889.

193. *DP*, February 28, 1890.

194. *DP*, October 25, 1889; emphasis in original. See also Factor, *The Black Response to America*, 122.

195. *NYA*, November 23, 1889.

196. Robert Factor makes a similar point. See Factor, *The Black Response to America*, 126.

197. Ibid., 127.

198. *NYF*, July 9, 1887; and *NYA*, January 2, 1892.

CHAPTER 3. INTERREGNUM AND RESURRECTION

Epigraph. Charles Hall, *IR* April 30, 1898.

1. For general information on Ida B. Wells-Barnett, see Ida B. Wells-Barnett, *Crusade for Justice: The Autobiography of Ida B. Wells* (Chicago: University of Chicago Press, 1970); Linda O. McMurry, *To Keep the Waters Troubled: The Life of Ida B. Wells* (New York: Oxford University Press, 1998); Mildred Thompson, *Ida B. Wells-Barnett: An Exploratory Study of an American Black Woman, 1893–1930* (Brooklyn, N.Y.: Carlson, 1990);

Patricia A. Schechter, *Ida B. Wells-Barnett & American Reform, 1880–1930* (Chapel Hill: University of North Carolina Press, 2001); Paula Giddings, *Ida: A Sword Among Lions: Ida B. Wells and the Campaign Against Lynching* (New York: Amistad, 2008); and Mia Bay, *To Tell The Truth Freely: The Life of Ida B. Wells* (New York: Hill and Wang, 2010).

2. Abraham Kendrick, "Ida B. Wells" *IF*, February 2, 1895.

3. Quoted in McMurry, *To Keep the Waters Troubled*, 245. McMurry incorrectly lists Jacks's first name as John.

4. Robert L. Factor, *The Black Response to America: Men, Ideals, and Organization, from Frederick Douglass to the NAACP* (Reading, Mass.: Addison-Wesley, 1970), 112; Deborah Gray White, *Too Heavy a Load: Black Women in Defense of Themselves, 1894–1994* (New York: Norton, 1999), 21–55. See also Crystal Nicole Feimster, *Southern Horrors: Women and the Politics of Rape and Lynching* (Cambridge, Mass.: Harvard University Press, 2009) and Beverly Guy-Sheffield, *Daughters of Sorrow: Attitudes Toward Black Women, 1880–1920* (Brooklyn, N.Y.: Carlson, 1990).

5. Anna Julia Cooper, *The Voice of Anna Julia Cooper: Including A Voice from the South and Other Important Essays, Papers, and Letters*, eds. Charles Lemert and Esme Bhan (Lanham, Md.: Rowman and Littlefield, 1998), 63.

6. For information on the NACW and the women's movement during this period, see White, *Too Heavy a Load*, 21–55; Elizabeth L. David, *Lifting as They Climb: National Association of Colored Women* (Washington, D.C.: NACW, 1933); Charles Harris Wesley, *The History of the National Association of Colored Women's Clubs: A Legacy of Service* (Washington, D.C.: NACW, 1984); Dorothy Salem, *To Better Our World: Black Women in Organized Reform* (New York: Carlson, 1990); Rosalyn Terborg-Penn, *African American Women in the Struggle for the Vote, 1850–1920* (Bloomington: Indiana University Press, 1998); and Guy-Sheffield, *Daughters of Sorrow.*

7. *Women's Era* 2 (August 1895): 10.

8. For a discussion of African American political ideologies at the turn of the century, see August Meier, *Negro Thought in America, 1880–1915* (Ann Arbor: University of Michigan Press, 1963). Though Meier's study remains the standard for examining the period, his work does give only short shrift to women. For a discussion of black women during the period, see White, *Too Heavy a Load*. For a more recent discussion of the ideology of racial uplift practiced by African Americans during the period, see Kevin K. Gaines, *Uplifting the Race: Black Leadership, Politics, and Culture in the Twentieth Century* (Chapel Hill: University of North Carolina Press, 1996).

9. For the most detailed study of Booker T. Washington, see Louis R. Harlan, *Booker T. Washington: The Making of a Black Leader, 1856–1901* (New York: Oxford University Press, 1972); and *Booker T. Washington: The Wizard of Tuskegee, 1901–1915* (New York: Oxford University Press, 1983). See also Meier, *Negro Thought in America.*

10. Booker T. Washington, *Up From Slavery: An Autobiography* (New York: Doubleday, 1901), 156.

11. Dorothy Drinkard Hawkshawe, "David Augustus Straker, Black Lawyer and Reconstruction Politician, 1842–1908." (PhD diss., Catholic University of America, 1974).

12. D. Augustus Straker, "The Organization Object and the Aim of the National Federation of Colored Men," *AMECR* 11 (December 1895): 499–511.

13. *CG*, February 29, 1896.

14. *CG*, March 21, 1896.

15. *VM*, August 1896.

16. See Desmond King and Stephen Tuck, "De-Centering the South: America's Nationwide White Supremacist Order After Reconstruction," *Past and Present* 194 (2007): 214–53; and Davison M. Douglas, *Jim Crow Moves North: The Battle over Northern School Desegregation, 1865–1954* (New York: Cambridge University Press, 2005).

17. Plessy v. Ferguson, 163 U.S. 537 (1896). For a full discussion of the decision, see Brook Thomas, ed., *Plessy v. Ferguson: A Brief History with Documents* (Boston: Bedford Books, 1997).

18. Plessy v. Ferguson, 163 U.S. 537 (1896). For the ruling on Dred Scott, see Scott v. Sandford, 60 U.S. 393 (1856). See also Paul Finkelman, ed., *Dred Scott v. Sanford: A Brief History with Documents* (Boston: Bedford Books, 1997).

19. *VM*, July and August 1896.

20. *VM*, August 1896.

21. D. Augustus Straker, "How the Anti-Lynching Plank Was Put into the Republican Platform," *AMECR* 13 (October 1896): 209–10.

22. Ibid., 208.

23. Ibid., 207–8; see also Hawkshawe, "David Augustus Straker," 141.

24. Straker. "How the Anti-Lynching Plank," 201–2. See also Hawkshawe, "David Augustus Straker," 139–54.

25. Rayford Whittingham Logan, *The Betrayal of the Negro: From Rutherford B. Hayes to Woodrow Wilson* (1965; rpr. New York: Da Capo 1997), 95–96, 100. George White introduced the first anti-lynching bill to Congress in January 1900. See Benjamin R. Justesen, *George Henry White: An Even Chance in the Race of Life* (Baton Rouge: Louisiana State University, 2001). See also Chapter 6.

26. *WB*, August 1 and October 10, 1896.

27. *WB*, October 10, 17, and 31, 1896. Chase's call for the revitalization of the League is of course curious since he once refused to join because of its nonpartisan position.

28. *WB*, November 14, 1896.

29. Ibid.

30. Ibid.

31. *WB*, November 28, 1896.

32. T. Thomas Fortune, "Are We Brave Men or Cowards?" *Monthly Review* 1, no. 6 (August 1894): 181.

33. Ibid.

34. *WB*, December 5, 12, and 19, 1896 and January 16, 1897.

35. *WB*, December 12, 1896.

36. *WB*, December 19, 1896.

37. Emma Thornbrough cites health and financial problems as the reason for Fortune's failure to call the Leagues to convention. However, this is an insufficient explanation, especially because Fortune continues to be hesitant to call the League into convention without the support of the masses. See Emma Thornbrough, *T. Thomas Fortune*, 178–79; and *NYS*, May 17, 1897.

38. *NYS*, May 17, 1897.

39. Fisher, "Political and Social Development of the Black Community," 165–66; and [AU: to be complete, the citation needs CAL. STAT. 1897, c. 108, 139. See also *Journal of the Assembly* (Sacramento, Calif.: Benjamin P. Avery, 1897), 455; *Journal of the Senate During the Thirty Second Session of the Legislature of the State of California 1897* (A. J. Johnston, Superintendent of State Printing, 1897), 713–14; and *LAT*, February 9, 24, and 26, 1897.

40. *NYS*, May 17, 1897; *WB*, April 17 and 24, and May 8, 22, and 29, 1897.

41. *CA*, May 14, 1898; and John F. Marszalek, *A Black Congressman in the Age of Jim Crow* (Gainsville: University Press of Florida, 2006), 114–15.

42. In the first half of 1898, the deaths of Frazier B. Baker, postmaster of Lake City, South Carolina, and Isaiah H. Loftin, postmaster of Hogansville, Georgia, had stunned the African American community. Both postmasters received intense opposition to their appointments by the white consistency of their communities, who alleged that neither could properly perform their duties. On February 22, 1898, a white mob set Baker's home on fire and shot at members of the family as they exited. The mob killed Baker and his infant son. Details of Loftin's death are not as readily available, though it is probable that he lost his life at the hands of a vigilante mob in late 1897 or early 1898. See Willard B. Gatewood, Jr., *Black Americans and the White Man's Burden, 1898–1903* (Urbana: University of Illinois Press, 1975), 31–33; Herbert Shapiro, *White Violence and Black Response: From Reconstruction to Montgomery* (Amherst: University of Massachusetts Press, 1988), 89–90; and George B. Tindall, *South Carolina Negroes, 1877–1900* (Baton Rouge: Louisiana State University Press, 1952), 255–56.

43. Walters, *My Life and Work*, 98; see also George Mason Miller, "'A This Worldly Mission': The Life and Career of Alexander Walters (1858–1917)" (PhD diss., State University of New York at Stony Brook, 1984), 165–66.

44. Walters, *My Life and Work*, 98.

45. Ibid., 102.

46. *CA*, April 1, 1898. See also *CG*, April 16, 1898.

47. *IR*, April 30, 1898.

48. *CA*, May 21 and 28 and June 18, 1898. For information on the Spanish-American War, see Gatewood, *Black Americans and the White Man's Burden*; Graham A. Cosmas, *An Army for Empire: The United States Army in the Spanish-American War* (Columbia: University of Missouri Press, 1971); Kristin L. Hoganson, *Fighting for American Manhood: How Gender Politics Provoked the Spanish-American and Philippine-American Wars* (New Haven: Yale University Press, 1998); and Louis A. Pérez, Jr., *The War of 1898: The United States and Cuba in History and Historiography* (Chapel Hill: University of North Carolina Press, 1998).

49. *CA*, June 18, 1898.

50. *Appeal*, June 18, 1898. It is not certain that the creation of the group is directly connected to Walters's call for the revival of the League, but the naming of the organization and the fact that the group folds into the Afro-American Council once it is formed suggests such a case. For information on previous activity by the Minnesota Afro-American League and Minnesota Equal Rights Association, see Chapters 1 and 2.

51. *Appeal*, June 18 and July 2, 9, and 23, 1898.

52. *CA*, July 2, 1895; and *IR*, August 20, 1898.

53. *IF*, July 30, 1898.

54. *IR*, April 30, May 7, and July 2, 1898. See also Sundiata Keita Cha-Jua, "'A Warlike Demonstration': Legalism, Armed Resistance, and Black Political Mobilization in Decatur, Illinois, 1894–1898," *Journal of Negro History* 83 (Winter 1998): 52–72, 61, 70. A number of chapters of the Afro-American League in Illinois continued their activities, including affiliates in Alton, Bloomington, Brooklyn, Cairo, Danville, Decatur, Jacksonville, Peoria, Rock Island, and Chicago.

55. Walters, *My Life and Work*, 98–102.

56. Ibid., 103. See also *WB*, August 27, 1898; *IF*, August 27, 1898; and *CA*, August 27, 1898.

57. Walters, *My Life and Work*, 103; and John W. Thompson, *An Authentic History of the Douglass Monument: Biographical Facts and Incidents in the Life of Frederick Douglass* (1903; rpr. Freeport, N.Y.: Books for Libraries Press, 1971), 196.

58. *CA*, August 27, 1898.

59. Ibid.

60. Thompson, *An Authentic History of the Douglass Monument*, 81–112. The monument was not unveiled at the ceremonies because it was not completed. It was unveiled on June 9, 1899, after some struggle; the statue had been in Rochester since October 4, 1898.

61. Walters, *My Life and Work*, 104–05; Thornbrough, *T. Thomas Fortune*, 179; Miller, "'A This Worldly Mission,'" 167; and Thompson, *An Authentic History of the Douglass Monument*, 199. Among those present were T. Thomas Fortune; Bishop Alexander Walters; Emily Howard; Sarah E. Blackall; Ida B. Wells-Barnett; W. Calvin Chase; John W. Thompson, Rochester businessman and organizer of the Douglass Monument project; John H. Smythe, president of the Negro Reformatory Association and ex-minister to Liberia; John C. Dancy, collector of customs at Wilmington, North Carolina; Reverend W. B. Bowens of Troy, New York; Chris Perry, editor of the *Philadelphia Tribune*; Bishop B. W. Arnett; Rochester Mayor George E. Warner; Susan B. Anthony; and Helen Douglass, the widow of Frederick Douglass. According to Emma Thornbrough, those who signed the call but were not able to attend included Booker T. Washington, ex-governor Pinckney Benton Stewart Pinchback, Judson Lyons, George White, and Archibald and Francis Grimké. Of those individuals, only Lyons can be found on the list published by Walters. See Walters, *My Life and Work*, 98–102; and Thornbrough, *T. Thomas Fortune*, 179. Washington, Pinchback, and the Grimkés are among a long list of individuals whom the *Indianapolis Freeman* encouraged to participate in the Council. See *IF*, October 1, 1898.

62. Thompson, *An Authentic History of the Douglass Monument*, 201.

63. For a discussion of the growth of Social Darwinism, see George M. Fredrickson, *The Black Image in the White Mind: The Debate on Afro-American Character and Destiny, 1817–1914* (Middletown, Conn.: Wesleyan University Press, 1987); and John S. Haller, Jr., *Outcasts from Evolution; Scientific Attitudes of Racial Inferiority, 1859–1900* (1971; rpr. Carbondale: Southern Illinois University Press, 1995).

64. Thompson, *An Authentic History of the Douglass Monument*, 202. See also Miller, " 'A This Worldly Mission,' " 167–68; and Thornbrough, *T. Thomas Fortune*, 180.

65. Thompson, *An Authentic History of the Douglass Monument*, 202–3.

66. Ibid., 203.

67. Ibid., 203–4.

68. Ibid. The Executive Committee consisted of Dancy, Wells-Barnett, Benjamin W. Arnett, J. W. Parker, Christopher J. Perry, H. T. Keating, and Walters.

69. Thompson, *An Authentic History of the Douglass Monument*, 203–4.

70. *IF*, October 1, 1898; *Colored American*, September 24 and October 1, 1898; *Appeal*, September 24, 1898; and *RP*, September 24, 1898.

71. *IF*, October 1, 1898.

72. *CA*, October 1, 1898.

73. *RP*, 8 October 1898; and *IW*, October 8, 1898.

74. *IW*, October 8, 1898.

75. Ibid.

76. *CA*, October 8 and 15, 1898; and *RP*, October 15, 1898.

77. *IW*, October 8, 1898.

78. *CA*, October 15, 1898.

79. *RP*, October 15, 1898.

80. *CA*, October 15, 1898.

81. Ibid. For another response, see also *WP*, October 17, 1898.

82. See T. Thomas Fortune, "The Latest Color Line," *Liberia Bulletin* 11 (November 1897): 60–65; and T. Thomas Fortune, "Race Absorption," *AMECR* 18, no. 1 (July 1901): 54–66. For more information on Fortune's position, see Shawn Leigh Alexander, ed., *T. Thomas Fortune the Afro-American Agitator: A Collection of Writings, 1880–1928* (Gainesville: University Press of Florida, 2008).

83. *CA*, October 15, 1898.

84. *IW*, October 8, 1898.

85. *CA*, October 29, 1898.

86. *CA*, November 19, 1898.

87. *CA*, October 2 and November 5, 1898.

88. *CA*, November 12 and 19, 1898; and *IF*, November 12, 1898.

89. Glenda E. Gilmore, "Murder, Memory, and the Flight of the Incubus," in *Democracy Betrayed: The Wilmington Race Riot of 1898 and Its Legacy*, eds. David S. Cecelski and Timothy B. Tyson (Chapel Hill: University of North Carolina Press, 1998), 76.

90. Ibid., 77–78.

91. Ibid., 79–80. For a romanticized, but widely popular version of a similar position, see Thomas Dixon's novel *The Clansman*. In this book, one of the African American males lusting after white women was the African American (mulatto) politician. See Thomas Dixon, *The Clansman: An Historical Romance of the Ku Klux Klan* (New York: Doubleday, 1905). It is also important to note that John C. Dancy is one of the individuals who disagreed with the position of the Council. See John C. Dancy to John Edward Bruce, 30 January 1899, *John Edward Bruce Papers*.

92. Quoted in Gilmore, "Murder, Memory, and the Flight of the Incubus," 84.

93. Ibid., 84–85.

94. See Glenda Elizabeth Gilmore, *Gender and Jim Crow: Women and the Politics of White Supremacy in North Carolina, 1896–1920* (Chapel Hill: University of North Carolina Press, 1996), 105–17; Robert Howard Wooley, "Race and Politics: The Evolution of the White Supremacy Campaign of 1898 in North Carolina." (PhD diss., University of North Carolina, 1977); and David S. Cecelski and Timothy B. Tyson, eds, *Democracy Betrayed: The Wilmington Race Riot of 1898 and Its Legacy* (Chapel Hill: University of North Carolina Press, 1998).

95. Gilmore, "Murder, Memory, and the Flight of the Incubus," 86–88.

96. Williams v. State of Mississippi, 170 U.S. 213 (1898). This Supreme Court decision and the McKinley Administration's refusal to step in are significant because the ruling basically seals the disfranchisement or virtually leaves no barriers to its expansion throughout the South. See Logan, *The Betrayal of the Negro*, 97–116. McKinley's silence on such issues led historian Rayford Logan to call the period during his administration the "nadir" in African American history. See Logan, *The Betrayal of the Negro*, 79–96.

97. T. Thomas Fortune to Booker T. Washington, 17 December 1898, *BTWPH* 4, 535–36; emphasis in original. See also Thornbrough, *T. Thomas Fortune*, 181.

98. *Washington Evening Star*, December 20, 1898.

99. Ibid. According to the *Star* article, a number of audience members exclaimed, "Stab him." See also *Washington Times*, December 20, 1898. It is important to note that some scholars have claimed that Fortune's speech and harsh rhetoric were due to his being under the influence of alcohol. However, there is no evidence of such; while Fortune's use of alcohol is well documented, it did not become a severe problem until after he contracted malaria during his trip to the Philippines, Hawaii, and Japan as a representative of the Roosevelt Administration. It does, however, seem that Fortune was expressing true frustration with the McKinley Administration no matter what he wrote to Booker T. Washington before the meeting. See Giddings, *Ida*, 402–3.

100. *Washington Times*, December 20, 1898. See also *TP*, January 6, 1899; and Thornbrough, *T. Thomas Fortune*, 181–84.

101. *Washington Evening Star*, December 20, 1898. Historian David W. Blight among others has claimed that no other president did as much as McKinley to reconcile the conflict in the post-bellum period. See David William Blight, *Race and Reunion: The Civil War in American Memory* (Cambridge: Harvard University Press, 2001).

102. *Washington Evening Star*, December 20, 1898.

103. Ibid. In the aftermath, Fortune claimed that the press had taken some of his comments out of context. W. Calvin Chase agreed with this statement and asserted that in his reference to stabbing McKinley, the *Age* editor by no means was proposing to assassinate the president, but was only speaking of "stabbing" the president at the ballot box. See *Washington Evening Star*, December 21, 1898.

104. T. Thomas Fortune to Booker T. Washington, 18 December 1898, *BTWPH* 4, 535–36; emphasis in original.

105. *CG*, December 24, 1898; *WB*, December 24, 1898; and *Washington Evening Star*, December 24, 1898.

106. *CG*, December 24, 1898.

107. Ibid.

108. *CA*, December 17 and 24, 1898 and January 7, 1899; *ISB*, December 30, 1898; and Walters, *My Life and Work*, 112.

109. Walters, *My Life and Work*, 113–14; *CA*, January 7, 1899.

110. Walters, *My Life and Work*, 125–26.

111. Ibid., 126.

112. Ibid., 126–27.

113. Ibid., 127.

114. Ibid., 127–28.

115. Ibid., 127.

116. Ibid., 129.

117. Ibid., 130.

118. Ibid., 124–25.

119. Ibid.

120. Ibid.

121. Ibid.

122. *CA*, January 14, 1899.

123. Cyrus Field Adams, *National Afro-American Council: A History of the Organization, Its Objects, Synopses of Proceedings, Constitution and By-Laws, Plan of Organization, Annual Topics, Etc.* (Washington D.C.: Cyrus Field Adams, 1902), 6; *Colored American*, January 14, 1899; *Afro-American Sentinel*, January 28, 1899; and John P. Green, *Fact Stranger Than Fiction: Seventy-Five Years of a Busy Life with Reminiscences of Many Great and Good Men and Women* (Cleveland: Rival, 1920), 267–68.

124. *CA*, January 14, 1899.

125. Adams, *National Afro-American Council*, 6. Among others, speeches were given by H. C. C. Astwood of New York, John Frank Blagburn of Iowa, Robert Pelham of Michigan, Mrs. Frederick Douglass of New York, Mary Church Terrell of Washington D.C., and William A. Pledger of Georgia. Pledger, for example, called for the creation of a daily newspaper that could serve as an organ of the Council as well as the daily voice of the race. See *CA*, January 14, 1899.

126. *CA*, January 14, 1899.

127. Adams, *National Afro-American Council*, 22. See also Walters, *My Life and Work*.

128. Adams, *National Afro-American Council*, 22.

129. Ibid., 24.

130. Ibid., 25.

131. Ibid., 15–21; Walters, *My Life and Work*, 104–9; and Factor, *The Black Response to America*, 129.

132. Adams, *National Afro-American Council*, 16–17.

133. Ibid., 17–18.

134. *CA*, January 7, 1898.

CHAPTER 4. NOT JUST "A BUBBLE IN SOAP WATER"

Epigraph. John Edward Bruce, *CA*, June 17, 1899. Representative George H. White, *CA*, May 13, 1899.

1. *RP*, January 7, 1899.

2. Ibid.; *CA*, January 7, 1899; *Star of Zion*, January 12, 1899; and *Afro-American Sentinel*, January 28, 1899. The delegation included, among others, Alexander Walters, John Mitchell, Jr., Daniel Murray, P. B. S. Pinchback, William Pledger, Edward E. Cooper, Jesse Lawson, and George H. White.

3. *RP*, January 7, 1899; *TP*, January 13, 1899; and *Star of Zion*, January 12, 1899.

4. *CA*, January 7, 1899.

5. Ibid.

6. *IW*, January 14, 1899.

7. *ISB*, January 13, 1899.

8. *IF*, January 28, 1899.

9. *CA*, January 14, 1899. See also Linda O. McMurry, *To Keep the Waters Troubled: The Life of Ida B. Wells* (New York: Oxford University Press, 1998), 254–55; and Patricia A. Schechter, *Ida B. Wells-Barnett & American Reform, 1880–1930* (Chapel Hill: University of North Carolina Press, 2001), 116. The *Colored American* editor's position was disingenuous since the organization did not have a separate national women's auxiliary—the group did have some local auxiliaries, but nothing on the national level—and as T. Thomas Fortune requested at the Rochester conference, the organization tried to integrate women into positions of power.

10. *IF*, March 4, 1899.

11. *RP*, January 14, 1899.

12. *Washington Evening Star*, January 15, 1899; and *Star of Zion*, February 16, 1899.

13. *Washington Evening Star*, January 25, 1899.

14. Ibid.

15. *CA*, February 25, 1899.

16. For more on Jesse Lawson, see Michael R. Hall, "Jesse Lawson and the National Sociological Society of 1903," in *Diverse Histories of American Sociology*, ed. Anthony J. Blasi (Boston: Brill, 2005), 127–40.

17. *CA*, February 4, 1899.

18. *CA*, February 11, 1899.

19. *Richmond Times*, January 31, 1899. Here the editors use the word "nationalist" in a location where the term "federalist" may have made more sense. The editors are implying that African Americans put too much weight on the federal government, not that they are nationalistic in the sense of the term as we understand it today.

20. *Richmond Times*, January 31, 1899.

21. *RP*, February 4, 1899.

22. Ibid.

23. Ibid.; *Richmond Times*, January 31, 1899.

24. *RP*, February 4, 1899.

25. Ibid.

26. Daniel Murray to Bishop Alexander Walters, 26 January 1899, *Daniel Murray Papers*. See also *CA*, March 25, 1899. These assistant counselors included, among others, advocates such as former Louisiana governor Pinckney B. S. Pinchback; E. M. Hewlett; Reuben S. Smith; St. Paul, Minnesota attorney Frederick McGhee, U.S. postage stamp agent and former Ohio state representative John P. Green; Detroit, Michigan attorney D. Augustus Straker; and U.S. Treasury register Judson W. Lyons.

27. Daniel Murray to Bishop Alexander Walters, 26 January 1899, *Daniel Murray Papers*.

28. Ibid.

29. Ibid.

30. Ibid. Participants at this meeting included Bishop Arnett, P. B. S. Pinchback, Henry P. Cheatham, John P. Green, George White, and Reuben S. Smith.

31. Ibid. For information on the Crumpacker Bill, which lingered in Congress for a number of years, see Michael Perman, *Struggle for Mastery: Disfranchisement in the South, 1888–1908* (Chapel Hill: University of North Carolina Press, 2001).

32. Daniel Murray et al., to Postmaster General, n.d., *Daniel Murray Papers*.

33. Ibid.

34. *CA*, March 8, 1899. See also Shawn Leigh Alexander, "The Afro-American Council and Its Challenge of Louisiana's Grandfather Clause," in *Racialism in the South Since Reconstruction*, eds. Chris Green, Rachel Rubin, and James Smethurst (New York: Palgrave, 2006), 13–36.

35. Perman, *Struggle for Mastery*, 124–72.

36. *CA*, March 4, 1899.

37. *WB*, April 15, 1899.

38. Hal Scripps Chase, "'Honey for Friends, Stings for Enemies': William Calvin Chase and the *Washington Bee*, 1882–1921," (PhD diss., University of Pennsylvania, 1973), 247.

39. *CA*, April 22, 1899. The *National Baptist Magazine* actually endorsed the League idea when Fortune called for the meeting in Rochester. The magazine's editor described the idea as grand and called on "every state, city and village, every church organization and

benevolent society" to send delegates and "a money contribution in order to make a strong National organization." See *National Baptist Magazine* 6, no. 2 (June 1898): 100.

40. *CA*, April 22, 1899.

41. See W. Fitzhugh Brundage, *Lynching in the New South: Georgia and Virginia, 1880–1930* (Urbana: University of Illinois Press, 1993); and Philip Dray, *At the Hands of Persons Unknown: The Lynching of Black America* (New York: Random House, 2002).

42. Brundage, *Lynching in the New South*, 82–83.

43. Dray, *At the Hands of Persons Unknown*, 5; and Brundage, *Lynching in the New South*, 83–84.

44. Brundage, *Lynching in the New South*, 83.

45. Dray, *At the Hands of Persons Unknown*, 9–14.

46. Ibid., 14. See also *Indianapolis Freeman*, April 29, 1899; *Baltimore Ledger*, April 29, 1899; *AC*, April 28, 1899; and *TP*, April 28 and May 5, 1899.

47. *AC*, April 30, 1899.

48. *ISB*, April 30, 1899.

49. *SLBA*, May 9. 1899.

50. *CA*, May 20, 1899.

51. Ibid.

52. *SLBA*, May 9, 1899.

53. *CA*, May 13, 1899.

54. Ibid., May 6, 1899; *Star of Zion*, May 4, 1899; and *BG*, May 4, 1899.

55. *CA*, May 13, 1899. Gertrude Mossell published her writings under her married name, Mrs. N. F. Mossell.

56. Ibid.

57. Ibid.

58. Ibid.

59. Ibid.

60. Ibid.

61. *WB*, May 13, 1899.

62. *SLBA*, May 23, 1899.

63. *SLBA*, June 6, 1899.

64. Ibid.

65. *RP*, May 20, 1899.

66. Ibid.

67. *TP*, May 11, 1899; *AAC*, May 12, 1899; *CR*, May 11, 1899; and *CA*, May 20, 1899.

68. *CA*, June 3, 1899. See also *Star of Zion*, April 13, 1899.

69. *CA*, June 3, 1899; *IW*, June 17, 1899; and *WP*, June 11 and 24, 1899. See also *IF*, June 17, 1899. For the text of the letter, see *WP*, June 11, 1899.

70. *CA*, June 3, 1899. In his biography of John E. Bruce, William Seraile only mentions Bruce's poem as an example of Bruce's comfort in placing things in the hands of God and as a plea for the Republican Party to not abandon the black community. Seraile does not connect the poem to Bruce's support for the Council and its event during the

weekend the poem was published. See William Seraile, *Bruce Grit: The Black Nationalist Writings of John Edward Bruce* (Knoxville: University of Tennessee Press, 2003), 102–3.

71. *CR*, May 11 and June 8, 1899; *Star of Zion*, April 27, May 11, and June 1, 1899. For David A. Graham's address, see Philip S. Foner and Robert J. Branham, eds., *Lift Every Voice: African American Oratory, 1787–1900* (Tuscaloosa: University of Alabama Press, 1998), 882–85. For Grimké's homily, see Francis J. Grimké, *The Works of Francis J. Grimké*, ed. Carter G. Woodson (Washington, D.C.: Associated Publishers, 1942), 1:294–303.

72. David A. Graham, "Some Facts About Southern Lynchings," in *Lift Every Voice*, 882–85.

73. *CA*, June 17, 1899.

74. Ibid.; emphasis in original. See also August Meier, "The Emergence of Negro Nationalism" (master's thesis, Columbia University, 1949), 107; and Seraile, *Bruce Grit*, 102.

75. *CA*, June 17, 1899.

76. Ibid.

77. Ibid.

78. *CA*, July 8, 1899. See also Murray, *To Keep the Waters Troubled*, 256.

79. *CA*, July 15, 1899.

80. Ibid.

81. *CBA*, July 29, 1899; *ISB*, August 4, 1899; *IF*, July 29, 1899; *CA*, July 22, 1899; and *RP*, July 29, 1899.

1. *WB*, August 5, 1899.

82. *IF*, July 29, 1899; *CA*, July 22, 1899; and *RP*, July 29, 1899.

83. *WB*, August 5, 1899.

84. Ibid. Chase's criticism of the partisan nature of the Council does not make sense, since unlike the Afro-American League, a number of prominent Republican insiders, including John P. Green and George White, were active members of the organization.

85. See Chapter 3.

86. *CA*, August 5, 1899.

87. *WB*, August 12, 1899.

88. *CA*, August 12, 1899.

89. *Appeal*, August 19, 1899.

90. W. E. B. Du Bois, "Two Negro Conventions," *The Independent* 51 (September 7, 1899): 2426; *Appeal*, August 19, 1899; and *CBA*, August 26, 1899.

91. *CA*, August 26, 1899. See also Cyrus Field Adams, *The National Afro-American Council*, 6–8; and Thornbrough, *T. Thomas Fortune*, 191.

92. *CA*, August 26, 1899; *ISB*, August 4, 1899; and Adams, *The National Afro-American Council*, 6–7.

93. Adams, *The National Afro-American Council*, 6–7; *CA*, August 26, 1899.

94. *CT*, August 19, 1899; *The Public* (August 26, 1899): 4–8. On Henry McNeal Turner and his positions on black emigration, see Edwin S. Redkey, *Black Exodus: Black Nationalist and Back-to-Africa Movements, 1890–1910* (New Haven, Conn.: Yale

University Press, 1969); and Stephen Ward Angell, *Bishop Henry McNeal Turner and African-American Religion in the South* (Knoxville: University of Tennessee Press, 1992).

95. Adams, *The National Afro-American Council*, 8; and *Appeal*, August 26, 1899.

96. Adams, *The National Afro-American Council*, 8; *CT*, August 19, 1899; and *Appeal*, August 26, 1899.

97. *CT*, August 19, 1899; *Appeal*, August 26, 1899; and Audrey A. Walker, "An Experiment in Non-Partisanship by the Negro 1884–1903" (master's thesis, Howard University, 1958), 57.

98. *CT*, August 19, 1899; and Adams, *The National Afro-American Council*, 8. Mohoney also introduced another resolution on the issue of nonpartisanship, which was not adopted by the delegation. In response to the notion that the race should not convene because it would disturb the peace of the Republican Party, Mohoney asserted that the suggestion came "from cowardly lips, and that it misrepresented the character of that party. If the Republican party cannot stand a demand for justice and fair play it ought to go down. We were men before that party was born, and our manhood is more sacred than any party can be. Parties were made for men—not men for parties." See *CT*, August 19, 1899.

99. *CT*, August 19, 1899; and Adams, *The National Afro-American Council*, 8.

100. "The Afro-American Council," *AMECR* 16, no. 2 (October 1899): 272–73.

101. Ibid.; Adams, *The National Afro-American Council*, 8; *CT*, August 21, 1899; and *AC*, August 25, 1899.

102. *AC*, August 25, 1899.

103. "The Afro-American Council," *AMECR* 16, no. 2 (October 1899), 272–73; and *CT*, August 20, 1899. In his autobiography, Ransom asserted that he saw Washington meeting with Walters outside Ransom's house and believed that the Wizard persuaded the bishop to soften the rhetoric at the convention. See Reverdy C. Ransom, *The Pilgrimage of Harriet Ransom's Son* (Nashville: Sunday School Union, 1949), 85; and Annetta L. Gomez-Jefferson, *The Sage of Tawawa: Reverdy Cassius Ransom, 1861–1959* (Kent, OH: Kent State University Press, 2002), 61.

104. For a description of McKinley's record, see Logan, *The Betrayal of the Negro*, 79–96 and Willard B. Gatewood, Jr., *Black Americans and the White Man's Burden, 1898–1903* (Urbana: University of Illinois Press, 1975), .

105. Thornbrough, *T. Thomas Fortune*, 191. See also T. Thomas Fortune to Booker T. Washington, 10 August 1899, *BTWPLC*.

106. Quoted in Thornbrough, *T. Thomas Fortune*, 191. For a brief discussion of the events, see David Levering Lewis, *W. E. B. Du Bois: A Biography of a Race, 1868–1919* (New York: Holt, 1993), 230–32. Du Bois does not mention his affiliation with the Afro-American Council in his autobiographical writings nor does David Levering Lewis mention Du Bois's post in his biography. For a discussion of this period Du Bois's life, see W. E. B. Du Bois, *The Autobiography of W. E. B. Du Bois: A Soliloquy on Viewing My Life from the Last Decade of Its First Century* (New York: International Publishers, 1968),

205–34. For a different take on the events, see Wells, *Crusade for Justice*, 259–60. See also Louis R. Harlan et al., *BTWPH* 5, 176–77, 181, 182, and 183.

107. *CT*, August 20, 1899. See also "The Afro-American Council," *AMECR* 16, no. 2 (October 1899), 272–73.

108. *Appeal*, August 26, 1899. See also Louis F. Post, "The American Negro," *The Public* 2 (August 26, 1899): 4–8; and Louis F. Post, "The National Afro-American Council," *Howard's American Magazine* 4 (November 1899): 33–41.

109. *Appeal*, August 26, 1899.

110. *WB*, August 19, 1899.

111. *IW*, August 26, 1899.

112. Louis R. Harlan, *Booker T. Washington: The Making of a Black Leader, 1856–1901* (New York: Oxford University Press, 1972), 265–66. For a complete discussion of the Washington controversy, see ibid., 264–67 and Thornbrough, *T. Thomas Fortune*, 191–92.

113. *NYT*, August 21,1899; *CT*, August 21, 1899; *Baltimore Ledger*, September 2, 1899; and *Indianapolis World*, September 2, 1899. See also Harlan, *Booker T. Washington*, 265.

114. *Appeal*, September 2, 1899. See also Reverdy C. Ransom, *The Pilgrimage of Harriet Ransom's Son*, 85 and Harlan, *Booker T. Washington*, 264–65.

115. Reverdy Ransom did write to Booker T. Washington after the Council convention to apologize for any inconvenience his actions may have caused the Tuskegee principal. See Reverdy Ransom to Booker T. Washington, 31 August 1899, *BTWPLC*.

116. *CA*, September 2, 1899.

117. *CG*, September 16, 1899.

118. *CA*, September 9, 1899.

119. *CA*, September 16, 1899. At the Chicago convention, Ida B. Wells-Barnett had stepped down from the position of secretary to become the director of the organization's Anti-Lynching Bureau. There was no controversy over Carter, a female, replacing Wells-Barnett as secretary. Carter resigned from her position for unspecified personal reasons.

120. *CA*, September 16, 1899.

121. *AC*, August 25, 1899; and Benjamin R. Justesen, *George Henry White: An Even Chance in the Race of Life* (Baton Rouge: Louisiana State University, 2001), 279.

122. *Appeal*, October 7 and 28, 1899; and *IF*, October 28, 1899. Ida B. Wells-Barnett willingly stepped down from her position as secretary of the Council to take the position of director of the director of the group's anti-lynching bureau.

123. *Appeal*, October 7, 1899. See also Schechter, *Ida B. Wells-Barnett & American Reform*, 116–17.

124. Wells-Barnett, *Lynch Law in Georgia* (Chicago: Ida B. Wells-Barnett, 1899), Preface. See also Schechter, *Ida B. Wells-Barnett & American Reform*, 116–17. For coverage of Wells-Barnett's findings in the Sam Hose case, see *RP*, October 14, 1899.

125. *Appeal*, October 7, 1899.

126. *CA*, January 6, 1900. On the Minnesota branch of the Afro-American Council, see Paul D. Nelson, *Frederick L. McGhee: A Life on the Color Line, 1861–1912* (Minneapolis: Minnesota Historical Society Press, 2002), 72–79. Nelson does not, however, discuss

this petition drive by McGhee and his colleagues of the Law Enforcement League—St. Paul's affiliate of the Afro-American Council in 1899.

127. *CA*, October 7, 1899.

128. *BG*, October 11, 1899; *LAT*, October 11, 1899; and *AC*, October 20, 1899.

129. *American Negro Academy Occasional Papers 1–22* (New York: Arno Press, 1969). On the Academy, see Alfred Moss, *The American Negro Academy: The Voice of the Talented Tenth* (Baton Rouge: Louisiana State University, 1981); Robert L. Factor, *The Black Response to America: Men, Ideals, and Organization, from Frederick Douglass to the NAACP* (Reading, Mass.: Addison-Wesley, 1970), 255; and August Meier, *Negro Thought in America, 1880–1915: Racial Ideologies in the Age of Booker T. Washington* (Ann Arbor: University of Michigan Press, 1963), 266–67. A number of individuals, including Walters, W. E. B. Du Bois, Kelly Miller, John Cromwell, Albert P. Miller, and John E. Bruce were members of both the American Negro Academy and the Afro-American Council. See Moss, *The American Negro Academy*, 92.

130. *American Negro Academy Occasional Papers 1–22*. See also Moss, *The American Negro Academy*, 99–100.

131. Alexander Walters to John W. Cromwell, 4 October 1899, *John Wesley Cromwell Papers*, cited in Moss, *The American Negro Academy*, 100. The American Negro Academy was selling Love's essay for 15 cents a piece. See *RP*, September 23, 1899.

132. *WP*, October 18, 1899. See also *WB*, October 21, 1899; and *Star of Zion*, November 9, 1899.

133. *WP*, October 18, 1899. See also George Mason Miller, "'A This Worldly Mission': The Life and Career of Alexander Walters (1858–1917)" (PhD diss., State University of New York at Stony Brook, 1984), 180–82. Bishop Walters's political strategy was not alien to the African American community as it was reflective of views held by many blacks since the Louisville Conference in 1883. See Chapters 1 and 2. See also Rayford Whittingham Logan, *The Betrayal of the Negro: From Rutherford B. Hayes to Woodrow Wilson* (1965 rpr., New York: Da Capo Press, 1997), 104; August Meier, "The Negro and the Democratic Party, 1875–1915," *Phylon* 17 (Summer, 1956): 173–91; and August Meier, *Negro Thought in America*.

134. *WB*, November 4, 1899.

135. *WB*, October 21 and 28 and November 4 and 11, 1899. Chief among the officeholders or strong Republican insiders were William Pledger, Judson W. Lyons, P. B. S. Pinchback, H. P. Cheatham, John P. Green, and George H. White.

136. *WB*, November 4, 1899; *IF*, November 18, 1899; and *Star of Zion*, November 9, 1899. See also *RP*, November 4, 1899.

137. *CA*, November 4, 1899.

138. Ibid. See also *Star of Zion*, November 9, 1899.

139. *CA*, November 11, 1899. See also *Star of Zion*, November 16, 1899.

140. *CA*, November 11, 1899.

141. For a discussion of the Afro-American League's struggles regarding the issue of the nonpartisan nature of the organization, see Chapter 2.

142. *CA*, November 11, 1899; and *Star of Zion*, November 16, 1899.

143. *CA*, November 11, 1899.

144. Ibid.

145. Ibid. Walters stressed clauses 2, 3, and 10 of the Council's constitution that called for the organization to test the constitutionality of laws that discriminate against blacks, promote work for securing legislation for the protection of the Reconstruction Amendments, and urge the appropriation for funds to black schools in areas where education is denied by discriminating laws.

146. *CA*, November 11, 1899. In his discussion, Walters takes special exception to Washington's argument in his then-recent *Atlantic Monthly* article. See Booker T. Washington, "The Case of the Negro," *Atlantic Monthly* 84 (November 1899): 577–87.

147. *CA*, November 11, 1899.

148. *CA*, November 18, 1899. See also *RP*, November 18, 1899.

149. *CA*, November 18, 1899.

150. Ibid.

151. *CA*, December 2, 1899.

152. Ibid.; and *RP*, December 2, 1899.

153. *CA*, December 2, 1899. The curious twist of the case is that W. Calvin Chase, who was a lawyer in addition to his job as editor of the *Bee*, was the attorney in the civil suit. As the *Colored American* stated, "the race for once is united and seems to be deadly in earnest in their prosecution" of this case. Editor Chase said nothing of the "Methodist Democratic Organization" aiding him and his client in the case; he simply quietly pressed forward with the Council's assistance.

154. Esther Hall Mumford, *Seattle's Black Victorians, 1852–1901* (Seattle: Ananse Press, 1980), 174–75; and Quintard Taylor, *The Forging of a Black Community: Seattle's Central District from 1870 Through the Civil Rights Era* (Seattle: University of Washington Press, 1994), 41–42.

155. *CA*, December 16, 1899; *Appeal*, December 23, 1899; and *WP*, December 29 and 30, 1899.

156. *CA*, December 16, 1899.

157. *CA*, January 6, 1900. See also Nelson, *Frederick L. McGhee*, 74. Nelson does mention McGhee's traveling to Washington, but he does not discuss any of McGhee's activity at the executive committee meeting.

158. *CA*, January 6, 1900.

159. For information about R. L. Smith, see Meier, *Negro Thought in America*, 123–24, 253.

160. *CA*, January 6, 1900.

161. Ibid. See also Moss, *The American Negro Academy*, 92. It is important to note that T. Thomas Fortune wrote to Booker T. Washington after the Executive Committee meeting and told him that he had done what he could to keep the group "in the middle of the road" and was successful. It is curious, however, what issues Fortune and Washington believed they were coming to control as the outline presented by the *Colored American*

before the meeting was basically the resolutions endorsed by the group. The only issue that may have concerned the two was for the Council to endorse the Democratic Party, but that was never the objective of Walters. Moreover, Fortune had certainly done his share of arraigning the president and the Republican Party over the past year. Another issue that Fortune disagreed with was the support of the Crumpacker Bill, but the Committee endorsed the proposed legislation. See T. Thomas Fortune to Booker T. Washington, 30 December 1899, *BTWPLC*; and Thornbrough, *T. Thomas Fortune*, 192. For Fortune's most recent attack on President McKinley at the time, see *Indianapolis World*, July 29, 1899; and Thornbrough, *T. Thomas Fortune*, 188–90.

CHAPTER 5. TO AWAKEN THE CONSCIENCE OF AMERICA

Epigraph. J. Francis Lee, "The Trojan," *CA* September 15, 1900. Alexander Walters, *Star of Zion*, August 30, 1900.

1. See Leon F. Litwack, *Trouble in Mind: Black Southerners in the Age of Jim Crow* (New York: Knopf, 1998); August Meier, *Negro Thought in America, 1880–1915: Racial Ideologies in the Age of Booker T. Washington* (Ann Arbor: University of Michigan Press, 1963); Rayford Whittingham Logan, *The Betrayal of the Negro: From Rutherford B. Hayes to Woodrow Wilson* (1965; rpr., New York: Da Capo Press, 1997); Edward L. Ayers, *Vengeance and Justice: Crime and Punishment in the 19th-Century American South* (New York: Oxford University Press, 1984); *Edward L. Ayers, The Promise of the New South: Life After Reconstruction* (New York: Oxford University Press, 1992); Herbert Shapiro, *White Violence and Black Response: From Reconstruction to Montgomery* (Amherst: University of Massachusetts Press, 1988); Leslie H. Fishel, Jr., "The North and the Negro, 1865–1900" (PhD diss., Harvard University, 1953); and Michael Perman, *Struggle for Mastery: Disfranchisement in the South, 1888–1908* (Chapel Hill: University of North Carolina Press, 2001).

2. *CA*, January 20, 1900.

3. Ibid., January 27, 1900.

4. Afro-American Council Circular Letter, 30 January 1900, *BTWPLC.*

5. Jesse Lawson to Booker T. Washington, 9 February 1900, *BTWPH* 5, 436–37. See also Louis R. Harlan, *Booker T. Washington: The Making of a Black Leader, 1856–1901* (New York: Oxford University Press, 1972), 296–98; Louis R. Harlan, "The Secret Life of Booker T. Washington," *Journal of Southern History* 37 (August 1971): 393–416; and August Meier, *Negro Thought in America*, 110–14.

6. For example, see Albert E. Pillsbury to Booker T. Washington, 25 February 1900 and Booker T. Washington to Francis J. Garrison, 27 February 1900, *BTWPH*, 5: 450–51.

7. *CA*, January 27, 1900.

8. Ibid. In his article, John E. Bruce published an actual petition that he asked the people to recreate and send to their congressional representatives.

9. *CA*, January 27, 1900.

10. *National Association Notes*, April 1900. See also Elizabeth McHenry. *Forgotten Readers: Recovering the Lost History of African-American Literary Societies* (Durham, N.C.: Duke University Press, 2002), 215.

11. *Appeal*, January 13 and 20 and February 3, 1900. See also Paul D. Nelson, *Frederick L. McGhee: A Life on the Color Line, 1861–1912* (St. Paul: Minnesota Historical Society Press, 2002), 74–75. As Nelson explains, it is doubtful that the group raised a tremendous amount for the Council, but it does demonstrate a unique means of collecting money for the struggle. In addition to this fund-raising activity, the local affiliate also hosted a luncheon for Booker T. Washington during his brief visit to St. Paul. *Appeal*, January 20, 1900. See also Nelson, *Frederick L. McGhee*, 75–76. Washington was in the region to give an address at Carlton College in Northfield, Minnesota.

12. *CA*, January 27, 1900. Other members of the committee included Daniel Murray, Alex L. Manly, T. C. Newsome, and H. P. Slaughter.

13. *CA*, January 27, 1900.

14. Benjamin R. Justesen, *George Henry White*: *An Even Chance in the Race of Life* (Baton Rouge: Louisiana State University, 2001), 278–79.

15. *Star of Zion*, February 1, 1900; *CA*, March 2, 1900.

16. Cong. Rec., 56th Cong., 1st Sess. 33 (1900) 1017, 1022.

17. *CA,* February 10 and 24, 1900.

18. Ida B. Wells-Barnett, "Lynch Law in America," *Arena* 23, no. 1 (January 1900): 15–24, 15, and 21; emphasis in original. See also Patricia A. Schechter, *Ida B. Wells-Barnett & American Reform, 1880–1930* (Chapel Hill: University of North Carolina Press, 2001), 117.

19. Wells-Barnett, "Lynch Law in America," 15.

20. Ibid., 21; emphasis in original.

21. Ibid., 22.

22. *CA*, February 10, 1900.

23. *IF*, February 24, 1900; and *Appeal*, February 24, 1900.

24. *CA*, March 10, 1900; *LAT,* March 5, 1900; and *WP*, March 5, 1900. The press coverage of the event did not mention Booker T. Washington's presence, but he told his secretary Emmett Scott that he attended the conference. Booker T. Washington to Emmett Scott, 11 March 1900, *BTWPH* 5, 457–58. In his letter to Scott, Washington also mentions that W. Calvin Chase believed that the "situation needed a conservative leader and that [Washington] ought to have the place occupied by Bishop Walters."

25. *CA*, March 10, 1899; and *WP*, March 5, 1899. See also Booker T. Washington to Emmett Scott, 11 March 1900, *BTWPH* 5, 457–58. At about the same time of the meeting in the District of Columbia, Washington was communicating with Francis J. Garrison about raising money for the Council's legal action. See Booker T. Washington to Francis J. Garrison, 11 March 1900, *BTWPH* 5, 459.

26. *IF*, March 10, 1900.

27. Cong. Rec. 2151–54. See also Justesen, *George Henry White*, 285–86. Congressman White did say 50,000 individuals had been lynched since the end of the Civil War.

The number seems exaggerated, but when the deaths in riots and mass kills are included, the figure seems less excessive.

28. Cong. Rec., 2151–54. See also Justesen, *George Henry White*, 286–88.

29. Cong. Rec., 2153.

30. Ibid., 2153–54. See also Justesen, *George Henry White*, 288–89. Albert E. Pillsbury did not send the letter to White; instead the congressman presented the letter, which White explained was sent to "a friend in the city" by permission. From the contents of the letter, it is safe to assume that Pillsbury sent the letter to one of White's Council colleagues, Daniel Murray or Edward Brown, as they were aiding White in drafting the anti-lynching bill. There is also a possibility that the Massachusetts lawyer sent the letter to Attorney General John Griggs who was aiding the Council members in the construction of the proposed legislation. Also, Booker T. Washington may have been instrumental in getting Pillsbury to comment on the legitimacy of an anti-lynching bill as he was already in contact with the Boston-based lawyer regarding the Council's proposed legal action in Louisiana. See Albert E. Pillsbury to Booker T. Washington, 25 February 1900, *BTWPH* 5, 449–50.

31. Cong. Rec., 2153–54.

32. Ibid., 2154.

33. *IF*, March 10, 1900.

34. *AC*, March 16, 1900; *BG*, April 4, 1900; and *CA*, April 7, 1900.

35. *CA*, April 7, 1900.

36. *CA*, May 12, 1900. See also *IF*, May 19, 1900; and *CG*, May 26, 1900.

37. George Mason Miller, "'A This Worldly Mission': The Life and Career of Alexander Walters (1858–1917)," (PhD diss., State University of New York at Stony Brook, 1984).

38. *CA*, May 12, 1900. See also *IF*, May 19, 1900; and *CG*, May 26, 1900.

39. *CA*, May 12, 1900. The delegation may have had some words with Senator Chandler regarding the White bill as well. Earlier in the year, Chandler had expressed his doubt on whether the federal government had the power "to prevent or punish crimes committed in the various states." *Colored American*, February 3, 1900.

40. *Daily Star Zion*, May 12, 1900.

41. Ibid. The Council collected the cash amount of $56.75 and took pledges for an additional $78.25.

42. *CA*, May 19, 1900. See also *NYT*, March 30, 1900; *Albany Evening Journal*, May 19, 1900; and Kathleen Dalton, *Theodore Roosevelt: A Strenuous Life* (New York: Knopf, 2002), 183.

43. *CA*, May 19, 1900.

44. *NYA*, May 4, 1900. See also Emma Lou Thornbrough, *T. Thomas Fortune: Militant Journalist* (Chicago: University of Chicago Press, 1972), 192–94; and Harlan, *Booker T. Washington: The Making of a Black Leader*, 292–96.

45. *CG*, May 19, 1900.

46. George Allen Mebane, *"The Negro Problem" as Seen and Discussed by Southern White Men in Conference, at Montgomery, Alabama; With Criticisms by the Northern Press* (New York: Alliance, 1900), 32.

47. Ibid, 35.

48. *CA*, June 9 and 16, 1900.

49. *CA*, June 16, 1900; and *IF*, June 23, 1900.

50. *NYA*, December 12, 1891. See also Thornbrough, *T. Thomas Fortune*, 202.

51. W. E. B. Du Bois, ed., *The Negro in Business*, Atlanta University Publications 4 (Atlanta: Atlanta University, 1899); Thornbrough, *T. Thomas Fortune*, 202; Louis Harlan, "Booker T. Washington and the National Negro Business League," in *Booker T. Washington in Perspective: Essays of Louis T. Harlan*, ed. Raymond W. Smock (Jackson: University of Mississippi Press, 1988), 98–109; Louis Harlan, *Booker T. Washington: The Making of a Black Leader*, 266–71; David Levering Lewis, *W. E. B. Du Bois: A Biography of a Race, 1868–1919* (New York: Holt, 1993), 220–21. See also Chapter 4.

52. W. E. B. Du Bois wrote William M. Trotter in 1905 that Du Bois's inaction was caused by T. Thomas Fortune's blocking the allocation of funds to the Business Bureau during the 1899 Afro-American Council Executive Committee meeting. See Du Bois to William Monroe Trotter, 20 May 1905, *W. E. B. Du Bois Papers*. There is no evidence to substantiate Du Bois's claim. In letters between Fortune and Washington regarding the Executive Committee meeting, there was no discussion of the Business Bureau; furthermore, in the news coverage of the meeting there was no discussion of the Business Bureau or the suppression of the group by Fortune. It is also curious to note that Du Bois does not mention the actions of Fortune until 1905, the year Du Bois and Trotter were organizing the Niagara Movement—a group they saw as an alternative to the Afro-American Council.

53. W. E. B. Du Bois to Booker T. Washington, 16 May 1900, *BTWPH* 5, 526.

54. *CC*, July 7, 1900. See also *IF*, July 14, 1900.

55. *CA*, July 21 and 14, 1900.

56. *IF*, July 14, 1900.

57. *WP*, June 18, 1900; and *CG*, June 30, 1900. See also Justesen, *George Henry White*, 292–94; and John R. Lynch, *Reminiscences of an Active Life: The Autobiography of John Roy Lynch* (Chicago: University of Chicago Press, 1970), 421–36.

58. *Official Proceeding of the Twelfth Republican National Convention, Held in the City of Philadelphia, June 19, 20 and 21, 1900* (Philadelphia: Dunlap Printing, 1900), 100–101; Kirk H. Porter and Donald B. Johnson, *National Party Platforms*, vol. 1, *1840–1956* (Urbana: University of Illinois Press, 1978), 124; and Richard B. Sherman, *The Republican Party and Black America: From McKinley and Hoover, 1896–1933* (Charlottesville: University Press of Virginia, 1973), 17.

59. Justesen, *George Henry White*, 293; and Sherman, *The Republican Party and Black America*, 13 and 17.

60. Kirk H. Porter and Donald B. Johnson, *National Party Platforms*, 121–24, 124. The Republican Party did call the violent acts "revolutionary," but gave no proposal on how to end the bloody murders. See also Chapter 3.

61. Porter and Johnson, *National Party Platforms*, 112–16. See also *CG*, July 21, 1900; and August Meier, "The Negro and the Democratic Party, 1875–1915," *Phylon* 17 (Summer, 1956): 173–91.

62. *WB*, July 7, 1900.

63. *IF*, July 7, 1900.

64. *CG*, July 21, 1900.

65. William Ivy Hair, *Carnival of Fury: Robert Charles and the New Orleans Race Riot of 1900* (Baton Rouge: Louisiana State University, 1976.); and Herbert Shapiro, *White Violence and Black Response*, 61–63.

66. Hair, *Carnival of Fury*, 171.

67. *New Orleans Times-Democrat*, July 28, 1900. See also Hair, *Carnival of Fury*, 171; and Shapiro, *White Violence and Black Response*, 62.

68. Ida B. Wells-Barnett, *Mob Rule in New Orleans: Robert Charles and His Fight to the Death*, in *Southern Horrors and Other Writings: The Anti-Lynching Campaign of Ida B. Wells, 1882–1900*, ed. Jacqueline Jones Royster (New York: Bedford Books, 1997), 158–208.

69. *WB*, August 11, 1900.

70. *IF*, August 11, 1900.

71. *CBA*, August 18, 1900. Taylor actually implicated Edward Cooper in the plot to take the money from the Republican administration.

72. *Indianapolis Freeman*, August18 and 25, 1900.

73. Alexander Walters to Booker T. Washington, 14 August 1900, *BTWPH* 5, 595.

74. Ibid. Such action gave some credence to the *Chicago Conservator*'s claim that Washington wanted nothing to do with an organization unless he had some control, but at least at this stage of the Council's life, the organization was still an autonomous group.

75. Peter Jefferson Smith, Jr., to Booker T. Washington, 28 August 1900, *BTWPH* 5, 609–10.

76. Cyrus Field Adams, *National Afro-American Council*, 9; *IW*, September 1, 1900; *CA*, September 1, 1900; *WB*, September 1 and 8, 1900; *IF*, September 1, 1900; *Appeal*, September 1, 1900; and *ISB*, September 7, 1900. Indiana's Governor Mount and Attorney General William L. Taylor as well as Indianapolis's Mayor Taggart all attended the convention.

77. *Star of Zion*, August 30, 1900.

78. *IW*, September 1, 1900.

79. *Atlanta Constitution*, August 30 and 31, 1900; *LAT*, August 30, 1900; and *IW*, September 1, 1900.

80. *IW*, September 1, 1900. See also *IF*, September 1, 1900; *CG*, October 6, 1900; and *IW*, October 13, 1900.

81. *IW*, September 1, 1900.

82. *IW*, September 1, 1900; and *IF*, September 1, 1900.

83. *IW*, September 1, 1900. See also *Appeal*, September 1, 1900; and *Iowa State Bystander*, September 7, 1900. Wells-Barnett stepped down from her position of chairman of the Anti-Lynching Bureau, but she did remain a member of the Bureau.

84. Adams, *National Afro-American Council*, 9; *IW*, September 1 and 8, 1900. See also Harlan, *Booker T. Washington: The Making of a Leader*, 270; John Coburn to Booker

T. Washington, 3 September 1900 and Richard W. Thompson to Booker T. Washington, 3 September 1900, *BTWPH* 5, 629–32.

85. *IW*, September 8, 1900; *BG*, September 1, 1900; and *WP*, September 1, 1900.

86. *IW*, September 8, 1900.

87. "An Address to the Metropolitan A. M. E. Church," May 22, 1900, *BTWPH* 5, 527–41.

88. *Indianapolis Journal*, September 1, 1900.

89. *IW*, September 8, 1900.

90. Alexander Walters to Booker T. Washington, 14 August 1900, *BTWPH* 5, 595.

91. *IW*, September 8, 1900; and *Appeal*, October 20, 1900. Those Council members that signed the document included Cyrus Field Adams and John P. Green of the post office department; John C. Dancy, collector of port; and Judson W. Lyons, register of the treasury.

92. *CG*, September 29, 1900.

93. Jesse Lawson to Booker T. Washington, 3 October 1900, *BTWPH* 5, 651–53.

94. Ibid.

95. Giles Beecher Jackson to Booker T. Washington, 5 October 1900, *BTWPH* 5, 649–51.

96. Alexander Walters to Booker T. Washington, 6 October 1900, *BTWPLC*. See also Miller, "'A This Worldly Mission,'" 179–80.

97. Jesse Lawson to Booker T. Washington, 8 October 1900, *BTWPH* 5, 651–53. There is no correspondence that discussed Washington personally contributing another $200 for the Council coffers. The conversation regarding the funds probably took place at the Council meeting when the two discussed the $100 that the Tuskegee principal collected from northern contributors.

98. *CA*, November 3, 1900.

99. *WB*, November 17, 1900; and *TP*, November 23, 1900.

100. *CA*, December 1, 1900.

101. Wells-Barnett explains in the introduction of the pamphlet that the Bureau had "no funds and is entirely dependent upon contributions from friends and members in carrying on the work." This led Patricia Schechter to conclude that Wells-Barnett "published the piece at her own expense." Though this may be correct, it is not entirely known. Wells-Barnett had toured the East Coast to raise money for the Bureau—which act would support her statement that the Bureau was dependent on donations—but it is not known how much money she collected for the cause. It is known, however, that none of the funds from her tour was turned over to the treasury. See Wells-Barnett, *Mob Rule*, 160; Schechter, *Ida B. Wells-Barnett and American Reform*, 117–18; and Adams, *National Afro-American Council*, 8–9.

102. Wells-Barnett, *Mob Rule*.

103. Schechter, *Ida B. Wells-Barnett and American Reform*, 117.

104. Wells-Barnett, *Mob Rule*, 202.

105. See Wells-Barnett, "Lynch Law in America."

106. Wells-Barnett, *Mob Rule*, 204.

107. Ibid., 206. See also Schechter, *Ida B. Wells-Barnett and American Reform*, 118.

108. Wells-Barnett, *Mob Rule*, 206.

109. *CG*, December 1, 1900. Wells-Barnett states that she is the chairman of the Council's Anti-Lynching Bureau. Although she may have been acting in this capacity, the group had elected another member of the organization, John Mitchell, Jr., to that position. See Adams, *National Afro-American* Council, 9.

110. *CG*, December 1, 1900.

111. *Star of Zion*, December 6, 1900.

112. Jesse Lawson to Booker T. Washington, 17, December 1900, *BTWPLC*.

113. Jesse Lawson to Booker T. Washington, 17 and 20 December 1900, and n.d., *BTWPLC*. See also Audrey A. Walker, "An Experiment in Non-Partisanship by the Negro 1884–1903" (master's thesis, Howard University, 1958), 92–93. The initial reaction by a number of individuals within the Council to Armand Romain was negative because of his high cost, but after being unable to retain the services of another local lawyer, the Council agreed to pay for his services.

114. *CA*, December 8 and 29, 1900. See also Perman, *Struggle for Mastery*, 224–25.

115. *CA*, December 8 and 29, 1900.

116. *Star of Zion*, January 10, 1901.

117. Giles Jackson to Booker T. Washington, 24 January and 28 January, 1901, *BT-WPH* 6, 14–17, 23–24.

118. *TP*, February 1, 1901. See also *WS*, January 19, 1901. For more on the lynching of Fred Alexander, see "Vengeance Without Justice—Injustice Without Retribution: The Afro-American Council's Struggle Against Racial Violence," *Great Plains Quarterly* 27, no. 2 (Spring 2007), 117–33.

119. *TP*, February 1 and 15, 1901. Black citizens of Kansas also met and drew up similar resolutions in Arkansas City, Emporia, and Edwardsville.

120. *TP*, February 15, 1901.

121. *ISB*, February 15, 1901.

122. *CA*, February 9, 1901. Wu Ting Fang, a Chinese minister touring the United States at the time of the Alexander lynching, was asked to comment on the incident. As he remarked on the disturbing nature of the Alexander murder, he also took the opportunity to express his thoughts on the racial situation of America. As he noted, he did not understand, "you brought the black man here against his will. You made him free . . . then you declared him equal to the white man, but you denied him equality. . . . he is still a slave socially," *Wichita Searchlight*, January 16, 1901.

123. *CA*, February 9, 1901; and *Star of Zion*, February 14, 1901.

124. *CA*, February 9, 1901; and *Star of Zion*, February 14, 1901.

125. *Star of Zion*, February 14, 1901; *CA*, February 16, 1901; and *CR*, February 28, 1901.

126. *TP*, March 1, 1901; and *Wichita Searchlight*, March 2, 1901. W. H. Hudson was a successful physician from Atchison and the head of the fraternal organization the True Eleven.

127. *TP*, March 1, 1901.

128. *CG*, March 16, 1901; *Washington Post*, March 3 and 8, 1901. Jesse Lawson wrote to Booker T. Washington on the day of the meeting informing him that the necessary money had been raised to initiate the case, and expressed relief that the Council would not have to call on the Tuskegeean for that money as he had contributed more for the case than any other individual. See Jesse Lawson to Booker T. Washington, 5 March 1901, *BTWPH* 6, 48–49. Before the Executive Committee meeting, Frederick McGhee was on a speaking tour to raise funds for the Council's Legal Bureau, but it is not known how much he raised for the cause. See Nelson, *Frederick L. McGhee*, 77.

129. *CG*, March 16, 1901.

130. Ibid. See also Miller, "'A This Worldly Mission.'"

131. *CG*, March 30, 1901.

132. Ibid. It is not clear whether this money was raised for the church or for the Council.

133. *Appeal*, April 5, 1901.

134. *TP*, March 22, 1901. Fred Roundtree, the Kansas Council secretary, did say the organization would use some of the funds to aid the national organization in its activities.

135. *TP*, April 5, 1901.

136. Jesse Lawson to Booker T. Washington, 12 March 1901, *BTWPLC*.

137. Jesse Lawson to Booker T. Washington, 12 and 15 March 1901, *BTWPLC*. Lawson wrote to Washington to attempt to get the Wizard to intervene. As he indicated, "I am free to admit that I do not understand the game these gentlemen are playing. If they are in earnest about the matter they are taking the wrong way of showing it." See also Walker, "An Experiment in Non-Partisanship by the Negro 1884–1903," 95.

138. Jesse Lawson to Booker T. Washington, 20 May 1901, *BTWPLC*.

139. Ibid. See also Walker, "An Experiment in Non-Partisanship by the Negro 1884–1903," 89–90.

140. Jesse Lawson to Booker T. Washington, 12 and, 30 April 1901, and 6 May 1901, *BTWPLC*.

141. Jesse Lawson to Booker T. Washington, 20 and 13 May 1901, *BTWPLC*. See also Walker, "An Experiment in Non-Partisanship by the Negro 1884–1903," 96.

142. Jesse Lawson to Booker T. Washington, 20 May and 13 May 1901, *BTWPLC*. See also Walker, "An Experiment in Non-Partisanship by the Negro 1884–1903," 96. The *AME Church Review* also published some material on the case in its April issue. See *AMECR* 17, no. 4 (April 1901), 390 and 393.

143. Though the Council had elected Ida B. Wells-Barnett as national organizer at the Indianapolis convention, it is unclear what her obligations were for that position. Furthermore, she continued to act in the capacity of the Council's Anti-Lynching Bureau—a position that, at least in the paper record of the convention, was in the hands of John Mitchell, Jr. To make matters even more confusing, in her own article on the organization, Wells-Barnett lists herself as the national organizer, but does not list anyone as

the director of the Anti-Lynching Bureau. Further confusion comes into play when the *Colored American* begins to call for the Council to appoint a national organizer in June 1901. See Ida B. Wells-Barnett, "National Afro-American Council," *Howard's American Magazine* 6, no. 10 (May 1901), 416; and *CA*, June 8 and 22, 1901.

144. Ida B. Wells-Barnett, "National Afro-American Council," 415–18.

145. Ibid., 418.

146. Ibid., 416. Wells-Barnett claims that the organization had already raised nearly $5000 for the case. This figure of course conflicts with the amount claimed by Jesse Lawson, the Financial Bureau director.

147. *WP*, May 13, 1901. See also *CA*, May 25, 1901; Jesse Lawson to Booker T. Washington, 13 May 1901, *BTWPH* 6, 108–9; and Jesse Lawson to Booker T. Washington, 20 May 1901, *BTWPLC*.

148. *Washington Post*, May 13, 1901. Besides being a current senator from Louisiana, Samuel Douglass McEnery was also a former governor and judge of the state.

149. Jesse Lawson to Booker T. Washington, 13 May 1901, *BTWPH* 6, 108–9.

150. *TP*, May 10, 1901.

151. *TP*, June 7, 1901. The Council desired the passage of legislation such as that in Ohio and South Carolina where the counties could be held responsible for injuries to persons and property committed by mobs.

152. *Star of Zion*, June 13, 1901. See also *CG*, June 22, 1901; *CA*, June 22, 1901; *CR*, July 11, 1901; and *Appeal*, July 20 and 27 and August 3, 1901.

153. *Star of Zion*, June 13, 1901.

154. Ibid.

155. *CA*, June 22 and 29, 1901.

156. Ibid., July 6 and 13, 1901.

157. Ibid., July 13, 1901.

158. Ibid., July 6, 1901.

159. *TP*, July 19, 1901. See also *ISB*, July 26, 1901. One affidavit claimed "Reddy McDonald, a deputy sheriff, rode into town ahead of the sheriff and party from the prison and told the crowd that Alexander was on the way." Along with the evidence collected by the Council and the Ministerial Union, many citizens of Leavenworth were convinced that the mob murdered an innocent man. A few days before the group met with the attorney general, 150 people held a vigil at the site of Alexander's murder. During the vigil, the minister asked the Lord to show them his divine wisdom and let it rain in the next twenty-four hours if Alexander was guilty of the crimes of which he was accused. As the *Topeka Plaindealer* and the *Topeka State Journal* reported, twenty-four hours passed without a drop of rain falling in Leavenworth. See *TP*, July 19, 1901.

160. *TP*, July 19, 1901. See also *ISB*, July 26, 1901.

161. Adams, *National Afro-American Council*, 26–27; *WB*, July 20, 1901; and *Star of Zion*, August 1, 1901.

162. Adams, *National Afro-American Council*, 26–27. Article 197 of the Louisiana constitution stated that Ryanes had to pass a literacy test, demonstrate that he owned

property assessed over $300, or prove that he or his ancestors had voted on or before January 1, 1897.

163. Ibid., 26–28. See also Walker, "An Experiment in Non-Partisanship by the Negro 1884–1903," 91–92.

164. Alexander Walters to Booker T. Washington, 27 June 1901, *BTWPH* 6, 160; and Alexander Walters to Booker T. Washington, 27 July 1901, *BTWPLC*

165. Alexander Walters to Booker T. Washington, 27 July 1901, *BTWPLC*. While Washington was declining to attend the Philadelphia convention, he was still working on the organization's Louisiana suit. In late July, he and attorney Albert E. Pillsbury corresponded regarding the filing of the Ryanes suit. At the same time Jesse Lawson wrote to Washington explaining that he would conceal the Tuskegeean's contributions to the Ryanes suit with the acronym X.Y.Z. and that all contributions that Washington secured from others would appeared as per X.Y.Z. See Albert E. Pillsbury to Booker T. Washington, 30 July 1901, *BTWPH* 6; and Jesse Lawson to Booker T. Washington, 30 July 1901, *BTWPLC*.

166. Gertrude Mossell, "The National Afro-American Council," *Colored American Magazine* 3 (August 1901): 291–305, 305.

167. *Star of Zion*, August 15, 1901.

168. Ibid. See also *CA*, August 17, 1901; and *AMECR* 28 (October 1901), 182–84.

169. *Star of Zion*, August 15, 1901.

170. Ibid.; and *CA*, August 17, 1901.

171. *Star of Zion*, August 15, 1901.

172. Ibid.; *CA*, August 17, 1901; *Atlanta Constitution*, August 10, 1901; and Adams, *National Afro-American Council*, 9–11. In addition to these topics of discussion, a number of elegant papers were read including "Negro Manhood" by T. Thomas Fortune, "The Schools of Today and Yesterday" by Walter H. Brooks, and "The Jim Crow Car and Its Remedy" by R. H. Boyd. See Adams, *National Afro-American Council*, 11 and *CA*, August 17, 1901. See also Alexander Walters to Booker T. Washington, 27 June 1901 and Emmett Scott to Booker T. Washington, 13 August 1901, *BTWPH* 6, 160, 186–87.

173. *CA*, August 17, 1901; and Emmett Scott to Booker T. Washington, 13 August 1901, *BTWPH* 6, 186–87.

174. *WB*, August 17 and 24, 1901.

175. *New Orleans Times-Democrat*, August 13, 1901.

176. Ibid. See also Walker, "An Experiment in Non-Partisanship by the Negro 1884–1903," 98–99.

177. *New Orleans Times-Democrat*, August 13, 1901; and Walker, "An Experiment in Non-Partisanship by the Negro 1884–1903," 99.

178. *New Orleans Times-Democrat*, August 20, 1901.

179. Ibid.; and Walker, "An Experiment in Non-Partisanship by the Negro 1884–1903," 100–101.

180. *New Orleans Times-Democrat*, August 20, 1901; and Walker, "An Experiment in Non-Partisanship by the Negro 1884–1903," 102.

181. The Louisiana Supreme Court would not render its decision until April 25, 1904. See Chapter 7.

182. *TP*, September 15, 1901.

183. Jesse Lawson to Booker T. Washington, 10 January 1901, *BTWPLC*. Louis Harlan does not mention the Council's discussion with Booker T. Washington, but for a look at Washington's position on the Alabama constitutional convention and suffrage, see Harlan, *Booker T. Washington: The Making of a Black Leader*, 292–96, 298–302. See also, Robert Volney Riser, "Prelude to the Movement: Disfranchisement in Alabama's 1901 Constitution and the Anti-Disfranchisement Cases" (PhD diss., University of Alabama, 2005).

184. Jesse Lawson to William C. Oates, 10 June 1901, *BTWPLC*. The proceedings of the convention took place over a few months. See *Proceedings of the Constitutional Convention of the State of Alabama, May 21st, 1901 to September 3rd, 1901*, 4 vols. (Wetumpka, Ala., 1941).

185. Jesse Lawson to William C. Oates, 10 June 1901, *BTWPLC*. The proceedings of the convention took place over a few months. See *Proceedings of the Constitutional Convention of the State of Alabama*. See also Walker, "An Experiment in Non-Partisanship by the Negro 1884–1903," 102.

186. *Proceedings of the Constitutional Convention of the State of Alabama* 4: 4303; and *New Orleans Times-Democrat*, July 25, 1901. See Harlan, *Booker T. Washington: The Making of a Black Leader*, 292–96, 300–301.

187. See Perman, *Struggle for Master*, 182–86; and C. Vann Woodward, *Origins of the New South, 1877–1913* (Baton Rouge: Louisiana State University Press, 1951), 339.

188. Jesse Lawson to Booker T. Washington, 20 and 26 December 1901, *BTWPLC*. See also Riser, "Prelude to the Movement."

189. *NYF*, December 6, 1884.

CHAPTER 6. INVASION OF THE TUSKEGEE MACHINE

Epigraph. Alexander Walters, *IF*, September 2, 1899; and *CG*, August 1, 1903.

1. Jesse Lawson to Booker T. Washington, 15, 16, 17, 20, 22, 23, 24, and 25 January 1902, *BTWPLC*. See also Audrey A. Walker, "An Experiment in Non-Partisanship by the Negro 1884–1903" (master's thesis, Howard University, 1958), 121–23. Legal Bureau of the Afro-American Council, *To the Colored Voters of the State of Alabama*, Broadside, *BTWPLC*.

2. Jesse Lawson to Booker T. Washington, 3 and 10 February 1902, *BTWPLC*.

3. *CG*, March 22, 1902; *WB*, March 15, 1902; *BAAL*, March 15, 1902; and *WP*, March 11, 1902.

4. *BAAL*, March 15, 1902.

5. Frederick McGhee to Emmett Scott, March 25, 1902, *BTWPH* 6, 424–26; and Frederick McGhee to Emmett Scott, March 29, 1902, *BTWPLC*. See also *BAAL*, March

29, 1902; *CA*, March 29, 1902; and *Appeal*, April 12, 1902. See also Paul D. Nelson, *Frederick L. McGhee: A Life on the Color Line, 1861–1912* (St. Paul: Minnesota Historical Society Press, 2002), 96–97.

6. Frederick McGhee to Emmett Scott, 5 April 1902, *BTWPLC*. See also Nelson, *Frederick McGhee*, 97.

7. Frederick McGhee to Emmett Scott, 5 April 1902, *BTWPLC*.

8. *CA*, April 26, 1902. Lawson does not give a figure on how many petitions had been returned at this time, but twenty-five petitions with 1,685 signatures were submitted to the committee. See HR57A-A 11.4.

9. *CA*, April 26, 1902. This delegation included Lawson, P. B. S. Pinchback, Daniel Murray, Bishop Grant, William A. Pledger, George H. White, Reverend Walter H. White, B. J. Bolding, H. P. Slaughter, A. M. Conway, and H. A. Thompson. See *Colored American*, May 3, 1902.

10. H.R. Rep. 2194, Ser. 8, 57th Cong., 1st Sess. and Cong. Rec., 57th Cong., 1st Sess., 3222.

11. Speech of Jesse Lawson before the House Committee on Labor, April 21, 1902. See also Walker, "An Experiment in Non-Partisanship by the Negro 1884–1903," 106–7.

12. *CA*, May 3, 1902.

13. Ibid.; and *WP*, April 21, 1902.

14. Speech of Jesse Lawson before House Committee on Labor, May 4, 1902. See also Walker, "An Experiment in Non-Partisanship by the Negro 1884–1903," 109.

15. Cong. Rec., 57th Cong., 1st Sess., 5898; H.R. Rep. 2194, Ser. 8, 57th Cong., 1st Sess.; and H.R. Rep. 2194, Part 2, Ser. 8, 57th Cong., 1st Sess..

16. H.R. Rep. 2194, Part 2, Ser. 8, 57th Cong., 1st Sess. See also Walker, "An Experiment in Non-Partisanship by the Negro 1884–1903," 110–11. The representatives who signed the minority report included Henry D. Flood of Virginia, W. Jasper Talbert of South Carolina, Ben Franklin Caldwell of Illinois, George Gilmore Gilbert of Kentucky, and William Henry Ryan of New York.

17. H.R. Rep. 2194, Part 2, Ser. 8, 57th Cong., 1st Sess. See also Walker, "An Experiment in Non-Partisanship by the Negro 1884–1903," 110–13.

18. *CA*, May 17, 1902.

19. *Hearings Before the U. S. Congress, House Committee on Interstate and Foreign Commerce of the House of Representatives* (Washington: Government Printing Office, 1902). The Council members who testified included Jesse Lawson, George H. White, Reverend Walter H. Brooks, and Cyrus Fields Adams.

20. *CA*, May 24, 1902.

21. Ibid. See also *Hearings Before the U. S. Congress, House Committee on Interstate and Foreign Commerce of the House of Representatives*, 437–39.

22. *Hearings Before the U. S. Congress, House Committee on Interstate and Foreign Commerce of the House of Representatives*, 437–38.

23. Ibid., 438–39. There were twenty-five petitions with 1,685 signatures submitted to the committee. See HR 57A-H11.4.

24. Ibid., 442.
25. Ibid., 445.
26. Ibid., 447.
27. Ibid., 448.
28. Ibid., 450.
29. Ibid.
30. Ibid., 452.
31. Ibid., 453.
32. *CA*, May 24, 1902.
33. *BG*, May 27, 1902; *Atlanta Constitution*, June 22, 1902; and *Wisconsin Advocate*, June 5, 1902.
34. See Michael Perman, *Struggle for Mastery: Disfranchisement in the South, 1888–1908* (Chapel Hill: University of North Carolina Press, 2001); August Meier, *Negro Thought in America, 1880–1915: Racial Ideologies in the Age of Booker T. Washington* (Ann Arbor: University of Michigan Press, 1963); Leon F. Litwack, *Trouble in Mind: Black Southerners in the Age of Jim Crow* (New York: Knopf, 1998); and C. Vann Woodward, *Origins of the New South, 1877–1913* (Baton Rouge: Louisiana State University Press, 1951).
35. Meier, *Negro Thought in America*; and Louis R. Harlan, *Booker T. Washington: The Wizard of Tuskegee, 1901–1915* (New York: Oxford University Press, 1983).
36. See Harlan, *Booker T. Washington*; and Emma Lou Thornbrough, "Booker T. Washington as Seen by His White Contemporaries," *Journal of Negro History* 53 (April 1968): 161–82.
37. Harlan, *Booker T. Washington*, 3–31; Robert L. Factor, *The Black Response to America: Men, Ideals, and Organization, from Frederick Douglass to the NAACP* (Reading, MA: Addison-Wesley, 1970), 211–19; and Emma Lou Thornbrough, *T. Thomas Fortune: Militant Journalist* (Chicago: University of Chicago Press, 1972), 226.
38. For a discussion of William Monroe Trotter, see Stephen R. Fox, *The Guardian of Boston: William Monroe Trotter* (New York: Atheneum, 1970). The *Guardian* started publication in November 1901.
39. Factor, *The Black Response to America*, 274. See also Fox, *The Guardian of Boston*, 21–46.
40. *Guardian*, November 9, 1901.
41. William Monroe Trotter to Reverend John Hagins, 10 April 1902, *William Monroe Trotter Papers*. Mugar Library, Boston University. C. H. Plummer to Booker T. Washington, 3 May 1902, *BTWPLC*. See also Factor, *The Black Response to America*, 277.
42. Frederick McGhee to Booker T. Washington, 27 June 1902, *BTWPLC*. The interesting thing about McGhee's statement is that he made reference to Washington's public position. As a member of the Council's Legal Bureau, he was more than likely aware that the Tuskegee principal was actively working with the group behind the scenes.
43. Peter J. Smith to Booker T. Washington, 3 July 1902, *BTWPH* 6, 492–93. See also Harlan, *Booker T. Washington*, 39.

44. T. Thomas Fortune to Booker T. Washington, 23 and 27 June, 1902, *BTWPLC*; and T. Thomas Fortune to Emmett Scott, 2 July 1902, *BTWPLC*. See also T. Thomas Fortune, "The Quick and the Dead," *AMECR* 32 (April 1916): 247–52.

45. *Appeal*, July 19, 1902.

46. Ibid.

47. *St. Paul Globe*, July 10, 1902; *Pioneer Press*, July 11, 1902; *Appeal*, July 19, 1902; *WS*, August 23 and 30, 1902; and Nelson, *Frederick L. McGhee*, 100.

48. *Pioneer Press*, July 10 and 11, 1902; and *St. Paul Globe*, July 11, 1902.

49. *Pioneer Press*, July 11, 1902; and *St. Paul Globe*, July 11, 1902. See also Nelson, *Frederick L. McGhee*, 101–2; Thornbrough, *T. Thomas Fortune*, 227; Harlan, *Booker T. Washington*, 38–39; and Factor, *The Black Response to America*, 278–79.

50. *Pioneer Press*, July 11, 1902; and *St. Paul Globe*, July 11, 1902.

51. See Thornbrough, *T. Thomas Fortune*; Meier, *Negro Thought in America*; Harlan, *Booker T. Washington*; and Factor, *The Black Response to America*.

52. *St. Paul Globe*, July 11, 1902.

53. Ibid.. See also Nelson, *Frederick L. McGhee*, 101–2.

54. *St. Paul Globe*, July 11, 1902; and *Appeal*, July 19, 1902.

55. *Appeal*, July 19, 1902; *WS*, August 23 and 30, 1902; and *St. Paul Dispatch*, July 11, 1902.

56. *St. Paul Dispatch*, July 11, 1902; and *Appeal*, July 19, 1902. See also Nelson, *Frederick L. McGhee*, 103.

57. *St. Paul Dispatch*, July 11, 1902; and *Appeal*, July 19, 1902.

58. *St. Paul Dispatch*, July 11, 1902; and *Appeal*, July 19, 1902.

59. *St. Paul Dispatch*, July 11, 1902; and *Pioneer Press*, July 11, 1902. See also Nelson, *Frederick L. McGhee*, 103.

60. *St. Paul Dispatch*, July 11, 1902. See also Nelson, *Frederick L. McGhee*, 103.

61. *St. Paul Dispatch*, July 11, 1902; and *Appeal* July 19, 1902.

62. *St. Paul Dispatch*, July 11, 1902. See also Nelson, *Frederick L. McGhee*, 104.

63. *Appeal*, July 19, 1902. The Address was drafted by, among others, William H. Steward, W. E. B. Du Bois, J. Madison Vance, Nelson Crews, Mrs. J. E. Porter, Bishop George W. Clinton, and John C. Dancy.

64. *Guardian*, July 19, 1902.

65. *Guardian*, July 19 and 26, 1902. See also Factor, *The Black Response to America*, 279; Thornbrough, *T. Thomas Fortune*, 228–29; and Harlan, *Booker T. Washington*, 40.

66. *CBA*, July 26, 1902.

67. *WB*, July 26, 1902. See also *IF*, July 19, 1902; *Illinois Idea*, August 3, 1902; and *Chicago Conservator*, August 3, 1902.

68. *CA*, July 19, 1902.

69. *RP*, August 2, 1902.

70. Ibid.

71. *CG*, August 9, 1902.

72. Emmett Scott to Booker T. Washington, 17 July 1902, *BTWPH* 6, 494–97.

73. T. Thomas Fortune to Booker T. Washington, 15 August 1902, *BTWPLC.*

74. Jesse Lawson to Booker T. Washington, 6 August 1902, *BTWPLC.*

75. John L. Mitchell, Jr., "Shall the Wheels of Race Agitation Be Stopped?," *The Colored American Magazine* 5 (September 1902): 386–91.

76. Ibid., 386.

77. Ibid, 386–87.

78. Ibid., 387.

79. Alexander Walters to Theodore Roosevelt, 6 October 1902, *BTWPLC.*

80. Alexander Waters to Booker T. Washington, 22 October 1902, *BTWPLC.* See also T. Thomas Fortune to Booker T. Washington, 17 October 1902, *BTWPLC*; Factor, *The Black Response to America*, 280; and George Mason Miller. " 'A This Worldly Mission': The Life and Career of Alexander Walters (1858–1917)" (PhD diss., State University of New York at Stony Brook, 1984), 232–34.

81. *NYT*, October 8, 1902; *WP*, October 8, 1902; *LAT*, October 8, 1902; and Thomas Dyer, *Theodore Roosevelt and the Idea of Race* (Baton Rouge: Louisiana State University Press, 1980).

82. *NYA*, October 23, 1902. Fortune's comments may have been a way for him to distance himself from any criticism of Roosevelt and the Republican Party. As some had feared at the St. Paul convention, the Council president was vying for a political appointment. See Thornbrough, *T. Thomas Fortune.*

83. *CA*, November 1, 1902.

84. Alexander Walters to Booker T. Washington, October 24, 1902, *BTWPH* 6, 557–58.

85. *CA*, November 16 and 22, 1902. See also Thornbrough, *T. Thomas Fortune*, 234–35.

86. *CG*, December 13, 1902.

87. *Appeal*, December 13, 1902. See also *Appeal*, December 20, 1902; *CG*, December 27, 1902; and Adams, *National Afro-American Council.*

88. *Appeal*, December 13, 1902.

89. See Adams, *National Afro-American Council.*

90. *CG*, December 20, 1902; *CA*, December 20, 1902; *Star of Zion*, January 1, 1903; and *Wichita Searchlight*, January 3, 1902. See also Miller. " 'A This Worldly Mission,' " 236–37. John S. Wise was the son of Governor Wise who executed John Brown in 1859.

91. *Cleveland Gazette*, December 20, 1902.

92. *ISB*, February 6, 1903; and *WP*, January 25, 1903.

93. *WB*, January 24 and 31 and February 7, 1903; *BAAL*, January 31, 1903; and *ISB*, February 6, 1903.

94. *WB*, January 31, 1903; and *CA*, February 14, 1903.

95. *WP*, January 27, 1903.

96. Ibid.,; *CA*, February 7, 1903.

97. *WP*, January 27, 1903; and *CA*, February 7, 1903.

98. *BAAL*, February 7, 1903.

99. *Appeal*, February 14, 1903.

100. *WB*, January 31, 1903. See also *WB*, February 7, 1903.

101. *CA*, February 14, 1903.

102. *BAAL*, February 7, 1903; *NYT*, January 31, 1903; and *WP*, January 30 and February 5, 1903.

103. *BAAL*, February 7, 1903; and *NYT*, January 31, 1903. It is not known if James H. Hayes actually went to New Orleans to speak at the Coliseum Club.

104. *Colored American*, February 28, 1903.

105. Cyrus Field Adams, "The Afro-American Council: The Story of its Organization—What It Stands For—Its Personnel," *The Colored American Magazine* 6 (March 1903): 331–38.

106. Ibid., 332. See also *WP*, January 30, 1903.

107. *Colored American*, March 21 and April 4, 1903.

108. W. E. B. Du Bois, *Dusk of Dawn: An Essay Toward an Autobiography of a Race Concept* (New York, 1940), 8.

109. See W. E. B. Du Bois, "The Relation of the Negroes to the Whites of the South," *Annals of the American Academy of Political and Social Science* 28, no. 1 (July 1901): 121–31; "The Talented Tenth," in *The Negro Problem*, ed. Booker T. Washington (New York: James Pott & Co., 1903); and "The Training of Black Men," *Atlantic Monthly* 49 (September 1902), 289–97. See also David Levering Lewis, *W. E. B. Du Bois*, 165–96; and August Meier, *Negro Thought in America*, 190–206.

110. W. E. B. Du Bois, *The Souls of Black Folk*, eds. David W. Blight and Robert Gooding-Williams (Boston: Bedford Books, 1997), 62–67.

111. Ibid., 71.

112. Ibid., 68.

113. Ibid., 70–71.

114. *CBA*, May 2, 1903. See also *IW*, May 2, 1903; *Guardian*, April 18, 1903; *BAAL*, May 2, 1903; *ISB*, May 8, 1903; and *CG*, May 16, 1903.

115. F. L. McGhee, "Report to the Financial Committee of the Afro-American Council," August 5, 1902 (Washington, 1902). See also Factor, *The Black Response to America*, 239.

116. See Factor, *The Black Response to America*, 239; Harlan, *Booker T. Washington* 245–47; and Thornbrough, *T. Thomas Fortune*, 241–42. In the correspondence concerning the case, Wilford Smith was J. C. May and Emmett Scott was R. C. Black.

117. *Giles v. Harris*, 189 U. S. 475 (1903). See also *CG*, May 30, 1903.

118. *Giles v. Harris*, 189 U. S. 475.

119. *CG*, May 30, 1903. *CG*, May 2, 1903.

120. *CG*, May 2, 1903.

121. *CA*, April 25, 1903.

122. "Resolutions and Minutes of the Colored Men's Meeting, Parker Memorial Hall, Boston, April 4, 1903," *William Monroe Trotter Papers*. See also Factor, *The Black Response to America*, 280–81.

123. *Chicago Broad Ax*, May 20, 1903; *NYT*, May 20, 1903; *Boston Guardian*, May 23, 1903; and *Brooklyn Eye*, June 6, 1903. See also Factor, *The Black Response to America*, 282.

124. *Brooklyn Eye*, June 6, 1903. See also Christopher Plummer to Booker T. Washington, 1 June 1903 and Wilford Scott to Emmett Scott 3 June 1903, *Booker T. Washington Papers*, Microfilm Collection *BTWPLC*, 282.

125. See Meier, *Negro Thought in America*, 207–47; Factor, *The Black Response to America*, 251–69; Thornbrough, *T. Thomas Fortune*, 233–34 and 242–43; Harlan, *Booker T. Washington*, 32–62; Dickson Bruce, Jr., *Archibald Grimké: Portrait of a Black Independent*, 93–106; and Fox, *Guardian of Boston*, 30–80.

126. Booker T. Washington, "Negro and the White" and "Suffrage Laws Unjust," *North American* June 7, 1903.

127. Of course what is not alluded to in this statement is Washington's active participation in the legal challenges brought by the Council in Louisiana and Alabama.

128. W. E. B. Du Bois, "Possibilities of the Negro: The Advance Guard of the Race," *Booklovers Magazine* 2, no. 7, (July 1903): 3–15. See also *CBA*, June 6, 13, and 27, 1903.

129. Cyrus Field Adams to Booker T. Washington, 2, 14, and 25 April, and 20 March 1903; Booker T. Washington to Emmett Scott, 6 and 9 April 1902, *BTWPLC*; Cyrus Field Adams to Booker T. Washington, n.d. 1903, *BTWPLC*; Booker T. Washington to Bishop Alexander Walters, 26 May 1903, *BTWPLC*; Booker T. Washington to William Pledger, 6 April 1903, *BTWPLC*; Charles W. Anderson to Emmett Scott, 22 June 1903, *BTWPLC*; and Booker T. Washington to T. Thomas Fortune, 26 June 1903, *BTWPLC*.

130. See August Meier, "Negro Racial Thought in the Age of Booker T. Washington, circa 1880–1915," 474–75; Booker T. Washington to William A. Pledger, 6 April 1903 and Booker T. Washington to Emmett J. Scott, 6 April 1903, *BTWPH* 7, 111–12.

131. Alexander Walters, "Disfranchisement," *AMECR* 20, no. 1 (July 1903): 20–30.

132. *CA*, July 11 and 19, 1903; *CG*, July 11, 1903; *Guardian*, July 11, 1903; and *Atlanta Constitution*, July 2, 1903. See also Meier, "Negro Racial Thought in the Age of Booker T. Washington," 496; Fox, *Guardian of Boston*, 47–49; and Harlan, *Booker T. Washington*, 40–44. The *Guardian* folks accused Washington of manipulating the backroom activity. John E. Bruce, a participant in the negotiations, did not see Washington as the overriding force. This seems to be the case as neither Washington nor Fortune was pleased with Hayes as the national organizer. See T. Thomas Fortune to Booker T. Washington, 7 July 1903, *BTWPH* 7, 200.

133. *St. Paul Dispatch*, July 11, 1902; and *Appeal*, July 19, 1902.

134. *CA*, July 11, 1903; *Guardian*, July 11, 1903. There is no record of Fortune's presidential address.

135. *Guardian*, July 11, 1903.

136. *Guardian*, July 11, 1903; and *CG*, July 11, 1903. See also Fox, *Guardian of Boston*, 47–48.

137. *Guardian*, July 11, 1903; *CG*, July 11, 1903; *NYA*, July 4, 1903; *Louisville Harold*, July 3, 1903; and William H. Ferris, *The African Abroad* (New Haven: Tuttle, Morehouse & Taylor Press, 1913), 375–76. See also Fox, *Guardian of Boston*, 47–48; Harlan, *Booker T.*

Washington, 42; Rudwick, *W. E. B. Du Bois*, 71–72; and Thornbrough, *T. Thomas Fortune*, 244–45.

138. *ISB*, July 3, 1903; *CA*, July 11, 1903; and *Guardian*, July 11, 1903.

139. *ISB*, July 3, 1903; and *WP*, July 3, 1903. See also E. Davidson Washington, ed., *Selected Speeches of Booker T. Washington* (Garden City, N.Y.: Doubleday, 1932), 92–99.

140. *ISB*, July 3, 1903. See also Thornbrough, *T. Thomas Fortune*, 245.

141. *Louisville Herald*, July 4, 1903. See also Thornbrough, *T. Thomas Fortune*, 246; and Fox, *Guardian of Boston*, 47–49.

142. *Guardian*, July 11, 1903; *CG*, July 11, 1903; and *CA*, July 11, 1903. See also Thornbrough, *T. Thomas Fortune*, 245–46; and Fox, *Guardian of Boston*, 47–49.

143. *CA*, July 11 and 18, 1903; *WP*, July 4, 1903; and *LAT*, July 4, 1903. See also Meier, "Negro Racial Thought in the Age of Booker T. Washington," 477.

144. *CA*, July 11 and 18, 1903. See also Meier, "Negro Racial Thought in the Age of Booker T. Washington," 477.

145. *ISB*, July 3, 1903.

146. *WB*, July 11, 1903.

147. *Guardian*, July 18, 1903.

148. *CA*, July 11, 1903.

149. Ibid.

150. *Guardian*, July 11, 1903.

151. The Council would not accept credit for its activity in the cases until 1905. National organizer Lewis G. Jordan would cite the group's efforts in the Louisiana and Alabama cases as evidence to support the Council. "Rev. L. G. Jordan Before the Afro-American Council," *Alexander's Magazine* 3 (December 15, 1905): 96–100.

152. *Guardian*, August 1, 1903. See also Fox, *Guardian of Boston*, 49–58; Factor, *The Black Response to America*, 285–87; and Rudwick, *W. E. B. Du Bois*, 72–76.

153. *Guardian*, August 1, 1903; and *Colored American*, August 22, 1903. See also *BG*, July 31, 1903; *Atlanta Constitution*, July 31, 1903; *LAT*, July 31, 1903; Fox, *Guardian of Boston*, 49–58; Factor, *The Black Response to America*, 285–87; and Rudwick, *W. E. B. Du Bois*, 72–76.

154. *Guardian*, August 1, 1903; and *CA*, August 22, 1903. See also Thornbrough, *T. Thomas Fortune*, 248–50; Fox, *Guardian of Boston*, 49–58; Factor, *The Black Response to America*, 285–87; and Rudwick, *W. E. B. Du Bois*, 72–76.

155. *Guardian*, August 1, 1903.

156. *Chicago Inter Ocean*, July 28, 1903; *Chicago Conservator*, August 8, 1903; *Guardian*, August 8, 1903; *WB*, August 8, 1903; *CG*, August 8, 1903; and *IW*, August 15, 1903. See also Factor, *The Black Response to America*, 287; and Booker T. Washington, *My Larger Education* (New York: Doubleday, 1911), 112–27.

157. *Guardian*, August 15, 1903. For a similar view, see Ida B. Wells-Barnett, "Booker T. Washington and His Critics," *The World Today* 4 (April 1904), 578. See also Factor, *The Black Response to America*, 287.

158. *Boston Evening Transcript*, September 3, 1903; *WB*, September 12, 1903; and *CBA*, September 12, 1903. See also Fox, *Guardian of Boston*, 67.

159. *ISB*, October 2, 1903.

160. *TP*, September 11, 1903.

161. *Boston Evening Transcript*, October 9, 1903; *ISB*, October 16, 1903; *CBA*, October 17 and 24, 1903; and *CA*, October 24, 1903. See also Fox, *Guardian of Boston*, 55–58.

162. Fox, *Guardian of Boston*, 57–58.

163. *WB*, October 24, 1903. See also Harlan, *Booker T. Washington*, 247. The Dan Rogers case was based on a murder trial where black jurors were excluded on the basis of their color and the suffrage provisions of the new constitution.

164. Ibid.

165. *WB*, October 3 and 10, 1903.

166. *WB*, November 7, 1903.

167. Booker T. Washington to T. Thomas Fortune, 3 November 1903, Emma Lou Thornbrough Papers. See also Thornbrough, *T. Thomas Fortune*, 250.

168. *IF*, December 26, 1903. See also Audrey A. Walker, "An Experiment in Non-Partisanship by the Negro 1884–1903" (master's thesis, Howard University, 1958), 78–82; Miller, "'A This Worldly Mission,'" 242–43; and Factor, *The Black Response to America*, 287–89.

169. *IF*, December 26, 1903.

170. Alexander Walters, "*Disenfranchisement*," 24.

171. "Objects and Plan of Organization of the National Republican Afro-American Council," Broadside (Washington, D.C., December 1903), *BTWPLC*. The organization also changed its name for a brief period from the Afro-American Council to the National Republican Afro-American Council.

172. *NYA*, December 24, 1903.

173. *WB*, December 12, 1903.

174. *CA*, December 19, 1903. See also *WB*, December 19, 1903.

CHAPTER 7. AN ARMY OF MICE OR AN ARMY OF LIONS?

Epigraph. Clarence Emery Allen, *WB*, September 2, 1905.

1. *New York Evening Post*, January 9, 1904.

2. See Louis R. Harlan, *Booker T. Washington: The Wizard of Tuskegee, 1901–1915* (New York: Oxford University Press, 1983), 63–83; Herbert Aptheker, "The Washington-Du Bois Conference of 1904," *Science and Society* 13 (Fall 1949): 344–51; Robert L. Factor, *The Black Response to America: Men, Ideals, and Organization, from Frederick Douglass to the NAACP* (Reading, Mass.: Addison-Wesley., 1970), 292–300; Elliott M. Rudwick, *W. E. B. Du Bois; A Study in Minority Group Leadership* (Philadelphia: University of Pennsylvania Press, 1960), 77–87; David Levering Lewis, *W. E. B. Du Bois: Biography of a Race, 1868–1919* (New York: Henry Holt, 1993), 304–11; and Stephen R. Fox, *The Guardian of Boston: William Monroe Trotter* (New York: Atheneum, 1971), 82–86.

3. W. E. B. Du Bois to Francis Grimké, 28 December 1903, *The Works of Francis J. Grimké*, ed. Carter G. Woodson (Washington, D.C.: Associated, 1942), 4: 89–90. See also Harlan, *Booker T. Washington*, 62–83; Aptheker, "The Washington-Du Bois Conference of 1904"; Factor, *The Black Response to America*, 293; and Rudwick, *W. E. B. Du Bois*, 78–79.

4. W. E. B. Du Bois to Francis Grimké, 28 December 1903, *Works of Francis J. Grimké*, 4: 89–90.

5. *Guardian*, January 9, 1904; and *WB*, January 16, 1904.

6. Factor, *The Black Response to America*, 293–94.

7. Kelly Miller, "Summary of the Proceedings of the Conference at Carnegie Hall," *BTWPH* 7, 384–87. See also *WB* 23, January 30, 1904; *IW*, January 30, 1904; and *Guardian*, January 30, 1904.

8. Miller, "Summary of the Proceedings."

9. Frederick McGhee to Booker T. Washington, 12 January 1904, *BTWPLC*. See also Paul D. Nelson, *Frederick L. McGhee: A Life on the Color Line, 1861–1912* (Minneapolis: Minnesota Historical Society Press, 2002), 127.

10. T. Thomas Fortune to Emmett Scott, 11, 12, 21, and 28 January 1904, *BTWPLC*; and Emmett Scott to T. Thomas Fortune 19 January 1904, *BTWPLC*. See also *IF*, January 30, 1904; *WB*, February 6, 1904; *NYA*, October 25, 1904; and Thornbrough, *T. Thomas Fortune*, 253–54.

11. *WB*, January 9, 1904.

12. Giles v. Teasley, 193 U.S. 146 (1904). See also *Guardian*, February 27, 1904; and Factor, *The Black Response to America*, 237–41.

13. *Guardian*, February 27, 1904.

14. *Appeal*, February 20, 1904.

15. Ibid. A few weeks later Adams was even more impressed by the spirit of the Japanese in coming to the aid of their nation as he reported that Kehoshiro Okahura was preparing to donate a million dollars to the Japanese cause: "a millionaire of Tokio [sic], Japan, offers his private museum worth $1,000,000, for sale in America, and he proposes to donate the amount to the Japanese war fund. It is this spirit of sacrifice which has made the Japanese a great people. We have no member of the race who is able to give $1,000,000, but there are 1,000,000 who could easily give $1 each and if the right spirit prevailed the sum would be raised in a week by the Afro-Americans as a fund to be used in the defense of the rights of the race. It ought to be raised." *Appeal*, March 5, 1904.

16. Harlan, *Booker T. Washington*, 78–79; and Factor, *The Black Response to America*, 299. See also Booker T. Washington to W. E. B. Du Bois, 27 January 1904 *BTWPH* 7, 459–60. See also *The Negro's Right to Jury Representation*, *Booker T. Washington Papers*, Tuskegee University.

17. *Rogers v. State of Alabama*, 192 U. S. 226 (1904).

18. *WB*, March 19, 1904.

19. Harlan, *Booker T. Washington*, 79–80; and Factor, *The Black Response to America*, 298.

20. T. Thomas Fortune to Emmett Scott, 28 March 1904, *BTWPLC*. See also T. Thomas Fortune to Emmett Scott, 26 March 1904, *BTWPLC*; and Thornbrough, *T. Thomas Fortune*, 258. According to Fortune, he was "thrown down by" a glass of brandy that he had consumed before attending a gathering at the home of Robert and Mary Church Terrell. It appears that once at the home, he became a bit loose-lipped and discussed the Council's activities and Washington's involvement. Fortune believed that he was with company who understood Washignton's actions, but he later discovered that he was not. See T. Thomas Fortune to Emmett Scott, 28 March 1904, *BTWPLC*; J. Douglass Wetmore to Booker T. Washington, 4 April 1904, *BTWPLC*; and Booker T. Washington to J. Douglass Wetmore, 14 April 1904, *BTWPLC*.

21. T. Thomas Fortune to William H. Steward, 28 March 1904, *BTWPLC*. See also T. Thomas Fortune, "The Quick and the Dead," *AMECR* 32, no. 4 (April 1916): 248–49.

22. T. Thomas Fortune to William H. Steward, 28 March 1904, *BTWPLC*. Fortune stayed in contact with the organization and continued to be a member of the local Council in New York City.

23. Factor, *The Black Response to America*, 315.

24. "The Negro Problem from the Negro Point of View," *World Today* 6 (April 1904): 511–23.

25. Booker T. Washington, "The Tuskegee Idea," *World Today* 6 (April 1904): 512.

26. Ida B. Wells-Barnett, "Booker T. Washington and His Critics," *World Today* 6 (April 1904): 518–21.

27. Ibid., 521.

28. W. E. B. Du Bois, "The Parting of the Ways," *World Today* 6 (April 1904): 521–23. See also *CG*, April 16, 1904; and *CBA*, April 23, 1904.

29. Du Bois, "The Parting of the Ways," 523.

30. Ibid., 523.

31. *NYA*, April 9, 1904. See also *BAAL*, April 16, 1904. For more on the lynchings in Saint Charles, see *Arkansas Gazette*, March 27, 1904; *Arkansas Democrat*, March 29, 1904; and Vincent Vinikas, "Specters in the Past: The Saint Charles, Arkansas, Lynching of 1904 and the Limits of Historical Inquiry," *Journal of Southern History* 65 (August 1999): 535–64.

32. *NYA*, April 9, 1904.

33. *CBA*, April 16, 1904; emphasis in original. See also *Appeal*, April 23, 1904.

34. *CBA*, April 16, 1904.

35. Ibid.

36. Ibid. In a comical aside, Julius Taylor of the *Chicago Broad Ax* agreed to publish the appeal out of respect for the women of the race and the cause. He did not agree to publish the appeal out of respect for Frederick McGhee because McGhee owed the *Broad Ax* "three dollars as subscription to *The Broad Ax*, and he must pay that honest debt first before we can respect him as an honorable leader of the Afro-American race."

37. *Appeal*, April 24, 1904.

38. *State ex rel. Ryanes v. Gleason*, 112 La. 612 (1903). See also Audrey A. Walker, "An Experiment in Non-Partisanship by the Negro 1884–1903" (master's thesis, Howard

University, 1958), 104. See also Shawn Leigh Alexander, "The Afro-American Council and Its Challenge of Louisiana's Grandfather Clause," in *Radicalism in the South Since Reconstruction*, eds. Chris Green, Rachel Rubin, and James Smethurst (New York: Palgrave, 2006), 13–36.

39. For information on John Milholland, see Brian W. Blaesser, "John E. Milholland" (senior thesis, Brown University, 1969).

40. John Milholland to Booker T. Washington, 9 October 1900, *BTWPLC.*

41. John Milholland to Booker T. Washington, 9 November 1903, *BTWPLC.* The group was launched by Milholland, Albert B. Humphrey of New York, John G. Carlisle of Kentucky, and John S. Wise of Virginia. See also Factor, *The Black Response to America*, 313.

42. Albert B. Humphrey to Theodore Roosevelt, 2 June 1904. *Theodore Roosevelt Papers*. Library of Congress, Washington, D.C.

43. *Guardian,* July 2, 1904. See also Harlan, *Booker T. Washington: The Wizard of Tuskegee*, 24–27.

44. Albert B. Humphrey to Booker T. Washington, 4 June 1904. *BTWPH* 7, 521–22. Albert B. Humphrey to Booker T. Washington, 9 June 1904. *BTWPLC.*

45. Albert B. Humphrey to Booker T. Washington, 4 June 1904. *BTWPH* 7, 521–22. Albert B. Humphrey to Booker T. Washington, 9 June 1904. *BTWPLC.* See also Robert Factor, *Black Response to America*, 314 and Harlan, *Booker T. Washington: The Wizard of Tuskegee*, 25–27.

46. Alexander Walters, "Civil and Political Status of the Negro," in *Proceedings of the National Negro Conference, 1909* (New York: Arno Press, 1969), 172.

47. Nina G. Du Bois to Booker T. Washington, 25 June 1904, *BTWPLC*; Harlan, *Booker T. Washington*, 80–81; Factor, *The Black Response to America*, 305; and Lewis, *W. E. B. Du Bois*, 308–11.

48. Harlan, *Booker T. Washington*, 80–81; Factor, *The Black Response to America*, 305; and Lewis, *W. E. B. Du Bois*, 308–11.

49. Booker T. Washington to Archibald Grimké, 8 July 1904, *BTWPH* 8, 9. See also Archibald Grimké to Booker T. Washington 13 July 1904, *BTWPH* 8, 16–17; Kelly Miller to W. E. B. Du Bois, 8 July 1904, *W. E. B. Du Bois Papers*; Harlan, *Booker T. Washington*, 81; and Dickson D. Bruce, Jr., *Archibald Grimké: Portrait of a Black Independent* (Baton Rouge: Louisiana State University Press, 1993), 108–10.

50. Harlan, *Booker T. Washington*, 80–81; Factor, *The Black Response to America*, 305; Bruce, *Archibald Grimké*, 109–10; and Lewis, *W. E. B. Du Bois*, 311–12. Du Bois was also disturbed by the fact that the Committee's financial support was coming from Andrew Carnegie, about whose racial position Du Bois was suspicious.

51. Archibald Grimké to W. E. B. Du Bois, 13 August 1904, *W. E. B. Du Bois Papers*; and Bruce, *Archibald Grimké*, 110.

52. *Appeal*, August 27 and September 4, 1904. See also *Wisconsin Advocate*, August 24, 1904.

53. *Appeal*, August 27, 1904.

54. *WB*, August 27, 1904. Ironically, W. Calvin Chase was upset that the Council had become a partisan organization—something that he had been calling for since the days of the Afro-American League. As he now stated, "The negro is beginning to learn how to play politics, and before many more years there will be as many negro Democrats as there are negro, Republicans, and equally as many Socialists. Now, let this bogus Council rest in peace."

55. Ibid.

56. *Appeal*, September 17, 1904; *BAAL*, September 17, 1904; *IW*, September 17, 1904; and *IF*, September 17, 1904. The St. Louis convention was the least publicized of the Council's previous seven national gatherings, but the sparse press descriptions do provide some information about the deliberations.

57. *IF*, September 17, 1904.

58. *Appeal*, September 17, 1904.

59. *IW*, September 17, 1904; *Appeal*, September 17, 1904; *BAAL*, September 17, 1904; *IF*, September 17, 1904; *Atlanta Constitution*, September 9, 1904; and *LAT*, September 10, 1904.

60. *IW*, September 17, 1904.

61. Cyrus Field Adams to Emmett Scott, 3 August 1904, *BTWPLC*. See also Factor, *The Black Response to America*, 318–19. In this section of *The Black Response to America*, historian Robert Factor confuses the activity of the Council and the National Negro Suffrage League at their meeting in Chicago with that of the two at their annual meeting in St. Louis.

62. *Appeal*, September 12, 1904. See also *Appeal*, September 26, October 31, November 7 and 14, and December 5, 1904.

63. *Appeal*, September 12, 1904. The *Appeal* ran the circular five more times. See *Appeal*, September 26, October 31, November 7 and 14, and December 5, 1904.

64. *Appeal*, April 23 and September 12, 1904.

65. *Guardian*, October 15, 1904; Factor, *The Black Response to America*, 321; and Fox, *Guardian of Boston*, 76–77.

66. *Guardian*, October 15, 1904.

67. *CG*, October 15, 1904.

68. W. E. B. Du Bois, "Credo," *Independent* 57 (October 6, 1904): 787. See also *Cleveland Gazette*, October 29, 1904 and *AMECR*, "A Negro's Creed," 21, no. 3 (January 1905): 279. See also Lewis, *W. E. B. Du Bois*, 311–13.

69. *Washington Bee*, September 24, 1904. The article was also used by Walters to counter the publication of information that he had switched his position on African Americans fighting against the sweeping disfranchisement legislation. See ibid., August 29, 1904. See also George Mason Miller, "'A This Worldly Mission': The Life and Career of Alexander Walters (1858–1917)" (PhD diss., State University of New York at Stony Brook, 1984), 249–50.

70. Miller, "'A This Worldly Mission," 253–54; and Thornbrough, *T. Thomas Fortune*, 270.

71. *Washington Bee*, December 10, 1904.

72. For a discussion of Roosevelt's hands-off policy and the general apathy regarding what was occurring in the South, see David W. Blight, *Race and Reunion: The Civil War in American Memory* (Cambridge, Mass: Harvard University Press, 2001).

73. *WB*, December 10, 1904. See also Miller, " 'A This Worldly Mission," 253–54.

74. *Appeal*, October 31, November 7 and 14, and December 5, 1904.

75. *NYA*, March 9, 1905; and Miller, " 'A This Worldly Mission,' " 255–56.

76. It is also at this time that W. E. B. Du Bois published his famous "Debits and Credits" article in the *VN*, which accused Washington of giving "hush money" as a subsidy of the black press. See *VN* 2 (January 1905): 677; *WB*, January 11, 1905; *NYA*, February 16, 1905; Harlan, *Booker T. Washington*, 85–86; and Lewis, *W. E. B. Du Bois*, 314–15, 320.

77. *NYA*, March 9, 1905. A copy of the letter is found in the Booker T. Washington Papers. The letter was sent to the recipients by J. Douglass Wetmore, lawyer and member of the Afro-American Council. The letter was signed by W. E. B. Du Bois, Kelly Miller, J. W. E. Bowen, Bishop Walters, and Henry T. Johnson. W. E. B. Du Bois et al., 24 January 1905, *BTWPLC*. The participants included Kelly Miller, W. E. B. Du Bois, William M. Trotter, J. W. E. Bowen, D. A. Straker, H. C. Smith, H. T. Johnson, and Walters. Nothing came of the overall plans of this committee.

78. *NYA*, March 2, 1905.

79. Nelson, *Frederick L. McGhee*, 127–29.

80. Leon F. Litwack, *Trouble in Mind: Black Southerners in the Age of Jim Crow* (New York: Knopf, 1998); Edward L. Ayers, *The Promise of the New South: Life After Reconstruction* (New York: Oxford University Press, 1992); C. Vann Woodward, *Origins of the New South, 1877–1913* (Baton Rouge: Louisiana State University Press, 1951); and Jack Abramowitz, "Accommodation and Militancy in Negro Life, 1876–1916" (PhD diss., Columbia University, 1950).

81. Charles Carroll, *The Negro a Beast* (1900; rpr. Miami: Mnemosyne, 1969); William P. Calhoun, *The Caucasian and The Negro in the United States. They Must Separate. If Not, Then Extermination. A Proposed Solution: Colonization* (Columbia, South Carolina: R. L. Bryan, 1902); Thomas Dixon, *The Leopard's Spots: A Romance of the White Man's Burden, 1865–1900* (New York: Doubleday, 1902); and *The Clansman: An Historical Romance of the Ku Klux Klan* (New York: Doubleday, 1905). See also I. A. Newby, *Jim Crow's Defense: Anti-Negro Thought in America, 1900–1930* (Baton Rouge: Louisiana State University Press, 1965); George M. Frederickson, *The Black Image in the White Mind: The Debate on Afro-American Character and Destiny, 1817–1914* (1971; rpr. Hanover, N. H.: Wesleyan University Press, 1987), 228–82; and Heather Cox Richardson, *The Death of Reconstruction: Race, Labor, and Politics in the Post-Civil War North, 1865–1901* (Cambridge, Mass.: Harvard University Press, 2001).

82. *NYA*, June 8, 15, and 29, 1905.

83. *ISB*, June 30 and July 6, 1905. The Des Moines, Iowa chapter in particular was becoming more active.

84. *CG*, June 3, 1905. The editors of the *Gazette* of course knew nothing about Booker T. Washington's association with the case.

85. Nelson, *Frederick McGhee*, 129; Rudwick, *W. E. B. Du Bois*, 94–97; Manning Marable, *W. E B. Du Bois, Black Radical Democrat* (Boston: Twayne, 1986), 52–74; Lewis, *W. E. B. Du Bois*, 315–16; Factor, *The Black Response to America*, 326; Ralph J. Bunche, "Extended Memorandum on the Programs, Ideologies, Tactics, and Achievements of Negro Betterment and Interracial Organizations" (manuscript prepared for Carnegie-Myrdal Study, June 1940).

86. W. E. B. Du Bois, "The Niagara Movement," *VN* 2, no. 9 (September 1905): 619–22. See also Herbert Aptheker, ed., *A Documentary History of the Negro People in the United States* (New York: Citadel Press, 1968), 904–7; Nelson, *Frederick McGhee*, 131; Fox, *Guardian of Boston*, 89–90; and Lewis, *W. E. B. Du Bois*, 315–22.

87. J. Max Barber, "The Significance of the Niagara Movement," *VN* 2 (August 1905)" 596. See also Factor, *The Black Response to America*, 327. Despite Barber and Du Bois's assertion that the group was not called to harangue Washington, the final sentence of Barber's comments certainly could be read as a direct challenge to Washington's leadership.

88. Barber, "The Significance of the Niagara Movement," 597.

89. "Declaration of Principles," *W. E. B. Du Bois Papers*; "Declaration of Principles," in *Pamphlets and Leaflets by W. E. B. Du Bois*, ed. Herbert Aptheker (New York: Kraus-Thomson Organization Limited, 1986), 55–58; *Cleveland Gazette*, July 22, 1905; Rudwick, *W. E. B. Du Bois*, 95–97; and Lewis, *W. E. B. Du Bois*, 321–23.

90. T. Thomas Fortune actually accused Du Bois of stealing his platform of 1887. See *NYA*, July 27, 1905; and Thornbrough, *T. Thomas Fortune*, 269–70.

91. See Meier, *Negro Thought in America*, 171–89; Rudwick, *W. E. B. Du Bois*, 95; and Factor, *The Black Response to America*, 327. Paul Nelson claims that the assertive language of the Declaration of Principles was one of the things that made the Niagara Movement new and militant. See Nelson, *Frederick McGhee*, 129–30.

92. W. E. B. Du Bois, "Outline for the Committee of Safety," February 20, 1904; and Booker T. Washington to W. E. B. Du Bois, 25 February 1904, *BTWPH* 7, 451–52. See also "Constitution and By-Laws of the Niagara Movement as Adopted July 12 and 13, at Buffalo, N. Y.," in *Pamphlets and Leaflets*, ed. Herbert Aptheker, 59–62; and Lewis, *W. E. B. Du Bois*, 322.

93. "Constitution and By-Laws of the Niagara Movement" in *Pamphlets and Leaflets*, 59–62; Lewis, *W. E. B. Du Bois*, 322; and Factor, *The Black Response to America*, 327.

94. "Constitution and By-Laws of the Niagara Movement," in *Pamphlets and Leaflets*, 61–62.

95. Harlan, *Booker T. Washington*, 84–106, 86–88; Rudwick, *W. E. B. Du Bois*, 98–99; Lewis, *W. E. B. Du Bois*, 322–24; Fox, *Guardian of Boston*, 94; and Christopher E. Forth, "Booker T. Washington and the 1905 Niagara Movement Conference," *Journal of Negro History* 72 (Summer–Autumn 1987): 52–54.

96. Forth, "Booker T. Washington and the 1905 Niagara Movement Conference," 52–54; Rudwick, *W. E. B. Du Bois*, 98–99; and Fox, *Guardian of Boston*, 94. While it is

certain that Washington moved to provide a media blackout of the proceedings—and in many ways he succeeded—historians have made too much out of this issue. When the amount of coverage or mentions of the Niagara Movement's opening conference and the republication of the new group's Declaration of Principles or the Address to the Nation are examined, it is comparable to that received by other civil rights organizations such as the Afro-American League, the Afro-American Council, the National Federation of Colored Men, and the National Negro Suffrage League. Therefore, it is uncertain whether Washington's call for media silence caused the lack of information or if it was a continuation of the inability or apathetic attitude of black editors that had plagued the League and the Council throughout the existence of the organizations. For a sampling of the initial press coverage of the Niagara conference, see *CG*, July 15 and 22, 1905; *WB*, July 22 and 29, 1905; *IF*, July 29, 1905; *Appeal*, July 29, 1905; *CBA*, August 5, 1905; and *Boston Evening Transcript*, July 15, 1905.

97. "Declaration of Principles," in *Pamphlets and Leaflets*, 55–58.

98. *BAAL*, July 15, 1905. The editors of the *Baltimore Afro-American-Ledger* may have also been responding to the Committee of Twelve's involvement with the Maryland Suffrage League's challenge of disfranchise legislation. Washington had approved the work of the Committee of Twelve in the region and had encouraged the distribution of Archibald Grimké's article "Why Disfranchisement Is Bad." See Archibald H. Grimké, "Why Disfranchisement Is Bad," *Atlantic Monthly* 94 (July 1904): 72–82.

99. *BAAL*, July 15, 1905.

100. Such a position is pragmatic and in no way should it be construed as being apologetic for the roads that both Washington and some Trotterites took to discredit each other.

101. *NYA*, July 27, 1905. The lynching, which included the murder of eight individuals (seven black and one white) took place on June 29, 1905. See W. Fitzhugh Brundage, *Lynching in the New South: Georgia and Virginia, 1880–1930* (Urbana: University of Illinois Press, 1993), 275.

102. *NYA*, July 27, 1905.

103. *NYA*, August 3, 1905.

104. August Meier and Elliott Rudwick, "Negro Boycotts of Segregated Streetcars in Florida, 1901–1905," *South Atlantic Quarterly* 64 (Autumn 1970): 525–33, 527. See also August Meier and Elliott Rudwick, "The Boycott Movement Against Jim Crow Streetcars in the South, 1900–1906," *Journal of American History* 55 (March 1969): 756–75.

105. *RP*, June 10, 1905. See also Meier and Rudwick, "Negro Boycotts of Segregated Streetcars in Florida."

106. The local Council in conjunction with other area groups such as the Interdenominational Minister's Group, which launched the boycott, planned the test case. *CG*, July 8, 1905; *NYA*, July 29, 1905; *BAAL*, July 29, 1905; and Meier and Rudwick, "Negro Boycotts of Segregated Streetcars in Florida," 528–29. While trying the case in court, Wetmore also was in conversation with George J. Baldwin, president of the Jacksonville Electric Company, to try to soften the blow of the boycott. Wetmore believed that

Baldwin was against the legislation because it damaged his profits, but also understood that the boycott could anger him. So while trying the case in court, Wetmore worked in collusion with Baldwin to notify the company of the boycott and protest locations. See J. D. Wetmore to George J. Johnson, 8 June 1905 and J. D. Wetmore to George J. Baldwin, 9 June 1905, *George Johnson Baldwin Papers*, The Southern Historical Collection, University of North Carolina.

107. *BAAL*, July 29, 1905; and Meier and Rudwick, "Negro Boycotts of Segregated Streetcars in Florida," 529.

108. *NYA*, August 3, 1905; *CG*, August 12, 1905; and Meier and Rudwick, "Negro Boycotts of Segregated Streetcars in Florida," 530–31.

109. *BAAL*, July 29, 1905; *RP*, August 5, 1905; *NYA*, August 3, 1905; *CG*, August 12, 1905; and Meier and Rudwick, "Negro Boycotts of Segregated Streetcars in Florida," 531.

110. *Florida v. Patterson*, 50 Fla. 127, 127–33 (1905).

111. *WB*, December 9, 1905; Meier and Rudwick, "Negro Boycotts of Segregated Streetcars in Florida," 532.

112. *NYA*, July 27 and August 3, 1905.

113. *CG*, August 12, 1905. As noted earlier, when the *Gazette* leveled a similar accusation, it certainly had no knowledge of Washington's involvement in the Louisiana case.

114. R. W. Thompson to Emmett Scott, 28 July 1905, and Emmett Scott to R. W. Thompson, 31 July 1905, *BTWPLC*. See also Rudwick, *W. E. B. Du Bois*, 99.

115. Emmett Scott to Booker T. Washington, 7 August 1905, *BTWPH* 8, 339.

116. *Washington Bee*, August 12, 1905. See also Nelson, *Frederick McGhee*, 132; and Miller, "'A This Worldly Mission,'" 258–59.

117. *WB*, August 12, 1905. Frederick McGhee certainly conveniently forgot that he had urged Washington to attend the 1902 Council convention in St. Paul.

118. *The Advance*, August 5, 1905; and *Chicago Broad Ax*, August 12, 1905.

119. *The Advance*, August 5, 1905.

120. *NYA*, August 31, 1905.

121. *Indianapolis World*, August 19, 1905.

122. W. E. B. Du Bois, "Growth of the Niagara Movement," *Voice of the Negro* 3 (January 1906): 43. See also Rudwick, *W. E. B. Du Bois*, 97.

123. *WB*, September 9, 1905. See also Rudwick, *W. E. B. Du Bois*, 97. There was no mention of whether Waller and his fellow Niagarites were working in conjunction with the Committee of Twelve and the Maryland Suffrage League, which as has already been mentioned was aided by Washington. If such an instance did occur, it adds a bit of irony to Waller's declaration that the Niagarites would no longer be fooled by the "hypocritical leaders . . . lulling the race to sleep with cries of Peace, Peace."

124. *Detroit Informer*, September 2, 1905; *Star of Zion*, September 7, 1905; and *ISB*, September 29, 1905.

125. *CG*, September 16, 1905; *IF*, September 16, 1905; *NYA*, September 21, 1905; *ISB*, September 29, 1905; and "Afro-American Council," *AMECR* 22 (October 1905): 183–184. For further evidence in support of the argument that Washington's controlled the press

coverage of the Niagara Movement, compare the coverage of the Niagara meeting with that of the Council's 1905 convention, an organization that Washington supported. The Council meeting only had coverage in the above newspapers and journals, which is two fewer than covered the activities of the race men in the Niagara region in July.

126. "Afro-American Council," *AMECR*, 183.

127. *ISB*, September 29, 1905; and "Afro-American Council," *AMECR*, 183–84.

128. William H. Lewis, "The Legal Status of the American Negro," *Colored American Magazine* 9, no. 4 (October 1905): 546. See also *Detroit Free Press*, September 1, 1905.

129. Lewis, "Legal Status of the American Negro," 552.

130. Ibid., 553. Lewis cites Alfred Lord Tennyson's poem "Freedom" in the text of his address.

131. *Detroit Free Press*, September 1, 1905; and Mary Church Terrell, Diary Entry 31 August 1905, Mary Church Terrell Papers.

132. "Afro-American Council," *AMECR*, 184.

133. *ISB*, September 29, 1905.

134. *Detroit Informer*, September 2, 1905; *Star of Zion*, September 7, 1905; and *ISB*, September 29, 1905. A. B. Humphreys of the Constitution League did attend the Council convention. See *Star of Zion*, September 7, 1905.

135. Clarence Emery Allen, "Stick Together," *WB*, September 2, 1905.

136. *NYA*, September 14, 1905. See also *IW*, September 23, 1905; and Bruce, *Archibald Grimké*, 142–44. The editors of the *Buxton Gazette* also called for the organizations to unify. See *Buxton Gazettee*, September 14, 1905.

137. *NYA*, September 14, 1905.

138. *WB*, September 23, 1905. See also Rudwick, *W. E. B. Du Bois*, 105. Elliott Rudwick claims that Mrs. Carrie W. Clifford was the first to lay out a plan of a merger between the Council and the Niagara Movement, but he cites the *Bee* article responding to Archibald Grimké's article in the *New York Age*.

139. *WB*, September 23, 1905.

140. "The Niagara Movement," *AMECR* 22 (October 1905): 180.

141. *The Advance*, August 5, 1905.

142. Booker T. Washington to J. Douglass Wetmore, 20 September 1905, *BTWPLC*.

143. Booker T. Washington to Alexander Walters, 18 September 1905, *BTWPT*.

144. *WB*, December 9, 1905; and "Rev. L. G. Jordan Before the Afro-American Council," *Alexander's Magazine* 3 (December 15, 1906): 96.

145. "Rev. L. G. Jordan Before the Afro-American Council," *Alexander's Magazine*, 96.

146. *WB*, October 28 and November 18 and 25, 1905; and W. E. B. Du Bois, "Growth of the Niagara Movement," *Voice of the Negro* 3 (January 1906): 43–44. See also Mark Elliott, *Color-Blind Justice: Albion Tourgée and the Quest for Racial Equality from the Civil War to* Plessy v. Ferguson (New York: Oxford University Press, 2006), 313–14.

147. Du Bois, "Growth of the Niagara Movement," 19–20. These memorial services took place in at least twenty-three locations, including Hartford and Bridgeport, Connecticut; Boston, New Bedford, and Fall River, Massachusetts; Atlanta, Georgia; Chicago

and Galesburg, Illinois; Mayville, New York; Baltimore, Maryland; Washington, D.C.; Minneapolis, Minnesota; Philadelphia, Pennsylvania; and Raleigh, North Carolina.

148. Pensacola had passed a municipal ordinance by the end of September, Jacksonville by mid-October. See Meier and Rudwick, "Negro Boycotts of Segregated Streetcars in Florida," 532 and Florida v. Patterson, 50 Fla. 127, 127–33 (1905). See also Paul Ortiz. *Emancipation Betrayed: The Hidden History of Black Organizing and White Violence in Florida from Reconstruction to the Bloody Election of 1920* (Berkeley: University of California Press, 2005); and Robert Cassanello, "Avoiding 'Jim Crow:' Negotiating Separate and Equal on Florida's Railroads and Streetcars and the Progressive Era Origins of the Modern Civil Rights Movement," *Journal of Urban History* 34 (March 2008): 435–57.

149. Meier and Rudwick, "Negro Boycotts of Segregated Streetcars in Florida," 532.

150. *NYA*, December 7, 1905; and *WB*, December 9, 1905.

151. *NYA*, December 7, 1905.

152. Ibid.

153. *BAAL*, November 25, 1905.

154. *WB*, December 9, 1905.

155. Meier and Rudwick, "Negro Boycotts of Segregated Streetcars in Florida," 533.

156. *NYA*, February 8, 1906.

157. *LAT*, November 21, 1905.

158. James Alexander to George C. Pardee, 11 December 1905, and Floyd H. Crumbly, 12 December 1905, *George C. Pardee Papers*, Bancroft Library, University of California, Berkeley; *LAT*, December 8, 1905; and Douglas Flamming, *Bound for Freedom: Black Los Angeles in Jim Crow America* (Berkeley: University of California Press, 2005), 132.

159. *IW*, November 18, 1905; John D. Swain, "A Protest Against Dixonism," *VN* 2, no. 12 (December 1905): 282–85; and NYA, December 28, 1905. For a critique of Dixon, see Kelly Miller's September 1905 open letter to Reverend Dixon, "As to the Leopard's Spots," in *Race Adjustment & The Everlasting Stain* (1908; rpr. 1928, New York: Arno Press, 1968), 28–56.

160. *NYA*, December 28, 1905.

161. Du Bois, "Growth of the Niagara Movement," 44–45.

162. Ibid. 45.

CHAPTER 8. "IT IS STRIKE NOW OR NEVER"

Epigraph. T. Thomas Fortune, "Let Us Organize Our Strength," *NYA*, July 12, 1906. W. E. B. Du Bois, "We Claim Our Rights," Philip S. Foner, *W. E. B. Du Bois Speaks: Speeches and Addresses, 1890–1919* (New York: Pathfinder, 1970), 173.

1. W. E. B. Du Bois, "Growth of the Niagara Movement," *VN* 3 (January 1906): 44.

2. *NYA*, January 18 and February 8 and 22, 1906.

3. *NYA*, February 8 and 22, 1906. Additionally, Jordan began discussions with Emmett Scott and Booker T. Washington about creating a "semi-monthly paper in the interest of the Council" to promote the organization's efforts and to counter Du Bois's "mouthpiece of the Niagara Movement," *The Moon*. See Lewis G. Jordan to Emmett Jay Scott, 12 February 1906, *BTWPH* 8, 520–21.

4. John Milholland Diary, 1 December 190 and 11 February 1906, *John Milholland Papers*. Brian W. Blaesser, "John E. Milholland" (senior thesis, Brown University, 1969), 58–66.

5. A. B. Humphrey, "Statement of Principles of the Constitution League," 22 January 1906, *W. E. B. Du Bois Papers*.

6. John Milholland Diary, 11 February 1906, *John Milholland Papers*. See also *NYT*, February 2, 1906; *NYA*, February 8, 1906; and Blaesser, "John E. Milholland," 59.

7. *NYT*, February 2, 1906; *New York Tribune*, February 2, 1905; and *NYA*, February 8, 1906.

8. John E. Milholland, *The Nation's Duty* (New York: Constitution League, 1906), 5–6; and *NYA*, February 8, 1906. See also Blaesser. "John E. Milholland," 60–61; and John E. Milholland, *The Negro and the Nation* (New York: Moore, 1905).

9. *NYA*, February 8, 1906; and *NYT*, February 2, 1906. See also John Milholland Diary, 11 February 1906, *John Milholland Papers*. Mary Church Terrell, *A Colored Woman in a White World* (1940; rpr. New York: Arno Press, 1980), 212.

10. *NYA*, February 8, 1906.

11. Ibid. See also Blaesser, "John E. Milholland," 62–63; and John Milholland Diary, 11 February 1906, *John Milholland Papers*.

12. John Milholland Diary, 11 February 1906, *John Milholland Papers*; Blaesser, "John E. Milholland," 72.

13. Blaesser, "John E. Milholland," 68.

14. "The Constitution League," *VN* 3, no. 4 (April 1906): 239. See also "Southern Representation," *VN*. 3, no. 4 (April 1906): 242–43; and General Secretary to Colleagues, 13 June 1906, *W. E. B. Du Bois Papers*.

15. *Jacksonville Florida Times-Union*, February 7, 1906; Patterson v. Taylor, 51 Fla. 275, 275–85 (1906); and Crooms v. Schad, 51 Fla. 168, 168–176 (1906). See also August Meier and Elliott Rudwick, "Negro Boycotts of Segregated Streetcars in Florida, 1901–1905," *South Atlantic Quarterly* 69, no. 4 (Autumn 1970): 532–33. Shortly after the decision Wetmore relocated to New York, which certainly diminished any hope of his working closely with another appeal.

16. *NYA*, February 8, 1906.

17. *WB*, February 10, 1906; *BAAL*, February 10, 1906; *NYA*, February 22, 1906. The *Baltimore Afro-American Ledger* refused to publish the full circular because of its length and because the Council sent insufficient funds to subsidize the use of space in the paper.

18. *NYA*, February 22, 1906.

19. Booker T. Washington to Bishop Alexander Walters, 1 March 1906, *BTWPH* 8, 535. See also "Rev. L. G. Jordan Before the Afro-American Council," *Alexander's Magazine* 3 (December 15, 1906): 97.

20. Bishop Alexander Walters to Booker T. Washington, 7 and 21 March 1906, *BTWPLC*; Booker T. Washington to Bishop Alexander Walters, 13 March 1906, *BTWPLC* and Emmett Scott to J. Douglas Wetmore, 15 March 1906, *BTWPLC.*

21. August Meier and Elliott Rudwick, "Negro Boycotts of Segregated Streetcars in Virginia, 1904–1907," *Virginia Magazine of History and Biography* 81, no. 4 (October 1973): 479–87. See also Blair Murphy Kelley, *Right to Ride: Streetcar Boycotts and African American Citizenship in the Era of* Plessy v. Ferguson (Chapel Hill: University of North Carolina Press, 2010).

22. Meier and Rudwick, "Negro Boycotts of Segregated Streetcars Virginia," 486–87.

23. *RP*, May 28, 1904. See also Meier and Rudwick, "Negro Boycotts of Segregated Streetcars Virginia," 485.

24. "*I Will Walk*," *AMECR* 22, no. 4 (April 1906): 387. See also Bishop Alexander Walters to Booker T. Washington, 7 and 21 March 1906, *BTWPLC*; Booker T. Washington to Bishop Alexander Walters, 13 March 1906, *BTWPLC*; and Emmett Scott to J. Douglas Wetmore, 15 March 1906, *BTWPLC*. The *New York Age* reported that the Newport News community was still boycotting the streetcars in late summer 1907. *NYA*, August 1, 1907. See also August Meier and Elliott Rudwick, "Negro Boycotts of Segregated Streetcars in Virginia," 487.

25. Charles Alexander, "The Afro-American Council," *Alexander's Magazine* 2, **no.** 3 (July 15, 1906): 22.

26. Ibid.

27. *NYA*, June 28, 1906.

28. Alexander, "The Afro-American Council," 26.

29. Ibid., 27.

30. Ibid., 22.

31. William A. Sinclair, *The Aftermath of Slavery* (New York: Arno Press, 1969); and *AME Church Review* 22, no. 2 (October 1905): 124–29, 124.

32. Sinclair, *The Aftermath of Slavery*, 215–58.

33. Alexander, "The Afro-American Council," 22–23.

34. Charles Alexander republished a number of the responses in his promotional piece on the Council. See Alexander, "The Afro-American Council," 23–26.

35. *NYA*, June 28, 1906; W. E. B. Du Bois, *Pamphlets and Leaflets*, ed. Herbert Aptheker (White Plains, N.Y.: Kraus-Thomson Organization, 1986), 67–68. The poem printed at the end of the appeal is from "What I Live For," by George L. Banks.

36. Du Bois, *Pamphlets and Leaflets*, 55–62, 67–68; and Du Bois, "The Niagara Movement," *VN* 3, no. 7 (July 1906): 476. See also General Secretary to Colleagues, 13 June 1906, *W. E. B. Du Bois Papers*.

37. "The Niagara Movement," *VN* 3, no. 7 (July 1906), 476.

38. J. Max Barber, "The Niagara Movement at Harper's Ferry," *VN* 3, no. 10 (October 1906): 408.

39. *Congregationalist*, April 7, 1906; Du Bois, *Pamphlets and Leaflets*, 66.

40. Du Bois, *Pamphlets and Leaflets*, 66.

41. "The Foraker Amendment to 'Rate Bill,'" *VN* 3, no. 7 (July 1906): 522. See also Percy E. Murray, "Harry C. Smith–Joseph B. Foraker Alliance: Coalition Politics in Ohio," *Journal of Negro History* 68 (Spring 1983), 176; and Michael Perman, *Struggle for Mastery: Disfranchisement in the South, 1888–1908* (Chapel Hill: University of North Carolina Press, 2001), 262–63. See also General Secretary to Colleagues, 13 June 1906, *W. E. B. Du Bois Papers*.

42. *NYA*, August 2, 1906; Barber, "The Niagara Movement at Harper's Ferry," *VN*, 406, 408; Perman, *Struggle for Mastery*, 263; and Stephen R. Fox, *The Guardian of Boston: William Monroe Trotter* (New York: Atheneum, 1971), 101. Barber credits the Illinois and Massachusetts branches for the protest against the Warner–Foraker amendment, but if one reads the article published by Kelly Miller and Archibald Grimké in the *New York Age*, it is obvious that it was a joint effort between members of all the civil rights organizations. See also Dickson D. Bruce, Jr., *Archibald Grimké: Portrait of a Black Independent* (Baton Rouge: Louisiana State University Press, 1993), 150–53.

43. "The Niagara Movement," *VN*, 476.

44. *NYA*, July 5 and 19, 1906. See also *NYA*, July 12, 1906.

45. Alexander, "The Afro-American Council," 26–27.

46. Ibid., 27.

47. *NYA*, July 19, 1906.

48. Ibid. See also Steven Hahn, *A Nation Under Our Feet: Black Political Struggles in the Rural South from Slavery to the Great Migration* (Cambridge, Mass.: Harvard University Press, 2003). Hahn does not discuss any activity of the Afro-American Council in the South.

49. *NYA*, July 19 and 26, 1906 and August 2 and 9, 1906.

50. *LAT*, August 28 and 30, 1906; James Alexander, "Appeal to Reason," attached to J. B. Wilson to George C. Pardee, 25 June 1906 and "Official Call of the Afro-American State Congress, to Convene at Riverside, California, August 27–29, 1906, *George C. Pardee Papers*, Bancroft Library, University of California, Berkeley; Douglas Flamming, *Bound for Freedom: Black Los Angeles in Jim Crow America* (Berkeley: University of California Press, 2005), 133–34; and James A. Fisher, "A History of the Political and Social Development of the Black Community in California, 1850–1950" (PhD diss., State University of New York at Stony Brook, 1971), 164–65.

51. *NYA*, July 26, 1906.

52. *NYA*, August 8, 1906. Disfranchisement also became an issue for the Niagara Movement as the date for its Harper's Ferry meeting drew closer. Claiming it was going to fight against the unjust suffrage legislation, the organization suffered a public relations setback when it was disclosed that two of the Movement's leaders, Du Bois and Lafayette M. Hershaw, a charter member of the Niagara Movement, had failed to pay their poll

taxes in their home state of Georgia. Many asked a simple question: why would individuals who asked blacks to stand up for their manhood rights essentially disfranchise themselves? Although the posing of the question was likely an attempt to discredit the two Niagara leaders, neither Du Bois nor Hershaw responded to the allegation, and the contradiction hung over the Harper's Ferry meeting. The failure of Du Bois and Hershaw to pay their poll tax would become more of an issue the following year as blacks in Georgia organized to get all eligible black male voters to mobilize against the Georgia legislature's attempts to institute more broad-based disfranchisement legislation. Du Bois and Hershaw never paid their poll tax, and curiously they never gave a reason for their failure to do so. Hershaw could have responded as he had relocated to Washington, D.C. See *NYA*, August 2, 1906. See also *NYA*, August 23, 1906.

53. *WB*, August 25, 1906; *Guardian*, August 25, 1906; *NYA*, August 23, 1906; *CG*, August 25, 1906; Barber, "The Niagara Movement at Harper's Ferry," *VN*, 402–11; Elliott Rudwick, *W. E. B. Du Bois: Voice of the Black Protest Movement* (Urbana: University of Illinois Press, 1982), 102–3; Manning Marable, *W. E. B. Du Bois: Black Radical Democrat* (New York: Twayne, 1986), 56–57; Stephen R. Fox, *Guardian of Boston*, 101–3; David Levering Lewis, *W. E. B. Du Bois: Biography of a Race, 1868–1919* (New York: H. Holt, 1993), 328–30; and Annetta L. Gomez-Jefferson, *The Sage of Tawawa: Reverdy Cassius Ransom, 1861–1959* (Kent, Ohio: Kent State University Press, 2002), 89–91.

54. Reverdy Ransom, "The Spirit of John Brown," in Reverdy Ransom, *Making the Gospel Plain: The Writings of Bishop Reverdy Ransom*, ed. Anthony B. Pinn (Harrisburg, Pa.: Trinity Press, 1999), 100–101.

55. W. E. B. Du Bois, "The Word," Reverdy C. Ransom, "*The Negro: The Hope or the Despair of Christianity* (Boston: Ruth Hill, 1935), cited in Gomez-Jefferson, *The Sage of Tawawa*, 91. See also Barber, "The Niagara Movement at Harper's Ferry," *VN*, 408.

56. Paul D. Nelson, *Frederick L. McGhee: A Life on the Color Line, 1861–1912* (Minneapolis: Minnesota Historical Society Press, 2002), 157. See also *Washington Bee*, August 25, 1906; and Arthur S. Gray (recorder), Minutes of Meeting, 18 August 1906, *W. E. B. Du Bois Papers*.

57. *WB*, August 25, 1906.

58. Ibid., and Arthur S. Gray (recorder), Minutes of Meeting, 18 August 1906, *W. E. B. Du Bois Papers*.

59. Nelson, *Frederick McGhee*, 160. See also *Pope v. Commonwealth of Virginia*, January 9, 1907, *Virginia Supreme Court of Appeals Order Book*, no. 34, 83; and J. Max Barber, "McGhee," *VN* 3, no. 11 (November 1906): 468.

60. *BAAL*, March 25, 1905; Daniel Murray, "The Overthrow of Jim Crow Car Laws," *VN* 3, no. 7 (July 1906): 521–22; and Perman, *Struggle for Mastery*, 256, 262. See also Arthur S. Gray (recorder), Minutes of Meeting, 18 August 1906, *W. E. B. Du Bois Papers*.

61. *NYA*, August 23, 1906; *WB*, August 25, 1906; *CG*, August 25, 1906; and "The Niagara Movement," *Alexander's Magazine* 2, no. 5 (September 15, 1906): 18–19. See also Philip S. Foner, *W. E. B. Du Bois Speaks: Speeches and Addresses, 1890–1919*, 170–73, 170–71;

W. E. B. Du Bois, *Pamphlets and Leaflets*, 63–65; Nelson, *Frederick McGhee*, 157–59; and Lewis, *W. E. B. Du Bois*, 330.

62. Foner, *W. E. B. Du Bois Speaks*, 172.

63. Ibid, 173. See also Lewis, *W. E. B. Du Bois*, 330.

64. Foner, *W. E. B. Du Bois Speaks*, 173.

65. *WB*, August 18, 1906; *Indianapolis Freeman*, August 23, 1906; and *NYA*, August 30, 1906.

66. Alexander Walters, "The Afro-American Council and Its Work," *The Colored American Magazine* 11, no. 3 (September 1906): 207.

67. Ibid.

68. Ibid., 210–11.

69. *WB*, June 30, July 14, and August 18, 1906; and *NYA*, August 30, 1906. See also Rudwick, *W. E. B. Du Bois*, 105. There was no criticism of W. Calvin Chase's position published in the *Bee* or any other paper, but he may have received letters responding to his comments that urged him to reconsider the organizations that needed to be unified. Like Chase, T. Thomas Fortune argued for the unification of the Niagara Movement and the Council. The Business League was left out of the discussion.

70. *WB*, August 18, 1906; *NYA*, September 6 and 13, 1906; and Walters, "The Afro-American Council and Its Work," 211.

71. *NYA*, September 6, 1906; and "Report on Brownsville Affray," *Senate Documents*, 59th Cong., 2 Sess., No. 155. See also Emma Lou Thornbrough, "The Brownsville Episode and the Negro Vote," *Mississippi Valley Historical Review* 44, no. 3, (December 1957): 469–93; James Tinsley, "Roosevelt, Foraker, and the Brownsville Affray," *Journal of Negro History* 61 (January 1956): 43–65; Ann J. Lane, *The Brownsville Affair; National Crisis and Black Reaction* (Port Washington, N.Y.: Kennikat Press, 1971); John D. Weaver, *The Brownsville Raid* (New York: Norton, 1970); and John D. Weaver, *The Senator and the Sharecropper's Son: Exoneration of the Brownsville Soldiers* (College Station: Texas A&M University Press, 1997). See also Factor, *The Black Response to America*, 330–34; Lewis, *W. E. B. Du Bois*, 330–32.

72. *NYA*, August 2 and September 6, 1906.

73. *NYA*, September 6, 1906.

74. *NYA*, September 27, 1906; and *New York World*, September 28, 1906. See also Mark Bauerlein, *Negrophobia: A Race Riot in Atlanta, 1906* (San Francisco: Encounter, 2001); Ray Stannard Baker, *Following the Color Line* (New York: Doubleday, 1908); Harlan, *Booker T. Washington*, 295–310; and Factor, *The Black Response to America*, 328–30. See also Gregory Mixon, *The Atlanta Riot: Race, Class, and Violence in a New South City* (Gainesville: University Press of Florida, 2005).

75. Bauerlein, *Negrophobia*; Factor, *The Black Response to America*, 329.

76. John Greenleaf Whittier, "Howard at Atlanta," in *Anti-Slavery Poems: Songs of Labor and Reform* (1888; rpr. New York: Arno Press, 1969). This stanza was used by Du Bois as the epigraph to his essay "Of the Wings of Atalanta," in *Souls of Black Folk*. See W. E. B. Du Bois, *The Souls of Black Folk*, ed. David W. Blight and Robert

Gooding-Williams (Boston: Bedford Books, 1997), 82. Whittier was an abolitionist. The poem was written in honor of General Oliver Otis Howard who commanded one corps of Sherman's forces as they captured Atlanta in September 1864.

77. W. E. B. Du Bois, "Litany of Atlanta," *Independent* 61 (1906): 856–58; and *Cleveland Gazette*, November 10, 1906. See also W. E. B. Du Bois, "The Tragedy of Atlanta. From the Point of View of the Negroes," *World Today* 11 (November 1906): 1173–75.

78. J. Max Barber, "The Atlanta Tragedy," *VN* 3, no. 11 (November 1906): 473–79, 473. See also Mixon, *The Atlanta Riot.*

79. *New York World*, September 25, 1906. See also *BTWPH* 9, 74–75; and Harlan, *Booker T. Washington*, 299.

80. Harlan, *Booker T. Washington*, 301.

81. Booker T. Washington to Charles Anderson, 4 October 1906, *BTWPLC.*

82. Theodore Roosevelt to Booker T. Washington, 8 October 1906, *BTWPLC*; and Harlan, *Booker T. Washington*, 300.

83. *NYA*, October 4, 1906; William L. Hunter, *Jesus Christ Had Negro Blood in His Veins* (Brooklyn: Hunter, 1901). Hunter's pamphlet went through nine editions between 1901 and 1913.

84. *WB*, November 10, 1906; and "Rev. L. G. Jordan Before the Afro-American Council," *Alexander's Magazine* 3, no. 2 (December 15, 1906): 96–100.

85. *WB*, November 10, 1906.

86. *NYA*, October 11, 1906. See also George Mason Miller, " 'A This Worldly Mission': The Life and Career of Alexander Walters (1858–1917)" (PhD diss., State University of New York at Stony Brook, 1984), 269; and *NYT*, October 10, 1906.

87. *NYA*, October 11, 1906. Such support for the work of the Constitution League and the Niagara Movement was important, as members of both groups were present—John Milholland and A. B. Humphrey for the Constitution League, and L. M. Hershaw for the Niagara Movement.

88. *NYT*, October 11, 1906; *New York Tribune*, October 11, 1906; *New York World*, October 11, 1906; and *NYA*, October 18, 1906. See also John Milholland Diary, 8–13 October 1906, *John Milholland Papers*; and Blaesser, "John E. Milholland," 72–73.

89. *NYA*, October 10, 1906. See also *NYT*, October 10, 1906.

90. *NYA*, October 10, 1906.

91. *New York Tribune*, October 11, 1906; *New York World*, October 11, 1906; *NYA*, October 11 and 18, 1906; Water F. Walker, "The Afro-American Council," *Alexander's Magazine* 3, no. 1 (November 15, 1906): 16–18.

92. Oswald Garrison Villard, "The Aims of the Afro-American Council," *The Colored American Magazine* 11 (November 1906): 349–53, 351.

93. *NYA*, October 18, 1906; *WP*, October, 12, 1906; and *Atlanta Constitution*, October 22, 1906. See also *BTWPH* 9, 94–96.

94. *NYA*, October 18, 1906.

95. *WB*, October 20, 1906.

96. *NYT*, October 11, 1906; and *Weekly Guide*, October 20, 1906. See also Miller, "'A This Worldly Mission,'" 272.

97. Blaesser, "John E. Milholland," 73.

98. Booker T. Washington to Charles Anderson, 17 October 1906, *BTWPLC*. See also John Milholland Diary, 8–13 October 1906, *John Milholland Papers*; and Blaesser. "John E. Milholland," 73.

99. *NYA*, October 11 and 18, 1906; and Emma Lou Thornbrough, *T. Thomas Fortune: Militant Journalist* (Chicago, University of Chicago Press, 1972), 280.

100. "Co-operation vs. Antagonism," *Alexander's Magazine* 2, no. 6 (October 15, 1906): 12–13. In hindsight, the National Association of Colored Women's Clubs, an organization that was gaining strength during the same time, should have been included in the *Alexander's Magazine* list of influential groups needing to unify. See Paula Giddings, *When and Where I Enter: The Impact of Black Women on Race and Sex in America* (New York: Bantam Books, 1985); and Deborah Gray White, *Too Heavy a Load: Black Women in Defense of Themselves, 1894–1994* (New York: W. W. Norton, 1999).

101. John Milholland Diary, 8–13 October 1906, *John Milholland Papers*; and Blaesser, "John E. Milholland," 72.

102. *NYA*, November 8, 1906. See also John Milholland Diary, 22 and 28 October 1906, *John Milholland Papers*; and Blaesser, "John E. Milholland," 73–76.

103. Weaver, *Brownsville Raid*, 97; Thornbrough, "Brownsville Episode and the Negro Vote"; Thornbrough, *T. Thomas Fortune*, 281–82; Tinsley, "Roosevelt, Foraker, and the Brownsville Affray"; Lane, *Brownsville Affair*; Factor, *The Black Response to America*, 330–34; Lewis, *W. E. B. Du Bois*, 330–32; and Harlan, *Booker T. Washington*, 309–10.

104. Harlan, *Booker T. Washington*, 309–10, 310. Washington wrote to his friend and confidant Charles Anderson, "Of course I am at a disadvantage in that I must keep my lips closed. The enemy will, as usual, to try to blame me for all this. They can talk, I cannot . . . ." See Booker T. Washington to Charles Anderson, 7 November 1906, *BTWPH* 9, 118.

105. *NYA*, November 8, 1906. See also Thornbrough, *T. Thomas Fortune*, 282–83.

106. *CG*, December 1, 1906; *IF*, December 8, 1906; Thornbrough, *T. Thomas Fortune*, 284. See also Miller, "'A This Worldly Mission,'" 265. Wetmore enlisted Alexander S. Bacon who also worked with the Constitution League. See *NYT*, January 3 and 7, 1907.

107. Blaesser, "John E. Milholland," 82–84; and Thornbrough, *T. Thomas Fortune*, 284. See also Miller, "'A This Worldly Mission,'" 265.

108. Terrell, *A Colored Woman in a White World*, 269, 271; John Milholland Diary, 18 and 28 November 1906, *John Milholland Papers*; and Blaesser, "John E. Milholland," 82–83. See also *WP*, November 18, 1906; and *Washington Evening Star*, November 18, 1906.

109. Gilchrist Stewart to Theodore Roosevelt, 29 November 1906, *Theodore Roosevelt Papers*, *NYT*, November 22, 1906; *NYA*, November 29, 1906; and Preliminary Report of Commission of the Constitution League of the United States on the Affray at Brownsville, Tex., 59th Cong. 2nd Sess., Senate Document 107. See also Blaesser. "John E. Milholland," 84.

110. Weaver, *The Brownsville Raid*, 103–44; and Lane, *The Brownsville Affair*, 28. See also Blaesser, "John E. Milholland," 86–87; Constitution League, *Inquiry Relative to Certain Companies of the Twenty-Fifth United States Infantry* (New York, 1906); and Preliminary Report of Commission of the Constitution League.

111. Horace Samuel Merrill and Marion Galbraith Merrill, *Republican Command, 1897–1913*, (Lexington: University Press of Kentucky, 1971), 241–42. See also Thomas Dyer, *Theodore Roosevelt and the Idea of Race* (Baton Rouge: Louisiana State University Press, 1980), 109–17; and Kelly Miller, "Roosevelt and the Negro," *Race Adjustment: Essays on Negro America* (1908; rpr. New York: Arno Press, 1969), 299–310.

112. Merrill and Merrill, *Republican Command*, 241–42. See also Harlan, *Booker T. Washington*, 319–20.

113. *WB*, December 29, 1906; and *WP*, December 21, 1906. See also *ISB*, December 7, 1906 and January 4, 1907.

114. *NYT*, January 3, 1907; *WB*, January 8, 1907; *WP*, January 8 and 11, 1907; and Thornbrough, *T. Thomas Fortune*, 284–85. The meeting was held at the AME Zion Church of S. L. Corrothers, a member of the Niagara Movement. Niagarite L. M. Hershaw was also present. Alexander S. Bacon and J. Douglas Wetmore drew up the report that was sent to Senator Foraker. See *NYT*, January 3, 1907.

115. *AMECR* 18, no. 3 (January 1907): 279–80

116. *WB*, January 9, 1907.

117. *WB*, January 9 and February 16, 1907; and *NYA*, January 17, 1907. See also Thornbrough, *T. Thomas Fortune*, 285; Booker T. Washington to James A. Cobb, 9 January 1907 and James A. Cobb to Booker T. Washington, 14 January 1907, *BTWPLC*.

118. At the same time the Constitution League held a rally in New York at Cooper Union. Members of both the Niagara Movement and the Afro-American Council were in attendance. See Blaesser, "John E. Milholland," 91–92. See also Charles W. Anderson to Booker T. Washington, 4 January 1907, *BTWPH* 9, 181–82.

119. Cong. Recc, 60th Cong., 1st Sess., 3122–24.

120. *WB*, February 16, 1907.

121. Ibid.

122. Ibid.

123. Ibid.

124. Meier, *Negro Thought in America*, 182. See also Miller, "'A This Worldly Mission,'" 273.

125. Booker T. Washington to James A. Cobb, 14 January 1907, *BTWPLC*; and James A. Cobb to Emmett Scott, 16 January 1907, *BTWPLC*; and Circular Letter from Jordan, 12 April 1907, *BTWPLC*.

126. Pope v. Commonwealth of Virginia, January 9, 1907, *Virginia Supreme Court of Appeals Order Book*, no. 34, 83.

127. Nelson, *Frederick L. McGhee*, 160.

128. Niagara Movement Circular Letter, 10 April 1907, *W. E. B. Du Bois Papers*. See also Nelson, *Frederick L. McGhee*, 160.

129. *CG*, May 25, 1907. See also *NYA*, June 13, 1907.

130. Alexander Walters to Booker T. Washington, 14 June 1907, *BTWPLC*; and Booker T. Washington to Alexander Walters, 18 June 1907, *BTWPLC*.

131. *WB*, June 27, 1907. See also Miller, "'A This Worldly Mission,'" 275.

132. *WB*, July 6, 1907.

133. *Washington Evening Star*, June 27, 1907; *WB*, July 6, 1907; and *WP*, June 27, 28, and 29 1907. See also Miller, "'A This Worldly Mission,'" 275.

134. *Washington Evening Star*, June 27, 1907. See also Miller, "'A This Worldly Mission,'" 275.

135. *WB*, July 6, 1907.

136. *Washington Evening* Star, June 27, 1907. See also Miller, "'A This Worldly Mission,'" 276.

137. *WB*, July 6, 1907; and *Washington Evening* Star, June 28, 1907.

138. Melvin Chisum to Booker T. Washington, 5 July 1907, *BTWPLC*.

139. *WB*, July 6, 1907. This uncovering of the spies is ironic since Chisum had been instrumental in getting the *Bee* to soften its anti-Washington stance the previous year. See Louis R. Harlan, "The Secret Life of Booker T. Washington," *The Journal of Southern History* 37, no. 3 (1971): 393–416.

140. *CG*, July 27, 1907.

141. *WB*, June 29, 1906 and *Baltimore Sun*, June 29, 1906. The coverage seems to indicate that W. Calvin Chase had something personal against William Hart. He attacked him for failing to hire black lawyers in his suit as well as all those who supported Hart's nomination. In the end, despite the nomination of a few other candidates, Bishop Walters, who was clearly annoyed with Chase, a constant critic of the Council, declared an end to the debate and named Hart the director of the Legal Bureau.

142. *WB*, July 6, 1906.

143. *Horizon* 2, no. 1 (July 1907): 20.

144. *CG*, July 20, 1907.

145. *WB*, July 6, 1906.

146. "Third Annual Meeting of the Niagara Movement," in Du Bois, *Pamphlets and Leaflets*, 74–76, 75. See also *CG*, September 7, 1907. Keeping with the symbolic imagery, the Niagarites made pilgrimages to the homes of William Lloyd Garrison and John Greenleaf Whittier.

147. "Third Annual Meeting of the Niagara Movement," in Du Bois, *Pamphlets and Leaflets*, 76.

148. "Department of Civil Rights Supplement to the Department's Annual Report for 1906–1907," in Du Bois, *Pamphlets and Leaflets*, 69–73.

149. "Niagara Movement Minutes" (Boston Mass., 1907 August 26–29), *W. E. B. Du Bois Papers*.

150. Ibid. See also Rudwick, *W. E. B. Du Bois*, 110. Socialism was a topic of discussion for Du Bois and member of the Movement in 1907. See, e.g., W. E. B. Du Bois,

"Socialist of the Path," *Horizon* 1 (February 1907); and Du Bois, "A Field for Socialists," *W. E. B. Du Bois Papers.*

151. Rudwick, *W. E. B. Du Bois*, 109. For information on Washington's attacks, see August Meier, "Booker T. Washington and the Rise of the NAACP," *The Crisis* 61 (February 1954): 69–76, 117–23; and Harlan, *Booker T. Washington*, 84–106, 295–337. See also Booker T. Washington to Richard L. Stokes, 27 August 1906 *BTWPH* 9, 62 and James A. Cobb to Booker T. Washington 26 August 1906 *BTWPLC*; and James A. Cobb to Emmett J. Scott, 5 September 1907 *BTWPH* 9, 334.

152. "A Brief Resume of the Massachusetts Trouble in the Niagara Movement," *W. E. B. Du Bois Papers*; Fox, *Guardian of Boston*, 104–5; Lewis, *W. E. B. Du Bois: Biography of a Race*, 340–41; and Rudwick, *W. E. B. Du Bois*, 109, 111–12. See also "Niagara Movement Minutes" (Boston Mass., 1907 August 26–29), *W. E. B. Du Bois Papers.*

153. "Third Annual Meeting of the Niagara Movement," in Du Bois, *Pamphlets and Leaflets*, 74, 75–76. The Movement was $250 dollars in the red after its two years of existence.

154. Ibid., 75–76.

155. J. Milton Waldron to W. E. B. Du Bois, 11 February 1908, *W. E. B. Du Bois Papers.*

156. W. E. B. Du Bois, "To Black Voters," *Horizon* (February 1908): 7; and W. E. B. Du Bois, "Bryan," *Horizon* (March 1908): 7. See also *NYA*, April 2, 1908; and Lewis, *W. E. B. Du Bois*, 341.

157. *Guardian*, July 23, 1908. See also Michael Kazin, *A Godly Hero: The Life of William Jennings Bryan* (New York: Knopf, 2006), 161.

158. *CG*, February 1, 1908. See also Miller, "'A This Worldly Mission,'" 298–305.

159. A frustrated Du Bois contemplated his resignation at the annual convention in Boston and again in December 1907. He wrote his resignation letter and had received a letter from Frederick McGhee agreeing to assume his post. Neither letter was sent. See "Niagara Movement Minutes," (Boston Mass., 1907 August 26–29), *W. E. B. Du Bois Papers*; W. E. B. Du Bois to J. Milton Waldron, 6 December 1907, *W. E. B. Du Bois Papers*; and W. E. B. Du Bois to the Niagara Movement Executive Committee, n. d., 1907, *W. E. B. Du Bois Papers.*

160. *Guardian*, March 21 and April 11, 1908; Alexander Walters to W. E. B. Du Bois, 31 March and 4 April 1908, *W. E. B. Du Bois Papers*; and W. E. B. Du Bois to Alexander Walters, 7 and 16 April and 12 June 1908; *W. E. B. Du Bois Papers.* See also Miller, "'A This Worldly Mission,'" 305–6; Rudwick, *W. E. B. Du Bois*, 114–15; Fox, *Guardian of Boston*, 111; and Connie Park Rice, "'For Men and Measures': The Life and Legacy of Civil Rights Pioneer J. R. Clifford" (PhD diss., West Virginia University, 2007), 131–33.

161. *Guardian*, April 11, 1908; Fox, *Guardian of Boston*, 110–14; and Mark R. Schneider, *Boston Confronts Jim Crow, 1890–1920* (Boston: Northeastern University Press, 1997), 115–16. See also W. E. B. Du Bois to Alexander Walters, 16 April 1908. *W. E. B. Du Bois Papers.*

162. W. E. B. Du Bois to Alexander Walters, 16 April 1908 *W. E. B. Du Bois Papers.* See also Rudwick, *W. E. B. Du Bois*, 115; and Miller, "'A This Worldly Mission,'" 306.

163. In 1908, Du Bois announced to Niagara members that Frederick McGhee had initiated another railcar segregation case, but there is no evidence that such a case was ever instituted. Again in 1909 Du Bois announced to members of the Movement that the group was working on a legal case in South Carolina, but there is no record of such a case. In the same year, Frederick McGhee told the delegates at the annual meeting at Sea Island, New Jersey, that the legal department was "unable to do anything owing to lack of funds." Frederick McGhee, "Report of the Fifth Annual Niagara Movement Convention," 14 August 1909, *W. E. B. Du Bois Papers*. See also "Dear Colleagues," in Du Bois, *Pamphlets and Leaflets*, 77, 79; and Nelson, *Frederick L. McGhee*, 164, 166.

164. Bishop Walters to W. E. B. Du Bois, 19 March, 1908, *W. E. B. Du Bois Papers*; Bishop Walters to W. E. B. Du Bois, 11 April 1908, *W. E. B. Du Bois Papers*; and W. E. B. Du Bois to Bishop Walters, 16 April 1908, *W. E. B. Du Bois Papers*.

165. W. E. B. Du Bois to Niagara Movement Colleagues, 14 March 1908, *W. E. B. Du Bois Papers*.

166. Marable, *W. E. B. Du Bois*, 69.

167. "Dear Colleagues," in Du Bois, *Pamphlets and Leaflets*, 77; and W. E. B. Du Bois, "Union," *Horizon* 3 (June 1908): 5–6. See also Nelson, *Frederick L. McGhee*, 164; Marable, *W. E. B. Du Bois*, 69–70; and Factor, *The Black Response to America*, 338.

168. W. E. B. Du Bois, "Union," 5–6.

169. William English Walling, "The Race War in the North," *Independent* 65 (September 3, 1908): 529–34; Charles F. Kellogg, *N.A.A.C.P.: A History of the National Association for the Advancement of Colored People, 1909–1920* (Baltimore: Johns Hopkins Press, 1967), 12; and Mary White Ovington, *The Walls Came Tumbling Down* (New York: Harcourt, Brace and Co., 1947), 103. See also August Meier and John H. Bracey, "The NAACP As a Reform Movement, 1909–1965: 'To Reach the Conscience of America,'" *The Journal of Southern History* 59 (February 1993): 3–30; Langston Hughes, *Fight for Freedom: The Story of the NAACP* (New York: Norton, 1962); and Patricia Sullivan, *Lift Every Voice: The NAACP and the Making of the Civil Rights Movement* (New York: New Press, 2009).

170. *Proceedings of the National Negro Conference, 1909* (New York: Arno Press, 1969).

171. Thornbrough, "Afro-American League," 511.

172. *Proceedings of the National Negro Conference*, 222–24.

173. Meier, *Negro Thought in America*, 183.

174. *NYG*, December 20, 1883.

EPILOGUE

Epigraph. Constitution of the African American League, January 1890, *Official Compilation of Proceedings of the Afro-American League National Convention, January 15, 16, 17, 1890* (Chicago: Battles and Cabbell, 1890), 38; W. E. B. Du Bois, *The Amenia Conference:*

An Historic Negro Gathering (Troutbeck Press, New York, September 1925.), in W. E. B. Du Bois, *Pamphlets and Leaflets*, ed. Herbert Aptheker (White Plains, N.Y.: Kraus-Thomson Organization, 1986), 211.

1. *Amsterdam News*, June 6, 1928. The *Amsterdam News* lists the Council in the obituary, but the time line of the paragraph demonstrates that the newspaper meant the League. The *Amsterdam News* mentions that years before the rise of Booker T. Washington, which many connect with his Atlanta speech in 1895, Fortune "had organized the Afro-American Council, the parent of the Niagara Movement."

2. W. E. B. Du Bois, "Social Planning for the Negro, Past and Present," *Journal of Negro Education* 5, no. 1 (1936): 110–25.

3. Julian Bond, lecture at the University of Massachusetts, Amherst, Fall 2009. Recording in author's procession.

4. Alexander Walters, "The Afro-American Council and Its Work," *Colored American Magazine* 11 (September 1906): 207.

5. *NYG*, December 20, 1883.

6. *NYA*, January 25, 1890.

Index

Acknowledgments

Extremely fortunate is a person who is able to do what he always dreamed of, even more so if that dream is to write history. To live every day with your heroes and heroines as you attempt to reconstruct the worlds they lived in – tracing their trials, tribulations, and triumphs along the way – is a joy and a blessing. Researching and writing history, however, is not accomplished alone; it comes together with significant assistance, and I have a number of people to thank, personally and professionally, for allowing me to follow my dream.

Reading, researching, and writing about African American history is a labor of love that became so much easier when I entered the W. E. B. Du Bois Department of Afro-American Studies at the University of Massachusetts in the fall of 1998. My six years in the department were enlightening and inspiring. The faculty, including Esther M. A. Terry, Ernest Allen Jr., John H. Bracey, Jr., Steve Tracy, Manisha Sinha, James Smethurst, Michael Thelwell, William Strickland, and Robert Paul Wolff, were supportive of my work and were willing to converse with me on any subject of black history and literature at the drop of a hat. From an intellectual standpoint, my years associated with the graduate program at UMass were everything a student would desire. It was truly a mentoring environment.

I have been the generous recipient of grants and fellowships that have assisted my research along the way. I thank the Gilder Lehrman Institute of American History, the Nellie Mae Education Foundation, and the Department of History at Yale University for the Cassius Marcellus Clay Fellowship. I also thank the University of Kansas for a grant from the New Faculty General Research Fund as well as the Department of African and African-American Studies for providing much-needed financial assistance to aid in the completion of this study.

I am indebted to Ernest Allen, Jr. and John H. Bracey, Jr., both of whom have extended themselves in invaluable ways. Professor Allen was always enthusiastic about this project and it greatly benefited from my extended colloquy with the exceptional Grandmaster E. He tirelessly read pieces, fragments, and drafts of this manuscript, as well as listening, critiquing, and offering heartfelt encouragement along the way. The prodigious Professor Bracey has also stood steadfast by this project, always providing sage advice and counsel, and offering copious reading recommendations and sources to push the study.

An ever-growing circle of vigorous intellectuals has inspired me to become a better scholar and writer through their conversations and examples. I would particularly like to thank David W. Blight for his assistance and conversations throughout the years. I also wish to single out David A. Goldberg, who read the entire manuscript multiple times with generous scrutiny and encouragement. Additionally, James Smethurst also closely read and shared his feedback regarding the manuscript.

I am grateful to those who have lent their support and advice about the individuals and organizations discussed in *An Army of Lions*. These individuals have taken valuable time over the years to discuss, read, and comment upon elements of this project and black intellectual history in general. I would especially like to thank Elsa Barkley Brown, Fitz Brundage, Randall Burkett, Cornelius Bynum, Susan Carle, Sundiata Cha-Jua, Deborah Dandridge, James Danky, Dennis Dickerson, Jacob Dorman, Jonathan Earle, Tom Edge, Bertis English, Stephanie Evans, Jeffery B. Ferguson, Ruben Flores, Kevin Gaines, Willard Gatewood, Glenda Gilmore, Eddie S. Glaude, Jr., Kenneth Hamilton, John Higginson, Darlene Clark Hine, Jonathon Holloway, Randal Jelks, Yemisi Jimoh, David Katzman, Clarence Lang, Minkah Makalani, Dan McClure, Zebulon Miletsky, Greg Mixon, Fred Morton, Bruce Mouser, David Peavler, David Roediger, Leslie Schwalm, John Stauffer, William Tuttle, and David W. Wills.

I also deeply appreciate my colleagues in the Department of African and African-American Studies at the University of Kansas. They have made KU a pleasant place to teach, as well as to conduct research and write. Furthermore, I am grateful to the extended African Americanist community at the University for their dialogue on black intellectual history.

My editor at the University of Pennsylvania Press, Robert Lockhart, provided careful guidance throughout the entire preparation of this manuscript. I thank him for his assistance and his patience. He promised me "hands-on attention" and he most certainly delivered on that promise. I truly thank him for his sagacious advice and keen editorial eye throughout the process. In addition I would like to thank Alison Anderson, Edward Wade,

Brian Desmond and Brooke Smith for their copyediting work as well as the readers for the Press who gave equal doses of criticism and encouragement. Finally, I am honored that this book is part of the Politics and Culture in Modern America series edited by Margot Canaday, Glenda Gilmore, Michael Kazin, and Thomas Sugrue. Their own work throughout the years has been an inspiration and I am humbled that they have endorsed this project.

My debt of gratitude also goes to my extended family, the Alexanders, Campbells, and Farrells, for their support and faith over the years.

I would also like to thank the lads, Leigham and Francis. You came into our lives during the final years of this project, and you have brought inspiration, encouragement, and needed, sometimes stressful, distractions. I appreciate all of your support, from the longing looks in the first year of your lives as I typed away, to the ability to name T. Thomas Fortune, W. E. B. Du Bois, and Frederick (Freddie D.) Douglass in a photo in your third year. And yes guys, Daddy really "did type all those a b c's."

Last, and most important, I must acknowledge the incredible support that I have received from Kelly Marie Farrell, who has literally lived with this book as long as I have. Words cannot express how much I appreciate the selfless love and support she has given me throughout these many years. She has tolerated living with an academic. She has made the process of writing and being an academic easy. She has generously allowed me to travel, research, and write while she became the rock and stability of our family. Without her love, support, and countless sacrifices I would not have been able to complete this study, let alone have achieved my dream of becoming an academic. It is to her that I dedicate this book.